Hands-On Blockchain for Python Developers

Python Developers

Gain blockchain programming skills to build decentralized applications using Python

Arjuna Sky Kok

BIRMINGHAM - MUMBAI

Hands-On Blockchain for Python Developers

Copyright © 2019 Packt Publishing

Commissioning Editor: Sunith Shetty
Acquisition Editor: Devika Battike
Content Development Editor: Athikho Sapuni Rishana
Technical Editor: Utkarsha Kadam
Copy Editor: Safis Editing
Language Support Editor: Storm Mann
Project Coordinator: Kirti Pisat
Proofreader: Safis Editing
Indexer: Manju Arasan
Graphics: Jisha Chirayil
Production Coordinator: Tom Scaria

First published: February 2019

Production reference: 1120219

Published by Packt Publishing Ltd.
Livery Place
35 Livery Street
Birmingham
B3 2PB, UK.

ISBN 978-1-78862-785-6

www.packtpub.com

`mapt.io`

Mapt is an online digital library that gives you full access to over 5,000 books and videos, as well as industry leading tools to help you plan your personal development and advance your career. For more information, please visit our website.

Why subscribe?

- Spend less time learning and more time coding with practical eBooks and Videos from over 4,000 industry professionals

- Improve your learning with Skill Plans built especially for you

- Get a free eBook or video every month

- Mapt is fully searchable

- Copy and paste, print, and bookmark content

Packt.com

Did you know that Packt offers eBook versions of every book published, with PDF and ePub files available? You can upgrade to the eBook version at `www.packt.com` and as a print book customer, you are entitled to a discount on the eBook copy. Get in touch with us at `customercare@packtpub.com` for more details.

At `www.packt.com`, you can also read a collection of free technical articles, sign up for a range of free newsletters, and receive exclusive discounts and offers on Packt books and eBooks.

Foreword

The Movement

This book you're holding in your hands is part of a new movement: The movement of mainstream decentralization. The movement of Blockchain, DLT, and distributed applications. The movement that will rearchitecting many of our future systems, very soon.

Decentralized and distributed architectures, consensus rules, and P2P networks, are of course much older than Blockchain itself. However, Blockchain perfected the integration of these elements with some really ingenious concepts, and showed the world that the previous traditional architecture was not the be-all-and-end-all.

Blockchain's first use-case was Bitcoin, and Bitcoin managed to be something very interesting and rare: a killer app. All technologies, whether they are databases, network devices, touch-screens, **high performance computing** (**HPC**), or Big Data, seek killer apps. The iPhone was a killer app for a ton of technologies, but primarily touchscreen and computing hardware miniaturization technologies. Google's search engine was arguably the killer app for Big Data, and then High-Performance Computing as well. IBM's Watson is trying to be the killer app for enterprise-class AI. Oculus Rift is trying to be the killer app for VR. A ton of technologies out there are still looking for their killer app.

My point is, Blockchain got lucky: It found its killer app very early—during its birth. This is why a huge number of people in the media and the general public (even so-called tech-savvy people) have trouble differentiating between Blockchain and Bitcoin and other cryptocurrencies.

Since you're holding this book, I'm confident you're not one of these people.

I'm sure you're familiar with the mantra: Bitcoin is Blockchain, but Blockchain is not [just] Bitcoin.

The Expansion

This book brings you an end-to-end overview for creating awesome solutions on the Blockchain. Arjuna has done an amazing job at gathering the topics and researching them. You'll learn to create everything from smart contracts to decentralized apps to Blockchain-based (and Blockchain-friendly) filesystems.

My suggestion for when you begin architecting these solutions is to keep Bitcoin in mind, just as a reference point. It is the killer app, after all. It's the longest running security experiment for a Blockchain consensus mechanism. It's the widest-adopted financial technology without a central banking system. It's helped a lot of people directly and indirectly, including myself.

But what you have to do is *expand* upon the concept, just like the ecosystem used to expand from just Bitcoin to the current explosion of technologies, platforms, and solutions. Let your mind be creative. Think of ways that Bitcoin brought value to millions of people and companies all over the world, and break it down into actual business value that you can implement in your solution. Identify the weaknesses of Bitcoin, and explore other technologies in the Blockchain jungle that you can use. Ethereum is just one of these technologies. Nxt, Hyperledger (from Fabric to Indy), and IOTA, and so on, are others. Explore technologies and explore the histories of these technologies, why they were created, and what value they bring.

The Garden

Blockchain itself is a garden of competing solutions. Your role is that of a botanist, who explores the outgrowth of these technologies as responses to other technologies; or organisms competing with other organisms. This book gives you a taste of multiple technologies you may use, and there are many more waiting for you.

This is the only way to understand Blockchain in full: Enter the garden.

Have a safe journey,

Pandu Sastrowardoyo
Secretary-General, Asosiasi Blockchain Indonesia
Chief Technology Officer of Kendi.io
Cofounder of Blockchain Zoo
Senior Consulting Partner at Blocksphere

Contributors

About the author

Arjuna Sky Kok has experience more than 10 years in expressing himself as a software engineer. He has developed web applications using Symfony, Laravel, Ruby on Rails, and Django. He also has built mobile applications on top of Android and iOS platforms. Currently, he is researching Ethereum technology. Other than that, he teaches Android and iOS programming to students.

He graduated from Bina Nusantara University with majors in Computer Science and Applied Mathematics. He always strives to become a holistic person by enjoying leisure activities, such as dancing Salsa, learning French, and playing StarCraft 2. He lives quietly in the bustling city of Jakarta.

In loving memory of my late brother, Hengdra Santoso (1979-2011).

About the reviewer

Jonathan Coignard is a scientific engineering associate at the Lawrence Berkeley National Laboratory since 2015. His work is focused on vehicle-to-grid interactions and distribution grid planning. He has developed simulation tools for distribution grid analysis, with a focus on standardization through the FMI standard. More recently, Jonathan has been exploring data ownership in power systems to foster power exchange at a distribution grid level. He graduated from the Technical University of Compiegne with a Masters in Urban Engineering (2010-2015).

Packt is searching for authors like you

If you're interested in becoming an author for Packt, please visit `authors.packtpub.com` and apply today. We have worked with thousands of developers and tech professionals, just like you, to help them share their insight with the global tech community. You can make a general application, apply for a specific hot topic that we are recruiting an author for, or submit your own idea.

Table of Contents

Section 4: Cryptocurrency and Wallets

Section 5: Decentralized Filesystem

Preface

Blockchain is seen as the main technological solution for a public ledger for all cryptocurrency transactions. This book serves as a practical guide to developing a fully-fledged decentralized application with Python to interact with the various building blocks of Blockchain applications.

Hands-On Blockchain for Python Developers starts by demonstrating how blockchain technology and cryptocurrency hashing works. You will understand the fundamentals and benefits of smart contracts, such as censorship resistance and transaction accuracy. As you steadily progress, you'll go on to build smart contracts using Vyper, which has a similar syntax to Python. This experience will further help you unravel the other benefits of smart contracts, such as reliable storage and backup, and efficiency. You'll also use web3.py to interact with smart contracts and leverage the power of both the web3.py and Populus frameworks to build decentralized applications that offer security and seamless integration with cryptocurrencies. As you explore later chapters, you'll learn how to create your own token on top of Ethereum and build a cryptocurrency wallet graphical user interface (GUI) that can handle Ethereum and Ethereum Request for Comments (ERC-20) tokens using the PySide2 library. This will enable users to seamlessly store, send, and receive digital money. Toward the end, you'll implement InterPlanetary File System (IPFS) technology in your decentralized application to provide a peer-to-peer filesystem that can store and expose media.

By the end of this book, you'll be well-versed in blockchain programming and be able to build end-to-end decentralized applications on a range of domains using Python.

Who this book is for

If you are a Python developer who wants to enter the world of blockchain, *Hands-On Blockchain for Python Developers* is for you. This book will be your go-to guide to becoming well-versed in the blockchain ecosystem and building your own decentralized applications using Python and library support.

What this book covers

Chapter 1, *Introduction to Blockchain Programming*, teaches the story of Bitcoin and what makes Bitcoin so valuable. You will learn the underlying technology that empowers Bitcoin, which is Blockchain technology. Also, you will learn why Ethereum was created in the first place.

Chapter 2, *Smart Contract Fundamentals*, shows the differences between traditional programs and smart contracts. You will see what flaws a traditional program has, and why a smart contract has the potential to overcome the flaws. You'll also see where smart contracts are being utilized nowadays.

Chapter 3, *Implementing Smart Contracts Using Vyper*, teaches you how to write a smart contract by using the Vyper programming language (which resembles Python). You will learn a number of important features of the Vyper programming language.

Chapter 4, *Interacting with Smart Contracts Using Web3*, shows you how to install the web3.py library, how to interact with a smart contract, and how to deploy a smart contract.

Chapter 5, *Populus Development Framework*, shows you how to use the Populus development framework and recognize its value to developers.

Chapter 6, *Building a Practical Decentralized Application*, teaches you how the web3.py library and Populus development framework are used to build a decentralized application.

Chapter 7, *Frontend Decentralized Application*, shows you how to build a Twitter-like decentralized application with a desktop frontend.

Chapter 8, *Creating Token in Ethereum*, teaches you how to create your own token. It is a hands-on learning guide on launching your own cryptocurrency.

Chapter 9, *Cryptocurrency Wallet*, shows you how to build an Ethereum wallet with a desktop frontend.

Chapter 10, *InterPlanetary – A Brave New File System*, is an introduction to the InterPlanetary File System, where people can store distributed files. In blockchain, storage is expensive. It is already prohibitive to store an image file (never mind a video file) on the blockchain. IPFS is a new technology designed to mitigate that problem. You will learn what IPFS is, and the state this technology is in at this very moment.

Chapter 11, *Using ipfsapi to Interact with IPFS,* teaches you how to use the Python library to connect to an IPFS node.

Chapter 12, *Implementing a Decentralized Applications Using IPFS,* shows you how to implement a decentralized video-sharing application that utilizes IPFS technology.

To get the most out of this book

A basic knowledge of Python is a must. This book is intended for Python developers who are looking to work on blockchain.

Download the example code files

You can download the example code files for this book from your account at www.packt.com. If you purchased this book elsewhere, you can visit www.packt.com/support and register to have the files emailed directly to you.

You can download the code files by following these steps:

1. Log in or register at www.packt.com.
2. Select the **SUPPORT** tab.
3. Click on **Code Downloads & Errata**.
4. Enter the name of the book in the **Search** box and follow the onscreen instructions.

Once the file is downloaded, please make sure that you unzip or extract the folder using the latest version of:

- WinRAR/7-Zip for Windows
- Zipeg/iZip/UnRarX for Mac
- 7-Zip/PeaZip for Linux

The code bundle for the book is also hosted on GitHub at https://github.com/PacktPublishing/Hands-On-Blockchain-for-Python-Developers. In case there's an update to the code, it will be updated on the existing GitHub repository.

We also have other code bundles from our rich catalog of books and videos available at https://github.com/PacktPublishing/. Check them out!

Download the color images

We also provide a PDF file that has color images of the screenshots/diagrams used in this book. You can download it here: http://www.packtpub.com/sites/default/files/downloads/9781788627856_ColorImages.pdf.

Conventions used

There are a number of text conventions used throughout this book.

CodeInText: Indicates code words in text, database table names, folder names, filenames, file extensions, pathnames, dummy URLs, user input, and Twitter handles. Here is an example: "If you are on the Linux platform, you will download this file: qt-unified-linux-x64-3.0.5-online.run."

A block of code is set as follows:

```
"compilation": {
    "backend": {
        "class": "populus.compilation.backends.VyperBackend"
    },
    "contract_source_dirs": [
        "./contracts"
    ],
    "import_remappings": []
},
```

Any command-line input or output is written as follows:

```
$ python3.6 -m venv qt-venv
$ source qt-venv/bin/activate
(qt-venv) $ pip install PySide2
```

Bold: Indicates a new term, an important word, or words that you see on screen. For example, words in menus or dialog boxes appear in the text like this. Here is an example: "Click **Next**. You will then be greeted with a login screen."

 Warnings or important notes appear like this.

Tips and tricks appear like this.

Get in touch

Feedback from our readers is always welcome.

General feedback: If you have questions about any aspect of this book, mention the book title in the subject of your message and email us at customercare@packtpub.com.

Errata: Although we have taken every care to ensure the accuracy of our content, mistakes do happen. If you have found a mistake in this book, we would be grateful if you would report this to us. Please visit www.packt.com/submit-errata, selecting your book, clicking on the Errata Submission Form link, and entering the details.

Piracy: If you come across any illegal copies of our works in any form on the internet, we would be grateful if you would provide us with the location address or website name. Please contact us at copyright@packt.com with a link to the material.

If you are interested in becoming an author: If there is a topic that you have expertise in, and you are interested in either writing or contributing to a book, please visit authors.packtpub.com.

Reviews

Please leave a review. Once you have read and used this book, why not leave a review on the site that you purchased it from? Potential readers can then see and use your unbiased opinion to make purchase decisions, we at Packt can understand what you think about our products, and our authors can see your feedback on their book. Thank you!

For more information about Packt, please visit packt.com.

Section 1: Blockchain and Smart Contracts

Introduction to blockchain technology, smart contracts, and decentralized applications.

The following chapters will be covered in this section:

- `Chapter 1`, Introduction to Blockchain Programming
- `Chapter 2`, Smart Contract Fundamentals
- `Chapter 3`, Implementing Smart Contracts Using Vyper

Introduction to Blockchain Programming

1

In this book, we'll learn blockchain programming so that you can become a force to be reckoned with when finding blockchain opportunities. To achieve this, you need to begin by understanding blockchain technology and what it entails. In this chapter, we will learn what blockchain technology is. How does blockchain empower Bitcoin and Ethereum? We will get an intuitive understanding of blockchain technology. We will also replicate some basic functions behind blockchain.

The following topics will be covered in this chapter:

- The rise of cryptocurrency and blockchain
- Blockchain technology
- Cryptography
- The hashing function
- Consensus
- Coding on the blockchain

The rise of cryptocurrency and blockchain

Assuming that you didn't live a secluded life as a hermit on a mountain in 2017, you would have heard all about cryptocurrency, especially Bitcoin. You didn't have to look far to hear about the soaring popularity of this topic, its terminology, and its growth in value. At this point, other cryptocurrencies also began to grow, making way for headlines such as **Ethereum reaches $1,000!** During this craze, people discussed everything about cryptocurrency, from the swinging price to the technology behind it, which is blockchain.

Blockchain was regarded as the technology that would bring the dawn of a new era of justice and prosperity for mankind. It would democratize wealth. It would take the power away from the oligarchy and give it back to the people. It would protect the data of the people. Then came 2018, and cryptocurrency went down. The party was over. Bitcoin now sits at $6,000, while Ethereum sits at less than $400.

However, despite the fact that the hype surrounding cryptocurrency had died down, it still continues to be a regular point of discussion. Blockchain conferences and meetups are cropping up in many places, while investments keep pouring into blockchain startups. Andreessen Horowitz, a giant name in Silicon Valley, secured as much as $300 million from its limited partner in a dedicated blockchain fund. [1] In this case, the opportunities lie where the money flows into. Katheryn Griffith Hill, a lead recruiter at Blockchain Developers, claims that [2] there are currently fourteen blockchain developer positions available for every blockchain developer. In addition, a friend of mine who attended a local blockchain event in Jakarta commented on this, stating that I could see around one hundred audience members, but there were only around four or five developers. 50% of the audience were investors. There are people who want to put money into blockchain, but there are fewer people who are capable of developing the product.

Blockchain started to be used as a payment solution without the middleman, namely Bitcoin. Then, people found out that blockchain has some other properties that are interesting. First, it is transparent, meaning people can audit it to check whether there is money laundering going on or not. Second, it gives to some extent privacy for users, which can be used to avoid profiling.

Then, after Ethereum was released, people suddenly became creative with how to apply blockchain in real life. From creating a token to represent ownership of something, such as an autonomous organization or payment with full privacy, to digital assets that cannot be duplicated (unlike MP3 files).

Blockchain technology

Most people know Bitcoin exists because of blockchain. But what is blockchain? It is an append-only database that consists of blocks that are linked by hashing. Here, each block contains many transactions of transferring value (but could be other things) between participants secured by cryptography; a consensus between many nodes that hold an identical database decides on which new block is to be appended next.

You don't have to understand the definition at this point; those are a lot of words to chew on! First, I'll explain blockchain to you so that you can adjust to this new knowledge as we move through this book.

Going back to the definition of blockchain, we can summarize the definition as an append-only database. Once you put something into the database, it cannot be changed; there is no Undo. We'll talk about the ramifications of this feature in Chapter 2, *Smart Contract Fundamentals*. This definition entails many things and opens up a whole new world.

So, what can you put into this append-only database? It depends on the cryptocurrency. For Bitcoin, you can store the transactions of transferring value. For example, Nelson sends one Bitcoin to Dian. However, we accumulate many transactions into one block before appending them to the database. For Ethereum, the things that you can put into the append-only database are richer. This not only includes the transaction of transferring value—it could also be a change of state. What I mean by state here is really general. For example, a queue for buying a ticket for a show can have a state. This state can be empty or full. Similarly to Bitcoin, in Ethereum, you gather all the transactions before appending them together in this append-only database.

To make it clearer, we put all these transactions into the block before appending them to the append-only database. Aside from the list of transactions, we store other things in this block, such as the time when we append the block into the append-only database, the target's difficulty (don't worry if you don't know about this), and the parent's hash (I'll explain this shortly), among many other things.

Now that you understand the block element of the blockchain, let's look at the chain element. As previously explained, aside from the list of transactions, we also put the parent's hash in the block. But for now, let's just use a simple ID to indicate the parent instead of using a hash. **Parent id** is just the previous block id. Here, think of the stack. In the beginning, there is no block. Instead, we put **Block A**, which has three transactions: **Transaction 1**, **Transaction 2**, and **Transaction 3**. Since **Block A** is the first block, it has no parent. We then apply **Block B** to **Block A**, which consists of two transactions: **Transaction 4** and **Transaction 5**. **Block B** is not the first one in this blockchain. Consequently, we set the parent section in **Block B** as the **Block A** id because **Block A** is the parent of **Block B**. Then, we put **Block C** in the blockchain, which has two transactions: **Transaction 6** and **Transaction 7**.

The parent section in **Block C** would be the **Block B** id, and so on. To simplify things, we increment the id from 0 by 1 for every new block:

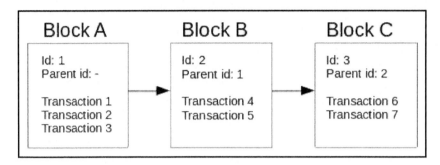

Let's implement a database to record the history of what people like and hate. This means that when you said you like cats at one point in history, you won't be able to change that history. You may add new history when you change your mind (for example, if you then hate cats), but that won't change the fact that you liked them in the past. So, we can see that in the past you liked cats, but now you hate them. We want to make this database full of integrity and secure against cheating. Take a look at the following code block:

```python
class Block:
    id = None
    history = None
    parent_id = None

block_A = Block()
block_A.id = 1
block_A.history = 'Nelson likes cat'

block_B = Block()
block_B.id = 2
block_B.history = 'Marie likes dog'
block_B.parent_id = block_A.id

block_C = Block()
block_C.id = 3
block_C.history = 'Sky hates dog'
block_C.parent_id = block_B.id
```

If you studied computer science, you will recognize this data structure, which is called a **linked list**. Now, there is a problem. Say Marie hates Nelson and wants to paint Nelson in a negative light. Marie can do this by changing the history of block A:

```
block_A.history = 'Nelson hates cat'
```

This is unfair to Nelson, who is a big fan of cats. So, we need to add a way in which only Nelson can write the history of his own preferences. The way to do this is by using a private key and a public key.

Signing data in blockchain

In blockchain, we use two keys to sign data, to authenticate a message and protect it from being altered by unauthorized users. The two keys are as follows:

- Private key
- Public key

The secrecy of the private key is guarded and it is not made known to the public. On the other hand, you let the public key be given out in public. You tell everyone, *hey, this is my public key.*

Let's generate the private key. To do this, we need openssl software. You can install this by doing the following:

```
$ sudo apt-get install openssl
```

So, Nelson generates the private key, which is the nelsonkey.pem file. He must keep this key secret. It is generated as follows:

```
$ openssl genrsa -out nelsonkey.pem 1024
```

From the private key, Nelson generates the public key:

```
$ openssl rsa -in nelsonkey.pem -pubout > nelsonkey.pub
```

Nelson can share this public key, nelsonkey.pub, with everyone. Now, in the real world we could set up a simple dictionary of the public key and its owner as follows:

```
{
'Nelson': 'nelsonkey.pub',
'Marie': 'mariekey.pub',
'Sky': 'skykey.pub'
}
```

We will now look at how Nelson can prove that he is the only one who can make changes to his history.

First, let's create a Python virtual environment:

```
$ python3 -m venv blockchain
$ source blockchain/bin/activate
(blockchain) $
```

Next, install the library:

```
(blockchain) $ pip install --upgrade pip
(blockchain) $ pip install wheel
(blockchain) $ pip install cryptography
```

This is the Python script that can be used to sign the message. Name this script verify_message.py (refer to the code file in the following GitLab link for the full code: https://gitlab.com/arjunaskykok/hands-on-blockchain-for-python-developers/blob/master/chapter_01/verify_message.py):

```
from cryptography.hazmat.primitives import hashes
from cryptography.hazmat.primitives.asymmetric import padding
from cryptography.hazmat.backends import default_backend
from cryptography.hazmat.primitives.asymmetric import rsa
from cryptography.hazmat.primitives import serialization

# Generate private key
#private_key = rsa.generate_private_key(
# public_exponent=65537,
# key_size=2048,
# backend=default_backend()
#)
...
...

# Message validation executed by other people
public_key.verify(
    signature,
    message,
    padding.PSS(mgf=padding.MGF1(hashes.SHA256()),
              salt_length=padding.PSS.MAX_LENGTH),
    hashes.SHA256())
```

When executing this script, nothing will happen, as expected. This means that the message is verified with the signature from the public key. The signature can only be created by Nelson because you need the private key in order to create a signature. However, to verify the message with the signature, you only need the public key.

Let's take a look at a case in which Marie tries to falsify the facts with a script named `falsify_message.py`. Marie tries to put `Nelson hates cat` in the history database as follows:

```
from cryptography.hazmat.primitives import hashes
from cryptography.hazmat.primitives.asymmetric import padding
from cryptography.hazmat.backends import default_backend
from cryptography.hazmat.primitives.asymmetric import rsa
from cryptography.hazmat.primitives import serialization

message = b'Nelson hates cat'
signature = b'Fake Signature'

with open("nelsonkey.pub", "rb") as key_file:
    public_key = serialization.load_pem_public_key(
        key_file.read(),
        backend=default_backend())

public_key.verify(
  signature,
  message,
  padding.PSS(mgf=padding.MGF1(hashes.SHA256()),
              salt_length=padding.PSS.MAX_LENGTH),
    hashes.SHA256())
```

Here's how the verify method works. Nelson calculates the hash from the message, then encrypts it with his private key. The result is the signature. For example, if Sky wants to verify the signature, he has the message and the signature. He calculates the hash of the message. Then, he decrypts the signature using the public key. The result is compared to the hash of the message. If it is the same, then everything is well. If not, either the message has been altered or the private key used to sign the message is different.

When doing this, you would get the following output:

```
Traceback (most recent call last):
  File "falsify_message.py", line 20, in <module>
    hashes.SHA256())
  File "/opt/Code/blockchain/blockchain_venv/lib/python3.6/site-packages/cryptography/hazmat/backends/openssl/rsa.py", line 474, in verify
    self._backend, padding, algorithm, self, signature, data
  File "/opt/Code/blockchain/blockchain_venv/lib/python3.6/site-packages/cryptography/hazmat/backends/openssl/rsa.py", line 268, in _rsa_sig_verify
    raise InvalidSignature
cryptography.exceptions.InvalidSignature
```

So, what does the signature look like? Go back to `verify_message.py` and append this line to the end of the file. Then, run the script again:

```
print(signature)
```

The signature looks like this:

```
b'/zD\x07A[1\x86K\xdd\xba\x1d\xba\xbc3\xddn\xf5"q\xedJ\xda\xf3\x1b\xc8\xcf\xb4\xbc\xa04\xa7_k\xa9\xc5\x90\x98\xaf\xc00o\x06J<\xe1\xdc$pBa\x83\xfcI\
xae2\x80\xcd\xb3\x8d\x0b\xfe5\x12\xf0/%\xceV,\x85\xe3>\xf8\xbd\xb6\xe6\xc0\x12\xabr\x99\xfa\x14t\xd7\xfej\x0c\xb0\x9e)B\x1cEj\x01\x92`\x99\xbb\xfa4
`K\x96r\\\x91@ZN\x04\xdf\x00}\x1fA\xa3?X\xdB\x11@pX\xdd\xcd'
```

Every message has a different signature, and it's impossible for Marie to guess the signature in order to falsify the message. So, with the private key and the public key, we can verify whether or not the message is indeed from someone authorized, even if we communicate on an unsecured channel.

So with the private key, Nelson could create a signature that is unique to the message it tries to sign:

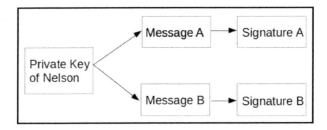

Everyone in the world who has Nelson's public key can verify that Nelson did indeed write **Message A**. Nelson can prove he did write **Message A** by showing **Signature A**. Everyone can take those two inputs and verify the truth:

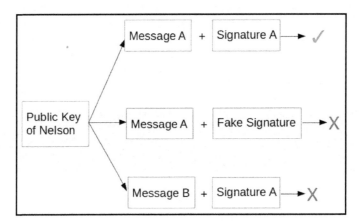

So, to validate whether or not it is Nelson who wrote `Nelson likes cat`, input the following (refer to the code file in the following GitLab link for the full code: `https://gitlab.com/arjunaskykok/hands-on-blockchain-for-python-developers/blob/master/chapter_01/validate_message.py`):

```
# validate_message.py
from cryptography.hazmat.primitives import hashes
from cryptography.hazmat.primitives.asymmetric import padding
from cryptography.hazmat.backends import default_backend
from cryptography.hazmat.primitives.asymmetric import rsa
from cryptography.hazmat.primitives import serialization

def fetch_public_key(user):
    with open(user + "key.pub", "rb") as key_file:
        public_key = serialization.load_pem_public_key(
            key_file.read(),
            backend=default_backend())
    return public_key

# Message coming from user
message = b"Nelson likes cat"

# Signature coming from user, this is very specific to public key.
# Download the public key from Gitlab repository of this code so this
signature matches the message.
# Otherwise, you should generate your own signature.
signature =
...
...
    padding.PSS(mgf=padding.MGF1(hashes.SHA256()),
                salt_length=padding.PSS.MAX_LENGTH),
    hashes.SHA256())
```

From linked list to blockchain

Now we know that only Nelson can write `Nelson likes cats` or `Nelson hates cats`, we can be at peace. However, to make the tutorial code short, we won't integrate the validation using the private key and the public key. We assume only authorized people are able to write the history in the block. Take a look at the following code block:

```
>>> block_A.history = 'Nelson likes cat'
```

When that happens, we assume it's Nelson who wrote that history. So, what is the problem in recording data with a linked list?

The problem is that the data can be altered easily. Say Nelson wants to be a senator. If many people in his district don't like cats, they may not be happy with the fact that Nelson likes them. Consequently, Nelson wants to alter the history:

```
>>> block_A.history = 'Nelson hates cat'
```

Just like that, the history has been changed. We can avoid this way of cheating by recording all history in the block every day. So, when Nelson alters the database, we can compare the data in the blockchain today to the data in the blockchain yesterday. If it's different, we can confirm that something fishy is happening. That method could work, but let's see if we can come up with something better.

Let's upgrade our linked list to the blockchain. To do this, we add a new property in the `Block` class, which is the parent's hash:

```python
import hashlib
import json

class Block:
    id = None
    history = None
    parent_id = None
    parent_hash = None

block_A = Block()
block_A.id = 1
block_A.history = 'Nelson likes cat'

block_B = Block()
block_B.id = 2
block_B.history = 'Marie likes dog'
block_B.parent_id = block_A.id
block_B.parent_hash =
hashlib.sha256(json.dumps(block_A.__dict__).encode('utf-8')).hexdigest()

block_C = Block()
block_C.id = 3
block_C.history = 'Marie likes dog'
block_C.parent_id = block_B.id
block_C.parent_hash =
hashlib.sha256(json.dumps(block_B.__dict__).encode('utf-8')).hexdigest()
```

Let's demonstrate what the `hashlib()` function does:

```
>>> print(block_B.__dict__)
{'parent_hash':
'880baef90c77ae39d49f364ff1074043eccb78717ecec85e5897c282482012f1',
'history': 'Marie likes dog', 'id': 2, 'parent_id': 1}
>>> print(json.dumps(block_B.__dict__))
{"parent_hash":
"880baef90c77ae39d49f364ff1074043eccb78717ecec85e5897c282482012f1",
"parent_id": 1, "history": "Marie likes dog", "id": 2}
>>> print(json.dumps(block_B.__dict__).encode('utf-8'))
b'{"id": 2, "parent_hash":
"69a1db9d3430aea08030058a6bd63788569f1fde05adceb1be6743538b03dadb",
"parent_id": 1, "history": "Marie likes dog"}'
>>> print(hashlib.sha256(json.dumps(block_B.__dict__).encode('utf-8')))
<sha256 HASH object @ 0x7f58518e3ee0>
>>>
print(hashlib.sha256(json.dumps(block_B.__dict__).encode('utf-8')).hexdiges
t())
25a7a88637c507d33ae1402ba6b0ee87eefe9c90e33e75c43d56858358f1704e
```

If we change the history of `block_A`, the following code look like this:

```
>>> block_A.history = 'Nelson hates cat'
```

Again, the history has been changed just like that. However, this time there is a twist. We can verify that this change has occurred by printing the original parent's hash of `block_C`:

```
>>> print(block_C.parent_hash)
ca3d23274de8d89ada13fe52b6000afb87ee97622a3edfa3e9a473f76ca60b33
```

Now, let's recalculate the parent's hash of each block:

```
>>> block_B.parent_hash =
hashlib.sha256(json.dumps(block_A.__dict__).encode('utf-8')).hexdigest()
>>> block_C.parent_hash =
hashlib.sha256(json.dumps(block_B.__dict__).encode('utf-8')).hexdigest()
>>> print(block_C.parent_hash)
10b7d80f3ede91fdffeae4889279f3acbda32a0b9024efccc9c2318e2771e78c
```

These blocks are different. By looking at these, we can be very sure that the history has been altered. Consequently, Nelson would be caught red-handed. Now if Nelson wants to alter the history without getting caught, it is not enough to change the history in `block_A` anymore. Nelson needs to change all the `parent_hash` properties in every block (except `block_A` of course). This is tougher cheating. With three blocks only, Nelson needs to change two `parent_hash` properties. With a 1,000 blocks, Nelson needs to change 999 `parent_hash` properties!

Cryptography

The most popular use of blockchain is to create a cryptocurrency. As the word **crypto** is in cryptocurrency, you would expect that you need to master cryptography in order to become a blockchain programmer. That is not true. You only need to know two things about cryptography:

- Private key and public key (asymmetric cryptography)
- Hashing

These two have been explained in the previous part of this chapter. You don't need to know how to design a hashing algorithm or private key and public key algorithm. You only need to get an intuitive understanding of how they work and the implications of these technologies.

The implication of private keys and public keys is that it enables decentralized accounts. In a normal application, you have a username and password. These two fields enable someone to access their account. But having a private key and public key enables someone to have an account in a decentralized manner.

For hashing, it is a one-way function, meaning that given an input, you can get the output easily. But given an output, you couldn't get the input. A simple version of a one-way function would be this:

$$f(x, y) \geq x + y$$

This is an addition process. If I tell you one of the outputs of this function is 999, and I ask you what the inputs are, you couldn't guess the answer. It could be anything from 1 and 998 to 500 and 499. A hashing function is something like that. The algorithm is clear as sky (you can read the algorithm of any hashing function on the internet), but it's hard to reverse the algorithm.

So, all you need to know about hashing is this: given input **input** you get this SHA-256 output (in hexadecimal):
`c96c6d5be8d08a12e7b5cdc1b207fa6b2430974c86803d8891675e76fd992c20`. If you don't know the input, you couldn't get the input based on this output alone. Say you know the input **input** it is very prohibitive to find another input that produces the same output. We wouldn't even know whether such input exists or not.

That is all you need to know about cryptography when you become a blockchain developer. But that's only true if you become a certain type of blockchain developer, who creates a program on top of Ethereum.

Symmetric and asymmetric cryptography

Symmetric cryptography uses the same key between sender and receiver. This key is used to encrypt and decrypt a message. For example, you want to create an encryption function to encrypt text. Symmetric cryptography could be as simple as adding 5 to the text to be encrypted. If A (or 65 in ASCII) is the text to be encrypted, then this encryption function will add 5 to 65. The encrypted text would be F (or 71 in ASCII). To decrypt it, you just subtract 5 from the encrypted text, F.

Asymmetric cryptography is a different beast. There are two keys: a public key and a private key. They are linked with a special mathematical relationship. If you encrypt a message with a public key, you can only decrypt it with a private key. If you encrypt a message with a private key, you can only decrypt it with a public key. There is no straight relationship as with symmetric keys (adding and subtracting the same number) between a public key and a private key. There are a couple of asymmetric cryptography algorithms. I'll explain the easiest one, the RSA algorithm.

Generate two prime numbers, called p and q. They should be really big numbers (with at least hundreds of digits), but for this example, we choose low numbers: 11 and 17. These are your private key. Don't let someone know these numbers:

```
n = p x q
```

n is a composite number. In our case, n is 187.

Then, we find e number, which should be relatively prime, with (p-1) x (q-1):

```
(p-1) x (q-1) = 160
```

Relatively prime means e and (p-1) x (q-1) cannot be factorized with any number except *1*. There is no number other than 1 that we can divide them by without a remainder. So, *e* is *7*. But, *e* can be *11* as well. For this example, we choose *7* for *e*.

e and *n* are your public key. You can tell these numbers to strangers you meet on the bus, your grandma, your friendly neighbor, or your date.

Let's say the message we want to encrypt is *A*. In the real world, encrypting a short message like this is not safe. We have to pad the short message. So, *A* would be something like xxxxxxxxxxxxxxxxxxxxA. If you check the previous script to encrypt a message earlier in this chapter, you would see there is a padding function. But for this example, we would not pad the message.

The encryption function is this:

```
encrypted_message = message° (mod n)
```

So, the `encrypted_message` would be *65 ** 7 % 187 = 142*.

Before we are able to decrypt the message, we need to find the `d` number:

```
e x d = 1 (mod (p-1) x (q-1))
```

`d` is *23*.

The decryption function is this:

```
decrypted_message = encrypted_message^d mod n
```

So, the `decrypted_message` would be *142 ** 23 % 187 = 65. 65* in ASCII is *A*.

Apparently, x^y `mod` n is easy to calculate, but finding the y root of integer module n is really hard. We call this trapdoor permutation. Factorization of n to find p and q is really hard (generating a private key from a public key). But, finding n from p and q is easy (generating a public key from a private key). These properties enable asymmetric cryptography.

Compared to symmetric cryptography, asymmetric cryptography enables people to communicate securely without needing to exchange keys first. You have two keys (private key and public key). You throw the public key out to anyone. All you need to do is to protect the secrecy of the private key. The private key is like a password to your Bitcoin/Ethereum account. Creating an account in any cryptocurrency is just generating a private key. Your address (or your username in cryptocurrency) is derived from the public key. The public key itself can be derived from the private key. An example of Bitcoin's private key in **Wallet Import Format (WIF)** is this:
5K1vbDP1nxvVYPqdKB5wCVpM3y99MzNqMJXWTiffp7sRWyC7SrG.

It has 51 hexadecimal characters. Each character can have 16 combinations. So, the amount of private keys is as follows: `16 ^ 51 =` 2571100870814384440867139347745860164035524790052468536482201 6 (it's not exactly this amount, because the first number of a private key in Bitcoin is always 5 in mainnet, but you get the idea). That is a huge number. So, the probability of someone finding another account that is filled with Bitcoin already when generating a private key with a strong random process is very, very low. But the kind of account generated by a private key and public key does not have a reset password feature.

If someone sends Bitcoin to your address, and you forgot your private key, then it's gone for good. So, while your public key is recorded on the blockchain that is kept in every Bitcoin node, people are not going to get the private key.

The hashing function

Hashing is a function that takes an input of any length and turns it into a fixed length output. So, to make this clearer, we can look at the following code example:

```
>>> import hashlib
>>> hashlib.sha256(b"hello").hexdigest()
'2cf24dba5fb0a30e26e83b2ac5b9e29e1b161e5c1fa7425e73043362938b9824'
>>> hashlib.sha256(b"a").hexdigest()
'ca978112ca1bbdcafac231b39a23dc4da786eff8147c4e72b9807785afee48bb'
>>> hashlib.sha256(b"hellohellohellohello").hexdigest()
'25b0b104a66b6a2ad14f899d190b043e45442d29a3c4ce71da2547e37adc68a9'
```

As you can see, the length of the input can be *1*, *5*, or even *20* characters, but the output will always be the length of *64* hexadecimal numeric characters. The output looks scrambled and it appears that there is no apparent link between the input and the output. However, if you give the same input, it will give the same output every time:

```
>>> hashlib.sha256(b"a").hexdigest()
'ca978112ca1bbdcafac231b39a23dc4da786eff8147c4e72b9807785afee48bb'
>>> hashlib.sha256(b"a").hexdigest()
'ca978112ca1bbdcafac231b39a23dc4da786eff8147c4e72b9807785afee48bb'
```

If you change the input by even just a character, the output would be totally different:

```
>>> hashlib.sha256(b"hello1").hexdigest()
'91e9240f415223982edc345532630710e94a7f52cd5f48f5ee1afc555078f0ab'
>>> hashlib.sha256(b"hello2").hexdigest()
'87298cc2f31fba73181ea2a9e6ef10dce21ed95e98bdac9c4e1504ea16f486e4'
```

Now that the output has a fixed length, which is 64 in this case, of course there will be two different inputs that have the same output.

Here is the interesting thing: it is very prohibitive to find two different inputs that have the same output as this hashing function. Mission Impossible: even if you hijack all the computers in the world and make them run the hashing computation, it is unlikely that you would ever find two different inputs with the same output.

Not all hashing functions are safe though. SHA-1 already died in 2017. This means that people can find two different long strings that have the same output. In this example, we will use SHA-256.

The output of the hashing function can be used as a digital signature. Imagine you have a string with a length of 10 million (say you are writing a novel), and to make sure this novel is not tampered with, you tell all your potential readers that they have to count the 10 million characters in order to ensure that the novel isn't be corrupted. Nobody would do that. But with hashing, you can publish the output validation with only 64 characters (through Twitter, for example) and your potential readers can hash the novel that they buy/download and compare them to make sure that their novel is legit.

So, we add the parent's hash in the block class. This way, we keep the digital signature of the parent's block in our block. This means that if we are ever naughty and change the content of any block, the parent's hash in any child's block will be invalid, and you would get caught red-handed.

But can't you change the parent's hash of the children's block if you want to alter the content of any block? You can, obviously. However, the process of altering the content becomes more difficult. You have to have two steps. Now, imagine you have 10 blocks and you want to change the content in the first block:

1. In this case, you have to change the parent's hash in its immediate child's block. But, alas, there are unseen ramifications with this. Technically speaking, the parent's hash in its immediate child is a part of the content in that block. That would mean that the parent's hash in its child (the grandchild of the first block) would be invalid.
2. Now, you have to change that grandchild's parent's hash, but this affects the subsequent block, and so on. Now, you have to change all blocks' parent's hashes. For this, ten steps need to be taken. Using a parent's hash makes tampering much more difficult.

Proof of work

So, we have three participants in this case: Nelson, Marie, and Sky. But there is another type of participant too: the one who writes into the blockchain is called—in blockchain parlance—the miner. In order to put the transaction into the blockchain, the miner is required to do some work first.

Previously, we had three blocks (`block_A`, `block_B`, and `block_C`), but now we have a candidate block (`block_D`), which we want to add into the blockchain as follows:

```
block_D = Block()
block_D.id = 4
block_D.history = 'Sky loves turtle'
block_D.parent_id = block_C.id
```

But instead of adding `block_D` to the blockchain just like that, we first require the miner to do some puzzle work. We serialize that block and ask the miner to apply an extra string, which, when appended to the serialization string of that block, will show the hash output with at least five zeros in the front, if it is hashed.

Those are a lot of words to chew on. First things first, we serialize the block:

```
import json
block_serialized = json.dumps(block_D.__dict__).encode('utf-8')
print(block_serialized)
b'{"history": "Sky loves turtle", "parent_id": 3, "id": 4}'
```

If the serialized block is hashed, what does it mean if we want the hash output to have at least five zeros at the front? It means that we want the output to look like this:

```
00000aa21def23ee175073c6b3c89b96cfe618b6083dae98d2a92c919c1329be
```

Alternatively, we want it to look like this:

```
00000be7b5347509c9df55ca35d27091b41a93acb2afd1447d1cc3e4b70c96ab
```

So, the puzzle is something like this:

```
string serialization + answer = hash output with (at least) 5 leading zeros
```

The miner needs to guess the correct answer. If this puzzle is converted to Python code, it would be something like this:

```
answer = ?
input = b'{"history": "Sky loves turtle", "parent_id": 3, "id": 4}' +
answer
output = hashlib.sha256(input).hexdigest()
// output needs to be
00000??????????????????????????????????????????????????????????????
```

So, how could the miner solve a problem like this? We can use brute force:

```
import hashlib

payload = b'{"history": "Sky loves turtle", "parent_id": 3, "id": 4}'
for i in range(10000000):
  nonce = str(i).encode('utf-8')
  result = hashlib.sha256(payload + nonce).hexdigest()
  if result[0:5] == '00000':
    print(i)
    print(result)
    break
```

The result would therefore be as follows:

```
184798
00000ae01f4cd7806e2a1fccd72fb18679cb07ede3a2a7ef028a0ecfd4aec153
```

This means that the answer is 184798, or the hash output of {"history": "Sky loves turtle", "parent_id": 3, "id": 4}184798 is the one that has five leading zeros. In that simple script, we iterate from 0 to 9999999 and append that into the input. This is a naive method, but it works. Of course, you could also append with characters other than numbers, such as a, b, or c.

Now, try to increase the number of leading zeros to six, or even ten. In this case, can you find the hash output? If there is no output, you could increase the range limit from 10000000 to an even higher number, such as 1000000000000. Once you get an appreciation of the hard work that goes into this, try to comprehend this: Bitcoin required around 18 leading zeros in the hash output at the time that this book was being written. The number of leading zeros is not static and changes according to the situation (but you don't need to worry about this).

So, why do we need proof of work? We need to take a look at the idea of consensus first.

Consensus

As we can see, the hashing function makes history tampering hard, but not too hard. Even if we have a blockchain that consists of 1000 blocks, it would be trivial to alter the content of the first block and change the 999 parent hashes on the other blocks with recent computers. So, to ensure that bad people cannot alter the history (or at least make it very hard), we distribute this append-only database to everyone who wants to keep it (let's call them miners). Say there are ten miners. In this case, you cannot just alter the blockchain in your copy because the other nine miners who would scold, saying something like *hey, our records say history A but your record says B*. In this case, the majority wins.

However, consensus is not just a case of choosing which blockchain has been chosen by the majority. The problem starts when we want to add a new block to the blockchain. Where do we start? How do we do it? The answer is that we broadcast. When we broadcast the candidate block that contains a new transaction, it will not reach every miner at the same time. You may reach the miner that stands beside you, but it will require time for your message to reach the miner that stands far away from you.

Here's where it gets interesting: the miner that stands far away from you may receive another new candidate block first. So, how do we synchronize all these things and make sure that the majority will have the same blockchain? The simple rule is to choose the longest chain. So if you are a miner in the middle, you may receive two different candidate blocks at the same time, as shown in the following figure:

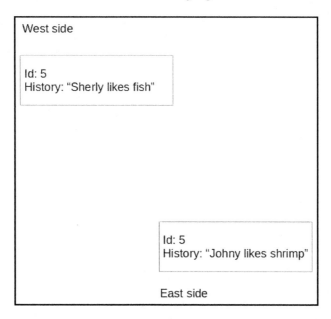

You get this from the West side:

```
block_E = Block()
block_E.id = 5
block_E.history = 'Sherly likes fish'
block_E.parent_id = block_D.id
```

And you get this from the East side:

```
block_E = Block()
block_E.id = 5
block_E.history = 'Johny likes shrimp'
block_E.parent_id = block_D.id
```

So, we will keep both versions of `block_E`. Our blockchain now has a branch. However, in a short time, other blocks have arrived from the East side. Here is the situation now:

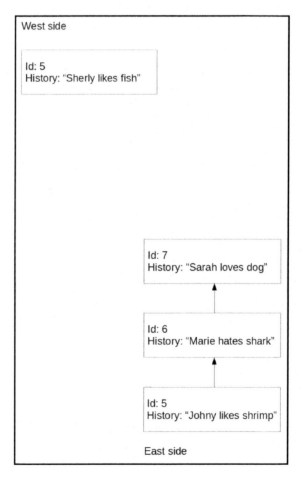

This is from the West side:

```
block_E = Block()
block_E.id = 5
block_E.history = 'Sherly likes fish'
block_E.parent_id = block_D.id
```

This is from the East side:

```
block_E = Block()
block_E.id = 5
block_E.history = 'Johny likes shrimp'
block_E.parent_id = block_D.id

block_F = Block()
block_F.id = 6
block_F.history = 'Marie hates shark'
block_F.parent_id = block_E.id

block_G = Block()
block_G.id = 7
block_G.history = 'Sarah loves dog'
block_G.parent_id = block_F.id
```

By this point, we can get rid of the West side version of the blockchain because we chose the longer version.

Here comes the problem. Say Sherly hates sharks but Sherly wants to get votes from a district where most people only vote for a candidate who loves sharks. To get more votes, Sherly broadcasts a block containing the following lie:

```
block_E = Block()
block_E.id = 5
block_E.history = 'Sherly loves shark'
block_E.parent_id = block_D.id
```

All is fine and dandy. The voting session takes one day. After one day has passed, the blockchain has gotten another two blocks:

```
block_E = Block()
block_E.id = 5
block_E.history = 'Sherly loves shark'
block_E.parent_id = block_D.id

block_F = Block()
block_F.id = 6
block_F.history = 'Lin Dan hates crab'
block_F.parent_id = block_E.id
```

```
block_G = Block()
block_G.id = 7
block_G.history = 'Bruce Wayne loves bat'
block_G.parent_id = block_F.id
```

The following figure illustrates the three blocks:

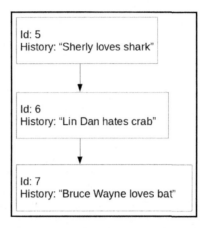

Now, Sherly needs to get votes from another district where most people only vote for candidates who hate sharks. So, how can Sherly tamper with the blockchain to make this work in her favor? Sherly could broadcast four blocks!

```
block_E = Block()
block_E.id = 5
block_E.history = 'Sherly hates shark'
block_E.parent_id = block_D.id

block_F = Block()
block_F.id = 6
block_F.history = 'Sherly loves dog'
block_F.parent_id = block_E.id

block_G = Block()
block_G.id = 7
block_G.history = 'Sherly loves turtle'
block_G.parent_id = block_F.id

block_H = Block()
block_H.id = 8
block_H.history = 'Sherly loves unicorn'
block_H.parent_id = block_G.id
```

The following figure illustrates the four blocks:

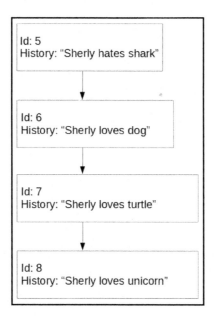

The miner will choose the blockchain from Sherly instead of the previous blockchain they kept, which contains the history of `Sherly loves sharks`. So, Sherly has been able to change the history. This is what we call a double-spending attack.

We can prevent this through proof of work (an incentive for adding blocks). We explained proof of work earlier in this chapter, but we haven't explained the incentive system yet. An incentive means that if the miner successfully adds a new block to the blockchain, the system gives them a digital reward. We can integrate it into the code as follows:

```
import hashlib

payload = b'{"history": "Sky loves turtle", "parent_id": 3, "id": 4}'
for i in range(10000000):
  nonce = str(i).encode('utf-8')
  result = hashlib.sha256(payload + nonce).hexdigest()
  if result[0:5] == '00000':
    // We made it, time to claim the prize
    reward[miner_id] += 1
    print(i)
    print(result)
    break
```

If Sherly wants to alter the history (by replacing some blocks), she needs to spend some resources by solving four puzzles in a short time. By the times she finishes doing this, the blockchain kept by the most miners would have likely added more blocks, making it longer than Sherly's blockchain.

This is the case because most miners want to get that reward we spoke of in the most efficient manner possible. To do this, they would get a new candidate block, work hard to find the answer in proof of work, and then add it to the longest chain as quickly as possible. But, why do they want to add it to the longest chain and not another chain? This is because it secures their reward.

Say we have two versions of the blockchain. One has three blocks, while the other has eight blocks. The most sensible way to add a new block is to add it to the blockchain that has eight blocks. If someone adds it to the blockchain that has three blocks, it is more likely to get discarded. Consequently, the reward would be taken away from the miner. The longest chain attracts the most miners anyway, and you want to be in the blockchain version that is kept by more people.

Some miners could persist in adding the block to the blockchain with three blocks, while other miners could also persist in adding the block to the blockchain with eight blocks. We call this a hard fork. Most of the time, miners will stick to the blockchain that has the longest chain.

To change the history, Sherly will need to outgun at least more than 50% of the miners, which is impossible. The older the block, the more secure the history in that block is. Say one person needs 5 minutes to do the puzzle work. In this case, to replace the last five blocks in the blockchain, Sherly needs more than 25 minutes (because Sherly needs at least six blocks to convince miners to replace the last five blocks in their blockchain). But in those 25 minutes, other miners would keep adding new blocks to the most popular blockchain. So when 25 minutes have passed, the most popular blockchain would have gained an additional five blocks! Maybe the miners take a nap for an hour and don't add any more blocks. In this case, Sherly could accumulate six blocks to tamper with the most popular blockchain. However, the incentive embedded in the blockchain keeps the miners awake 24/7 as they want to get the reward as much as possible. Consequently, it's a losing battle for Sherly.

Coding on the blockchain

As this book is being written, the two most popular cryptocurrencies are Bitcoin and Ethereum (once in a while, Ripple will take second place). If you ask a simple question to someone who knows a lot about cryptocurrencies, you may get an answer: Bitcoin is just for sending money, but you can create a program on Ethereum. The program can be tokens, auction, or escrow, among many other things. But that is a half-truth. You can also create a program on Bitcoin. Usually, people call this program a script. In fact, it is a must to provide a script in a Bitcoin transaction. A transaction in Bitcoin can be mundane, so if I want to send you 1 BTC (a unit of currency in Bitcoin) and your Bitcoin address is Z, I need to upload a script like this into Bitcoin blockchain:

```
What's your public key? If the public key is hashed, does it equal Z? If
yes, could you provide your private key to prove that you own this public
key?
```

But it could be a little bit fancier. Let's say you want to require at least two signatures from four authorized signatures to unlock this account; you can do that with Bitcoin script. Think creative and you can come up with something like this:

```
This transaction is frozen until 5 years from now. Then business will be as
usual, that the spender must provide public key and private key.
```

But a Bitcoin script is created with a simple programming language, incapable of even looping. It is stack-based. So, you put instructions: hash the public key, check a signature, and check the current time. Then, it will be executed on the Bitcoin node from left to right.

This means that you cannot create a fancy program, such as an auction, on Bitcoin. Bitcoin is designed just to store and transfer value (money). So it is purposely designed to avoid a complex program. In a Bitcoin node, every script is executed. Without a loop, a Bitcoin script will be so simple and you know when it will stop. But if you have a loop in a Bitcoin script, you don't know when it will stop. It could stop in the fourth iteration, or the millionth iteration, or in a far away future.

Some people were not satisfied with this limitation, so Ethereum was created. The programming language that you are equipped with on the Ethereum blockchain is much more sophisticated than the programming language in Bitcoin (there is a `while` or `for` construct). Technically speaking, you could create a program that runs forever in the Ethereum blockchain.

You can do what you can do in Bitcoin, which is store and transfer values. But there is so much more that you can do in Ethereum. You could create a voting program, an escrow service, an online auction, and even another cryptocurrency on top of it. So, people like to differentiate the currencies of **Bitcoin (BTC)** and **Ethereum (ETH)**. BTC is like digital gold. ETH is like oil and gas. Both are valuable, if we take that analogy. But, you can use oil and gas to create a whole new world, such as by creating plastics, fuel, and so on. On the other hand, what you can do with gold is quite limited, other than creating jewelry.

Creating a cryptocurrency on top of Ethereum is very easy. All you need is a weekend if you are a skilled programmer. You just inherit a class, and set your token's name and supply limit. Then, you compile it and launch to the Ethereum production blockchain, and you would have your own cryptocurrency. Prior to this, creating another cryptocurrency meant forking Bitcoin. The skill level required to do that is quite deep (C++, CMake, and replacing many parts of files in the Bitcoin core).

Other types of blockchain programmers

This chapter intended to give you an intuitive understanding of how blockchain works. However, it's not a complete scope of how it works. My explanation differs quite a lot from how Bitcoin works (and even Ethereum). Ethereum does not use `SHA-256` for hashing; it commonly uses the `Keccak-256` algorithm. In our case, we only put one history/transaction/payload in one block, but Bitcoin can save more than 1,000 transactions in one block. Then, we generate a private key and public key by using RSA cryptography, while Bitcoin and Ethereum use elliptic curve cryptography. In our case, the payload is history (who likes/loves/hates an animal), but in Bitcoin it's a transaction that has a dependency on the previous payload. In Ethereum itself, it's a state of programs. So, if you have variable a as equal to integer 5 in the payload, it could be something like change variable a to integer 7. In the Bitcoin consensus, we choose the blockchain that has the most hashing rate power, not the one that has the longest chain. For example, blockchain A has two blocks, but each block has the answer to solve the puzzle with 12 leading zeros, while blockchain B has ten blocks but each block has the answer to solving the puzzle with only five leading zeros. In this situation, blockchain A has the most hash rate power.

Now, we go back to the following questions: what does it mean to be a blockchain programmer? How many types of Blockchain programmers are there? What is the scope of this book?

Blockchain programming could mean that you are working on improving the state of Bitcoin or creating a fork of Bitcoin, such as Bitcoin Cash. You need C++ and Python. If you are creating a Bitcoin fork, such as Bitcoin Gold, you need to dig deeper into cryptography. In Bitcoin Gold, the developers changed the proof of work hashing function from SHA-256 to Equihash because Equihash is ASIC resistant. ASIC resistance means you cannot create a specific machine to do the hashing. You need a computer with a GPU to do the Equihash hashing function, but this book will not discuss that.

Furthermore, Blockchain programming could mean that you are working on improving the Ethereum Virtual Machine. You need Go, C++, or Python. You need to understand how to interact with low-level cryptographic library functions. An intuitive understanding of how basic cryptography works is not enough, but this book will not discuss that either.

Blockchain programming could mean that you are writing the program on top of Ethereum. You need Solidity or Vyper for this, which this book will discuss. You only need an intuitive understanding of how basic cryptography works. You have been abstracted away from low-level cryptography. Once in a while, you might use a hashing function in a program you write, but nothing fancy.

Blockchain programming could mean that you are writing a program to interact with the program on top of Ethereum, which sounds meta. But what you will need for this depends on the platform. If it is a mobile app, you need Kotlin, Java, Swift, Obj-C, or even C++. If it is a web frontend, you will most likely need JavaScript. Only an intuitive understanding of how basic cryptography works is needed. This book will discuss some of this.

This is the same as if I asked you, *what does it entail when someone wants to become a web developer?* The answer is quite diverse. Should I learn Ruby, Java, PHP, or Python? Should I learn Ruby on Rails, Laravel, or Django?

This book is going to teach you how to build a program on top of Ethereum (not to be confused with building Ethereum itself). Comparing this with web development, this is like saying that this book is going to teach you how to build a web application using Ruby on Rails, but the book does not teach you how to dissect the Ruby on Rails framework itself. This does not mean that the internals of Ruby on Rails are not important, it just means that most of the time, you don't need them.

This book will teach you to use the Python programming language, assuming that you have basic knowledge of Python already. But why Python? The answer is a cliché: Python is one of the easiest and most popular programming languages. It lowers the barrier to entry for someone who wants to jump into blockchain.

Summary

In this chapter, we looked into the technology behind cryptocurrencies such as Bitcoin and Ethereum. This technology enables the decentralization of storing values or code. We also covered cryptography by using private and public keys to secure the integrity of any data. Further on, we learned about hash functions, proof of work, consensus, and the basic concepts of blockchain programming.

In the next chapter, we will learn about a smart contract, a kind of program that lives in Ethereum. A smart contract is different than a kind of program that lives in a server, such as an application written with Ruby on Rails, Laravel, or Django. The differences are more than just the syntax; the concept is radically different than a normal web application.

References

- https://techcrunch.com/2018/06/25/andreessen-horowitz-has-a-new-crypto-fund-and-its-first-female-general-partner-is-running-it-with-chris-dixon/
- https://bitcoin.org/bitcoin.pdf
- https://bitcoin.org/en/development

Smart Contract Fundamentals 2

In this chapter, we will explore the basics of smart contracts. While in Bitcoin we store value, in Ethereum we store code. The code that we store in Ethereum is called a **smart contract**. A smart contract is a trustless code, meaning the integrity of the code is guarded by algorithms and cryptography. We can store, the code which is censorship-resistant and is able to avoid third-party interference even from the developer of the smart contract. This opens possibilities of creating many types of application, such as transparent digital tokens, trustless crowdsale, secure voting systems, and autonomous organization.

The following topics will be covered in this chapter:

- Installing an Ethereum development environment
- Writing a smart contract
- Deploying a smart contract to Ethereum blockchain
- Interacting with smart contracts
- Why smart contracts?

Installing an Ethereum development environment

It's time to create a smart contract. If you are familiar with Solidity, Truffle, Ganache, and the smart contract fundamentals, you can skip ahead to `Chapter 3`, *Implementing Smart Contracts Using Vyper*. Here, we will focus on the content of a smart contract created with Solidity. Throughout the remainder of the book, we will use the Vyper programming language to develop a smart contract. However, we will still use the same development environment (such as Ganache) in the rest of the book.

Installing Node.js

Node.js is a popular framework for developing web applications, mobile applications, and decentralized applications. Head to `https://nodejs.org` and download the latest version (which is version 10 at the time of writing). Here is how to install Node.js on the Ubuntu Linux platform:

```
$ curl -sL https://deb.nodesource.com/setup_10.x | sudo -E bash -
$ sudo apt-get install -y nodejs
$ node --version
v10.15.0
```

Installing Truffle and Solidity

Truffle is a development framework for developing a smart contract with Solidity. You can create one without Truffle, but Truffle makes it easier. Without Truffle, you can still write a smart contract, but to compile it, you have to launch the Solidity compiler with certain flags. Then, in order to deploy this smart contract to the blockchain, you have to create a script to send the bytecode to the blockchain. With Truffle, in order to compile, you call the, `truffle compile` command, and to deploy a smart contract to the blockchain, you call the `truffle migrate` command after writing a simple migration script. Truffle also provides you with a tool for interacting with the smart contract in the blockchain network. It has everything you need to develop a smart contract. As stated previously, however, we will not be using this framework in the next chapter.

We are going to start by installing Truffle using the Node.js package manager. In Ubuntu Linux, in order to install Truffle globally, we have to use `sudo`. As described in the previous paragraph, Truffle is a smart contract development framework containing many tools, including a console application to interact with the blockchain network and the development blockchain software. On top of that, with Truffle, you get the Solidity compiler as well.

But first, you need to make sure `npm` installs software globally in your home directory:

```
$ mkdir ~/.npm-global
$ npm config set prefix '~/.npm-global'
```

Then append this line to the `~/.` profile file:

```
export PATH=~/.npm-global/bin:$PATH
```

Now, open a new Terminal so that the new profile file takes effect or, alternatively, do the following:

```
$ source ~/.profile
```

Then, we can install Truffle as follows:

```
$ npm install -g truffle
$ truffle version
Truffle v5.0.2 (core: 5.0.2)
Solidity v0.5.0 (solc-js)
Node v10.15.0
```

Installing Ganache

For developing a smart contract, people usually use Ganache. Ganache is a private, developmental Ethereum network that you can only use in the Ethereum development phase. The Truffle framework already includes the Ethereum blockchain network, which has the same purpose as Ganache. The difference between the two is that Ganache has a frontend GUI and a more user-friendly interface.

When you launch Ganache, you are equipped with 10 accounts, each filled with 100 ethers, which is the currency in Ethereum blockchain. As you will see later in this chapter, the concept of money (such as holding, sending, and receiving money, and tracking the balance) in Ethereum programming is important. You need to spend money in order to launch a smart contract in Ethereum blockchain. You can send money from an account to a smart contract, and a smart contract can, in turn, send money to other smart contracts or other accounts.

To download the software, go to the Ganache website: `https://www.truffleframework.com/ganache`. For the Linux platform, the software is called `ganache-1.2.3-x86_64.AppImage`. After downloading this, you must set the correct permission before executing it:

```
$ chmod a+x ganache-1.2.3-x86_64.AppImage
$ ./ganache-1.2.3-x86_64.AppImage
```

Writing a smart contract

Once all the requisite software is installed, we can start writing a smart contract. First, we will create a new directory, and then initialize it with the Truffle development tool:

```
$ mkdir my_first_smart_contract
$ cd my_first_smart_contract
$ truffle init
```

The output of the `truffle init` command is as follows:

```
✓ Preparing to download
✓ Downloading
✓ Cleaning up temporary files
✓ Setting up box

Unbox successful. Sweet!

Commands:

  Compile:        truffle compile
  Migrate:        truffle migrate
  Test contracts: truffle test
```

This will command Truffle to initialize your directory to be a smart contract development project. A couple of directories are available to you when developing a smart contract in this project directory:

```
$ ls
contracts migrations test truffle-config.js
```

You usually incorporate a smart contract's source code in the `contracts` folder. The `migrations` folder holds the files that are used in the deployment of smart contracts, and the `test` folder holds the `test` files. You can configure the smart contract deployment settings in the `truffle-config.js` file. We will create the first smart contract and name it `donation.sol` using the following code:

```solidity
pragma solidity ^0.5.0;

contract Donation {
    address public donatur;
    address payable donatee;
    uint public money;
    string public useless_variable;
```

```
constructor() public {
  donatee = msg.sender;
  useless_variable = "Donation string";
}

function change_useless_variable(string memory param) public {
  useless_variable = param;
}

function donate() public payable {
  donatur = msg.sender;
  money = msg.value;
}

function receive_donation() public {
  donatee.transfer(address(this).balance);
}
}
```

If you are new to smart contracts, there may be some unfamiliar keywords in the preceding example. In this chapter, we are not going to discuss everything to do with Solidity. Instead, we will only look into the features of Solidity that are necessary for building a smart contract and learning the concept of a smart contract.

But first, let's compile this smart contract written in Solidity to Ethereum bytecode and an **application binary interface (abi)**. To do this, we will run the following command in the Truffle project directory:

```
$ truffle compile
```

The result of the compilation can be seen in the build/contracts folder, named Donation.json:

```
Compiling ./contracts/Migrations.sol...
Compiling ./contracts/donation.sol...
Writing artifacts to ./build/contracts
```

If you open the file, you can see a number of interesting things. This .json file is 1,530 lines long. The json object in this file has 14 keys. You only need to think about two keys for now. The first one is the interface (called **abi**), and the second one is the binary that can be executed on the Ethereum Virtual Machine (called bytecode). Refer to the code file in the following GitLab link for the code in this section: https://gitlab.com/arjunaskykok/hands-on-blockchain-for-python-developers/blob/master/chapter_02/my_first_smart_contract/build/contracts/Donation.json.

We cannot run this binary file in the same way as when we compile the C code and execute the binary directly. We need to put this binary into the Ethereum virtual machine. The interface itself is needed for us to interact with the smart contract later when we develop a decentralized application. When you deploy a smart contract to Ethereum blockchain, you need the bytecode. When you want to interact with a smart contract already deployed in Ethereum blockchain, you need the `abi` interface.

Deploying a smart contract to Ethereum blockchain

These are the steps for deploying a smart contract to Ethereum blockchain with Truffle:

1. **Write a migration script**: To deploy your smart contract, you need to write a migration file. Create a new file named `migrations/2_deploy_donation.js`. Then, we fill this file with the following script:

   ```
   var Donation = artifacts.require("./Donation.sol");

   module.exports = function(deployer) {
     deployer.deploy(Donation);
   };
   ```

   As for the `migrations/1_initial_migration.js` and `contracts/Migrations.sol` files, we leave these as they are for now. Truffle needs these files in order to deploy a smart contract.

2. **Launch Ganache (the blockchain for Ethereum development)**: Now you need to launch Ganache. Assuming you have been given proper permission, run the following command line to execute the file:

   ```
   ./ganache-1.2.3-x86_64.AppImage
   ```

As you can see in the following screenshot, you have numerous accounts, each with a balance of 100 ethers:

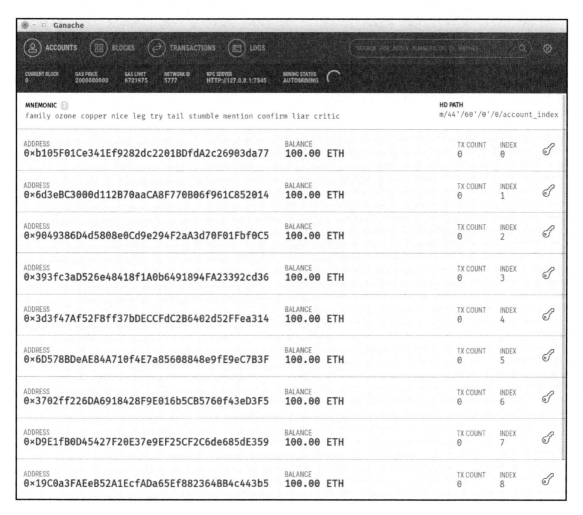

One thing you will notice from the Ganache screen is the **RPC SERVER**, which is located in `http://127.0.0.1:7545`. This is where your Ethereum blockchain is located in the `Truffle` project directory.

3. **Edit the Truffle configuration file**: If you open `truffle-config.js`, the code will look like this after removing the comment lines:

```
module.exports = {
  networks: {
  },
  mocha: {
  },
  compilers: {
    solc: {
    }
  }
};
```

Wipe it out and add the following lines of code to the `truffle-config.js` file:

```
module.exports = {
  networks: {
    "development": {
      network_id: 5777,
      host: "localhost",
      port: 7545
    },
  }
};
```

The `host` and `port` is taken from the RPC server in the Ganache screen, and `network_id` is taken from Network ID in the Ganache screen.

4. **Execute migration scripts**: To deploy your smart contract, you can execute it as follows:

```
$ truffle migrate
```

The Truffle framework will take your bytecode defined in the `Donation.json` file and send it to Ethereum blockchain or Ganache. This will provide you with the following output:

```
⚠ Important ⚠
If you're using an HDWalletProvider, it must be Web3 1.0 enabled or your migration will hang.


Starting migrations...
======================
> Network name:    'development'
> Network id:      5777
> Block gas limit: 6721975


1_initial_migration.js
======================

   Deploying 'Migrations'
   ----------------------
   > transaction hash:    0xc265c6afb14e3a5d409d7bf66ed3d3f8fe4654d04ef55d854190daacdc943e03
   > Blocks: 0           Seconds: 0
   > contract address:    0x9Dc44aa8d05c86388E647F954D00CaA858837804
   > account:             0xb105F01Ce341Ef9282dc2201BDfdA2c26903da77
   > balance:             99.99430184
   > gas used:            284908
   > gas price:           20 gwei
   > value sent:          0 ETH
   > total cost:          0.00569816 ETH


   > Saving migration to chain.
   > Saving artifacts
   ---------------------------------------
   > Total cost:          0.00569816 ETH


2_deploy_donation.js
====================

   Deploying 'Donation'
   --------------------
   > transaction hash:    0xfdc69335e7cf2974529d298202fd2ecbce8f4756f444de2cc20fff898f3fef18
   > Blocks: 0           Seconds: 0
   > contract address:    0x3E9417399786347B6Ab38f59d3f00829d6bba7b8
   > account:             0xb105F01Ce341Ef9282dc2201BDfdA2c26903da77
   > balance:             99.98444338
   > gas used:            450889
   > gas price:           20 gwei
   > value sent:          0 ETH
   > total cost:          0.00901778 ETH


   > Saving migration to chain.
   > Saving artifacts
   ---------------------------------------
   > Total cost:          0.00901778 ETH

Summary
=======
> Total deployments:   2
> Final cost:          0.01471594 ETH
```

In the `2_deploy_donation.js` section, take note of the hexadecimal number after the word `contract address:`, which is `0x3e9417399786347b6ab38f59d3f00829d6bba7b8`. This is the smart contract's address, which is similar to the URL of a web application.

If `Network is up to date.` was output when you tried to deploy your smart contract, you can delete the files inside the `build/contracts` directory and run this version using the `truffle migrate` command:

```
$ truffle migrate --reset
```

Now, we will take a look at the changes on the Ganache screen:

The most important thing to note is that the first
account, `0xb105F01Ce341Ef9282dc2201BDfdA2c26903da77`, has lost money. The
balance is no longer 100 ETH; it is **99.98 ETH**. So where did the 0.02 ETH go? Miners need to
be incentivized in order to write your smart contract into the Ethereum blockchain. Note
that, the **CURRENT BLOCK** is no longer 0, but **4**. So, 0.02 ETH will be the fee for the miner
who successfully puts the block containing your smart contract into the blockchain. But, of
course, in this case, there is no miner because we use Ganache, the Ethereum development
blockchain. Ganache just simulates the transaction fee by incorporating a smart contract
into the blockchain.

If you click the **TRANSACTIONS** tab, you will see something like this:

You have now created two contracts (Donation and Migrations). Once a smart contract is
deployed, unless you apply a method to shut it down, it will be in the blockchain forever. If
there is a bug in your smart contract, you cannot patch it. You have to deploy a fixed smart
contract in a different address.

Interacting with smart contracts

To interact with your smart contract that resides in Ethereum blockchain, execute this command inside your `Truffle` project directory:

```
$ truffle console
```

Then, in the `truffle` console prompt, execute the following command:

```
truffle(development)> Donation.deployed().then(function(instance) { return
instance.useless_variable.call(); });
'Donation string'
```

If you are confused about `then`, the Truffle console uses the concept of callback, on which accessing the smart contract object is executed asynchronously. This statement in the Truffle console returns immediately before the callback is being executed. In the callback function, you will accept the smart contract instance as an `instance` parameter. Then, we can access our `useless_variable` variable from this `instance` parameter. Then, to retrieve the value, we have to execute the `call` method on that variable.

The Truffle framework would use the **abi** defined in the `Donation.json` file to understand what interfaces are available in your smart contract. Recall that you define the `useless_variable` in your smart contract and set it to `Donation string` in the constructor (or initialization) function. It is free to read a public variable in this way; it does not cost any ether because it is stored in blockchain.

Let me remind you what it means if the variable is stored in blockchain. If you incorporate this smart contract in the Ethereum production blockchain, the `useless_variable` variable will be stored in every Ethereum node. At the time of writing, there are around 10,000 nodes. This number keeps changing, as can be seen here: https://www.ethernodes.org. A node can be in one computer, and a computer can hold a couple of nodes. However, it is most likely that one computer holds only one node because the requirement to become the host of a node is pretty high. You need a node if you want to interact with the blockchain (there are also other options for this, such as using API to interact with someone else's node). For this reason, it is free to read the `useless_variable` variable because you just read it from your computer.

If you are confused by this free concept, let's make it clearer by changing the `useless_variable` variable into something else:

```
truffle(development)> Donation.deployed().then(function(instance) { return
instance.change_useless_variable("sky is blue", {from:
"0xb105F01Ce341Ef9282dc2201BDfdA2c26903da77" }); });
```

You would get the following output:

```
truffle(development)> Donation.deployed().then(function(instance) { return instance.change_useless_variabl
e("sky is blue", {from: "0xb105F01Ce341Ef9282dc2201BDfdA2c26903da77" }); });
{ tx:
   '0xbbbffcb848999907c55c5ae5f5e7e0f4c8f73316bfc66170f018a5bf52a6d1b6',
  receipt:
   { transactionHash:
      '0xbbbffcb848999907c55c5ae5f5e7e0f4c8f73316bfc66170f018a5bf52a6d1b6',
     transactionIndex: 0,
     blockHash:
      '0x31875d328acfa552bfe8705cf930037c0061bba5770ce38d3ae5eecad2b33118',
     blockNumber: 5,
     from: '0xb105f01ce341ef9282dc2201bdfda2c26903da77',
     to: '0x3e9417399786347b6ab38f59d3f00829d6bba7b8',
     gasUsed: 33684,
     cumulativeGasUsed: 33684,
     contractAddress: null,
     logs: [],
     status: true,
     logsBloom:
      '0x000000000000000000000000000000000000000000000000000000000000000000000000000000000000000000000000000
00000000000000000000000000000000000000000000000000000000000000000000000000000000000000000000000000000000000
000000000000000000000000000000000000000000000000000000000000000000000000000000000000000000000000000000000000
000000000000000000000000000000000000000000000000000000000000000000000000000000000000000000000000000000000000
000000000000000000000000000000000000000000000000000000000000000000000000000000000000000000000000000000000',
     v: '0x1c',
     r:
      '0xe8a28af0553506b18c860a46e970fec181a3d1d6a784362cd28c814a72f04f45',
     s:
      '0x7b3406452158e26078a066ee85928112753698462ed7d080076857b904d853f3',
     rawLogs: [] },
  logs: [] }  _
```

There is another cryptic hexadecimal number after the word `from`, which is `0xb105F01Ce341Ef9282dc2201BDfdA2c26903da77`. This is the public address of the first account in Ganache. You can confirm it by looking at the Ganache screen. Here, there is a difference in the way you read the `useless_variable` variable and set it with different content. Changing the content of the variable requires different syntax and, more importantly, an account to use. An account is required because you need to spend some money when changing the variable in blockchain. When you change the value of this `useless_variable` variable in the smart contract in the blockchain, you are basically broadcasting to all Ethereum nodes in the Ethereum production blockchain, which has around 10,000 nodes available to update the content of `useless_variable`. We are using Ganache, which is an Ethereum development blockchain, but in a production setting, you need to sign your transaction to change the content of the variable with a private key. A private key's purpose is similar to a password on an account, but a private key cannot be changed, while you can update your password as many times as you like. If you forget your password, you could reset it and click the link in your confirmation email to update it. In blockchain, this is not an option.

If you check Ganache now, your balance stays the same; only the block number increases from 4 to 5:

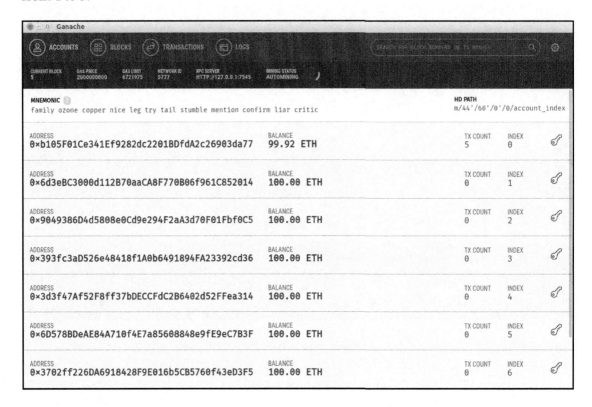

This happens because the amount of money required is so small. You can look at the output of the command to change the value of `useless_variable` after you execute the last command. Look at the **gas used** field; this is what you spent when executing a function in a smart contract. The amount of gas used is 33684, but this is in gwei, not in ether. 1 ether is equal to 1,000,000,000 gwei, so it is around 0.00003 ether. In this case, the gas is calculated automatically but, later, you can set how much gas you want to allocate when executing any function in Ethereum blockchain. If you do not contribute much ether, and the amount of gas allocated is small, there is a big chance your execution will be accorded lower priority. It will take longer for the transaction to be confirmed (meaning the value of the variable has been changed). It could get rejected by miners if the network is experiencing heavy traffic.

This concept of spending money to change the state of the program is new. Reading everything from blockchain is free because all the data is in your computer (if you have Ethereum node), but to change or add something in blockchain requires money. This occurs because you change the data in all Ethereum nodes across the globe, which is expensive! As well as changing the state of the smart contract, computation that runs in memory also requires money.

Sending ether to smart contracts

Now, let's send some ether to the smart contract. Let's use the second account for this. The second account wants to donate 5 ether using a smart contract as follows:

```
truffle(development)> Donation.deployed().then(function(instance) { return
instance.donate({ from: "0x6d3eBC3000d112B70aaCA8F770B06f961C852014",
value: 5000000000000000000 }); });
```

You would get the following output:

```
truffle(development)> Donation.deployed().then(function(instance) { return instance.donate({ from: "0x6d3e
BC3000d112B70aaCA8F770B06f961C852014", value: 5000000000000000000 }); });
{ tx:
  '0x5aa91711451be98ee2aa496e0c5e256cc3130548752ecde956562d910ed39f58',
  receipt:
  { transactionHash:
    '0x5aa91711451be98ee2aa496e0c5e256cc3130548752ecde956562d910ed39f58',
    transactionIndex: 0,
    blockHash:
    '0xc00e847b4828be83b1480df758aed02d98b3e8a3cd39d867a820eac03b6f9269',
    blockNumber: 6,
    from: '0x6d3ebc3000d112b70aaca8f770b06f961c852014',
    to: '0x3e9417399786347b6ab38f59d3f00829d6bba7b8',
    gasUsed: 61770,
    cumulativeGasUsed: 61770,
    contractAddress: null,
    logs: [],
    status: true,
    logsBloom:
    '0x00000000000000000000000000000000000000000000000000000000000000000
00000000000000000000000000000000000000000000000000000000000000000000000000
00000000000000000000000000000000000000000000000000000000000000000000000000
00000000000000000000000000000000000000000000000000000000000000000000000000
0000000000000000000000000000000000000000000000000000000000000000000000000',
    v: '0x1b',
    r:
    '0x4b96902ef07e8797251f1260f50ea93d2b9fd1d0fb40d9137592d748684e74ff',
    s:
    '0x72862773e36b7230215fa709f002d5274b2818bed1b87face0184d4f399822e0',
    rawLogs: [] },
  logs: [] }
```

As well as the `from` field, you need to add a `value` field. In this `value` field, you input how much money you want to send to the smart contract. You may wonder why this number has so many zeros. When you transfer money in Ethereum blockchain, you must use the lowest currency unit (similarly to converting from dollars to cents), which is called **wei**. 1 ether is 1,000,000,000,000,000,000 wei (18 zeros). You want to send 5 ether, making it 5,000,000,000,000,000,000. Now, if you look at your Ganache screen, you will notice that the balance drops to 95 ether. So 5 ether is now held in the smart contract, as demonstrated in the following screenshot:

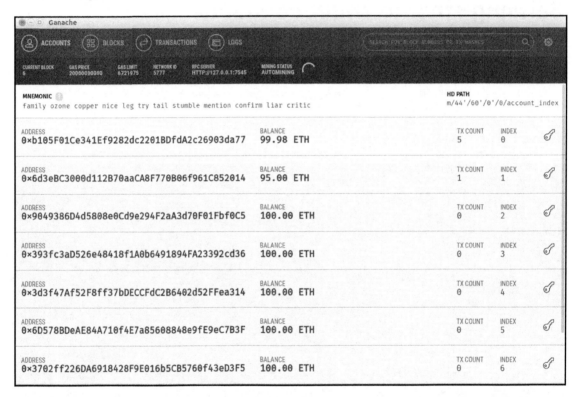

Let's withdraw this using the first account:

```
truffle(development)> Donation.deployed().then(function(instance) { return
instance.receive_donation({ from:
"0xb105F01Ce341Ef9282dc2201BDfdA2c26903da77" }); });
```

You will get the following output:

```
truffle(development)> Donation.deployed().then(function(instance) { return instance.receive_donation({ fro
m: "0xb105F01Ce341Ef9282dc2201BDfdA2c26903da77" }); });
{ tx:
   '0x358d305690351679d395d0fcc731d7cf870dba35ed04baaf4285b911b2f8034e',
  receipt:
   { transactionHash:
      '0x358d305690351679d395d0fcc731d7cf870dba35ed04baaf4285b911b2f8034e',
     transactionIndex: 0,
     blockHash:
      '0x4ce9350d10e5f09620419bee25e5f9c690f52ab8067a64d9302093c7823d6c4f',
     blockNumber: 7,
     from: '0xb105f01ce341ef9282dc2201bdfda2c26903da77',
     to: '0x3e9417399786347b6ab38f59d3f00829d6bba7b8',
     gasUsed: 29616,
     cumulativeGasUsed: 29616,
     contractAddress: null,
     logs: [],
     status: true,
     logsBloom:
      '0x000000000000000000000000000000000000000000000000000000000000000000000000000000000000000000000000
00000000000000000000000000000000000000000000000000000000000000000000000000000000000000000000000000000000
00000000000000000000000000000000000000000000000000000000000000000000000000000000000000000000000000000000
00000000000000000000000000000000000000000000000000000000000000000000000000000000000000000000000000000000
0000000000000000000000000000000000000000000000000000000000000000000000000000000000000000000000',
     v: '0x1b',
     r:
      '0xe203637d37c1624324d62ed8f5aa76e4a4c4fd59b513e062dcd980d5fd6cb500',
     s:
      '0x6b5674c93031e247f7c16042d17d0dab437c57b437c9c8c7615db5a044c19e83',
     rawLogs: [] },
  logs: [] }
```

This execution has the same syntax as before, minus the `value` field. Now take a look at the Ganache screen. The first account has between 104 and 105 ether (such as 104.8 or 104.9 ether). It is not 105 ether because we already outlaid some money launching the smart contract using the first account, and for paying the transaction fee when executing some functions in the smart contract:

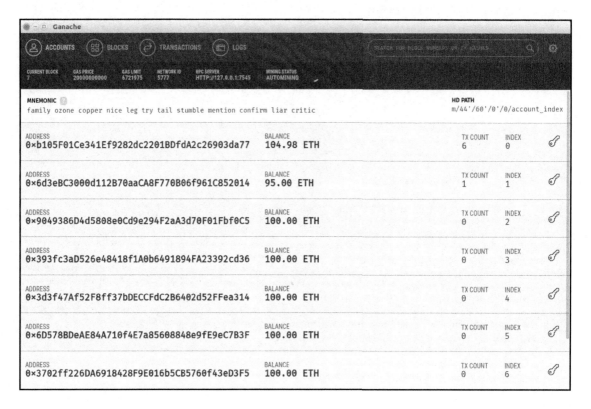

Why smart contracts?

You have now seen a smart contract in action. So what is all the fuss about? What can smart contracts do that traditional programs (normal web applications) can't? When it comes to changing the value of a variable in a program that lives on the network, we can use remote procedure call. More commonly, we can store a variable in a database and people can change the value in the database from a web application. When sending money, we can integrate our web application with Stripe or PayPal, giving us the means to send money. Alternatively, you could create a table in a database for storing digital money. Ether in Ethereum is basically digital money. In fact, a normal web application can do everything a smart contract can do, but faster and cheaper. The key difference is that blockchain solutions can be trustless. This means that you can put trust in the program itself, but not the operator.

In a normal web application, we rely on trusting the operators (developers or system administrators) of the web application. We hope that they develop and deploy the web application honestly. There is no way for us, as a user of the web application, to make sure the web application does what it tells everyone it is trying to do.

Let's say we have a web application that hosts videos (such as YouTube or Vimeo). The web application can increase the number of likes on a video if a user clicks the **Like** button. The rule is that a user can only like a video once. Consequently, you would expect a video that contains 400 likes to have 400 users who have liked that video. What if I tell you that behind the scenes, a system administrator can increase the number of likes artificially? This means that among 400 likes, it could be that only 300 likes come from genuine users. The other 100 likes are inflated by the system administrator. It does not have to be as raw as updating a table in a database directly, for example, through `UPDATE video_likes SET likes_amount = 400 WHERE video_id = 5;`. The way to inflate the number of likes could be embedded inside the system.

Normal users would not notice this. The company behind the web application could publish the source code on GitHub. But how do you make sure the web application is indeed built from the source code hosted on GitHub? What if, after deploying the web application, the system administrator or the developer patches the system?

There are a number of ways to prevent this digital cheating. First of all, we can introduce an IT auditor. These could be from governmental or non-governmental organizations. They will audit the source code of the system and, more importantly, check what the code does in the production system. In this situation, you move your trust from the developers or system administrators to third-party auditors.

As an IT consultant, I make a livelihood by building web applications and mobile applications. I once encountered a prospective client who wanted to make a digital newspaper (along the lines of the Guardian or the New York Times). This client asked me whether there is a way to move any article into the most viewed articles section as desired. The motive here was to promote specific articles, even if it meant that the system would be lying to users about what the most frequently viewed articles are.

The CEO of Reddit recently issued a public apology for being caught modifying comments made about him on the website. More information on this is provided at the following link: https://techcrunch.com/2016/11/23/reddit-huffman-trump/.

Even well-known websites play with digital cheating. For instance, some cryptocurrency exchanges fake trading volumes. More information is provided on this at the following link: https://medium.com/@sylvainartplayribes/chasing-fake-volume-a-crypto-plague-ea1a3c1e0b5e.

Smart contracts are another means of preventing digital cheating. A developer of a smart contract could publish the source code and deploy the smart contract into Ethereum blockchain. People can verify whether the source code being published and the smart contract being deployed are one and the same. A developer could create a method to cheat inside the smart contract, but this will be caught by users because they could reconstruct the source code of the smart contract from the smart contract's bytecode in the blockchain. A developer could not patch the smart contract that is already being deployed.

There are other smart contract properties, such as autonomy and censorship resistance. However, none of these properties beat its transparency. Alternatively, you must have greater power than all 10,000 nodes working together to protect the credibility of the Ethereum system. To make the math simple, you need to buy more than 5,000 computers with high-end GPUs. Let's say you have that amount of resources in order to cheat. Honest miners will be alarmed when you cheat in the Ethereum system, and they will make a noise on the internet. So if you have the means to cheat in Ethereum, you cannot do it sneakily. Furthermore, if you have the means to obtain 5,000 computers with high-end GPUs, you could become a miner in the Ethereum platform and generate a nice income. Consequently, it is very hard to cheat in the Ethereum platform.

Summary

In this chapter, we explored how to install Solidity development tools: Node.js, Truffle, or Ganache. We then learned how to write a smart contract and compile it. After that, we looked at the concept of deploying a smart contract to Ethereum blockchain, followed by interacting with a smart contract being deployed with the Truffle console tool. We gained an understanding of the concept of sending ether to a smart contract and gas usage when executing a function in a smart contract. In the last step, we familiarized ourselves with why the smart concept works so well, with the potential to create a program that is censorship-resistant and transparent, and that cannot be circumvented.

In the next chapter, we will learn how to implement smart contracts using Vyper.

Further reading

Ethereum yellow paper: `https://ethereum.github.io/yellowpaper/paper.pdf`

Ethereum white paper: `https://github.com/ethereum/wiki/wiki/White-Paper`

Implementing Smart Contracts Using Vyper

3

Many programmers who are learning how to write a smart contract will learn about the Solidity programming language. There are abundant sources of online tutorials and books that can teach you about Solidity. When combined with the Truffle framework, Solidity forms a killer combo for developing a smart contract. Almost all smart contracts that live on the Ethereum blockchain are written in the Solidity programming language.

In this chapter, we will explore how to write a smart contract. However, we are not going to use the Solidity programming language for this. Instead, we will use the Vyper programming language.

The following topics will be covered in this chapter:

- Motivations behind Vyper
- Installing Vyper
- Creating a smart contract using Vyper
- Deploying a smart contract to Ganache
- Going deeper into Vyper
- Interacting with other smart contracts
- Compiling code programmatically
- Other tricks

Motivations behind Vyper

Writing a smart contract is different than developing a normal web application. When developing a normal web application, the motto is *move fast and break things*. The speed of developing a web application is paramount. If there is a bug in the application, you can always upgrade the application later. Alternatively, if the bug is catastrophic, you can patch it online or take the application offline before introducing a fix. There is a very popular word to describe the ideal mindset in developing a normal web application—agile. You need to be flexible in order to change the software as the requirements change.

However, writing a smart contract requires a different mindset. The application of smart contracts can range from writing a financial application to launching a rocket into space. Fixing an error once a smart contract is deployed is very difficult. You cannot replace a smart contract because once it is deployed, it is deployed. You can destroy a smart contract if you write a function to do so, but the only way to fix a faulty smart contract is to deploy a new smart contract that has the fix to the error in a new address, and then communicate this situation to all concerned parties. But you cannot replace a smart contract.

So, the ideal situation would be a smart contract deployed on the blockchain with no bugs, or at least without malignant bugs. However, bugs still appear in smart contracts that are released in the real world.

So, what kind of bugs can appear in smart contracts? The first kind is the one that will make your money disappear. Let's say you are writing a smart contract for an **initial coin offering (ICO)**. An ICO is the accumulation of capital by selling tokens that you have created on top of an Ethereum blockchain. So basically, people buy your token with ethers. You can set the price as you like—for example, *1 ETH = 100 YOURTOKEN*. This means that people would get 100 of your tokens if they pay you 1 ether.

The first bug that you can introduce is that people can send money (ethers) to your smart contract, but you cannot withdraw it (either you forgot to implement the withdrawal method or the withdrawal method is faulty). This would mean that you could check your smart contract's balance, and the ether balance could well be worth $1 million, but it would be stuck there forever and no one would be able to claim it.

Another bug could be that you forgot to secure the method to destroy a smart contract. In Ethereum, you are incentivized to remove stuff from the blockchain because storage is expensive. So if you deploy a smart contract, you will pay a gas fee because your smart contract will be kept. You can experiment with it, and then if you get bored with your smart contract, you can destroy it. To do that, Ethereum will give some gas back to your account. This is to discourage spamming the Ethereum blockchain. So, going back to our case of the smart contract's bug, imagine that you have accumulated $1 million worth of ether in your smart contract, and then someone destroys your smart contract account by accessing a function to destroy it. In this case, your ether balance will be destroyed as well.

The last type of bug is one that allows a hacker to steal your ether balance and move it to their account. This could occur under many different circumstances. For example, maybe you forgot to the set correct permissions in the withdrawal function, or maybe the permission in the withdrawal function is too open.

Of course, all of these bugs can be traced back to the fault of the programmers. To avoid these kinds of bugs, a new kind of job was born—a smart contract auditor, who audits your smart contract to make sure it does not have bugs. However, Vitalik Buterin (the inventor of Ethereum) then looked at the tool (the programming language, in this case) and wondered whether this situation could be mitigated by improving the tool itself. The culprit in this case is the Solidity programming language. Vitalik argued that Solidity has some features that are powerful, but have the potential to create bugs. Although the developers of Solidity had a plan to improve the safety of Solidity, Vitalik wanted some freedom to experiment with a fresh perspective. From this, Vyper was born.

Say that you created a parent class that has an important function. In your current or child class, you use this function without checking its definition. Perhaps the parent class was written by someone else in your team. Programmers are sometimes too lazy to check function definitions in other files; they will scroll up and down in a source code file to read the code, but programmers often will not check code in other files enabled by the inheritance feature.

Another Solidity feature that could really make a smart contract complicated and hard to read is a modifier, which is like a preliminary function. The following code shows how a modifier is used in Solidity:

```
modifier onlyBy(address _account)
{
  require(msg.sender == _account, "Sender not authorized.");
  _;
}
function withdraw() public onlyBy(owner)
{
  //withdraw money;
}
```

If we want to use the `withdraw()` method, the smart contract will execute the `onlyBy()` modifier method first. The `require` phrase is used to ensure that `msg.sender` (which calls this method) is the same as the `account` variable that was sent as a parameter. This example is simple. You can read all of the code in the blink of an eye. However, consider the fact that these functions are separated by many lines, or even defined in another file. Programmers have a tendency to overlook the definition of the `onlyBy()` method.

Function overloading is one of the most powerful features in programming languages. This is a feature that enables you to send different parameters to get different functions, as shown in the following code:

```
function flexible_function(uint _in) public {
    other_balance = _in;
}

function flexible_function(uint _in, uint _in2) public {
    other_balance = _in + _in2;
}

function flexible_function(uint _in, uint _in2, uint _in3) public {
    other_balance = _in + _in2 - _in3;
}
```

However, the function overloading feature can mislead programmers, causing them to execute a function with a different intention. A programmer might only remember that the `flexible_function` function does this, but could innocently execute a different kind of function than `flexible_function`.

Consequently, some smart people decided that while all of these features make it possible to create a really complex program, these features should be limited to developing a smart contract. Perhaps they got this idea from those who write programs on spacecraft, where there are rules as to which features of C++ are forbidden to be used. Alternatively, they could have been inspired by the reason why Java was created to replace C++. In Java, direct manipulation of the memory feature was not possible. Bjarne Stroustoup (the creator of C++) said that C++ is so powerful that with C++, people can shoot themselves in their foot.

These smart people decided to create a new programming language that is simpler than Solidity. Python is their main inspiration because the syntax of this programming language is derived from Python. This programming language is called **Vyper**. In Vyper, features such as inheritance, function overloading, modifiers, and many others are removed. The creator of the Vyper programming language argued that the removal of these features can make the development of a smart contract easier. Importantly, it also makes the code easier to read. Code is read much more than it is written. With all of these factors, they hope that programmers could create fewer bugs when using the Vyper programming language to create a smart contract.

Installing Vyper

By default, Ubuntu Xenial has Python 3.5 installed. Vyper needs Python 3.6 software, and so you will need to install Python 3.6 first if you want to use Ubuntu Xenial. A newer version of Ubuntu, such as Bionic Beaver, will have Python 3.6 installed already.

So, if you don't have Python 3.6 software installed, you must install it first using the following commands:

```
$ sudo apt-get install build-essential
$ sudo add-apt-repository ppa:deadsnakes/ppa
$ sudo apt-get update
$ sudo apt-get install python3.6 python3.6-dev
```

It's not just Python 3.6 that is required by Vyper; you need to install the development files `python3.6-dev` as well. Then you can create a virtual environment for Python 3.6 by going through the following steps:

1. First, you must install the `virtualenv` tool using the following code:

```
$ sudo apt-get install virtualenv
```

2. Then, create a virtual environment for Python 3.6 using the following code:

```
$ virtualenv -p python3.6 vyper-venv
```

3. Now, execute the virtual environment script as follows:

```
$ source vyper-venv/bin/activate
```

4. Next, install Vyper using `pip` as follows:

```
(vyper-venv) $ pip install vyper
```

5. If you don't have any errors here, you are set to go. You can test the Vyper compiler as follows:

```
(vyper-venv) $ vyper --version
0.1.0b6
```

Then you are ready to embark on the next step of your journey.

Creating a smart contract with Vyper

Now let's create a smart contract with Vyper. First, we will create a file with the `.vy` extension and name it `hello.vy`, as follows:

```
name: public(bytes[24])

@public
def __init__():
    self.name = "Satoshi Nakamoto"

@public
def change_name(new_name: bytes[24]):
    self.name = new_name

@public
def say_hello() -> bytes[32]:
    return concat("Hello, ", self.name)
```

If you come from a Solidity or Python background, you will notice a peculiarity: there is no class (as in the Python programming language) and there is no contract (as in the Solidity programming language) in a smart contract written with the Vyper programming language. However, there is an `initializer` function. The name of the `initializer` function is the same as it is in the Python programming language, which is __init__.

While using Python, you can create as many classes as you want in one file. In Vyper, the rule is one smart contract per one file. There is also no class or contract here; the file itself is a class.

This is how you compile this `vyper` file:

```
(vyper-venv) $ vyper hello.vy
```

From this, you will get the following output:

```
0x600035601c527401000000000000000000000000000000000000000060205267ffffffffffffffffffffffffffffffffff6040527ffffffff
ffffffffffffffffffffffffff80000000000000000000000000000000000000060605274012a05f1ffffffffffffffffffffffffffffffffdabf41c006080
527fffffffffffffffffffffffffffffed5fa0e00000000000000000000000000000000000060a052341561009e57600080fd5b6010610140527f53
61746f736869204e616b616d6f746f0000000000000000000000000000006101605261014080600060c0526020600202082510161016101
20600060028183520156b82610120516020021115601600fb5761011d565b610120516020028501561610120518501555b815160010180835281
14156100e8575b50505050506104785660003560c1c52740100000000000000000000000000000000000000020526f7fffffffffffffffff
ffffffffffffffffff6040527fffffffffffffffffdabf41c006080527fffffffffffffffffffffffffffffed5fa0e00000000000000000000000000000060a052634596
d11f60005114156101305760206004610140373415610b457600080fd5b60386004356004016101603760186004356004013511156100d4
57600080fd5b610160806000060c0526020600202082510161012060006002818352015b82610120516020021115610106576101285655b
610120516020028501516101201205185015556b81516001018083528114156100f3575b50505050505005b63b45985036000511415610276577
3415610149576000080fd5b600060007610140527f48656c6c2000000000000000000000000000000000006101052
6101406007806020846101a00101826020850160006046012f15050805182019150506006001816c052602060c0200160208360101a001
018260c052602060c0205461012060000600181835320156b82610120516020021115610168576101fa565b6101205185015461012051602002
8501525b815160010180835281141561010c5575b5050505050508060c052602060c02054820191505080601a0526101a090506026020620208203
526102002008151601f81835201536b601f6102005111156102303c576102595565b600061020051846020015358155b81516001018083528114156102
2b575b50560604081510160206001820306601f820103905060208203f350005b6306fdde036000511141561034a573415610128f57600080fd
5b610180600008060c0526020610180602540161012060000600281835201536b826101201205160200211156102c4576102e6565b6101
20518501546101205160200280150180835281141561b1575b505050505050602610160526260140815160188183520156b
600181810405111156103f5761032c565b60006101405184602015358155b816100601014051846200101535b81516001018083528114156102fe575b50506000406101018051602
0601820306601f820103905001610160f350005b60006000fd5b6101286104780361012860003961012861047803600f3
```

This is the bytecode of the smart contract. Keep in mind that to deploy a smart contract, you need bytecode, but to access a smart contract, you need `abi`. So how do you get `abi`? You can do this by running the following command:

```
(vyper-venv) $ vyper -f json hello.vy
```

From this, you will get the following output:

[{"name": "__init__", "outputs": [], "inputs": [], "constant": false, "payable": false, "type": "constructor"}, {"name": "change_name", "outputs": [], "inputs": [{"type": "bytes", "name": "new_name"}], "constant": false, "payable": false, "type": "function", "gas": 70954}, {"name": "say_hello", "outputs": [{"type": "bytes", "name": "out"}], "inputs": [], "constant": false, "payable": false, "type": "function", "gas": 7371}, {"name": "name", "outputs": [{"type": "bytes", "name": "out"}], "inputs": [], "constant": true, "payable": false, "type": "function", "gas": 5286}]

If you want to get both `abi` and `bytecode` together in a single compilation process, you could combine both flags in the compilation process as follows:

```
(vyper-venv) $ vyper -f json,bytecode hello.vy
```

This will give you the following output:

[{"name": "__init__", "outputs": [], "inputs": [], "constant": false, "payable": false, "type": "constructor"}, {"name": "change_name", "outputs": [], "inputs": [{"type": "bytes", "name": "new_name"}], "constant": false, "payable": false, "type": "function", "gas": 70954}, {"name": "say_hello", "outputs": [{"type": "bytes", "name": "out"}], "inputs": [], "constant": false, "payable": false, "type": "function", "gas": 7371}, {"name": "name", "outputs": [{"type": "bytes", "name": "out"}], "inputs": [], "constant": true, "payable": false, "type": "function", "gas": 5286}]
0x600035601c52740100000000000000000000000000000000000000006020526f7ffffffffffffffffffffffffffffffff6040527ffffffffffffffffffffffffffffffff8000000000000000000000000000000060605274012a05f1fffffffffffffffffffffffffffffdabf41c006080527ffffffffffffffffffffffffffffffffed5fa0e00000000000000000000000000000060a052341561009e57600080fd5b6010610140527f5361746f736869204e616d6616d6f746f000000000000000000000000000061016052610140806600c052602060c0206020825101610120600060028183520150826101205160200211156100fb5761011d565b6010205160200285015161012051850155b8151600010180835281141561000e8575b505050505050610478566000035601c527401000000000000000000000000000000000000000000006020526f7fffffffffffffffffffffffffffffffff6040527ffffffffffffffffffffffffffffffff8000000000000000000000000000000060605274012a05f1fffffffffffffffffffffffffffffdabf41c006080527ffffffffffffffffffffffffffffffffed5fa0e00000000000000000000000000000060a052634596d11f600051141561013057602060004601403734156100b4576000080fd5b60386004356004016101016037601860004356004013511156100d457600080fd5b6101016080600060c052602060c02060208251016101012060000600281835201 5b82610120516020021115610106576101285650b610120516020028501516101012051850155b8151600010180835281141561000e57575b505050505050508060c06c6c6f2c200000000000000000000000000000000000000000000000000000000610160526101406007806020846101a00101826020850160000600460 12f1505080518201915050600060018160c052602060c0200160208361010a001018260c052602060c02054610120600060006001818352015b826101 205160200211156101d8576101fa565b6101205185015461012051602002850152b8151600101808352811141561022b575b505060040815101602060001820306601f820103905060208203f350005b 6306fdde0360005114156103a57341561028f57600080fd5b610180600808060c052602060c020601860002082540161016120600060028183520 15b826101205160200211156102c4576102e6565b6101205185015461012051602002850152b8151600010180835281141561021b1575b505050 50506002601610526101408151601808183520155b6018610140511115610030f5761032c565b60006010140518460200101535b8151600010180835281 14156102fe575b5050604061016180516020602001820306601f820103905001610160f350005b60006000fd5b6101286104780361012860003961 0128610478036000f3

Deploying a smart contract to Ganache

So how do you deploy this smart contract to the Ethereum blockchain? There are few ways to do this, but let's employ a familiar way using Truffle:

1. Create a directory and initialize it with `truffle init` as follows:

```
$ mkdir hello_project
$ cd hello_project
$ truffle init
```

2. Just as you did in the previous chapter, set `truffle-config.js` as the following:

```
module.exports = {
  networks: {
    "development": {
      network_id: 5777,
      host: "localhost",
      port: 7545
    },
  }
};
```

3. Create a `build` directory, as follows:

```
$ mkdir -p build/contracts
$ cd build/contracts
```

4. Then create a `Hello.json` file there, as follows:

```
{
  "abi":
  "bytecode":
}
```

5. Then fill the `abi` field with `abi` or `json` output from the compilation process, and fill the `bytecode` field with the `bytecode` output from the compilation process. You need to quote the `bytecode` value with double quote marks . Don't forget to put comma between the `abi` field and the `bytecode` field. This will give you something similar to the following:

```
{
   "abi": [{"name": "__init__", "outputs": [], "inputs": [],
"constant": false, "payable": false, "type": "constructor"},
{"name": "change_name", "outputs": [], "inputs": [{"type": "bytes",
"name": "new_name"}], "constant": false, "payable": false, "type":
"function", "gas": 70954}, {"name": "say_hello", "outputs":
[{"type": "bytes", "name": "out"}], "inputs": [], "constant":
false, "payable": false, "type": "function", "gas": 8020}, {"name":
"name", "outputs": [{"type": "bytes", "name": "out"}], "inputs":
[], "constant": true, "payable": false, "type": "function", "gas":
5112}],
   "bytecode":
"0x600035601c5274010000000000000000000000000000000000000000006020526f
7ffffffffffffffffffffffffffffffff6040527fffffffffffffffffffffffffffff
fffff80000000000000000000000000000000060605274012a05f1ffffffffffffffff
fff...
...
1600101808352811415610319575b5050602061016052604061018051016020600 1
820306601f820103905061016 0f3005b60006000fd5b6101286104 9703610128600
0396101286104 97036000f3"
}
```

6. You can then create a migration file to deploy this smart contract by creating a new file in `migrations/2_deploy_hello.js`, as follows:

```
var Hello = artifacts.require("Hello");
module.exports = function(deployer) {
  deployer.deploy(Hello);
};
```

After everything is set up, fire up Ganache!

7. Then, inside the `hello_project` directory, you could just run the migration process, as follows:

```
$ truffle migrate
```

You will see something similar to the following:

```
Compiling ./contracts/Migrations.sol...
Writing artifacts to ./build/contracts

⚠ Important ⚠
If you're using an HDWalletProvider, it must be Web3 1.0 enabled or your migration will hang.


Starting migrations...
======================
> Network name:    'development'
> Network id:      5777
> Block gas limit: 6721975


1_initial_migration.js
======================

   Deploying 'Migrations'
   ---------------------
   > transaction hash:    0x707a30979acaa7a3900f14b9dc611e20c2faf8a64d1abd82e0898a51d99e302e
   > Blocks: 0           Seconds: 0
   > contract address:    0x9Dc44aa8d05c86388E647F954D00CaA858837804
   > account:             0xb105F01Ce341Ef9282dc2201BDfdA2c26903da77
   > balance:             99.99430184
   > gas used:            284908
   > gas price:           20 gwei
   > value sent:          0 ETH
   > total cost:          0.00569816 ETH


   > Saving migration to chain.
   > Saving artifacts
   -------------------------------------
   > Total cost:          0.00569816 ETH

2_deploy_hello.js
=================

   Deploying 'Contract'
   ---------------------
   > transaction hash:    0xf410b462cf3786dbbef3e37397d697263663558300a43e824cc8fcac144294c1
   > Blocks: 0           Seconds: 0
   > contract address:    0x3E9417399786347B6Ab38f59d3f00829d6bba7b8
   > account:             0xb105F01Ce341Ef9282dc2201BDfdA2c26903da77
   > balance:             99.9866772
   > gas used:            339198
   > gas price:           20 gwei
   > value sent:          0 ETH
   > total cost:          0.00678396 ETH


   > Saving migration to chain.
   > Saving artifacts
   -------------------------------------
   > Total cost:          0.00678396 ETH


Summary
=======
> Total deployments:   2
> Final cost:          0.01248212 ETH
```

Your smart contract written with Vyper has been deployed to Ganache. Your smart contract address is as follows:

```
0x3E9417399786347B6Ab38f59d3f00829d6bba7b8
```

Interacting with smart contracts

Just as we did before, you can use the Truffle console to interact with your smart contract, as follows:

```
$ truffle console
```

Your smart contract is always given the name `Contract`. We can access the smart contract using the following statement:

```
truffle(development)>
Contract.at("0x3E9417399786347B6Ab38f59d3f00829d6bba7b8")
```

You will get a long output in which you can see `abi`, `bytecode`, and so on, as shown in the following screenshot:

```
truffle(development)> Contract.at("0x3E9417399786347B6Ab38f59d3f00829d6bba7b8")
TruffleContract {
  constructor:
   { [Function: TruffleContract]
     _constructorMethods:
      { setProvider: [Function: setProvider],
        new: [Function: new],
        at: [Function: at],
        deployed: [Function: deployed],
        defaults: [Function: defaults],
        hasNetwork: [Function: hasNetwork],
        isDeployed: [Function: isDeployed],
        detectNetwork: [Function: detectNetwork],
        setNetwork: [Function: setNetwork],
        setWallet: [Function: setWallet],
        resetAddress: [Function: resetAddress],
        link: [Function: link],
        clone: [Function: clone],
        addProp: [Function: addProp],
        toJSON: [Function: toJSON],
        decodeLogs: [Function: decodeLogs] },
     _properties:
      { contract_name: [Object],
        contractName: [Object],
        gasMultiplier: [Object],
        timeoutBlocks: [Object],
        autoGas: [Object],
        numberFormat: [Object],
        abi: [Object],
        network: [Function: network],
        networks: [Function: networks],
        address: [Object],
        transactionHash: [Object],
        links: [Function: links],
        events: [Function: events],
        binary: [Function: binary],
        deployedBinary: [Function: deployedBinary],
        unlinked_binary: [Object],
        bytecode: [Object],
        deployedBytecode: [Object],
        sourceMap: [Object],
        deployedSourceMap: [Object],
        source: [Object],
        sourcePath: [Object],
        legacyAST: [Object],
        ast: [Object],
        compiler: [Object],
        schema_version: [Function: schema_version],
        schemaVersion: [Function: schemaVersion],
        updated_at: [Function: updated_at],
        updatedAt: [Function: updatedAt],
        userdoc: [Function: userdoc],
        devdoc: [Function: devdoc] },
     _property_values: {},
     _json:
      { contractName: undefined,
        abi: [Array],
        bytecode:
```

Let's look at the value of the `name` variable of the smart contract using the following statement:

```
truffle(development)>
Contract.at("0x3E9417399786347B6Ab38f59d3f00829d6bba7b8").then(function(ins
tance) { return instance.name.call(); });
'0x5361746f736869204e616b616d6f746f'
```

You may notice that the cryptic output does not look like Satoshi Nakamoto. However, it actually is Satoshi Nakamoto, but written in hexadecimal. Let's throw away `0x` from the cryptic output; this is just an indicator that this string is in hexadecimal form. You now have the `5361746f736869204e616b616d6f746f` string. Take the first two numbers, which are `53`, and convert them into a decimal number. In Python, you can do this as follows:

```
>>> int(0x53)
83
```

So, the decimal number is `83`. Do you remember the ASCII table? This is a data table that holds the relations between decimal numbers and characters. So, the decimal number `65` represents the character A (capital A) and the decimal number `66` represents the character B (capital B).

So what is the character of the decimal number `83`? You can use Python to find out as follows:

```
>>> chr(83)
'S'
```

If you do this for all other hexadecimal characters on which each hexadecimal character takes two number characters, it would spell out Satoshi Nakamoto.

Let's execute another method in this smart contract using the following code:

```
truffle(development)>
Contract.at("0x3E9417399786347B6Ab38f59d3f00829d6bba7b8").then(function(ins
tance) { return instance.say_hello.call(); })
'0x48656c6c6f2c205361746f736869204e616b616d6f746f'
```

That cryptic output is just `Hello, Satoshi Nakamoto`.

Let's change the name as follows:

```
truffle(development)>
Contract.at("0x3E9417399786347B6Ab38f59d3f00829d6bba7b8").then(function(ins
tance) { return instance.change_name(web3.utils.fromAscii("Vitalik
Buterin"), { from: "0x6d3eBC3000d112B70aaCA8F770B06f961C852014" }); });
```

You will get the following as the output:

```
truffle(development)> Contract.at("0x3E9417399786347B6Ab38f59d3f00829d6bba7b8").then(function(instance) {
  return instance.change_name(web3.utils.fromAscii("Vitalik Buterin"), { from: "0x6d3eBC3000d112B70aaCA8F7
70B06f961C852014" }); });
{ tx:
   '0xdee0ff14d73c2c10aff074cae5fca71bf0f2b252ca62612b9dd1d106f3af719c',
  receipt:
   { transactionHash:
      '0xdee0ff14d73c2c10aff074cae5fca71bf0f2b252ca62612b9dd1d106f3af719c',
     transactionIndex: 0,
     blockHash:
      '0x7208e3eeb70ef544e5abd9a11aed07445a1c2fedda4e049f6d3775534fdb0130',
     blockNumber: 5,
     from: '0x6d3ebc3000d112b70aaca8f770b06f961c852014',
     to: '0x3e9417399786347b6ab38f59d3f00829d6bba7b8',
     gasUsed: 33304,
     cumulativeGasUsed: 33304,
     contractAddress: null,
     logs: [],
     status: true,
     logsBloom:
      '0x00000000000000000000000000000000000000000000000000000000000000000000000000000000000000000000000000
000000000000000000000000000000000000000000000000000000000000000000000000000000000000000000000000000000000000
000000000000000000000000000000000000000000000000000000000000000000000000000000000000000000000000000000000000
000000000000000000000000000000000000000000000000000000000000000000000000000000000000000000000000000000000000
000000000000000000000000000000000000000000000000000000000000000000000000000000000000000000000000000000000',
     v: '0x1b',
     r:
      '0xbd7cc34be918d05deca365562fd9d47250ac8d92cc5bcd9819e59bd94a995281',
     s:
      '0x0614fd8b39778567d638f33c3c4a9b49f7ec011832434ede5b7157df3b19fcb7',
     rawLogs: [] },
  logs: [] }
```

The value in the `from` field is taken from one of the accounts in Ganache. You can just look at the Ganache window and choose any account you like.

We cannot send a string directly to the `change_name` method; we have to convert it to a hexadecimal string with the `web3.utils.fromAscii` method first.

Now has the name been changed? Let's find out. Run the following command:

```
truffle(development)>
Contract.at("0x3E9417399786347B6Ab38f59d3f00829d6bba7b8").then(function(ins
tance) { return instance.name.call(); });
'0x566974616c696b204275746572696e'
```

Yup, the name has been changed. If you transform that hexadecimal string to an ASCII string, you will get Vitalik Buterin.

Going deeper into Vyper

Let's take a look at our smart contract:

```
name: public(bytes[24])

@public
def __init__():
    self.name = "Satoshi Nakamoto"

@public
def change_name(new_name: bytes[24]):
    self.name = new_name

@public
def say_hello() -> bytes[32]:
    return concat("Hello, ", self.name)
```

Take a look at the first line:

```
name: public(bytes[24])
```

The array of bytes is basically a string. The variable called `name` has a type of array of `bytes` or `string`. Its visibility is `public`. If you want to set it to `private`, then just omit the public keyword, as follows:

```
name: bytes[24]
```

Now, take a look at the next lines:

```
@public
def __init__():
    self.name = "Satoshi Nakamoto"
```

If you are coming from a Python background, then you will recognize the Python decorator function. There are four of these in Vyper:

- `@public` means you can execute this method as a user (just as you did in the Truffle console in the previous chapter).
- `@private` means that only other methods inside the same smart contract can access this method. You cannot call the method as a user (in the Truffle console).
- `@payable` means that you can send some ethers to this method.
- `@const` is an indicator that this method should not modify the state of a smart contract. It means that it will not cost ether to execute this method. It's like reading a public variable's value.

Going back to the __init__() method, you could pass a parameter to this method like this:

```
i: public(uint256)

@public
def __init__(int_param: uint256):
    self.i = int_param
```

Don't forget to send the parameter when you deploy a smart contract. In our case, we use migration in Truffle software, so modify your migration file, 2_deploy_hello.js, to be as follows:

```
var Hello = artifacts.require("Hello");
module.exports = function(deployer) {
    deployer.deploy(Hello, 4);
};
```

Let's move on to the following lines of the smart contract to understand the public method:

```
@public
def change_name(new_name: bytes[24]):
    self.name = new_name
```

This method modifies the state of the smart contract, which is the name variable. This would incur gas.

Let's move on to the next lines of the smart contract to learn about returning a value inside the public method:

```
@public
def say_hello() -> bytes[32]:
    return concat("Hello, ", self.name)
```

A concat is a built-in function that combines the strings. Refer to https://vyper.readthedocs.io/en/latest/built-in-functions.html for a complete list of built-in functions.

You must be careful with the return value of the method indicated by the right arrow (→). You might set this to an array of bytes that does not have enough length. For example, take a look at the following code:

```
@public
def say_hello() -> bytes[28]:
    return concat("Hello, ", self.name)
```

In this case, it would fail in compilation, although "Hello, Satoshi Nakamoto" is definitely less than 28 characters. The string has a length of 23 characters; however, you must remember that `self.name` is defined as `bytes[24]`, and `Hello,` has a length of 7 characters. Because 24 + 7 is 31 characters, you must set this to a bigger array.

Since this method does not change the state of this smart contract, you can add `@const` on top of this method, as follows:

```
@public
@const
def say_hello() -> bytes[32]:
    return concat("Hello, ", self.name)
```

Data types

Let's create a more complex smart contract and name it `donation.vy`, as follows. You can refer to the followng GitLab link for the full code: `https://gitlab.com/arjunaskykok/hands-on-blockchain-for-python-developers/blob/master/chapter_03/donation.vy`:

```
struct DonaturDetail:
    sum: uint256(wei)
    name: bytes[100]
    time: timestamp

donatur_details: public(map(address, DonaturDetail))

...
...

@public
def withdraw_donation():
    assert msg.sender == self.donatee

    send(self.donatee, self.balance)
```

Compile and deploy the smart contract as before. Don't forget to remove all of your files in the `build/contracts` directory and restart your Ganache if you reuse the project directory.

Take a look at the following lines:

```
struct DonaturDetail:
    sum: uint256(wei)
    name: bytes[100]
    time: timestamp
```

Let's discuss the Vyper data types one by one:

- **Struct**: The first one is called the struct. A struct in Vyper is just like a struct in another programming language; it is a container of different data types. You can access its members as follows:

  ```
  DonaturDetail.name = "marie curie"
  ```

- **Wei**: The second data type that we are going to learn about is a `uint256(wei)`. This refers to a specific amount of ether that can be held. As you know, 1 ether is 1,000,000,000,000,000,000 wei (18 zeros). To hold that large an amount, a specific data type is required.
- **Timestamp**: The third data type is the `timestamp` data type. This is designed to hold time values.
- **Address**: The fourth one is the address data type. This is designed to hold the address value (such as `0xdCad3a6d3569DF655070DEd06cb7A1b2Ccd1D3AF`). This could be the address of an account or a smart contract. If you want to know what an address data type looks like, you can take a look at Ganache in the following screenshot. The address of the account is an example of the address data type. You could send ethers to the variable with this data type:

- **Map**: The fifth one is the `map` data type. This is like a dictionary. A simple map would be look as follows:

```
simple_map: map(address, uint256)
```

Here, the key is `address` and the value is `uint256`. Here's how you fill the value to this map:

```
self.simple_map[0x9049386D4d5808e0Cd9e294F2aA3d70F01Fbf0C5] = 10
```

There is a twist with this map data type if you are accustomed to the dictionary data type in Python: you cannot iterate this map. So, don't expect to iterate a variable that has a mapping data type in Vyper, like you did with variables using the `dictionary` data type in Python. You can see how this works by looking at the following code:

```
for key in self.simple_map:
    // do something with self.simple_map[key]
```

The **Ethereum virtual machine** (**EVM**) doesn't keep track of all the keys of a variable that has the mapping data type. In Python, you could get all keys from a variable that has the dictionary data type, as shown in the following code:

```
self.simple_map.keys()
```

But you cannot do this in Vyper.

If you access a nonexistent key, it will return the default value of the value data type. In our case, if we do something like this, we would get 0, as shown in the following code:

```
self.simple_map[0x11111111111111111111111111111111111111111] => 0
```

It makes no difference if you never set the value for the `0x11111111111111111111111111111111111111111` key or if you set it with a value of 0. If you want to keep track of the keys, you need to keep them in a separate array. The mapping data type is like the default dictionary in Python, as shown in the following code:

```
>>> from collections import defaultdict
>>> d = defaultdict(lambda: 0, {})
>>> d['a']
0
>>> d['a'] = 0
>>> d['a']
0
```

So, going back to our second defined variable, let's look at the following code:

```
donatur_details: public(map(address, DonaturDetail))
```

This code shows the map of an address to a struct that contains the `wei`, `string`, and `timestamp` data types. We want to record a donator's name, the amount of the donation, and the time of the donation with this data type.

- **Array**: The fifth data type is the array data type, which does not have infinite size. The size of the array must be set in the beginning.

Take a look at these lines:

```
donaturs: public(address[10])
```

This is an array of addresses with size `10`.

Let's take a look at the following lines to learn how to keep the owner's account in the smart contract:

```
donatee: public(address)
```

- **Integer**: The sixth data type is integer. It's something like `uint256` or `int128`. Please note that `uint256` and `uint256(wei)` are different. The difference between uint256 and int128 is that the int128 data type can hold zero, positive numbers, and negative. The uint256 data type can only hold zero and positive numbers, but its upper limit is higher than int128.

The following code will hold the address of someone who launched this smart contract:

```
index: int128
```

This is designed to keep track of how many donators have donated. Note that it does not have a public modifier. This means that you cannot access the variable from the Truffle console.

Let's take a look at the ___init___() method:

```
@public
def __init__():
    self.donatee = msg.sender
```

Inside every method, there are special objects. One of these is `msg`. You can access the account that accesses this method with `msg.sender`. You can also find the amount of ethers (in `wei`) with `msg.value`. In the following code, we want to save the address of the launcher of this smart contract:

```
@payable
@public
def donate(name: bytes[100]):
    assert msg.value >= as_wei_value(1, "ether")
    assert self.index < 10

    self.donatur_details[msg.sender] = DonaturDetail({
                                        sum: msg.value,
                                        name: name,
                                        time: block.timestamp
                                     })

    self.donaturs[self.index] = msg.sender
    self.index += 1
```

Here, `@payable` indicates that this method accepts payment in ether. The `assert` phrase is like `assert` in the Python programming language. If the condition is `false`, then the execution of the method will be aborted. After the `assert` lines, we just set the `self.donatur_details` map with the `msg.sender` key to a `DonaturDetail` struct. Inside of the struct, you set the property of the time with `block.timestamp`, which indicates the current time. The `as_wei_value` phrase is a built-in function. Since we must deal with ether payment using the wei unit in this smart contract, it is a good idea to use this built-in function. If not, you have to use a lot of zeros, as follows:

```
assert msg.value >= 1000000000000000000
```

Withdrawing ethers

The last lines of the smart contract will be a method to withdraw donation to the `donatee` account, as shown in the following code:

```
@public
def withdraw_donation():
    assert msg.sender == self.donatee

    send(self.donatee, self.balance)
```

Here, `self.balance` represents all ethers that are accumulated in this smart contract. The `send` phrase is a built-in function to transfer money to the first parameter, in this case, the `donatee`.

So let's test this smart contract in the Truffle console. Make sure you change the address in the method to the address of your smart contract. You can get it with the `truffle migrate` command, as follows:

```
truffle(development)>
Contract.at("0x3E9417399786347B6Ab38f59d3f00829d6bba7b8").then(function(ins
tance) { return instance.donatee.call(); });
'0xb105f01ce341ef9282dc2201bdfda2c26903da77'
```

This is the first account in Ganache, as shown in the following screenshot:

Let's donate 2 ether from the second account in Ganache, as follows:

```
truffle(development)>
Contract.at("0x3E9417399786347B6Ab38f59d3f00829d6bba7b8").then(function(ins
tance) { return instance.donate(web3.utils.fromAscii("lionel messi"),
{from: "0x6d3eBC3000d112B70aaCA8F770B06f961C852014", value:
2000000000000000000}); });
```

Now donate 3.5 ether from the third account in Ganache, as follows:

```
truffle(development)>
Contract.at("0x3E9417399786347B6Ab38f59d3f00829d6bba7b8").then(function(ins
tance) { return instance.donate(web3.utils.fromAscii("taylor swift"),
{from: "0x9049386D4d5808e0Cd9e294F2aA3d70F01Fbf0C5", value:
3500000000000000000}); });
```

Now take a look at the donator's donation using the following code:

```
truffle(development)>
Contract.at("0x3E9417399786347B6Ab38f59d3f00829d6bba7b8").then(function(ins
tance) { return
instance.donatur_details__sum.call("0x9049386D4d5808e0Cd9e294F2aA3d70F01Fbf
0C5"); });
<BN: 30927f74c9de0000>
```

The way you access a property of a struct is by using two underscores after the `donatur_details` struct. You put the key of the map inside the `call` function. If you are wondering what `30927f74c9de0000` in `<BN: 30927f74c9de0000>` means, it's not the memory's location—it's a number in hexadecimal format. Because the number is very big (BN is a short for big number), EVM has to display the number in hexadecimal format, as follows:

```
truffle(development)> web3.utils.toBN(15);
<BN: f>
truffle(development)> web3.utils.toBN(9);
<BN: 9>
truffle(development)> web3.utils.toBN(100);
<BN: 64>
truffle(development)> web3.utils.toBN(3500000000000000000);
<BN: 30927f74c9de0000>
```

If you look at Ganache, the second and third accounts have lost some money, as shown in the following screenshot:

So, let's withdraw the donation using the following code:

```
truffle(development)>
Contract.at("0x3E9417399786347B6Ab38f59d3f00829d6bba7b8").then(function(ins
tance) { return instance.withdraw_donation({from:
"0xb105F01Ce341Ef9282dc2201BDfdA2c26903da77"}); });
```

Take a look at your Ganache. The first account, in my case, has 105.48 ETH, as shown in the following screenshot:

Other data types

Vyper has other data types that have not been used in the donation smart contract, as shown in the following list:

- `bool`: This data type is like a normal Boolean. It holds true or false values, as shown in the following code:

  ```
  bull_or_bear: bool = True
  ```

- `decimal`: This data type is like `float` or `double` in Python, as shown in the following code:

  ```
  half_of_my_heart: decimal = 0.5
  ```

- `bytes32`: This data type is like `bytes32`, with a peculiarity. If the length of the value is less than 32 bytes, it will be padded with zero bytes. So, if you set the `messi` value (5 characters/bytes) to the `bytes32` data type variable (as shown in the following code), it will become `messi\x00\x00\x00\x00\x00\x00\x00\x00\x00\x00\x00\x00\x00\x00\x00\x00\x00\x00\x00\x00\x00\x00\x00\x00\x00\x00\x00`:

  ```
  goat: bytes32 = convert('messi', bytes32)
  ```

- `Constant`: This data type cannot be changed after being declared:

  ```
  GOAT: constant(bytes[6]) = 'messi'
  ```

Unlike the C++ programming language, where an uninitialized variable can have a garbage value, all uninitialized variables in the Vyper programming language have default values. The default integer data type value is `0`. The default Boolean data type value is `false`.

Useful built-in functions

You have used built-in functions, such as `send`, `assert`, `as_wei_value`, `concat`, and `convert`. However, there are other useful functions, such as the following:

- `slice`: The `slice` phrase is the bytes data type. It's used for tasks such as getting a substring from a string, as shown in the following code:

  ```
  first_name: bytes[10] = slice(name, start=0, len=10)
  ```

- `len`: This function is used to get the length of values, as shown in the following code:

  ```
  length_of_name: int128 = len(name)
  ```

- `selfdestruct`: This function is used to destroy the smart contract, as shown in the following code. The argument is the address that this smart contract sends its ethers to:

  ```
  selfdestruct(self.donatee)
  ```

- `ceil`: This function is used to round the integer to the upper limit, as shown in the following code:

  ```
  round_heart: int128 = ceil(half_of_my_heart)
  ```

- `floor`: This function is used to round the integer to the lower limit, as shown in the following code:

```
round_heart: int128 = floor(half_of_my_heart)
```

- `sha3`: This is a built-in hashing function, as shown in the following code:

```
secret_hash: bytes32 = sha3('messi')
```

Events

Vyper supports events. You can broadcast an event in your method to any subscriber of this event. For example, when people donate ethers with the smart contract, you can broadcast a donation event. To declare an event, you can use the following statement:

```
Donate: event({_from: indexed(address),  _value: uint256(wei)})
```

Then, in our `donate` method, you can broadcast the event after the donation transaction has occurred, as shown in the following code:

```
@public
def donate(name: bytes[100]):
    log.Donate(msg.sender, msg.value)
```

We'll talk more about events in later chapters.

Interacting with other smart contracts

Did you know that your smart contract doesn't have to be lonely out there? Your smart contract can interact with other smart contracts on the blockchain.

The address data type is not only used for normal accounts, but it can also be used for smart contract accounts. So, a smart contract can donate ethers to our donatee via the donation smart contract!

Restart your Ganache; we will start our blockchain anew. Remember your `hello.vy` Vyper file? We want to deploy our `Hello` smart contract with a custom name.

Our migration file, `migrations/2_deploy_hello.js`, is still the same, as shown in the following code:

```
var Hello = artifacts.require("Hello");
module.exports = function(deployer) {
  deployer.deploy(Hello);
};
```

Compile your `hello.vy` file again to get the interface and the bytecode. Open our contracts JSON file, the `build/contracts/Hello.json` file. Wipe out all the content's and replace it with the following code:

```
{
  "contractName": "Hello",
  "abi": <your Hello smart contract's interface>,
  "bytecode": "<your Hello smart contract's bytecode>"
}
```

You have to give a name to your smart contract because this time, you are going to deploy two smart contracts. If you don't give a name to your smart contract, it will have a default name, `Contract`. It's not a problem if you only want to deploy one smart contract.

Then, for your `donation.vy`, edit it, and add the following lines of code (highlighted in bold) to the code file (refer to the code file in the following GitLab link for a complete code file of `donation.vy` at https://gitlab.com/arjunaskykok/hands-on-blockchain-for-python-developers/blob/master/chapter_03/donation.vy):

```
struct DonaturDetail:
    sum: uint256(wei)
    name: bytes[100]
    time: timestamp

contract Hello():
    def say_hello() -> bytes[32]: constant

donatur_details: public(map(address, DonaturDetail))

...
...

@public
def withdraw_donation():
    assert msg.sender == self.donatee

    send(self.donatee, self.balance)

@public
```

```
@constant
def
donation_smart_contract_call_hello_smart_contract_method(smart_contract_add
ress: address) -> bytes[32]:
    return Hello(smart_contract_address).say_hello()
```

Note the changes in bold. These changes are how you declare the interface of the smart contract you want to interact with; you declare the contract object and the methods you want to interact with. You don't need to know the implementation of the say_hello method, only the interface (that is, the arguments it expects and the return value).

Then call the external smart contract's donation_smart_contract_call_hello_smart_contract_method method. Send the address as the argument for the contract object and call the method as usual. If you already know the address of the smart contract you want to interact with, you can hardcode it. But I use an arguments because I don't know the address of the Hello smart contract yet.

Using the following code, create another migration file for our upgraded Donation smart contract, migrations/3_deploy_donation.js:

```
var Donation = artifacts.require("Donation");
module.exports = function(deployer) {
  deployer.deploy(Donation);
};
```

Compile your donation.vy and get the interface and the bytecode of the smart contract.

Then, using the following code, create another contract JSON file for our Donation smart contract, build/contracts/Donation.json:

```
{
  "contractName": "Donation",
  "abi": <your Donation smart contract's interface>,
  "bytecode": "<your Donation smart contract's bytecode>"
}
```

Run the migration. You may have to use --reset flag, as follows:

```
$ truffle migrate --reset
```

You will get the following output:

```
2_deploy_hello.js
=================

   Replacing 'Hello'
   -----------------
   > transaction hash:    0x35f141e349184d28bdc2b226a7ed0d5917761224b7c7d1148980501213d43998
   > Blocks: 0            Seconds: 0
   > contract address:    0xBc932d934cfE859F9Dc903fdd5DE135F32EbC20E
   > account:             0xb105F01Ce341Ef9282dc2201BDfdA2c26903da77
   > balance:             99.97281372
   > gas used:            339198
   > gas price:           20 gwei
   > value sent:          0 ETH
   > total cost:          0.00678396 ETH


   > Saving migration to chain.
   > Saving artifacts
   -------------------------------------
   > Total cost:          0.00678396 ETH


3_deploy_donation.js
====================

   Deploying 'Donation'
   --------------------
   > transaction hash:    0xb691f88223487b40ffe7fa6588c037e98e4f47669e2d917521092ada4aa63d5d
   > Blocks: 0            Seconds: 0
   > contract address:    0x98Db4235158831BF9133faC1c4e1829021ecEB67
   > account:             0xb105F01Ce341Ef9282dc2201BDfdA2c26903da77
   > balance:             99.96359732
   > gas used:            433786
   > gas price:           20 gwei
   > value sent:          0 ETH
   > total cost:          0.00867572 ETH


   > Saving migration to chain.
   > Saving artifacts
   -------------------------------------
   > Total cost:          0.00867572 ETH
```

Note the address of the Donation smart contract and the address of the Hello smart
contract. The address of the Donation smart contract is
0x98Db4235158831BF9133faC1c4e1829021ecEB67 and the address of the Hello smart
contract is 0xBc932d934cfE859F9Dc903fdd5DE135F32EbC20E. Yours could be different.

Run the Truffle console as follows:

```
$ truffle console
```

Now our smart contract is not lonely anymore, as shown in the following code:

```
truffle(development)>
Donation.at("0x98Db4235158831BF9133faC1c4e1829021ecEB67").then(function(ins
tance) { return
instance.donation_smart_contract_call_hello_smart_contract_method.call("0xB
c932d934cfE859F9Dc903fdd5DE135F32EbC20E"); } );
'0x48656c6c6f2c205361746f736869204e616b616d6f746f'
```

One of the use cases of the interaction between smart contracts is to create a decentralized exchange smart contract. Say that your grandma launched a token smart contract named power grid token and your uncle launched a token smart contract named Wi-Fi access token. You could create a smart contract that interacts with power grid token and Wi-Fi access token. In your smart contract, you could create a method to enable the trade between these two tokens; you just have to get their smart contract's addresses and interfaces. Of course, you also need to write the logic of the trade.

Compiling code programmatically

You could create a script to compile Vyper code, instead of using a command-line utility. Make sure that you are in the same directory containing hello.vy and donation.vy. Create a script named compiler.vy, as follows:

```
import vyper
import os, json

filename = 'hello.vy'
contract_name = 'Hello'
contract_json_file = open('Hello.json', 'w')

with open(filename, 'r') as f:
    content = f.read()

current_directory = os.curdir

smart_contract = {}
smart_contract[current_directory] = content

format = ['abi', 'bytecode']
compiled_code = vyper.compile_codes(smart_contract, format, 'dict')

smart_contract_json = {
    'contractName': contract_name,
    'abi': compiled_code[current_directory]['abi'],
    'bytecode': compiled_code[current_directory]['bytecode']
```

```
}

json.dump(smart_contract_json, contract_json_file)

contract_json_file.close()
```

If you execute this script using the following command, you will get a `Hello.json` file that you could use with Truffle, as shown in the following code:

(vyper-venv) $ python compiler.py

Now, let's study the script bit by bit. First, import the `Vyper` library and some Python standard libraries so we can write a JSON file, as follows:

```
import vyper
import os, json
```

You need a Vyper file, the name that you want to give to your smart contract, and the output JSON file. The following code will do this task:

```
filename = 'hello.vy'
contract_name = 'Hello'
contract_json_file = open('Hello.json', 'w')
```

Use the following lines of code to get the content of the Vyper file:

```
with open(filename, 'r') as f:
    content = f.read()
```

Then you create a dictionary object where the key is a path to your Vyper file and the value is the content of the Vyper file, as follows:

```
current_directory = os.curdir

smart_contract = {}
smart_contract[current_directory] = content
```

To compile the Vyper code, all you need to do is use the `compile_codes` method from the `vyper` module, as follows:

```
format = ['abi', 'bytecode']
compiled_code = vyper.compile_codes(smart_contract, format, 'dict')
```

The first argument of the `compile_codes` method is a dictionary with the key points to the path and the value representing the Vyper code in a string. The second argument is `format`, which consists of the interface and the bytecode. The third argument is optional. If you use `'dict'`, then you will get a dictionary. If you don't give a third argument, then you will get an array. Let's look at the following code:

```
smart_contract_json = {
    'contractName': contract_name,
    'abi': compiled_code[current_directory]['abi'],
    'bytecode': compiled_code[current_directory]['bytecode']
}
```

Because we used `'dict'` as our third argument, we get the result of a dictionary object. The key of the result is our path to the Vyper files. Technically speaking, you can set it to any string you like. Some developers use the file path to differentiate their Vyper files, which are scattered inside a project directory.

The last code is used to write the result to an output JSON file:

```
json.dump(smart_contract_json, contract_json_file)

contract_json_file.close()
```

By compiling Vyper code programmatically, you can build a framework on top of Vyper. In the later chapters of this book, you will use a framework called Populus to compile and deploy Vyper files. But you may want to build a better framework, or you could build a Vyper **integrated development environment** (IDE), such as the JetBrains IDE, but for the Vyper programming language.

Other tricks

Vyper is not as liberal as Python; there are some limitations that you must live with. To overcome these limitations, you need to make peace with them or you need to unlock your creativity. Here are some hints as to how to do this.

The first limitation is that the array must have a fixed size. In Python, you might be very accustomed to having a list that you can extend on your whim, as shown in the following code:

```
>>> flexible_list = []
>>> flexible_list.append('bitcoin')
>>> flexible_list.append('ethereum')
>>> flexible_list
['bitcoin', 'ethereum']
```

There is no such thing in Vyper. You have to declare how big your array is. Then you must use an integer variable to track how many items you have inserted into this fixed-size array. You used this strategy in the Donation smart contract.

If you are itching to have an infinite-sized array, there is a way that you can achieve this. You can use the mapping data type with an integer as the key. You still use an integer variable to track how many items you have inserted into this mapping data type variable, as shown in the following code:

```
infinite_array_of_strings: map(uint256, bytes[100])
index: int128
```

But since infinite_array_of_strings is a mapping data type, it's your responsibility to guard this variable from the noninteger keys.

The second limitation is that the mapping data type cannot accept the composite data type as the key. So you cannot put a mapping data type or struct data type as the key. But it can accept a mapping data type or struct data type as the value, as shown in the following code:

```
mapping_of_mapping_of_mapping: map(uint256, map(uint256, map(uint256,
bytes[10])))
```

If you want to use the struct as the key of the mapping data type variable, you could serialize them first. For example, if you want to use two strings as the key of the mapping data type variable, you can concatenate the strings to make the key for your mapping data type variable, as shown in the following code:

```
friend1_str: bytes32 = convert(friend1, bytes32)
friend2_str: bytes32 = convert(friend2, bytes32)
key: bytes[100] = concat(friend1_str, friend2_str)

dating[key] = True
```

Or you could use a nested array, as follows:

```
dating[friend1_address][friend2_address] = True
```

Which approach is better depends on the situation and your preference.

The third limitation is that the Vyper programming language cannot access the real world. So, don't imagine something like the following in your smart contract:

```
nba_final_winner = nba.get_json_winner('2019/2020')
```

Summary

In this chapter, we learned how to write a smart contract using the Vyper programming language. First, we installed the Vyper compiler. Then we developed a smart contract. By doing this, we learned about most of the features of the Vyper programming language, including the function decorator, initialization function, and function permission modifier. There are also some data types such as address, integer, timestamp, map, array, and array of bytes (string). We learned how to compile a Vyper source to a smart contract and then deploy it to Ganache with the Truffle tool. We also interacted with that smart contract through the Truffle console.

In the next chapter, we are going to learn about web3.py. This is the first step towards building a decentralized application.

Section 2: Web3 and Populus

This section comprises a practical project for learning blockchain programming, which will revolve around a secure voting application.

The following chapters will be covered in this section:

- Chapter 4, Interacting with Smart Contracts Using Web3
- Chapter 5, Populus Development Framework
- Chapter 6, Building a Practical Decentralized Application

4
Interacting with Smart Contracts Using Web3

In this chapter, you're going to learn how to connect to a smart contract programmatically. Here, you'll use the Python programming language to execute a method in a smart contract. To achieve that, you will use the web3.py library. In the previous chapter, you built a smart contract and deployed it to the Ethereum blockchain. You also used Vyper to write a smart contract. To interact with that smart contract, you fired up the Truffle console and typed in a number of commands. Those commands are sent to the smart contract in the blockchain. Depending on what command you type in, this could either read the state of the smart contract or change it. In this chapter, you are going to move beyond the Truffle console.

This chapter will cover the following topics:

- Introduction to decentralized applications
- Geth
- Understanding the web3.py library
- Interacting with smart contracts using web3.py

Introduction to decentralized applications

You'll build a program using Python to execute methods in a smart contract programmatically, and we call this program a decentralized application. So, there's a smart contract, and there's a decentralized application. A smart contract written with the Vyper or Solidity programming languages lives in an Ethereum blockchain. This means that if you deploy your smart contract to the Ethereum production blockchain, the bytecode of your smart contract is written in every Ethereum node. So, if we have 10,000 Ethereum nodes in this world, your smart contract is duplicated 10,000 times.

However, a decentralized application doesn't live in Ethereum blockchain. It lives in your computer, in your neighbor's computer, in a cloud, but it does not live on the blockchain, and it does not have to be duplicated all over the world in the same way as a smart contract. People build a decentralized application using various programming languages. In the case of Ethereum, the most popular programming languages for building a decentralized application are Javascript in the Node.js environment and Python. In our case, we are going to use Python to build a decentralized application. To do this, we need a library. In the case of Javascript , we need a web3.js library. In our case, which is Python, we need a web3.py library. All of the library names include the word web3.

People like to think of web3 as a third version of the internet: a decentralized internet. So, if this is the third version, what are the first and second ones, you ask? The first version of the internet is the internet that you use to consume content passively (think static websites.) The second version of the internet is the social one, where you generate content and co-create experiences (think Facebook, Twitter, or Instagram):

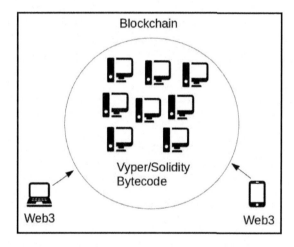

In the preceding screenshot, we can see that the Vyper or Solidity bytecode lives (duplicated) in many Ethereum nodes (system). But a program using the web3 library can live in a single computer (such as a laptop or smartphone).

Installing web3

Without further ado, let's install the web3 library. Create a virtual environment with Python 3.6 as follows:

```
$ virtualenv -p python3.6 web3-venv
```

Activate the virtual environment and install Vyper as follows:

```
$ source web3-venv/bin/activate
(web3-venv) $ pip install vyper
```

Then, install the `web3.py` library using `pip`:

```
(vyper-venv) $ pip install web3
```

Now, verify whether it works as follows:

```
(vyper-venv) $ python
>>> import web3
>>> web3.__version__
'4.8.2'
```

If you don't encounter any errors, it works. Let's connect to the Ganache blockchain with `web3`. To do this, first fire up Ganache, and then go back to your Python Command Prompt:

```
>>> from web3 import Web3, HTTPProvider
>>> w3 = Web3(HTTPProvider('http://localhost:7545'))
>>> w3.eth.blockNumber
0
>>> w3.eth.getBlock('latest')
AttributeDict({'number': 0, 'hash':
HexBytes('0x0bbde277e2147d93f12852a370e70e2efe9c66f45db6e80e0cba584508d3eba
c'), 'parentHash':
HexBytes('0x00000000000000000000000000000000000000000000000000000000000000
0'), 'mixHash':
...
...
HexBytes('0x56e81f171bcc55a6ff8345e692c0f86e5b48e01b996cadc001622fb5e363b42
1'), 'stateRoot':
HexBytes('0x31740a2d8b535c624aa481ba7d6d696085438037246b7501b4f24f77f94f399
4'), 'receiptsRoot':
HexBytes('0x56e81f171bcc55a6ff8345e692c0f86e5b48e01b996cadc001622fb5e363b42
1'), 'miner': '0x0000000000000000000000000000000000000000', 'difficulty':
0, 'totalDifficulty': 0, 'extraData': HexBytes('0x'), 'size': 1000,
'gasLimit': 6721975, 'gasUsed': 0, 'timestamp': 1548300279, 'transactions':
[], 'uncles': []})
```

What we have done here is connecting to Ganache blockchain with the `web3` library. We can retrieve the information on the blockchain, such as how many blocks have been mined on this particular blockchain. Because we are using Ganache, a development blockchain, `w3.eth.blockNumber` returns 0 because we have not created any transaction on Ganache.

Geth

Go Ethereum (Geth) is an implementation of the Ethereum protocol written in Go. You can use Geth to sync an Ethereum node, or even build a private Ethereum blockchain. If you want to be a miner, this is a software that you would use. Your Ethereum node is a gateway and a part of Ethereum blockchain. Your program with the `web3` library requires the Ethereum node to be able to interact with a smart contract that lives inside the blockchain.

Using Ganache is all fine and dandy. But Ganache is a fake blockchain. There are no miners, so it's hard to simulate some situations that we would encounter on real Ethereum blockchain. As a result, let's step up our game. We don't need to use Ethereum production blockchain now, but we can use something in between development and production blockchain—the **Rinkeby network**. If the Ethereum production blockchain is akin to a production server, the Rinkeby network is like a staging server. In DevOps lingua franca, a staging server is a test server that mimics a production server as closely as possible.

So, Rinkeby is not a software like Ganache. It lives on the internet. As a result, using the Rinkeby network, we can get a feel for what it is like to deal with the Ethereum production blockchain. One of the situations you could encounter in Etherum blockchain in the Rinkeby network is that it takes time to confirm a transaction. In Ganache, it takes a fraction of a second to confirm a transaction. In the Rinkeby network, it takes maybe 20-30 seconds, or even a minute, to confirm a transaction, so you need to get used to it. Of course, not everything in the Ethereum production blockchain can be replicated on the Rinkeby network. Another situation that specifically happens in the Ethereum production blockchain is that it includes the high traffic that the Ethereum production blockchain sometimes gets. For example, a decentralized application named Cryptokitties slowed down the Ethereum network because there are many users interacting with the application, as can be seen here: `https://techcrunch.com/2017/12/03/people-have-spent-over-1m-buying-virtual-cats-on-the-ethereum-blockchain/`.

There is another Ethereum testing network similar to the Rinkeby network—the **Ropsten network**. The difference here is that the Rinkeby network uses **Proof-of-Authority (PoA)** in confirming transactions, while the Ropsten network uses **Proof-of-Work (PoW)**. Right now, there is no need to worry about this difference, since using the Rinkeby network is similar to using the Ropsten network.

There are two ways to connect to this kind of Ethereum blockchain—by running Ethereum node yourself, or by using other people's nodes. Each method comes with its own advantages and disadvantages. Running an Ethereum node takes up a lot of storage. A node connecting to the Rinkeby network requires around 6 GB of storage. As regards the Ethereum production network, it requires a whopping 150 GB of storage. Depending on your internet connection, to be fully operational, you need a night or a couple of days to make the node fully synchronized with all other nodes.

Another method is to use someone else's node. Some people build a web service to connect to their Ethereum node, so you can use an API to connect to their Ethereum node. One of the most popular services for this is Infura. All you need to do here is register on their website to get their API.

To run our own Ethereum node for the Rinkeby network, go to `https://geth.ethereum.org/downloads/` to download the software for your operating system. For Ubuntu Linux, this is in `tar.gz` format, so you have to extract it. Then, put the binary file somewhere convenient (something such as `/opt/bin` or `/home/yourusername/Program` or `/user/local/bin`).

After doing this, synchronize the node as follows:

```
$ ./geth --rinkeby
```

You can use a different data directory. By default, Geth stores the data in the `~/.ethereum` directory:

```
$ ./geth --rinkeby --datadir /opt/data/ethereumdata
```

In my case, this takes a night. Your experience may be different depending on how fast your internet connection is.

If it is fully synced (you know this is the case when the output no longer changes that often), then you can run Python inside the `web3-venv` virtual environment as follows:

```
(web3-venv) $ python
>>> from web3 import Web3, IPCProvider
>>> w3 = Web3(IPCProvider("/home/yourusername/.ethereum/rinkeby/geth.ipc"))
```

Here, we are using a different provider to the one we used in the previous example. With the Ganache example, we use an HTTP provider. Remember that Ganache uses http://localhost:7545 and you use this information in the Truffle configuration. However, in our case, when we connect to the Ethereum node, we use **Inter Process Communication provider (IPC)**. You can also see a parameter of IPCProvider , which is a file path. So your Python program communicates with the Ethereum node by means of that file. In computer science, that file is called a pipe. You just search where the geth.ipc file lives on your local computer. Remember that geth.ipc only shows up if you run geth software. If you stop it, the geth.ipc file will disappear.

Then, before you run business as usual, you need to inject something into the web3 middleware. This should be done because the block size in the Ethereum production blockchain is different to the block size in the Rinkeby blockchain:

```
>>> from web3.middleware import geth_poa_middleware
>>> w3.middleware_stack.inject(geth_poa_middleware, layer=0)
```

Then, you can test it, as shown in the following code block:

```
>>> w3.eth.getBlock('latest')
AttributeDict({'difficulty': 2, 'proofOfAuthorityData':
HexBytes('0xd88301081384676574688867 6f312e31312e32856c696e75780000000000000000
01c62ac5af9b2ea6bf897a99fff40af6474cd5680fc8239853f03db116b2154594d2ab77a6f
18c41132ee819143d2d41819237468924d29cb4b1252d2385a862400'), 'gasLimit':
7000000, 'gasUsed': 1373640, 'hash':
HexBytes('0xa14b569f874eefc75fe734bc28b7457755eff1da26794d6615f15e173920406
7'), 'logsBloom':
...
...
HexBytes('0x66e75c91271b45f5271d2fe2fd0efc66f48f641632e83a086fc57646a0c0bc3
f'), 'uncles': []})
```

The output you got is the information regarding the latest block of blockchain in the Rinkeby network. There are a couple of things that you can learn from the block of blockchain. You can find all the transactions that have been confirmed in this block; the gas used, the gas limit, and so on. In the Rinkeby network, the miner is always the zero address (0x0000000000000000000000000000000000000000), because blockchain in the Rinkeby network uses proof of authority. But in mainnet (production network), you can find out who got the reward to confirm the blockchain. You can find the information from the latest block in mainnet (the Ethereum production network) from https://etherscan.io/blocks. Of course, you could find the same information from the Ethereum production node if you are willing to sync the node.

Geth console

Before we continue to use the `web3` library, let's play around with Geth software. Geth software can act like the Truffle console:

```
$ ./geth --rinkeby --verbosity 0 console
```

The keyword is `console` in that statement, but in order to make it a more pleasant experience, you should add another `--verbosity` flag with a value of `0`. This will prevent you from getting bogged down with a lot of output from the `geth` software:

```
Welcome to the Geth JavaScript console!
instance: Geth/v1.8.16-stable-477eb093/darwin-amd64/go1.11
modules: admin:1.0 clique:1.0 debug:1.0 eth:1.0 miner:1.0 net:1.0
personal:1.0 rpc:1.0 txpool:1.0 web3:1.0
>
```

In the Geth console, you can do anything that you can do in the Truffle console. However, we now want to create an Ethereum account. When you launch Ganache, you are equipped with 10 accounts that are ready to be used. However, this is not the case in the Rinkeby blockchain. You need to create an account manually in Rinkeby:

```
> personal.newAccount("password123")
"0x28f5b56b035da966afa609f65fd8f7d71ff68327"
```

This is the command to create a new Ethereum account. You need to supply a password to create an account in the Geth console. Don't forget the password for this account, as there is no option to recover it. The output of this command is your account's public address.

The private key is encrypted in a file inside the following directory: `/home/yourusername/.geth/rinkeby/keystore`.

The file name is something like this: `UTC—2018-10-12T09-30-20.687898000Z—28f5b56b035da966afa609f65fd8f7d71f f68327`. This is a combination of a timestamp and public key. You can open it, but you will not be able to find the private key inside it:

```
{"address":"28f5b56b035da966afa609f65fd8f7d71ff68327","crypto":{"cipher":"a
es-128-
ctr","ciphertext":"38b091f59f879369a6afdd91f21c1a82deb59374677144c94dd529d3
c9069d39","cipherparams":{"iv":"b168482d467df6e1fe4bdb5201a64a6a"},"kdf":"s
crypt","kdfparams":{"dklen":32,"n":262144,"p":1,"r":8,"salt":"bd94440d3f2bb
9313a0020331bac9410ff3cdc9f32756f41f72dde1ef7bf32e1"},"mac":"3313b72603e85e
73f84a47ef7ed0e931db85441e1702e0d96f2f001c54170cb6"},"id":"7a033367-92fe-42
d3-bec5-970076f35d8a","version":3}
```

To decrypt it, you can use the web3 library. Name the script extract_private_key.py:

```
from web3 import Web3
w3 = Web3()

# Change the filepath to your keystore's filepath
with open('/opt/data/ethereumdata/keystore/UTC-
-2018-10-12T09-30-20.687898000Z--28f5b56b035da966afa609f65fd8f7d71ff68327')
as keyfile:
    encrypted_key = keyfile.read()
    private_key = w3.eth.account.decrypt(encrypted_key, 'password123')
    print(private_key)
```

If you execute the script, you will see your private key, which can be used in another situation:

```
(web3-venv) $ python extract_private_key.py
b'\xa0\xe2\xa2\xf0$j\xe9L\xb3\xc0\x14Q\xb0D\xec\xa16\xa1\xca\xdd\x07.\x0f\x
0f=5\xbd\xc5mb(r'
```

Please do not use this account in a production setting any more because the private key is already exposed. Use it for development purposes only.

This private key is in bytes format. If you want to convert it to a hex string, you can do it like this:

```
(web3-venv) $ python
>>>
b'\xa0\xe2\xa2\xf0$j\xe9L\xb3\xc0\x14Q\xb0D\xec\xa16\xa1\xca\xdd\x07.\x0f\x
0f=5\xbd\xc5mb(r'.hex()
'a0e2a2f0246ae94cb3c01451b044eca136a1cadd072e0f0f3d35bdc56d622872'
```

Understanding the web3.py library

Now, let's write a decentralized application with this library. The simplest decentralized application script would be sending money from one account to another. Name the script send_money_ganache.py:

```
from web3 import Web3, HTTPProvider


w3 = Web3(HTTPProvider('http://localhost:7545'))
```

```
private_key =
'59e31694256f71b8d181f47fc67914798c4b96990e835fc1407bf4673ead30e2'

transaction = {
  'to':
Web3.toChecksumAddress('0x9049386D4d5808e0Cd9e294F2aA3d70F01Fbf0C5'),
  'value': w3.toWei('1', 'ether'),
  'gas': 100000,
  'gasPrice': w3.toWei('1', 'gwei'),
  'nonce': 0
}

signed = w3.eth.account.signTransaction(transaction, private_key)
tx = w3.eth.sendRawTransaction(signed.rawTransaction)
```

Before you execute this script, launch Ganache first. After doing so, take any public address you like and put it into the `to` field in the transaction dictionary. This account will be the receiver. Then find another account, look at its private key, and input the value in the `private_key` variable:

Put one ether in the `value` field. This means you want to send 1 ether to another account. This is a simple script to illustrate how sending a transaction works. It does not show best practice because you shouldn't put a private key embedded in the code like this. You could read a private key from the file with restricted permission, for example, or you could request the private key from the standard input.

If you execute this script, you would notice that the receiver's balance would increase by 1 ETH, while the sender's balance would decrease by 1 ETH:

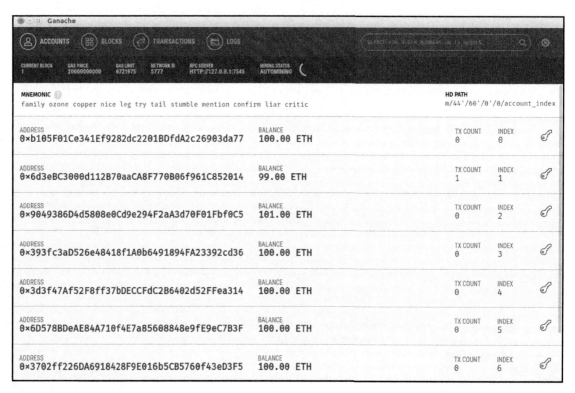

Here is the following output:

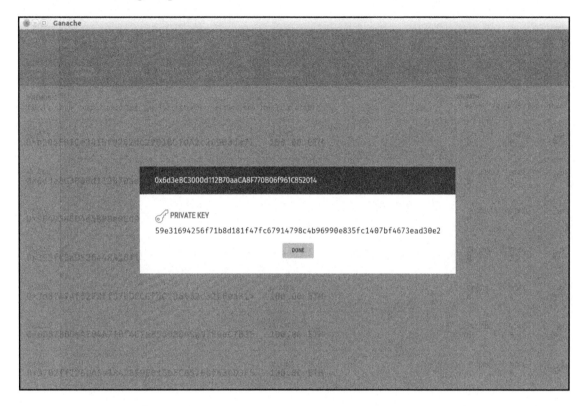

Gas and gas price

As you will know, Ethereum blockchain is not free; someone has to maintain it. I am not talking about developers who write Ethereum software, but miners who run Ethereum nodes to confirm transactions. They are rewarded with money (ETH) from Ethereum software itself. On top of that, they are rewarded with the fee of the transaction. This fee is the gas and gas price.

Why do we need a fee on top of a reward in Ethereum software? This is to prevent spam from users. If a transaction is free, a troller could set up two accounts, sending the money back and forth between them. In addition, this gives high priority to users who want to pay more. If there are two similar transactions, but the first transaction is backed with more gas, it would be of higher priority in a miner's to-do list. The transaction with less gas will be confirmed in the end; it just needs to wait a little bit longer.

So there is gas and there is a gas price. Gas is the amount of gas you are willing to allocate in this transaction. In a previous script, you allocate 20,000 gas to create a transaction to send the money. For a more complex transaction, such as executing a complex method in a smart contract, it could require more gas. If you don't allocate enough gas, your transaction would be rejected and you could lose gas as well. But if you put more than enough gas, if your transaction is successful, the remaining gas would be returned to you. So, you would think: Why not just set gas aside as much as possible? There is a catch. If, somehow, your call of a method in a smart contract fails assertion (for example: assert 1 == 2), you would lose all the gas you use up until the assertion line (but the remaining gas will be refunded). So you need to hit the middle ground.

Gas price is the price of the gas, so gas is not free. It's separated from Ethereum itself. You buy gas with the ETH you have. You could check the gas price in historical transactions. In the Ethereum production blockchain, you could check the price of the gas in `https://www.ethgasstation.info/`.

How do you estimate the gas you need for your transaction? You need to learn all the intricacy of the Solidity or Vyper programming languages. If I allocate a variable of integer with 256 bits and store it in storage, how much would it cost? What about looping? What about constructing a struct? This sounds complicated, but luckily, the `web3` library has a method to estimate gas usage. First, create a script named `estimate_gas.py`:

```
from web3 import Web3, HTTPProvider


w3 = Web3(HTTPProvider('http://localhost:7545'))

transaction = {
  'to':
Web3.toChecksumAddress('0x9049386D4d5808e0Cd9e294F2aA3d70F01Fbf0C5'),
  'value': w3.toWei('1', 'ether'),
  'gas': 100000,
  'gasPrice': w3.toWei('1', 'gwei'),
  'nonce': 0
}

print("Estimating gas usage: " + str(w3.eth.estimateGas(transaction)))
print("Gas price: " + str(w3.eth.gasPrice))
```

You would get this output:

```
Estimating gas usage: 21000
Gas price: 2000000000
```

If you find an error related to nonce, change nonce to 1 or higher until it works. Well talk about nonce in the following section.

Nonce

You may have observed that you get errors related to nonce if you try to execute the sending money script more than once. If you haven't, try it. You have to increase nonce to make it work again. Nonce is like an indicator of how many transactions you have made with an account. For the first transaction (just after creating a new account), you put zero value in nonce. Then, for the second transaction, you put a value of 1 in nonce. Then, for the third transaction, you put a value of 2 in nonce.

But keeping track of the nonce value becomes silly, especially if you want to use an old account on which you don't know how high the nonce value is. Fortunately, there is a way of obtaining the latest nonce value from Ethereum blockchain. Create a script named `get_latest_nonce.py`:

```
from web3 import Web3, HTTPProvider
w3 = Web3(HTTPProvider('http://localhost:7545'))
transaction_count =
w3.eth.getTransactionCount("0xcc6d61988CdcF6eB510BffAeD4FC0d904f8d3e7D")
print(transaction_count)
```

Try to send money again with a higher nonce, and then execute this script. Do it again. This will show you the value tallies.

With this new knowledge, you must be careful to create a transaction in Ethereum blockchain. In the real world, transactions could take time to be confirmed. Imagine you create two different transactions in parallel with the same nonce. If both transactions are valid, only one of them will be recorded on Ethereum blockchain. The other one will be rejected because of a nonce issue. Which transaction of these two will be confirmed? It would be quite random.

Instead, you must decide which transaction you want to be confirmed first. Give it a lower nonce. For the second transaction, you accord a higher nonce. However, if the first transaction fails, the second transaction will be rejected because the nonce is too high (the nonce skips one number). This is something you need to bear in mind.

So why all of this nonce bureaucracy? It is to prevent the same transaction from happening again. Imagine you broadcast a transaction where you send one ETH to your neighbor. I could copy this transaction and broadcast it again. Since this transaction is validated with your signature, I could drain your account.

Creating a transaction on Rinkeby

Now that you have had fun with Ganache, let's try to create a transaction on the Rinkeby network. You may notice a problem here—unlike Ganache, where you get 10 accounts each with a 100 ETH balance, here you get nothing. You have to create an account by default. Creating 10 accounts is easy. But what about the balance? Each account you created on the Rinkeby network with Geth software comes with a balance of 0 ETH. But sending money requires well, money, to pay the transaction fee.

In the Ethereum production blockchain, you get ETH from the cryptocurrency exchange or from mining. But in the Rinkeby network, you get money by begging. And here's how to do it.

Go to `https://faucet.rinkeby.io/`, and then, using one of the social media platforms, such as Twitter, Google+, or Facebook, you create a post containing your public address in the Rinkeby network. Then, post your social media post in the form on the Rinkeby faucet website. You have three options: 3 ethers in 8 hours, 7.5 ethers in 1 day, or 18.5 ethers in 3 days:

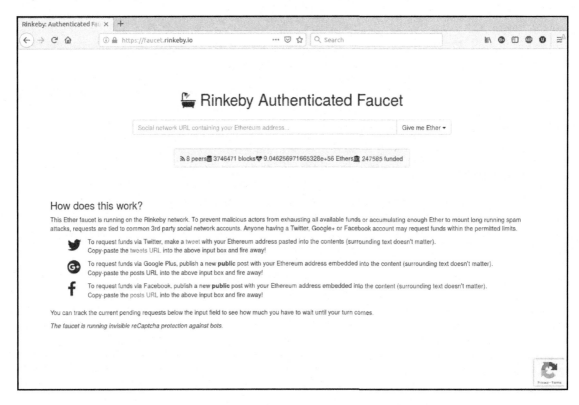

To make sure you got the balance, you can check the balance from the Geth software. Sync it first. As I said before, this process could take a long time, perhaps several hours, or one night in my case:

```
$ ./geth --rinkeby
```

After your local blockchain node is fully synced with the Rinkeby network, kill the geth process first and launch geth again, but with different flags:

```
$ ./geth --rinkeby --verbosity 0 console
```

Execute this command inside the geth console:

```
> web3.eth.getBalance('0x28f5b56b035da966afa609f65fd8f7d71ff68327')
3000000000000000000
```

Change this address to your address. You should get some ETH from the faucet.

Assuming you have the ETH already, you can create a transaction in the Rinkeby network. Here is the script to send ethers in the Rinkeby network. You can refer to the code file on the following GitLab link for the full code:
https://gitlab.com/arjunaskykok/hands-on-blockchain-for-python-developers/blob/master/chapter_04/send_money_rinkeby.py:

```
from web3 import Web3, IPCProvider
from web3.middleware import geth_poa_middleware

# Change the path of geth.ipc according to your situation.
w3 = Web3(IPCProvider('/opt/data/ethereumdata/geth.ipc'))

w3.middleware_stack.inject(geth_poa_middleware, layer=0)

...
...

nonce = w3.eth.getTransactionCount(Web3.toChecksumAddress(from_account))

transaction = {
    'to': Web3.toChecksumAddress(to_account),
    'value': w3.toWei('1', 'ether'),
    'gas': 21000,
    'gasPrice': w3.toWei('2', 'gwei'),
    'nonce': nonce
}

signed = w3.eth.account.signTransaction(transaction, private_key)
w3.eth.sendRawTransaction(signed.rawTransaction)
```

Change the account receiver's address, your private key encrypted file location, your password, and the `geth.ipc` file location according to your situation.

Remember that our private key is encrypted in a file. So we read that file, and then unlock it with a password. Remember, you should not embed the password in the code directly. Then you can check your destination account's balance in the `geth` console after waiting a couple of minutes:

```
> web3.eth.getBalance('0x99fb2eee85acbf878d4154de73d5fb1b7e88c328')
100000000000000000
```

You send a transaction by signing it with a private key. This is the most versatile way to create a transaction in Ethereum. But there is another way, which involves using just a password.

You can use a private key like this:

```
signed = w3.eth.account.signTransaction(transaction, private_key)
w3.eth.sendRawTransaction(signed.rawTransaction)
```

Or, instead, you can use a password when signing a transaction, as follows:

```
w3.personal.sendTransaction(transaction, password)
```

Using password can only be done when you control the node because it requires an encrypted private key file. I have created a couple of accounts in my Ethereum node. I can only use a password when signing a transaction for these accounts only. But with a private key, I can use any account.

Interacting with smart contracts using web3.py

You've sent ethers using a Python script with the `web3` library in Ganache and the Rinkeby network. Now, let's create a script to interact with a smart contract. But before doing that, you need to learn how to launch a smart contract with `geth` and a Python script with the `web3` library. Previously, in Chapter 3, *Implementing Smart Contracts Using Vyper,* you launched a smart contract using Truffle.

Launching a smart contract with Geth

In the next section, we are going to connect to a smart contract with `web3`. Here's how to deploy a smart contract to the Rinkeby blockchain:

```
$ ./geth --rinkeby --verbosity 0 console
```

In the `geth` console, list all of your accounts with Geth software:

```
> eth.accounts
["0x8b55f0a88a1c53a8976953cde4f141752e847a00",
"0x1db565576054af728b46ada9814b1452dd2b7e66",
"0x28f5b56b035da966afa609f65fd8f7d71ff68327",
"0x5b0d65b07a61c7b760bf372bbec1b3894d4b0225",
"0x99fb2eee85acbf878d4154de73d5fb1b7e88c328"]
```

All of these accounts come from the keystore files you created with this command: `personal.newAccount("password")`. Say you want to unlock the first account, then you can use the `personal.unlockAccount` method:

```
> personal.unlockAccount(eth.accounts[0], "password123")
true
```

Now, get `bytecode` and put it in a variable. Remember that you get `bytecode` when you compile the source code with the Vyper compiler:

```
> bytecode = "smart contract bytecode"
> tx = eth.sendTransaction({from: eth.accounts[0], data: bytecode, gas:
500e3}
```

Then, check whether your smart contract has been confirmed on the blockchain:

```
> web3.eth.getTransactionReceipt(tx)
```

If it has been confirmed, then you should get the following output:

```
{
 blockHash:
"0xfed7dcbd5e8c68e17bff9f42cd30d95588674497ae719a04fd6a2ff219bb001d",
 blockNumber: 2534930,
 contractAddress: "0xbd3ffb07250634ba413e782002e8f880155007c8",
 cumulativeGasUsed: 1071323,
 from: "0x1db565576054af728b46ada9814b1452dd2b7e66",
 gasUsed: 458542,
 logs: [],
 logsBloom: "0x00000...",
 status: "0x1",
 to: null,
```

```
transactionHash:
"0x1a341c613c2f03a9bba32be3c8652b2d5a1e93f612308978bbff77ce05ab02c7",
 transactionIndex: 4
}
```

Launching a smart contract with web3

You can also launch a smart contract using a Python script with the web3 library. Name this script deploy_smart_contract_to_ganache.py. You can refer to the code file on the following GitLab link for the full code, https://gitlab.com/arjunaskykok/hands-on-blockchain-for-python-developers/blob/master/chapter_04/deploy_smart_contract_to_ganache.py:

```
from web3 import Web3, HTTPProvider
from vyper import compile_codes


contract_source_code = '''
name: public(bytes[24])

@public
def __init__():
    self.name = "Satoshi Nakamoto"


...
...


# Change the account to your situation.
tx_hash = HelloSmartContract.constructor().transact({'from':
'0xb105F01Ce341Ef9282dc2201BDfdA2c26903da77'})

tx_receipt = w3.eth.waitForTransactionReceipt(tx_hash)
print(tx_receipt)
```

Run the script. But make sure you have Ganache running. You should get the following output:

```
AttributeDict({'transactionHash':
HexBytes('0xcfce0a28d0f8232735f99bcf871762f9780f19ab916e92c03d32fdabfd6b9e9
a'), 'transactionIndex': 0, 'blockHash':
HexBytes('0x84139a5c9ad050cf7be0678feb4aefc9e8b2806636245f16c790048e50347df
e'), 'blockNumber': 1, 'from':
'0xb105f01ce341ef9282dc2201bdfda2c26903da77', 'to': None, 'gasUsed':
339198, 'cumulativeGasUsed': 339198, 'contractAddress':
'0x9Dc44aa8d05c86388E647F954D00CaA858837804', 'logs': [], 'status': 1,
'logsBloom':
```

```
HexBytes('0x0000000000000000000000000000000000000000000000000000000000000000
000000000000000000000000000000000000000000000000000000000000000000000000000000
000000000000000000000000000000000000000000000000000000000000000000000000000000
000000000000000000000000000000000000000000000000000000000000000000000000000000
000000000000000000000000000000000000000000000000000000000000000000000000000000
000000000000000000000000000000000000000000000000000000000000000000000000000000
0000000000000000000000000000000000000000000000000000000000000000000000000000'
), 'v': '0x1c', 'r':
'0x74c63921055bd2fed65a731356b30220c6de3a28ec5fd26e296bf609d76d25ce', 's':
'0x655395f422fa7b419caf87f99e2da09296b123eceb99aed4d19195e542b01bcd'})
```

First, you create a smart contract object with this statement:

```
HelloSmartContract = w3.eth.contract(abi=abi, bytecode=bytecode)
```

Then, in order to deploy a smart contract, you just have to use the `constructor` method:

```
tx_hash = HelloSmartContract.constructor().transact({'from':
'0xb105F01Ce341Ef9282dc2201BDfdA2c26903da77'})
```

The final step is quite important, which is to wait for the transaction to be confirmed. It's important because you need to get the smart contract's address after the transaction has been confirmed.

If you want to deploy a smart contract to the Rinkeby network, you need to modify this script. Create a new file named `deploy_smart_contract_to_rinkeby.py`. You can refer to the code file on the following GitLab link for the full code: https://gitlab.com/arjunaskykok/hands-on-blockchain-for-python-developers/blob/master/chapter_04/deploy_smart_contract_to_rinkeby.py:

```
from web3 import Web3, IPCProvider
from vyper import compile_codes


contract_source_code = '''
name: public(bytes[24])

...
...

signed = w3.eth.account.signTransaction(transaction, private_key)
tx_hash = w3.eth.sendRawTransaction(signed.rawTransaction)

tx_receipt = w3.eth.waitForTransactionReceipt(tx_hash)
print(tx_receipt)
```

The difference (other than using `IPCProvider` instead of `HTTPProvider`) when deploying a smart contract to the Rinkeby network is that you have to set `gas`, `gasPrice`, and `nonce` as well. On top of that, you use the `buildTransaction` method, get the `transaction` object, and sign it with a private key. Because this script runs in the Rinkeby network, you need to make sure you've allocated sufficient gas. It's a common mistake to deploy a smart contract to the Rinkeby network with insufficient gas. Then, developers are confused as to why the smart contract can't be accessed afterward. When you deploy this smart contract to the Rinkeby network, you need to wait a while.

Playing with a smart contract

In the previous chapter, we have developed a simple smart contract using Vyper named `hello.vy`. Let's create a script using `web3` to interact with this smart contract. If you have forgotten the content of `hello.vy`, here is the content of the file:

```
name: public(bytes[24])

@public
def __init__():
    self.name = "Satoshi Nakamoto"

@public
def change_name(new_name: bytes[24]):
    self.name = new_name

@public
def say_hello() -> bytes[32]:
    return concat("Hello, ", self.name)
```

Compile it and deploy it to Ganache or the Rinkeby network. Now, depending on whether you want to connect to your smart contract in Ganache or Rinkeby, choose one of the following options.

The first script is for interacting with the smart contract in the Rinkeby network. Name the script `play_with_smart_contract_in_rinkeby.py`. You can refer to the code file on the following GitLab link for the full code: https://gitlab.com/arjunaskykok/hands-on-blockchain-for-python-developers/blob/master/chapter_04/play_with_smart_contract_in_rinkeby.py:

```
from web3 import Web3, IPCProvider
from vyper import compile_codes

contract_source_code = '''
```

```
name: public(bytes[24])

...
...

signed_txn_hash = w3.eth.sendRawTransaction(signed_txn.rawTransaction)

w3.eth.waitForTransactionReceipt(signed_txn_hash)

print(Hello.functions.say_hello().call())
```

The second script is to interact with the smart contract in Ganache. Name the script `play_with_smart_contract_in_ganache.py`. You can refer to the code file on the following GitLab link for the full code: `https://gitlab.com/arjunaskykok/hands-on-blockchain-for-python-developers/blob/master/chapter_04/play_with_smart_contract_in_ganache.py`:

```
from web3 import Web3, HTTPProvider
from vyper import compile_codes


contract_source_code = '''
name: public(bytes[24])

...
...

signed_txn_hash = w3.eth.sendRawTransaction(signed_txn.rawTransaction)

w3.eth.waitForTransactionReceipt(signed_txn_hash)

print(Hello.functions.say_hello().call())
```

We'll discuss the code line by line to understand the concept better:

```
from web3 import Web3, IPCProvider
from vyper import compile_codes


contract_source_code = '''
name: public(bytes[24])

...
...

smart_contract = {}
smart_contract['hello'] = contract_source_code
```

```
format = ['abi', 'bytecode']
compiled_code = compile_codes(smart_contract, format, 'dict')

abi = compiled_code['hello']['abi']
```

This part of the script is designed to get the `abi` and `bytecode` of the smart contract:

```
# Change the path of geth.ipc according to your situation.
w3 = Web3(IPCProvider('/opt/data/ethereumdata/geth.ipc'))

from web3.middleware import geth_poa_middleware
w3.middleware_stack.inject(geth_poa_middleware, layer=0)

# Change the address of the smart contract, the account, the password, and
the path to the keystore according to your situation,
address = "0x58705EBBc791DB917c7771FdA6175b2D9F59D51A"
password = 'password123'
w3.eth.defaultAccount = '0x28f5b56b035da966afa609f65fd8f7d71ff68327'
with open('/opt/data/ethereumdata/keystore/UTC-
-2018-10-12T09-30-20.687898000Z--28f5b56b035da966afa609f65fd8f7d71ff68327')
as keyfile:
    encrypted_key = keyfile.read()
    private_key = w3.eth.account.decrypt(encrypted_key, password)

Hello = w3.eth.contract(address=address, abi=abi)
```

This script is for the Rinkeby network option. You get the `web3` connection object and the private key. Then, you initialize the smart contract object based on the `abi` and the address from the deploying smart contract script:

```
w3 = Web3(HTTPProvider('http://localhost:7545'))

# Change the address of the smart contract, the private key, and the
account according to your situation
address = "0x9Dc44aa8d05c86388E647F954D00CaA858837804"
private_key =
'0x1a369cedacf0bf2f5fd16b5215527e8c8767cbd761ebefa28d9df0d389c60b6e'
w3.eth.defaultAccount = '0xb105F01Ce341Ef9282dc2201BDfdA2c26903da77'

Hello = w3.eth.contract(address=address, abi=abi)
```

This script is for the Ganache option. You get the `web3` connection object and set the private key. Then, you initialize the smart contract object based on the `abi` and the `address` from the deploying smart contract script.

In both (Ganache and Rinkeby) scripts, you set the value to `w3.eth.defaultAccount`. If you set the address to `w3.eth.defaultAccount`, this means that this address is the account that is going to broadcast transactions. It will also execute methods in a smart contract. If you remember what you did in Truffle console, you specified the account that will execute methods in a smart contract with the `from` parameter, as follows:

```
Donation.at("0x3e9417399786347b6ab38f59d3f00829d6bba7b8").change_useless_va
riable("sky is blue", {from: "0xb105F01Ce341Ef9282dc2201BDfdA2c26903da77"
});
```

If you don't use the default account, you would need to specify the `from` field, too, when you build a transaction:

```
print(Hello.functions.name().call())

print(Hello.functions.say_hello().call())
```

To obtain the value from a public variable or public method that does not change the state of the smart contract, you use the contract object's `functions` method, followed by the public variable and public method (both must be executed using `()`), followed by executing the `call` method:

```
nonce = w3.eth.getTransactionCount(w3.eth.defaultAccount)

txn = Hello.functions.change_name(b"Vitalik Buterin").buildTransaction({
  'gas': 70000,
  'gasPrice': w3.toWei('1', 'gwei'),
  'nonce': nonce
})
```

If you remember what to do with nonce, it is necessary to get the updated one. For a transaction that is going to change the state of the smart contract, instead of `call`, you use `buildTransaction`, which supplies parameters that you recognize already: `gas`, `gasPrice`, and `nonce`. If you don't use `w3.eth.defaultAccount`, then you need to add another parameter here: `from`. If you want to send some ethers to the smart contract (for example, the `donate` method in Donation Smart Contract), you add another parameter as well: `value`.

If you notice, the `gas` and `gasPrice` parameters in the script for the Rinkeby network are much higher:

```
txn = Hello.functions.change_name(b"Lionel Messi").buildTransaction({
        'gas': 500000,
        'gasPrice': w3.toWei('30', 'gwei'),
        'nonce': nonce
    })
```

In Ganache, you can get away with 70,000 gas and a gas price set to `1 gwei`. In the Rinkeby network, however, you must be careful. To be safe, I bumped up the gas and the gas price when interacting with a smart contract in the Rinkeby network. If you fail to change the state of the smart contract in the Rinkeby network, sometimes it means you haven't allocated sufficient gas and the gas price is not high enough:

```
signed_txn = w3.eth.account.signTransaction(txn, private_key=private_key)
```

You sign this transaction with your private key. However, in Ganache, you don't have to do this. Instead, you could make a transaction directly without a private key:

```
Hello.functions.change_name(b"Vitalik Buterin").transact()
```

In contrast, for the Rinkeby network or the Ethereum production blockchain, you have to sign your transaction:

```
signed_txn_hash = w3.eth.sendRawTransaction(signed_txn.rawTransaction)
```

Then, you broadcast your transaction:

```
w3.eth.waitForTransactionReceipt(signed_txn_hash)
```

In Ganache, the execution of the method will be very fast, but in Rinkeby, it could take a few minutes. In a proper decentralized application, you would handle this with asynchronous programming or threading:

```
print(Hello.functions.say_hello().call())
```

The last line is there to ensure that it has changed the `name` variable in the smart contract.

Summary

In this chapter, you learned how to install a web3 library. This is the library that is designed to connect to a smart contract. On top of that, you learned how to run an Ethereum node on the Rinkeby network. You configured web3 to connect to the Ethereum blockchain on the Rinkeby network. You also learned how to tell web3 to connect to an Ethereum testing network, such as Ganache. In addition, you created a script to send ethers from one account to another. Finally, you created a script to execute methods on a smart contract, either to read the value of public variables or to change the state of the smart contract.

In the next chapter, you are going to use a smart contract development framework called **Populus** that takes care of the manual work you've undertaken in relation to a smart contract, such as compiling the code and deploying it. In addition, the Populus framework offers an integrated way to test the smart contract.

5
Populus Development Framework

In this chapter, you're going to learn how to use Populus, which is a smart contract development framework. Populus, like Truffle, is a tool designed to make it easier for you to develop a smart contract. If we cast our minds back to Chapter 3, *Implementing Smart Contracts Using Vyper*, you may recall that we had to manually create a .json file and then copy the abi output in the console to the .json file. With Populus, you can avoid repeating manual jobs that you've executed previously.

This chapter will explore the following topics:

- Setting up Populus
- Smart contract unit test
- Deploying a smart contract with Populus

Setting up Populus

Populus is a smart contract development framework, just like Truffle. So why should we use Populus instead of Truffle? Basically, this is a personal choice. Populus is written with Python and supports unit testing with Python by default. If you use Truffle, you use unit testing with JavaScript by default. This is like choosing web3.py (Python) or web3.js (JavaScript) to build a decentralized application.

To set up Populus, let's observe the following steps:

1. Create a virtual environment from scratch:

```
$ virtualenv -p python3.6 populus-venv
$ source populus-venv/bin/activate
```

2. We install web3, populus, and vyper:

```
(populus-venv) $ pip install eth-abi==1.2.2
(populus-venv) $ pip install eth-typing==1.1.0
(populus-venv) $ pip install py-evm==0.2.0a33
(populus-venv) $ pip install web3==4.7.2
(populus-venv) $ pip install -e
git+https://github.com/ethereum/populus#egg=populus
```

 The reason why we have to install the specific version of web3 is because the latest version of web3 (4.8.2) breaks Populus.

3. Install the Solidity compiler:

```
(populus-venv) $ python
>>> from solc import install_solc
>>> install_solc('v0.4.25')
```

4. Create a symbolic link:

```
(populus-venv) $ ln -s /home/yourusername/.py-solc/solc-
v0.4.25/bin/solc populus-venv/bin/
```

5. Create a project directory:

```
(populus-venv) $ mkdir populus_tutorial
(populus-venv) $ cd populus_tutorial
```

6. Initialize this project directory with populus:

```
(populus_venv) $ populus init
```

This command is like truffle init. After learning populus, you may not even need this command any more. This command will put two directories in your project directory—contracts and tests.

Inside `contracts`, there is a sample Solidity file: `Greeter.sol`. Inside the `tests` directory, there is a sample test file: `test_greeter.py`.

Open `Greeter.sol`, a simple smart contract, as follows:

```
pragma solidity ^0.4.0;

contract Greeter {
    string public greeting;

    // TODO: Populus seems to get no bytecode if `internal`
    function Greeter() public {
        greeting = 'Hello';
    }

    function setGreeting(string _greeting) public {
        greeting = _greeting;
    }

    function greet() public constant returns (string) {
        return greeting;
    }
}
```

Before you can compile the smart contract, you have to create a project configuration called `project.json`. You must enter the project directory first:

```
(populus-venv) $ cp ../populus-
    venv/src/populus/populus/assets/defaults.v9.config.json project.json
```

`populus-venv` is where you create a virtual environment. If you take a look at it, it's a significant file, containing 255 lines. You can compile it by using the following command:

```
(populus-venv) $ populus compile
```

The result of the compilation is `build/contracts.json`. You can find `abi` and `bytecode` in that `.json` file. There's additional information that you can find in that `.json` file, apart from `abi` and `bytecode`, such as the compiler version.

You'll already be familiar with the workflow of smart contract development. Compile `Solidity/Vyper` files so we can get `abi` and `bytecode`. Then, use `abi` and `bytecode` with the `web3` library.

Now, you'll encounter something new. There is another directory that you haven't seen yet: the `tests` directory. Inside that directory, there is a test file called `test_greeter.py`, which is a unit test. Take a look at it here:

```
def test_greeter(chain):
    greeter, _ = chain.provider.get_or_deploy_contract('Greeter')

    greeting = greeter.call().greet()
    assert greeting == 'Hello'


def test_custom_greeting(chain):
    greeter, _ = chain.provider.get_or_deploy_contract('Greeter')

    set_txn_hash = greeter.transact().setGreeting('Guten Tag')
    chain.wait.for_receipt(set_txn_hash)

    greeting = greeter.call().greet()
    assert greeting == 'Guten Tag'
```

You can execute this test file as follows:

```
(populus-venv) $ py.test tests
```

This will give you the following output:

```
============================== test session starts
==============================
platform linux -- Python 3.6.6, pytest-3.9.1, py-1.7.0, pluggy-0.8.0
rootdir: /tmp/pop_tut, inifile:
plugins: populus-2.2.0
collected 2 items

tests/test_greeter.py ..
[100%]

============================== warnings summary
==============================

...

====================== 2 passed, 3 warnings in 0.88 seconds
======================
```

Your test will now pass. We'll discuss smart contract unit testing in more depth later in this chapter.

Adding support for Vyper

As you know, we aren't focusing on Solidity in this book, but Vyper. We need to add support for Vyper. First, because this is a new virtual environment, install `vyper`:

```
(populus-venv) $ pip install vyper
```

Then, in the project directory, create a `.vy` file called `Greeter.vy` in the `contracts` directory:

```
greeting: bytes[20]


@public
def __init__():
    self.greeting = "Hello"


@public
def setGreeting(x: bytes[20]):
    self.greeting = x


@public
def greet() -> bytes[20]:
    return self.greeting
```

Before you can compile this Vyper code, you need to change something in the `project.json` file.

Go to `compilation` key. The value of the key is an object with these keys: `backend`, `backends`, `contract_source_dirs`, and `import_remappings`. Delete the `backends` key and then change the `backend` key to the following code:

```
"backend": {
        "class": "populus.compilation.backends.VyperBackend"
},
```

Hence, the content of the `compilation` key appears as follows:

```
"compilation": {
  "backend": {
    "class": "populus.compilation.backends.VyperBackend"
  },
  "contract_source_dirs": [
    "./contracts"
  ],
  "import_remappings": []
},
```

Then, run the compilation as usual:

```
(populus-venv) $ populus compile
```

To make sure it is indeed a Vyper compilation and not a Solidity compilation, you could open `build/contracts.json`. Inside, you will be able to see the following:

```
{
  "Greeter": {
    ...
    "source_path": "contracts/Greeter.vy"
  }
}
```

 The latest version of Vyper is 0.1.0b6 and it breaks Populus. The developer needs some time to fix this. If the bug hasn't yet been fixed while you're reading this book, you could patch Populus yourself.

First, check whether the bug is fixed or not using the following command:

```
(populus-venv) $ cd populus-venv/src/populus
(populus-venv) $ grep -R "compile(" populus/compilation/backends/vyper.py
 bytecode = '0x' + compiler.compile(code).hex()
 bytecode_runtime = '0x' + compiler.compile(code,
bytecode_runtime=True).hex()
```

In our case here, the bug has not been fixed. So, let's patch Populus to fix the bug. Make sure you're still in the same directory (`populus-venv/src/populus`):

```
(populus-venv) $ wget
https://patch-diff.githubusercontent.com/raw/ethereum/populus/pull/484.patc
h
(populus-venv) $ git apply 484.patch
(populus-venv) $ cd ../../../
```

Our Populus development framework now has Vyper support.

Smart contract unit test

If you run unit testing, you will receive an error due to the incorrect data type. The solution here would be to change all string data types to a bytes data type. Then, owing to a deprecation warning, you should change the way you call methods in a smart contract.

Ultimately, your unit test, which is located in `tests/test_greeter.py`, should look like this:

```
def test_greeter(chain):
    greeter, _ = chain.provider.get_or_deploy_contract('Greeter')

    greeting = greeter.functions.greet().call()
    assert greeting == b'Hello'


def test_custom_greeting(chain):
    greeter, _ = chain.provider.get_or_deploy_contract('Greeter')

    set_txn_hash = greeter.functions.setGreeting(b'Guten Tag').transact()
    chain.wait.for_receipt(set_txn_hash)

    greeting = greeter.functions.greet().call()
    assert greeting == b'Guten Tag'
```

Then, if you were to run your unit test again, it would be successful.

Let's take a look at the first method:

```
def test_greeter(chain):
    greeter, _ = chain.provider.get_or_deploy_contract('Greeter')

    greeting = greeter.functions.greet().call()
    assert greeting == b'Hello'
```

Your unit test function should accept the `chain` argument most of the time. From the `chain` object, you could get a provider. If you remember, a provider is an object that connects to an Ethereum blockchain, be it through HTTP or IPC. From there, you could get the contract object. Whether the test framework gets the contract object directly from the blockchain or whether it deploys the contract first before fetching the contract depends on the situation. In our case, it is the latter option. The test framework creates a contract object in memory and interacts with it. After unit testing, everything vanishes.

Later, you would fetch the contract object from a permanent blockchain.
`get_or_deploy_contract` from the `provider` object returns two objects. You only need
to concern yourself with the first one, the contract object, most of the time.

From the `contract` object, executing the methods on the smart contract should be familiar
to you. To execute the `public` method or to get the value of public variables, you would
use `functions`, followed by the method or the public variables added with `()` and ending
with `call()`.

After executing the public method, you would get the return value. In this case, you get as a
`byte` object, unlike `string` in the Solidity example. In Vyper, there is no first class string
support. String is stored as `byte` object. Vyper is still in active development mode, but
expect this to change in the future.

On the second unit test, you would test a method in the smart contract to change the state
of a variable:

```
def test_custom_greeting(chain):
    greeter, _ = chain.provider.get_or_deploy_contract('Greeter')

    set_txn_hash = greeter.functions.setGreeting(b'Guten Tag').transact()
    chain.wait.for_receipt(set_txn_hash)

    greeting = greeter.functions.greet().call()
    assert greeting == b'Guten Tag'
```

Everything is the same as the first unit test, except that here are two new lines in the
middle:

```
    set_txn_hash = greeter.functions.setGreeting(b'Guten Tag').transact()
    chain.wait.for_receipt(set_txn_hash)
```

This is the way to use a transaction. Remember, a transaction is anything that involves
changing the state of the contract. You call `functions`, followed by the method that's going
to change the state of the contract augmented by `()`, ending with `transact()` with the
necessary parameters. After that, using the `chain` object, you wait for the transaction to
finish. During testing, this has been very fast. But if you test this on another Ethereum
blockchain, say, in the Rinkeby network, the transaction could last a couple of minutes.

Let's move to a more complicated example. Remember our donation smart contract that
you wrote in `Chapter 3`, *Implementing Smart Contracts Using Vyper*. Why don't we test that
smart contract?

Let's save the donation smart contract in the source code folder that you developed in Chapter 3, *Implementing Smart Contracts Using Vyper*. You can save the code in `contracts/donation.vy`. If you've forgotten this, you can refer to the code file on the following GitLab link for the full code, `https://gitlab.com/arjunaskykok/hands-on-blockchain-for-python-developers/blob/master/chapter_05/populus_tutorial/contracts/Donation.vy`:

```
struct DonaturDetail:
    sum: uint256(wei)
    name: bytes[100]
    time: timestamp

donatur_details: public(map(address, DonaturDetail))

donaturs: public(address[10])

donatee: public(address)

index: int128

...
...

@public
def withdraw_donation():
    assert msg.sender == self.donatee

    send(self.donatee, self.balance)
```

We want to test a number of different things here.

To begin with, let's take a look at the constructor method:

```
@public
def __init__():
    self.donatee = msg.sender
```

We want to test whether the `donatee` variable will contain the address of the account that launches the smart contract or not.

Let's write our first unit test. You can save this unit test in `tests/test_donation.py`:

```
def test_donatee(web3, chain):
    donation, _ = chain.provider.get_or_deploy_contract('Donation')

    donatee = donation.functions.donatee().call()
    assert donatee == web3.eth.coinbase
```

In this unit test, we're using the two arguments version because we want to get the `web3` object. It does not actually matter if you switch the order of the parameters. `def test_donatee(web3, chain):` is the same as `def test_donatee(chain, web3):`.

The argument in `get_or_deploy_contract` is taken from the name of your `.vy` file. So be careful naming your source code filename.

One thing that's new (but not really new since you already encountered this in Chapter 4, *Interacting With Smart Contracts Using Web3*, is `web3.eth.coinbase`. This is the default account. In this context (unit test), it means the address of the account that launched the smart contract.

If this unit test succeeds, let's continue testing another method in this smart contract:

```
@payable
@public
def donate(name: bytes[100]):
    assert msg.value >= as_wei_value(1, "ether")
    assert self.index < 10
    self.donatur_details[msg.sender] = DonaturDetail({
                                        sum: msg.value,
                                        name: name,
                                        time: block.timestamp
                                      })

    self.donaturs[self.index] = msg.sender
    self.index += 1
```

In this method, you're forced to send at least 1 ether to the smart contract.

Let's test the fail case by writing the second unit test:

```
def test_donate_less_than_1_eth(web3, chain):
    donation, _ = chain.provider.get_or_deploy_contract('Donation')

    with pytest.raises(eth_tester.exceptions.TransactionFailed):
        donation.transact({'value': web3.toWei('0.8',
'ether')}).donate(b'Taylor Swift')
```

Now, you need to add two `import` statements:

```
import pytest
import eth_tester
```

Let's learn how to deal with an exception in this unit test. You can put a troubled transaction inside the `with` statement that will catch an exception. Basically, you expect the transaction to fail. When something fails in the program, it returns a special code (for example, -1) or it throws an exception. In this case, it throws an exception.

Run the test to see whether it works. Then, let's test the success case, meaning the donation is accepted (refer to the code file in the following GitLab link for the full code: `https://gitlab.com/arjunaskykok/hands-on-blockchain-for-python-developers/blob/master/chapter_05/populus_tutorial/tests/test_donation.py`):

```
def test_donate_1_eth(web3, chain):
    import time

    donation, _ = chain.provider.get_or_deploy_contract('Donation')

    t = eth_tester.EthereumTester()
    account2 = t.get_accounts()[1]

...
...

    assert donatur == account2
    assert donation_sum == web3.toWei('1', 'ether')
    assert donation_name == donatur_name
    assert (int(time.time()) - donation_time) < 600 # could be flaky

    assert web3.eth.getBalance(donation.address) == web3.toWei('1',
'ether')
```

This is a lot to digest, so let's discuss it step by step.

```
import time
```

We're going to use the `time` library to check the timestamp later in this unit test:

```
donation, _ = chain.provider.get_or_deploy_contract('Donation')
```

You already know this statement. Using the `chain` object, you could get the provider and then you use the `get_or_deploy_contract` method from this provider. The result is a donation smart contract object:

```
t = eth_tester.EthereumTester()
account2 = t.get_accounts()[1]
```

`eth_tester` is a library designed to make you test a smart contract easier. To do that, you create an object of `EthereumTester`. There are many helper functions in this library. One of them is there to give you some accounts loaded with a lot of ETH, sort of like Ganache. The first account is the manager account or the account that launched the smart contract. As demonstrated previously, you could also get that account from `web3.eth.coinbase`. The second account and so on are testing accounts that you could use in your unit test.

`t.get_accounts()` gives you a lot of accounts. However, don't use the first account because that would be the manager account. Here, you use the second account:

```
donatur_name = b'Taylor Swift'
set_txn_hash =
donation.functions.donate(donatur_name).transact({'from': account2,
'value': web3.toWei('1', 'ether')})
    chain.wait.for_receipt(set_txn_hash)
```

You've seen the `transact` function in the previous unit test with the greeter smart contract. In this `transact` method, you could specify an ether amount that you want to send to the smart contract. You could also use a different account. In these `transact` parameters, we also use the helper function, `web3.toWei`. Otherwise, you have to use a number with a lot of zeros. Then, you wait for the transaction to be confirmed:

```
donatur = donation.functions.donaturs(0).call()
donation_sum = donation.functions.donatur_details__sum(donatur).call()
donation_name = donation.functions.donatur_details__name(donatur).call()
donation_time = donation.functions.donatur_details__time(donatur).call()
```

After doing this, you can access the public variables to confirm the change in state.

For an array, you put an index inside the array method, as in `donation.functions.donaturs(0).call()`.

For mapping, instead of the integer index, you provide the key inside the parameter of the mapping method, as in `donation.functions.donatur_details__sum(donatur).call()`.

For a struct, you access the member by appending two underscores, as in `donation.functions.donatur_details__sum(donatur).call(`*).*

Then, we test the donation by asserting all of these variables as follows:

```
assert donatur == account2
```

We then check that the donator address is recorded correctly:

```
assert donation_sum == web3.toWei('1', 'ether')
```

We then check that the donation amount is recorded correctly:

```
assert donation_name == donatur_name
```

We then check that the donator's name is recorded correctly:

```
assert (int(time.time()) - donation_time) < 600 # could be flaky
```

We then check the time when the donation occurred. We do this because the time is recorded when the transaction is confirmed in blockchain, so you never know when the transaction is being confirmed. In our case, it would be fast. However, if you test it in the Rinkeby network, that's something to keep in mind. Here, I make sure that the difference between the unit test time and the timestamp recorded in the smart contract doesn't differ by more than 10 minutes (600 seconds).

We then check the donation amount directly from the balance of the smart contract:

```
assert web3.eth.getBalance(donation.address) == web3.toWei('1', 'ether')
```

This is different from the previous test, where you test the balance by checking the value of the public variable. In our case, we have many donations, so they'll be different.

Let's take a look at the last method in the smart contract:

```
@public
 def withdraw_donation():
     assert msg.sender == self.donatee

     send(self.donatee, self.balance)
```

This is the method to withdraw the donation. Don't laugh; some people launched a smart contract that does not have a way to withdraw the ethers in it. All ethers in those smart contracts are locked forever, which is why testing is important. It ensures that you don't make stupid mistakes like this.

In this withdrawal method, you want to test that you can withdraw ethers in the smart contract. Then, you need to make sure that only a certain account (in this case, it is the manager account) is able to withdraw ethers from the smart contract.

Let's create a unit test for that. First, we create a unit test to make sure that another account can't withdraw ethers from the smart contract:

```python
def test_other_account_could_not_withdraw_money(web3, chain):
    donation, _ = chain.provider.get_or_deploy_contract('Donation')

    t = eth_tester.EthereumTester()
    account2 = t.get_accounts()[1]

    donatur_name = b'Taylor Swift'
    set_txn_hash =
donation.functions.donate(donatur_name).transact({'from': account2,
'value': web3.toWei('1', 'ether')})
    chain.wait.for_receipt(set_txn_hash)

    with pytest.raises(eth_tester.exceptions.TransactionFailed):
        donation.functions.withdraw_donation().transact({'from': account2})
```

Everything should look familiar to you now. You wrap the fail case of withdrawing ethers in the `with` statement that catches the exception.

Now, let's test the success case that the manager account could indeed withdraw ethers to their account:

```python
def test_manager_account_could_withdraw_money(web3, chain):
    donation, _ = chain.provider.get_or_deploy_contract('Donation')

    t = eth_tester.EthereumTester()
    account2 = t.get_accounts()[1]

    donatur_name = b'Taylor Swift'
    set_txn_hash =
donation.functions.donate(donatur_name).transact({'from': account2,
'value': web3.toWei('1', 'ether')})
    chain.wait.for_receipt(set_txn_hash)

    initial_balance = web3.eth.getBalance(web3.eth.coinbase)
    set_txn_hash =
donation.functions.withdraw_donation().transact({'from':
web3.eth.coinbase})
    chain.wait.for_receipt(set_txn_hash)

    after_withdraw_balance = web3.eth.getBalance(web3.eth.coinbase)

    assert abs((after_withdraw_balance - initial_balance) -
web3.toWei('1', 'ether')) < web3.toWei('10', 'gwei')
```

Everything here will be familiar to you, except maybe the last line. The manager's account balance after withdrawal minus the `initial_balance` wouldn't be exactly `1 ether` because the manager's account needs to pay the fee. In this case, we just use a rough measurement to ensure that the withdrawal is successful. As long as the difference is below 10 gwei, that should be fine. Gwei is the currency we use to calculate the fee for sending a transaction. 1 gwei is 1,000,000,000 wei. If you find this confusing, you could assert it using ether currency, as follows:

```
assert abs((after_withdraw_balance - initial_balance) - web3.toWei('1',
'ether')) < web3.toWei('0.00000001', 'ether')
```

Run the test:

```
(populus-venv) $ py.test tests/test_donation.py
```

You should get a successful result:

```
================================ test session starts =================================
platform linux -- Python 3.6.7, pytest-4.1.1, py-1.7.0, pluggy-0.8.1
rootdir: /home/arjuna/Documents/WritingBook/hands-on-blockchain-for-python-developers/chapter_05/populus_tutorial, inifile:
plugins: populus-2.2.0
collected 5 items

tests/test_donation.py .....                                              [100%]

============================== 5 passed in 2.41 seconds ==============================
```

Using arguments in the constructor

Both smart contracts that we test have no arguments in the constructor. But what if we write a smart contract that has arguments in the constructor? How do we test that?

Let's write a simple smart contract that has arguments in the constructor. Name it `contracts/Greeter2.vy`:

```
greeting: bytes[20]


@public
def __init__(greeting_param: bytes[20]):
    self.greeting = greeting_param


@public
def setGreeting(x: bytes[20]):
    self.greeting = x
```

```
@public
def greet() -> bytes[20]:
    return self.greeting
```

Then, write the following test. Name it `tests/test_greeter2.py`:

```
import pytest

@pytest.fixture()
def greeter2_contract(chain):
    Greeter2Factory = chain.provider.get_contract_factory('Greeter2')
    deploy_txn_hash = Greeter2Factory.constructor(b'Hola').transact()
    contract_address = chain.wait.for_contract_address(deploy_txn_hash)
    return Greeter2Factory(address=contract_address)

def test_greeter2(greeter2_contract):
    greeting2 = greeter2_contract.functions.greet().call()
    assert greeting2 == b'Hola'
```

Here, you customize the deployment of your smart contract using the `fixture` feature from `pytest`. First, you get the contract factory from the chain's provider, and then you put your argument in the `constructor` method of the `factory` object, ending with the `transact()` method. Then, wait until it is deployed on the blockchain. Finally, you will receive the address.

In the test function, you put the argument exactly as the fixture function's name. Here, our fixture function is `greeter2_contract`. Inside the test function, you just use this object as a smart contract object that's similar to an object returned by `chain.provider.get_or_deploy_contract('Donation')`.

Now, test this as follows:

```
(populus-venv) $ py.test tests/test_greeter2.py
```

You should get a successful result:

```
================================= test session starts =================================
platform linux -- Python 3.6.7, pytest-4.1.1, py-1.7.0, pluggy-0.8.1
rootdir: /home/arjuna/Documents/WritingBook/hands-on-blockchain-for-python-developers/chapter_05/populus_tutorial, inifile:
plugins: populus-2.2.0
collected 1 item

tests/test_greeter2.py .                                                        [100%]

============================== 1 passed in 0.66 seconds ================================
```

There are still many things you could test. We only test for one donation, but we could accept up to 10 donations. This should be checked as well. How complete you want the test coverage to be is up to you and the requirements of the project. There are still a plethora of unit testing aspects that we haven't discussed here, such as setup, tear down, and test-driven development.

Deploying a smart contract with Populus

Populus isn't just a framework designed to easily develop and test a smart contract. It has a tool to deploy a smart contract to a blockchain, including a private chain.

A private chain is basically your private Ethereum blockchain, similar to Ganache, except that you build it yourself. It's like blockchain in the Rinkeby network, but you're the sole miner. You can create a private blockchain manually using geth software; `populus` just makes it easier for you.

The command to create a new private `chain` is as follows:

```
(populus-venv) $ populus chain new localblock
```

This command will create some files in your project directory. All generated files are located inside the `chains` directory. One of the files generated is `chains/localblock/genesis.json`. The purpose of the genesis file is to dictate the initial configuration of the Ethereum blockchain:

```
{
    "parentHash":
"0x0000000000000000000000000000000000000000000000000000000000000000",
    "coinbase": "0xcb22827ab291b3094076de25d583c49b902a5606",
    "extraData": "0x686f727365",
    "config": {
        "daoForkBlock": 0,
        "daoForSupport": true,
        "homesteadBlock": 0
    },
    "timestamp": "0x0",
    "mixhash":
"0x0000000000000000000000000000000000000000000000000000000000000000",
    "nonce": "0xdeadbeefdeadbeef",
    "alloc": {
        "0xcb22827ab291b3094076de25d583c49b902a5606":{
            "balance": "1000000000000000000000000000000"
        }
    },
```

```
    "gasLimit": "0x47d5cc",
    "difficulty": "0x01"
}
```

You don't need to know all of the meanings of these keys. `coinbase` means all mining rewards should go into this account. `alloc` means the initial balance of the accounts.

Apart from the genesis file, you should get `chains/localblock/init_chain.sh`. Open it and you should have the following content:

```
#!/bin/sh
geth --rpc --rpcaddr 127.0.0.1 --rpcport 8545 --rpcapi
admin,debug,eth,miner,net,personal,shh,txpool,web3,ws --ws --wsaddr
127.0.0.1 --wsport 8546 --wsapi
admin,debug,eth,miner,net,personal,shh,txpool,web3,ws --datadir
/home/yourusername/populus_tutorial/chains/localblock/chain_data --maxpeers
0 --networkid 1234 --port 30303 --ipcpath
/home/yourusername/populus_tutorial/chains/localblock/chain_data/geth.ipc -
-nodiscover --mine --minerthreads 1 init
/home/yourusername/populus_tutorial/chains/localblock/genesis.json
```

This script is basically running geth software with certain parameters. The most important parameter is `init`, which you feed to your `genesis.json` file. Then, run the initialization of your private blockchain:

(populus-venv) $ ./chains/localblock/init_chain.sh

Then, open the `chains/localblock/run_chain.sh` file and you should have this content:

```
#!/bin/sh
geth --rpc --rpcaddr 127.0.0.1 --rpcport 8545 --rpcapi
admin,debug,eth,miner,net,personal,shh,txpool,web3,ws --ws --wsaddr
127.0.0.1 --wsport 8546 --wsapi
admin,debug,eth,miner,net,personal,shh,txpool,web3,ws --datadir
/home/yourusername/populus_tutorial/chains/localblock/chain_data --maxpeers
0 --networkid 1234 --port 30303 --ipcpath
/home/yourusername/populus_tutorial/chains/localblock/chain_data/geth.ipc -
-unlock 0xcb22827ab291b3094076de25d583c49b902a5606 --password
/home/yourusername/populus_tutorial/chains/localblock/password --nodiscover
--mine --minerthreads 1
```

The important flags that you need to note for now are `--mine`, `--password`, `--ipcpath`, `--unlock`, and `--datadir`. `--mine` indicates that you want to mine in this private blockchain, `--password` is the location of the password file, `--unlock` unlocks the account with the password file, `--datadir` is the location of your private Ethereum blockchain directory, and `--ipcpath` is where your `geth.ipc` will be located when you run your private Ethereum blockchain.

Before running the blockchain, edit the `chains/localblock/run_chain.sh` script, change the value of the `--ipcpath` flag to `/tmp/geth.ipc`, and then run the blockchain:

```
(populus-venv) $ ./chains/localblock/run_chain.sh
```

Now, edit the `project.json` file. The `chains` key has one object that has four keys: `tester`, `temp`, `ropsten`, and `mainnet`. Add the `localblock` key with its value in this object. Hence, the `localblock` key must be adjacent to the `tester`, `mainnet`, `temp`, and `ropsten` keys, as demonstrated in the following code block:

```
"localblock": {
  "chain": {
    "class": "populus.chain.ExternalChain"
  },
  "web3": {
    "provider": {
      "class": "web3.providers.ipc.IPCProvider",
    "settings": {
      "ipc_path":"/tmp/geth.ipc"
    }
    }
  },
  "contracts": {
    "backends": {
      "JSONFile": {"$ref": "contracts.backends.JSONFile"},
      "ProjectContracts": {
        "$ref": "contracts.backends.ProjectContracts"
      }
    }
  }
}
```

Then, you could deploy your smart contract to your private blockchain as follows:

```
(populus_venv) $ populus deploy --chain localblock Donation
> Found 2 contract source files
  - contracts/Donation.vy
  - contracts/Greeter.vy
> Compiled 2 contracts
```

```
    - contracts/Donation.vy:Donation
    - contracts/Greeter.vy:Greeter
Beginning contract deployment. Deploying 1 total contracts (1 Specified, 0
because of library dependencies).

Donation
Deploying Donation
Deploy Transaction Sent:
b'v\xc4`\x06h\x17\xf6\x10\xd7\xb2\x7f\xc6\x94\xeb\x91n\xae?]-
\xf43\xb8F\xdc=}\xb33\x03|\xd4'
Waiting for confirmation...

Transaction Mined
==================
Tx Hash : b'v\xc4`\x06h\x17\xf6\x10\xd7\xb2\x7f\xc6\x94\xeb\x91n\xae?]-
\xf43\xb8F\xdc=}\xb33\x03|\xd4'
Address : 0xab3B30CFeC1D50DCb0a13671D09d55e63b7cFf40
Gas Provided : 467715
Gas Used : 367715


Verified contract bytecode @ 0xab3B30CFeC1D50DCb0a13671D09d55e63b7cFf40
Deployment Successful.
```

Then, you can play around with your smart contract such as you did in Chapter 4, *Interacting with Smart Contracts Using Web3*. You can refer to the code file at the following GitLab link: https://gitlab.com/arjunaskykok/hands-on-blockchain-for-python-developers/blob/master/chapter_05/populus_tutorial/interact_smart_contract_in_private_chain.py, for the complete code of the following code block:

```
>>> from web3 import Web3, IPCProvider
>>> w3 = Web3(IPCProvider(ipc_path="/tmp/geth.ipc"))
>>> w3.eth.coinbase
'0xcB22827aB291b3094076DE25D583C49b902a5606'
>>> w3.eth.getBalance(w3.eth.coinbase)
100000001187500000000000000000000
>>> address = "0xab3B30CFeC1D50DCb0a13671D09d55e63b7cFf40"
>>> false = False
>>> true = True
>>> abi = [
...
...
>>> donation = w3.eth.contract(address=address, abi=abi)
>>> donation.functions.donatee().call()
'0xcB22827aB291b3094076DE25D583C49b902a5606'
```

Are you still attached to Ganache? If so, we can deploy to a Ganache blockchain. Start by firing up Ganache and then add this content to the `chains` key object in the `projects.json` file:

```
"ganache": {
  "chain": {
    "class": "populus.chain.ExternalChain"
  },
  "web3": {
    "provider": {
      "class": "web3.providers.HTTPProvider",
      "settings": {
        "endpoint_uri": "http://localhost:7545"
      }
    }
  },
  "contracts": {
    "backends": {
      "JSONFile": {"$ref": "contracts.backends.JSONFile"},
      "ProjectContracts": {
        "$ref": "contracts.backends.ProjectContracts"
      }
    }
  }
}
```

Run the deployment as follows:

```
(populus_venv) $ populus deploy --chain ganache Donation
> Found 2 contract source files
  - contracts/Donation.vy
  - contracts/Greeter.vy
> Compiled 2 contracts
  - contracts/Donation.vy:Donation
  - contracts/Greeter.vy:Greeter
Beginning contract deployment. Deploying 1 total contracts (1 Specified, 0
because of library dependencies).

Donation
Deploying Donation
Deploy Transaction Sent: b'\xd4\xeb,{\xa0d\n\xb2\xb0\xb2\x1b\x18\xdd
\xa1A\x89\xea`\xa8b?A\x14L\x99\xd1rR4\xc7\xfa'
Waiting for confirmation...

Transaction Mined
=================
Tx Hash : b'\xd4\xeb,{\xa0d\n\xb2\xb0\xb2\x1b\x18\xdd
\xa1A\x89\xea`\xa8b?A\x14L\x99\xd1rR4\xc7\xfa'
```

```
Address : 0x9Dc44aa8d05c86388E647F954D00CaA858837804
Gas Provided : 467715
Gas Used : 367715


Verified contract bytecode @ 0x9Dc44aa8d05c86388E647F954D00CaA858837804
Deployment Successful.
```

Then, when you want to play around with your smart contract in Ganache, you just have to adjust the provider as you learned in Chapter 4, *Interacting with Smart Contracts Using Web3:*

```
>>> from web3 import Web3, HTTPProvider
>>> w3 = Web3(HTTPProvider('http://localhost:7545'))
```

The remainder of the code is the same. You can name the script interact_smart_contract_in_ganache.py. In Ganache, the coinbase account and the manager account are the first accounts in Ganache. Refer to the GitLab link for the full code to interact with the smart contract in Ganache, https://gitlab.com/ arjunaskykok/hands-on-blockchain-for-python-developers/blob/master/chapter_05/ populus_tutorial/interact_smart_contract_in_ganache.py:

```
from web3 import Web3, HTTPProvider
w3 = Web3(HTTPProvider("http://localhost:7545"))

print(w3.eth.coinbase)
print(w3.eth.getBalance(w3.eth.coinbase))

# Change this address to your smart contract address
address = "0x9Dc44aa8d05c86388E647F954D00CaA858837804"
false = False
true = True
abi = [
...
...
donation = w3.eth.contract(address=address, abi=abi)
print(donation.functions.donatee().call())
```

Summary

In this chapter, you learned how to develop a smart contract with the Populus development framework. Populus isn't equipped with Vyper support, only Solidity. Consequently, you need to add Vyper support by installing Vyper and editing the Populus project configuration file. You also learned how to create unit tests for a smart contract. In this unit test, you used the `web3` object to interact with a smart contract and test it programmatically. After this, you learned how to create a private chain. Finally, you deployed a smart contract to this private chain and Ganache.

In the next chapter, you're going to build an application on top of a blockchain that's more complicated than the donation smart contract. This application is the voting decentralized application.

6
Building a Practical Decentralized Application

In this chapter, we are going to write a popular application on the blockchain, which will be a secure voting application powered by the blockchain. You have all the tools to develop this application, namely, populus and `web3.py`.

Here are the topics that we are going to cover in this chapter:

- Developing a simple voting application
- Learning about an event in a smart contract
- Developing a commercial voting application
- Developing a token-based voting application
- Discussing another type of voting application

Developing a simple voting application

First, we are going to build the simplest voting application, simpler than the voting application example that comes with the Vyper software source code. Let's set up our Populus project directory:

```
$ virtualenv -p python3.6 voting-venv
$ source voting-venv/bin/activate
(voting-venv) $ pip install eth-abi==1.2.2
(voting-venv) $ pip install eth-typing==1.1.0
(voting-venv) $ pip install web3==4.7.2
(voting-venv) $ pip install -e
git+https://github.com/ethereum/populus#egg=populus
(voting-venv) $ pip install vyper
(voting-venv) $ mkdir voting_project
(voting-venv) $ cd voting_project
(voting-venv) $ mkdir tests contracts
```

```
(voting-venv) $ cp ../voting-
venv/src/populus/populus/assets/defaults.v9.config.json project.json
```

Then, add Vyper support to `project.json` by changing the value of the key compilation to the following:

```
"compilation": {
    "backend": {
        "class": "populus.compilation.backends.VyperBackend"
    },
    "contract_source_dirs": [
        "./contracts"
    ],
    "import_remappings": []
},
```

 The latest version of Vyper is 0.1.0b6 which, breaks Populus. The developer needs some time to fix this problem. If the bug has still not been fixed by the time you are reading this book, you can patch Populus yourself.

First, check whether the bug has been fixed by using the following command:

```
(voting-venv) $ cd voting-venv/src/populus
(voting-venv) $ grep -R "compile(" populus/compilation/backends/vyper.py
            bytecode = '0x' + compiler.compile(code).hex()
            bytecode_runtime = '0x' + compiler.compile(code,
bytecode_runtime=True).hex()
```

In our case here, the bug has not been fixed. So, let's patch Populus to fix the bug. Make sure you are still in the same directory (`voting-venv/src/populus`):

```
(voting-venv) $ wget
https://patch-diff.githubusercontent.com/raw/ethereum/populus/pull/484.patc
h
(voting-venv) $ git apply 484.patch
```

Now, create a simple voting smart contract inside the `contracts` directory. Name it `SimpleVoting.vy`. Refer to the following GitLab link for the full code – `https://gitlab.com/arjunaskykok/hands-on-blockchain-for-python-developers/blob/master/chapter_06/voting_project/contracts/SimpleVoting.vy`:

```
struct Proposal:
    name: bytes32
    vote_count: int128

Voting: event ({_from: indexed(address), _proposal: int128})
```

```
proposals: public(map(int128, Proposal))

proposals_count: public(int128)
voters_voted: public(map(address, int128))

...
...

@public
@constant
def winner_name() -> bytes32:
    return self.proposals[self.winning_proposal()].name
```

Let's discuss this simple voting smart contract. It is inspired by the voting example in the Vyper source code, but this example is simplified even further. The original example has a delegation feature that would make things hard to understand. We start with the struct data type variable declaration:

```
struct Proposal:
    name: bytes32
    vote_count: int128
```

The data structure is a variable that has a composite data type that holds the name of the proposal and the amount that the proposal has. The vote_count in the Proposal struct has a data type of int128, while name in the Proposal struct has a data type of bytes32. You could also use uint256 instead of the int128 data type for vote_count in the Proposal struct. It would not make any difference, though. However, bytes32 is a new data type. As you may recall from Chapter 3, *Implementing Smart Contracts With Vyper*, if you want to use the string (or array of bytes) data type in Vyper, you use bytes[20] if the length of that string is less than 20.

bytes32 is another string data type similar to bytes[32], but with one peculiarity; if you set the b'messi' string to a variable with the bytes[32] type and retrieve it with web3, you would get b'messi'. However, if you set the b'messi' string to a variable with the bytes32 type and retrieve it with web3, you would get b'messi\x00\x00\x00\x00\x00\x00\x00\x00\x00\x00\x00\x00\x00\x00\x00\x00\x00\x00\x00\x00\x00\x00\x00\x00\x00\x00\x00'. This string would be padded until we reach 32 bytes. By default, you should use bytes[20] or bytes[256] as the string data type, as opposed to using bytes32. Then why am I using bytes32 in this smart contract? I have a good reason for doing so, but we need to move on to the constructor function first to understand the reason why I use bytes32 to keep the name of proposals:

```
Voting: event ({_from: indexed(address), _proposal: int128})
```

This is the first time we are using an event in a smart contract. `event` is a keyword in Vyper that is designed to create an event. An event is something that happens inside smart contract that our client (the `web3` program) wants to subscribe to. In this statement, `Voting` is the name of the event and it has two parameters. The first parameter is `_from`, which has the type of `address`. `indexed` is used to make filtering events possible using `_from` as a filter. The second parameter is `_proposal`, which is of the type `int128`. Remember, `int128` is a 128-bit integer. This event will become clearer when we subscribe to it in our client program. For now, let's move on to the following:

```
proposals: public(map(int128, Proposal))
```

This variable is a mapping data type variable that maps an `int128` data type variable to a `Proposal` struct variable. Basically, it's a list of proposals:

```
proposals_count: public(int128)
```

This is a helper variable to count how many proposals are in this smart contract:

```
voters_voted: public(int128[address])
```

This is used to check whether an account has already voted or not. We don't want an account to vote for the same proposal more than once. Remember, this is a mapping data type. By default, a non-existent value points to a null value. Null in the context of `int128` is 0:

```
@public
def __init__(_proposalNames: bytes32[2]):
    for i in range(2):
        self.proposals[i] = Proposal({
            name: _proposalNames[i],
            vote_count: 0
        })
        self.proposals_count += 1
```

This constructor got an argument, which is an array of `bytes32`. Inside the constructor, it will iterate twice (we hardcoded the number of proposals into two). Each iteration will set a new member into the `proposals` mapping variable. `name` is set from the argument, and `vote_count` is initialized as 0. Then, the `proposals_count` is increased by one for each iteration.

Here's why I use `bytes32` as a data type for a proposal name: If I used `bytes[128]` as a data type for a proposal name, I could not send it as an argument.

The method in a smart contract in the Vyper programming language cannot accept nested arrays such as `bytes[128][2]` as an argument (at least at the moment in the latest version of Vyper):

```
@public
def vote(proposal: int128):
    assert self.voters_voted[msg.sender] == 0
    assert proposal < self.proposals_count

    self.voters_voted[msg.sender] = 1
    self.proposals[proposal].vote_count += 1

    log.Voting(msg.sender, proposal)
```

This is the function to vote. It accepts an argument named `proposal`. Here, the user votes for a proposal with an integer. So, if the user calls the `vote` method with an argument of 0, such as `vote(0)`, it means the user votes for the first proposal. Of course, you could use the string to vote, as in `vote(b'proposal1')` when you design your own voting smart contract. Here, I use an integer to make things simpler.

In this function, we assert that the voter has not yet voted with this statement: `assert self.voters_voted[msg.sender] == 0`. After voting, we set the value of `voters_voted` with the voter's address as the key to 1: `self.voters_voted[msg.sender] = 1`. We also verify that the voting is valid by checking that the value of the voting is less than the number of proposals, which is 2. The nitty-gritty of this function is the following statement: `self.proposals[proposal].vote_count += 1`. At the end of this function, our `Voting` event is used in this statement: `log.Voting(msg.sender, proposal)`. This is similar to broadcasting that something important has happened—Hey, world! There is a `Voting` event that has two parameters, `msg.sender` as the `address` parameter, and `proposal` as the `int128` parameter. Then, anyone who subscribes to this event will be notified. The subscription of the event happens on the client side, using the `web3` library, as demonstrated in the following code:

```
@private
@constant
def winning_proposal() -> int128:
    winning_vote_count: int128 = 0
    winning_proposal: int128 = 0
    for i in range(2):
        if self.proposals[i].vote_count > winning_vote_count:
            winning_vote_count = self.proposals[i].vote_count
            winning_proposal = i
    return winning_proposal
```

This private function is designed to check which proposal has the most votes:

```
@public
@constant
def winner_name() -> bytes32:
    return self.proposals[self.winning_proposal()].name
```

This `public` function is designed to get the name of the proposal that has the most votes. This function uses the private function described previously.

This smart contract is simple but not perfect, as there is a bug present. For example, in the `vote` function, we did not handle the negative value of voting. On top of that, the number of proposals is hardcoded into 2. However, it will get the job done.

Then, you can compile the smart contract's code in the usual manner:

```
(voting-venv) $ populus compile
```

As a good citizen, let's write a test for this smart contract. Create a file named `test_simple_voting_app.py` in the `tests` directory. Refer to the following GitLab link for the full code of the following code block: `https://gitlab.com/arjunaskykok/hands-on-blockchain-for-python-developers/blob/master/chapter_06/voting_project/tests/test_simple_voting_app.py`:

```
import pytest
import eth_tester


@pytest.fixture()
def voting(chain):
    SimpleVotingFactory =
chain.provider.get_contract_factory('SimpleVoting')
    deploy_txn_hash = SimpleVotingFactory.constructor([b'Messi',
b'Ronaldo']).transact()
    contract_address = chain.wait.for_contract_address(deploy_txn_hash)
    return SimpleVotingFactory(address=contract_address)
...
...
    assert voting.functions.proposals__vote_count(0).call() == 2
    assert voting.functions.proposals__vote_count(1).call() == 1
    assert voting.functions.winner_name().call()[:5] == b'Messi'
```

Let's discuss this test one function at a time:

```
@pytest.fixture()
def voting(chain):
    SimpleVotingFactory =
```

```
chain.provider.get_contract_factory('SimpleVoting')
    deploy_txn_hash = SimpleVotingFactory.constructor([b'Messi',
b'Ronaldo']).transact()
    contract_address = chain.wait.for_contract_address(deploy_txn_hash)
    return SimpleVotingFactory(address=contract_address)
```

Because our simple voting smart contract's constructor requires an argument, we need to use a fixture in the test, as discussed in Chapter 5, *Populus Development Framework*. Then, our fixture can be used as an argument in the test method:

```
def test_initial_state(voting):
    assert voting.functions.proposals_count().call() == 2

    messi = voting.functions.proposals__name(0).call()
    assert len(messi) == 32
    assert messi[:5] == b'Messi'
    assert voting.functions.proposals__name(1).call()[:7] == b'Ronaldo'
    assert voting.functions.proposals__vote_count(0).call() == 0
    assert voting.functions.proposals__vote_count(1).call() == 0
```

This is to check the state of the smart contract after it is deployed. One thing is very unique here; the length of the name's variable in the struct data inside the proposals variable is 32, even if we set it with the value b'messi', such is the peculiarity of the bytes32 data type. This is why we slice the variable to get what we want. Then, for the next test method, we use the chain parameter in addition to the voting parameter:

```
def test_vote(voting, chain):
    t = eth_tester.EthereumTester()
    account2 = t.get_accounts()[1]

    assert voting.functions.proposals__vote_count(0).call() == 0

    set_txn_hash = voting.functions.vote(0).transact({'from': account2})
    chain.wait.for_receipt(set_txn_hash)

    assert voting.functions.proposals__vote_count(0).call() == 1
```

This is used to test the vote function. We test whether the vote function indeed changes the vote_count property of the proposals variable:

```
def test_fail_duplicate_vote(voting, chain):
    t = eth_tester.EthereumTester()
    account2 = t.get_accounts()[1]

    set_txn_hash = voting.functions.vote(0).transact({'from': account2})
    chain.wait.for_receipt(set_txn_hash)
```

```
    with pytest.raises(eth_tester.exceptions.TransactionFailed):
        voting.functions.vote(1).transact({'from': account2})

    with pytest.raises(eth_tester.exceptions.TransactionFailed):
        voting.functions.vote(0).transact({'from': account2})
```

This ensures that we cannot vote more than once using the same account. As we learned in Chapter 5, *Populus Development Framework,* you wrap the fail case with the `pytest.raises` with statement. The last test case is to check the winning proposal:

```
def test_winning_proposal(voting, chain):
    t = eth_tester.EthereumTester()
    account2 = t.get_accounts()[1]
    account3 = t.get_accounts()[2]
    account4 = t.get_accounts()[3]

    set_txn_hash = voting.functions.vote(0).transact({'from': account2})
    chain.wait.for_receipt(set_txn_hash)

    set_txn_hash = voting.functions.vote(0).transact({'from': account3})
    chain.wait.for_receipt(set_txn_hash)

    set_txn_hash = voting.functions.vote(1).transact({'from': account4})
    chain.wait.for_receipt(set_txn_hash)

    assert voting.functions.proposals__vote_count(0).call() == 2
    assert voting.functions.proposals__vote_count(1).call() == 1
    assert voting.functions.winner_name().call()[:5] == b'Messi'
```

In this test, you use three accounts with the `t.get_accounts` helper methods.

Deploying a smart contract that has arguments in its constructor

Let's deploy this smart contract to the Ethereum blockchain. However, we must first be aware that there are some things that complicate the situation. First, the `event` does not work in Ganache, so we have to deploy it to the Rinkeby network or the private Ethereum blockchain. Second, our smart contract has an argument in the constructor. To deploy a smart contract with arguments, we need to use a different method; we cannot use the normal method as demonstrated in Chapter 5, *Populus Development Framework.* In Chapter 5, *Populus Development Framework,* we deployed a smart contract using Populus this way: `populus deploy --chain localblock Donation`.

The Populus method can only deploy a smart contract with a constructor without arguments. Let's overcome these obstacles one by one. The first thing we need to do is deploy it to the private Ethereum blockchain, as follows:

1. Inside the `voting_project` directory, run the following command:

   ```
   (voting-venv) $ populus chain new localblock
   ```

2. Then, initialize the private chain using the `init_chain.sh` script:

   ```
   (voting-venv) $ ./chains/localblock/init_chain.sh
   ```

3. Edit `chains/localblock/run_chain.sh` and change the value of the `--ipcpath` flag to `/tmp/geth.ipc`. Then, run the blockchain:

   ```
   (voting-venv) $ ./chains/localblock/run_chain.sh
   ```

4. Now, edit the `project.json` file. The `chains` key has one object that has 4 keys: `tester`, `temp`, `ropsten`, and `mainnet`. Add one key named `localblock` with its value to this object:

```
"localblock": {
  "chain": {
    "class": "populus.chain.ExternalChain"
  },
  "web3": {
    "provider": {
      "class": "web3.providers.ipc.IPCProvider",
      "settings": {
        "ipc_path":"/tmp/geth.ipc"
      }
    }
  },
  "contracts": {
    "backends": {
      "JSONFile": {"$ref": "contracts.backends.JSONFile"},
      "ProjectContracts": {
        "$ref": "contracts.backends.ProjectContracts"
      }
    }
  }
}
```

Running a blockchain requires a dedicated terminal. So open a new terminal, execute a virtual environment script, and then go inside the `voting_project` directory. Create this file and name it `deploy_SmartVoting.py`:

```python
from populus import Project
from populus.utils.wait import wait_for_transaction_receipt


def main():

    project = Project()

    chain_name = "localblock"

    with project.get_chain(chain_name) as chain:

        SimpleVoting = chain.provider.get_contract_factory('SimpleVoting')

        txhash = SimpleVoting.deploy(transaction={"from":
chain.web3.eth.coinbase}, args=[[b'Messi', b'Ronaldo']])
        receipt = wait_for_transaction_receipt(chain.web3, txhash)
        simple_voting_address = receipt["contractAddress"]
        print("SimpleVoting contract address is", simple_voting_address)


if __name__ == "__main__":
    main()
```

Now, let's discuss what this program does:

```python
from populus import Project
from populus.utils.wait import wait_for_transaction_receipt
```

We import tools from the `populus` library, and `Project` represents the `project.json` configuration file. `wait_for_transaction_receipt` is a function that waits until our transaction has been confirmed in the Ethereum blockchain:

```python
def main():

    project = Project()

    chain_name = "localblock"

    with project.get_chain(chain_name) as chain:
```

Inside the `main` function, we initialize a `Project` instance and then we get the `localblock` chain:

```
"localblock": {
  "chain": {
    "class": "populus.chain.ExternalChain"
  },
  "web3": {
    "provider": {
      "class": "web3.providers.ipc.IPCProvider",
      "settings": {
        "ipc_path":"/tmp/geth.ipc"
      }
    }
  },
  "contracts": {
    "backends": {
      "JSONFile": {"$ref": "contracts.backends.JSONFile"},
      "ProjectContracts": {
        "$ref": "contracts.backends.ProjectContracts"
      }
    }
  }
}
```

The `chain` object is now representing this `json` object in the `project.json` file.

We get the `SimpleVoting` smart contract factory from `build/contracts.json`:

```
SimpleVoting = chain.provider.get_contract_factory('SimpleVoting')
```

Then, we deploy our smart contract to the private Ethereum blockchain:

```
txhash = SimpleVoting.deploy(transaction={"from": chain.web3.eth.coinbase},
args=[[b'Messi', b'Ronaldo']])
```

It receives two keyword arguments, `transaction` and `args`. The transaction argument is a dictionary of transactions. Here, we set the `from` parameter. `chain.web3.eth.coinbase` is our default account, which is common in a `testing/development` scenario. Here, we use the default account without the private key. In this transaction object, we can also set `gas`, gasPrice, and other transaction parameters. The `args` keyword argument allows us to send an argument to the constructor of a smart contract. It is a nested array, `[[b'Messi', b'Ronaldo']]`, because the inner array is the `_proposalNames` argument in the constructor of the smart contract.

The outer array is designed to encapsulate other parameters in the constructor, but we only have one argument in this case:

```
@public
def __init__(_proposalNames: bytes32[2]):
    for i in range(2):
        self.proposals[i] = {
            name: _proposalNames[i],
            vote_count: 0
        }
        self.proposals_count += 1

receipt = wait_for_transaction_receipt(chain.web3, txhash)
```

We wait for the transaction to be confirmed. Then, we get the address of the smart contract from the deployment process:

```
simple_voting_address = receipt["contractAddress"]
print("SimpleVoting contract address is", simple_voting_address)
```

The `receipt` object is an object from the blockchain that describes the confirmation of the transaction. What we are concerned with in this context is the address, that is, the `contractAddress` key in the receipt object:

```
if __name__ == "__main__":
    main()
```

This is designed to execute the `main` function.

Unlike Ganache, where you are given 10 accounts (each equipped with 100 ethers), in this private Ethereum blockchain with default settings from Populus, you only have one account equipped with 1 trillion ethers! The following script allows you to find out how many ethers the default account has:

```
from web3 import Web3, IPCProvider

w3 = Web3(IPCProvider(ipc_path='/tmp/geth.ipc'))

print(w3.fromWei(w3.eth.getBalance(w3.eth.coinbase), 'ether'))
```

In this smart contract, we want to play with our smart contract with more than 1 account. So let's create 10 accounts in this Ethereum private blockchain. Creating a new account is possibly not the appropriate term here because all accounts are already created in the Ethereum blockchain, so perhaps **finding new accounts** is more appropriate. Create a new file inside the `voting_project` directory and name it `create_10_accounts_on_private_chain.py`:

```python
from web3 import Web3, IPCProvider

w3 = Web3(IPCProvider(ipc_path='/tmp/geth.ipc'))

with open('10_accounts.txt', 'w') as f:
    for i in range(10):
        f.write(w3.personal.newAccount('password123') + "\n")
```

We will write our new accounts' addresses in the file so we can reuse them later. The function that you need to notice is `w3.personal.newAccount('password123')`. This will give you the public address. The private key will be encrypted with `password123`. This will be saved in the `chains/localblock/chain_data/keystore` directory. The name of the encrypted file is something like this—UTC—2018-10-26T13-13-25.731124692Z—36461a003a03f857d60f5bd0b8e8a6 4aab4e4535. The end part of the name of the file is the `public` address. In that filename example, the `public` address is `36461a003a03f857d60f5bd0b8e8a64aab4e4535`. Execute this script. The `public` address of the 10 accounts will be written in the `10_accounts.txt` file.

If you take a look at the `chains/localblock/chain_data/keystore` directory, you will see at least 11 files.

Each of these new 10 accounts are equipped with 0 ethers. To vote in our smart contract, you should not have an empty balance. So, why don't we distribute our money from the default account to these 10 accounts? Create a file inside `voting_project`, and name it `distribute_money.py`. Refer to the code file in the following GitLab link for the full code — https://gitlab.com/arjunaskykok/hands-on-blockchain-for-python-developers/blob/master/chapter_06/voting_project/distribute_money.py:

```python
from web3 import Web3, IPCProvider
from populus.utils.wait import wait_for_transaction_receipt
import glob

w3 = Web3(IPCProvider(ipc_path='/tmp/geth.ipc'))

address = 'fa146d7af4b92eb1751c3c9c644fa436a60f7b75'
```

```
. . .
. . .
            signed = w3.eth.account.signTransaction(transaction, private_key)
            txhash = w3.eth.sendRawTransaction(signed.rawTransaction)
            wait_for_transaction_receipt(w3, txhash)
```

Now, let's discuss this script line by line:

```
from web3 import Web3, IPCProvider
from populus.utils.wait import wait_for_transaction_receipt
import glob
```

You already know about `Web3`, `IPCProvider`, and `wait_for_transaction_receipt`.
`glob` is from the Python standard library. Its purpose is to filter files from the directory:

```
w3 = Web3(IPCProvider(ipc_path='/tmp/geth.ipc'))
```

We connect to the Ethereum node using a socket:

```
address = 'fa146d7af4b92eb1751c3c9c644fa436a60f7b75'
```

This is our default account's address. How do you know? You can find it with
`w3.eth.coinbase` in a script connecting to this private Ethereum blockchain, or you can
take a look at the filename inside the `chains/localblock/chain_data/keystore`
directory. There is only one filename after you initialize and run the private Ethereum
blockchain. Now, after you initialize another 10 accounts, naturally, the number of files will
be 11:

```
with open('chains/localblock/password') as f:
    password = f.read().rstrip("\n")
```

The password to unlock the default account is stored in a plain text file in
`chains/localblock/password`:

```
    encrypted_private_key_file =
glob.glob('chains/localblock/chain_data/keystore/*' + address)[0]
    with open(encrypted_private_key_file) as f2:
        private_key = w3.eth.account.decrypt(f2.read(), password)
```

After finding this, we decrypt the encrypted file using the `w3.eth.account.decrypt`
method:

```
w3.eth.defaultAccount = w3.eth.coinbase
```

This is to avoid the obligation of providing the `from` parameter to a method when creating a transaction:

```
with open('10_accounts.txt', 'r') as f:
    accounts = f.readlines()
    for account in accounts:
```

We opened `10_accounts.txt`, containing all the new accounts that we have, and then we iterated these one by one:

```
        nonce =
w3.eth.getTransactionCount(Web3.toChecksumAddress(w3.eth.defaultAccount))
        transaction = {
            'to': Web3.toChecksumAddress(account.rstrip("\n")),
            'value': w3.toWei('10', 'ether'),
            'gas': 1000000,
            'gasPrice': w3.toWei('20', 'gwei'),
            'nonce': nonce
        }
```

We check the latest nonce value with `w3.eth.getTransactionCount` before feeding it to transaction object. The transaction object has `to`, `value`, `gas`, and `gasPrice`, as well as the `nonce` key. Here, we want to send 10 ethers to each account:

```
        signed = w3.eth.account.signTransaction(transaction, private_key)
        txhash = w3.eth.sendRawTransaction(signed.rawTransaction)
```

We sign the transaction with our private key, and then we broadcast the transaction to the miners using the `w3.eth.sendRawTransaction` method:

```
wait_for_transaction_receipt(w3, txhash)
```

This is very important. If you only send money to one account, you could skip it. However, since we broadcast 10 transactions in a sequential manner, you must wait for each transaction to be confirmed first before broadcasting the next transaction.

Think of it this way: you broadcast a transaction of sending 10 ethers with nonce 3, and then miners will need time to confirm this transaction. But, in a short space of time, you broadcast a new transaction with nonce 4. Miners who get this transaction will complain to you because you tried to skip from nonce 2 to nonce 4. Remember, the transaction with nonce 3 takes time to be confirmed.

After executing the file, you can check that your 10 accounts have 10 ethers each.

Let's create our simple decentralized voting application based on the smart contract. Go outside `voting_project` and create a new directory to contain our application. After creating the directory, enter the following inside it:

```
(voting-venv) $ mkdir voting_dapp
(voting-venv) $ cd voting_dapp
```

Let's create a program to subscribe to a `Voting` event. Name this file `watch_simple_voting.py`:

```python
from web3 import Web3, IPCProvider

w3 = Web3(IPCProvider(ipc_path='/tmp/geth.ipc'))

false = False
true = True
abi = .... # Take the abi from voting_projects/build/contracts.json.

with open('address.txt', 'r') as f:
    content = f.read().rstrip("\n")

address = content

SimpleVoting = w3.eth.contract(address=address, abi=abi)

event_filter = SimpleVoting.events.Voting.createFilter(fromBlock=1)

import time
while True:
    print(event_filter.get_new_entries())
    time.sleep(2)
```

Now, let's discuss this program line by line:

```python
from web3 import Web3, IPCProvider

w3 = Web3(IPCProvider(ipc_path='/tmp/geth.ipc'))

We connect to private Ethereum blockchain using socket.

false = False
true = True
abi = .... # Take the abi from voting_projects/build/contracts.json.
```

We need `abi` to connect to a smart contract. You can get this from the smart contract's complication. Since `abi` is a `json` object that has a Boolean set as `true` and `false`, while Python's Boolean values are `True` and `False` (notice the capitalization), we need to adjust it:

```
with open('address.txt', 'r') as f:
    content = f.read().rstrip("\n")

address = content
```

To connect to a smart contract, you need an address. This is the address from the deployment script. You can also set the address to the one hardcoded in the code, as follows:

```
address = '0x993FFADB39D323D8B134F6f0CdD83d510c45D306'
```

However, I prefer to put it in an external file:

```
event_filter = SimpleVoting.events.Voting.createFilter(fromBlock=1)
```

This is designed to create a subscription to the `Voting` event of the `SimpleVoting` smart contract. The syntax is as follows:

```
<name of smart contract>.events.<name of event>.createFilter(fromBlock=1)
```

`fromBlock` is the historical pointer. The lower the block, the earlier the history:

```
import time
while True:
    print(event_filter.get_new_entries())
    time.sleep(2)
```

Then, we subscribe to the voting event. You would get something like this:

```
[]
[]
[]
```

Let this script run. Don't exit the application. Open a new Terminal, execute our virtual environment script, and go inside the `voting_dapp` project. After doing so, create a new script and name it `simple_voting_client.py`. Refer to the code file in the following GitLab link for the full cod: `https://gitlab.com/arjunaskykok/hands-on-blockchain-for-python-developers/blob/master/chapter_06/voting_dapp/simple_voting_client.py`:

```
from web3 import Web3, IPCProvider
from populus.utils.wait import wait_for_transaction_receipt
```

```
import glob

w3 = Web3(IPCProvider(ipc_path='/tmp/geth.ipc'))

with open('client_address.txt', 'r') as f:
    content = f.read().rstrip("\n")

address = content.lower()

...
...

signed = w3.eth.account.signTransaction(txn, private_key=private_key)
w3.eth.sendRawTransaction(signed.rawTransaction)
```

Now, let's discuss this line by line. We start from the top part of the script:

```
from web3 import Web3, IPCProvider
from populus.utils.wait import wait_for_transaction_receipt
import glob

w3 = Web3(IPCProvider(ipc_path='/tmp/geth.ipc'))

with open('client_address.txt', 'r') as f:
    content = f.read().rstrip("\n")

address = content.lower()

encrypted_private_key_file =
glob.glob('../voting_project/chains/localblock/chain_data/keystore/*' +
address)[0]
with open(encrypted_private_key_file) as f:
    password = 'password123'
    private_key = w3.eth.account.decrypt(f.read(), password)
    w3.eth.defaultAccount = '0x' + address
```

The logic here is the same as the previous script. You started by opening the encrypted file using `password123`. You then set the voter's account address in the `client_address.txt` file to make this script flexible. You are welcome to hardcode the voter's account address in the script:

```
false = False
true = True
abi = ...
```

Here, you set the `abi` from the smart contract compilation in the usual manner:

```
with open('address.txt', 'r') as f:
    content = f.read().rstrip("\n")

smart_contract_address = content

SimpleVoting = w3.eth.contract(address=smart_contract_address, abi=abi)
```

Remember, in this script, there are two addresses. The first is the address of the voter or the client. The second is the address of the smart contract. Then, you need to get the nonce:

```
nonce =
w3.eth.getTransactionCount(Web3.toChecksumAddress(w3.eth.defaultAccount))
```

You use this nonce when building a transaction:

```
txn = SimpleVoting.functions.vote(0).buildTransaction({
        'gas': 70000,
        'gasPrice': w3.toWei('1', 'gwei'),
        'nonce': nonce
    })
```

This is the `vote` function. Here, we vote for the proposal with the index 0, which is `b'messi'`. You submit `gas`, `gasPrice`, and `nonce`, and you omit `from` because you already set `w3.eth.defaultAccount`:

```
signed = w3.eth.account.signTransaction(txn, private_key=private_key)
w3.eth.sendRawTransaction(signed.rawTransaction)
```

The last lines are dedicated to signing and broadcasting transactions.

Execute the script, and then go to the Terminal in which you ran the `watch_simple_voting.py` script. You would then get something like this:

```
[]
[]
[]
[]
[AttributeDict({'args': AttributeDict({'_from':
'0xf0738EF5635f947f13dD41F34DAe6B2caa0a9EA6', '_proposal': 0}), 'event':
'Voting', 'logIndex': 0, 'transactionIndex': 0, 'transactionHash':
HexBytes('0x61b4c59425a6305af4f2560d1cd10d1540243b1f74ce07fa53a550ada2e649e
7'), 'address': '0x993FFADB39D323D8B134F6f0CdD83d510c45D306', 'blockHash':
HexBytes('0xb458542d9bee85ed7673d94f036e55f8daca188e5871cc910eb49cf4895964a
0'), 'blockNumber': 3110})]
[]
[]
```

```
[]
[]
[]
[]
```

There you have it. In a real-world application, this event can be used to give a notification in a decentralized application. Then, you could update the standings of the voting or whatever you like.

You can also get all events from the beginning. Remember the code to get the event? This is as follows:

```
import time
while True:
    print(event_filter.get_new_entries())
    time.sleep(2)
```

Instead of using `get_new_entries`, you could use `get_all_entries` to retrieve all events from the beginning, demonstrated as follows:

```
event_filter.get_all_entries()
```

Developing a commercial voting application

Let's upgrade our smart contract to a commercial one. To vote, the voter needs to pay a small amount of money. This is similar to American Idol, in which people vote for who they want to win by text-messaging their choice.

Go back to the `voting_project` directory and open a new file in the `contracts` directory and name this `CommercialVoting.vy`. Refer to the code file in the following GitLab link for the full code of this code block: https://gitlab.com/arjunaskykok/hands-on-blockchain-for-python-developers/blob/master/chapter_06/voting_project/contracts/CommercialVoting.vy:

```
struct Proposal:
    name: bytes32
    vote_count: int128

proposals: public(map(int128, Proposal))

voters_voted: public(map(address, int128))

manager: public(address)

...
```

```
. . .

@public
def withdraw_money():
    assert msg.sender == self.manager

    send(self.manager, self.balance)
```

This smart contract is similar to `SimpleVoting.vy`, but with an additional payment feature. We won't discuss it line by line, but we will look at the differences between the previous smart contract and this one:

```
@public
def __init__(_proposalNames: bytes32[2]):
    for i in range(2):
        self.proposals[i] = Proposal({
            name: _proposalNames[i],
            vote_count: 0
        })
    self.manager = msg.sender
```

In this constructor function, we save the address of the account that launched the smart contract:

```
@public
@payable
def vote(proposal: int128):
    assert msg.value >= as_wei_value(0.01, "ether")
    assert self.voters_voted[msg.sender] == 0
    assert proposal < 2 and proposal >= 0

    self.voters_voted[msg.sender] = 1
    self.proposals[proposal].vote_count += 1
```

In this `vote` function, we added the `@payable` decorator so people can send money when they want to vote. As well as that, we require the minimum payment to be `0.01` ether using this statement: `assert msg.value >= as_wei_value(0.01, "ether")`:

```
@public
def withdraw_money():
    assert msg.sender == self.manager

    send(self.manager, self.balance)
```

Naturally, we have to create a function to withdraw ethers from the smart contract. Here, we send ethers to the manager account.

Now, let's move on to testing the smart contract. Create the test file inside the `tests` directory and name it `test_commercial_voting.py`. Refer to the code file in the following GitLab link for the full code: https://gitlab.com/arjunaskykok/hands-on-blockchain-for-python-developers/blob/master/chapter_06/voting_project/tests/test_commercial_voting.py:

```
import pytest
import eth_tester


@pytest.fixture()
def voting(chain):
    CommercialVotingFactory =
chain.provider.get_contract_factory('CommercialVoting')
    deploy_txn_hash = CommercialVotingFactory.constructor([b'Messi',
b'Ronaldo']).transact()
    contract_address = chain.wait.for_contract_address(deploy_txn_hash)
    return CommercialVotingFactory(address=contract_address)


...
...


    assert abs((after_withdraw_balance - initial_balance) - web3.toWei('1',
'ether')) < web3.toWei('10', 'gwei')
```

Let's discuss the test functions one by one:

```
def test_initial_state(voting, web3):
    assert voting.functions.manager().call() == web3.eth.coinbase
```

This is designed to test the manager variable points to the account that launched the smart contract. Remember that `web3.eth.coinbase` is the default account. Testing whether to vote requires a number of ethers and accounts, which we can get from `t.get_accounts()`:

```
def test_vote_with_money(voting, chain, web3):
    t = eth_tester.EthereumTester()
    account2 = t.get_accounts()[1]
    account3 = t.get_accounts()[2]

    set_txn_hash = voting.functions.vote(0).transact({'from': account2,
                                                      'value':
web3.toWei('0.05', 'ether')})
    chain.wait.for_receipt(set_txn_hash)

    set_txn_hash = voting.functions.vote(1).transact({'from': account3,
                                                      'value':
```

```
web3.toWei('0.15', 'ether')})
    chain.wait.for_receipt(set_txn_hash)

    assert web3.eth.getBalance(voting.address) == web3.toWei('0.2',
'ether')
```

This is to test that you can send ethers in the `vote` function. You also test the balance of the ethers that are accumulated in the smart contract:

```
def test_vote_with_not_enough_money(voting, web3):
    t = eth_tester.EthereumTester()
    account2 = t.get_accounts()[1]

    with pytest.raises(eth_tester.exceptions.TransactionFailed):
        voting.functions.vote(0).transact({'from': account2,
                                           'value': web3.toWei('0.005',
'ether')})
```

This is to test that you need to send a minimum of `0.01` ether when you want to vote:

```
def test_manager_account_could_withdraw_money(voting, web3, chain):
    t = eth_tester.EthereumTester()
    account2 = t.get_accounts()[1]

    set_txn_hash = voting.functions.vote(0).transact({'from': account2,
'value': web3.toWei('1', 'ether')})
    chain.wait.for_receipt(set_txn_hash)

    initial_balance = web3.eth.getBalance(web3.eth.coinbase)
    set_txn_hash = voting.functions.withdraw_money().transact({'from':
web3.eth.coinbase})
    chain.wait.for_receipt(set_txn_hash)
    after_withdraw_balance = web3.eth.getBalance(web3.eth.coinbase)

    assert abs((after_withdraw_balance - initial_balance) - web3.toWei('1',
'ether')) < web3.toWei('10', 'gwei')
```

This is one of the most important tests in this smart contract. It is designed to test whether or not you can correctly withdraw ethers from the smart contract. You can check the balance before and after withdrawal, and make sure that the difference is roughly around 1 ether (because you have to pay for gas).

Developing a token-based voting application

Now, let's develop a token-based voting application on the blockchain. What I mean by token-based voting is that in order to vote, you must have a token that is created in the smart contract. If you vote with this token, then the token is burnt, meaning that you cannot vote twice. In this smart contract, the number of tokens are also limited, unlike previous voting applications where unlimited accounts can vote. Let's write a smart contract in the `contracts` directory and name the file `TokenBasedVoting.vy`. Refer to the code file in the following GitLab link for the full code: https://gitlab.com/arjunaskykok/hands-on-blockchain-for-python-developers/blob/master/chapter_06/voting_project/contracts/TokenBasedVoting.vy:

```
struct Proposal:
    name: bytes32
    vote_count: int128

proposals: public(map(int128, Proposal))


...
...
@public
@constant
def winner_name() -> bytes32:
    return self.proposals[self.winning_proposal()].name
```

Let's discuss this script line by line:

```
struct Proposal:
    name: bytes32
    vote_count: int128

proposals: public(map(int128, Proposal))

token: public(map(address, bool))
index: int128
maximum_token: int128
manager: address
```

You have familiarized yourself with the `proposals` variable, which has the same purpose as the previous voting application. `token` is a new variable that is intended to track the token's owner. `index` and `maximum_token` are variables to count how many tokens we have assigned. Remember, we want to limit the number of tokens. The manager is the one who launched the smart contract:

```
@public
def __init__(_proposalNames: bytes32[2]):
```

```
for i in range(2):
    self.proposals[i] = Proposal({
        name: _proposalNames[i],
        vote_count: 0
    })
self.index = 0
self.maximum_token = 8
self.manager = msg.sender
```

In the constructor, after setting up the `proposals` variable, we initialize the `index` to be 0, and `maximum_token` to be 8. Only 8 tokens are available in this smart contract, meaning that only 8 vote attempts can be attempted. The `manager` variable is initialized to the one that launched the smart contract:

```
@public
def assign_token(target: address):
    assert msg.sender == self.manager
    assert self.index < self.maximum_token
    assert not self.token[target]
    self.token[target] = True
    self.index += 1
```

In this function, the owner can assign the token to any account. To indicate the owner of the token, we set the `true` value to the `token` variable, with its key points to `target`. The `index` is increasing by one, so later, we cannot create more than the `maximum_token` variable:

```
@public
def vote(proposal: int128):
    assert self.index == self.maximum_token
    assert self.token[msg.sender]
    assert proposal < 2 and proposal >= 0

    self.token[msg.sender] = False
    self.proposals[proposal].vote_count += 1
```

In this `vote` function, we burn the token by setting the `token` mapping variable with the voter's address key to `false`. But first, we must ensure that the voter is the valid owner of the token using this statement: `assert self.token[msg.sender]`. We must also ensure that people can vote after all tokens have been assigned. Of course, just like the previous voting application, we increase the vote count of the proposal that the voter votes for.

Let's create a test for the token-based voting application. To do this, create a file named `test_token_based_voting.py` in the `tests` directory. Refer to the code file in the following GitLab link for the full code: `https://gitlab.com/arjunaskykok/hands-on-blockchain-for-python-developers/blob/master/chapter_06/voting_project/tests/test_token_based_voting.py`. Add the following code into the new file:

```
import pytest
import eth_tester


@pytest.fixture()
def voting(chain):
    TokenBasedVotingFactory =
chain.provider.get_contract_factory('TokenBasedVoting')
    deploy_txn_hash = TokenBasedVotingFactory.constructor([b'Messi',
b'Ronaldo']).transact()
    contract_address = chain.wait.for_contract_address(deploy_txn_hash)
    return TokenBasedVotingFactory(address=contract_address)


...
...


    set_txn_hash = voting.functions.vote(0).transact({'from': account2})
    chain.wait.for_receipt(set_txn_hash)
```

Let's discuss this script line by line. We start from the `fixture` function:

```
import pytest
import eth_tester


@pytest.fixture()
def voting(chain):
    TokenBasedVotingFactory =
chain.provider.get_contract_factory('TokenBasedVoting')
    deploy_txn_hash = TokenBasedVotingFactory.constructor([b'Messi',
b'Ronaldo']).transact()
    contract_address = chain.wait.for_contract_address(deploy_txn_hash)
    return TokenBasedVotingFactory(address=contract_address)
```

As usual, we create a `fixture` of this smart contract by deploying the smart contract manually:

```
def assign_tokens(voting, chain, web3):
    t = eth_tester.EthereumTester()
    accounts = t.get_accounts()
```

```
    for i in range(1, 9):
        set_txn_hash =
voting.functions.assign_token(accounts[i]).transact({'from':
web3.eth.coinbase})
        chain.wait.for_receipt(set_txn_hash)
```

This is a `helper` function for assigning 8 tokens to different accounts:

```
def test_assign_token(voting, chain):
    t = eth_tester.EthereumTester()
    account2 = t.get_accounts()[1]

    assert not voting.functions.token(account2).call()

    set_txn_hash = voting.functions.assign_token(account2).transact({})
    chain.wait.for_receipt(set_txn_hash)

    assert voting.functions.token(account2).call()
```

This `test` function is designed to check that the `assign_token` function can assign a token to the target's address:

```
def test_cannot_vote_without_token(voting, chain, web3):
    t = eth_tester.EthereumTester()
    account10 = t.get_accounts()[9]

    assign_tokens(voting, chain, web3)

    with pytest.raises(eth_tester.exceptions.TransactionFailed):
        voting.functions.vote(0).transact({'from': account10})
```

This `test` function is designed to ensure that only the owner of the token can vote in this smart contract:

```
def test_can_vote_with_token(voting, chain, web3):
    t = eth_tester.EthereumTester()
    account2 = t.get_accounts()[1]

    assign_tokens(voting, chain, web3)

    assert voting.functions.proposals__vote_count(0).call() == 0

    set_txn_hash = voting.functions.vote(0).transact({'from': account2})
    chain.wait.for_receipt(set_txn_hash)

    assert voting.functions.proposals__vote_count(0).call() == 1
```

This `test` function is intended to ensure that the owner of the token can vote for the proposal successfully.

Let me explain why this token-based voting is quite amazing. There are only 8 tokens that are available, and these can be used to vote in this smart contract. The programmer who wrote and deployed this smart contract cannot even change the rule after this smart contract goes live. The voter can verify that the rule is fair by demanding the source code of the smart contract from the programmer, and verifying that the bytecode from the compilation is indeed the same as the bytecode in the smart contract's address. To get the bytecode from the smart contract's address, you could do something like this:

```
from web3 import Web3, HTTPProvider

w3 = Web3(HTTPProvider('http://127.0.0.1:8545'))
print(w3.eth.getCode('0x891dfe5Dbf551E090805CEee41b94bB2205Bdd17'))
```

Then, you compile the smart contract's source code from the author and compare them. Are they the same? If they are, then you can audit the smart contract to make sure there is no cheating. If not, then you can complain to the author or decide not to participate in their smart contract.

Achieving this transparency in traditional web applications is no small feat. Verifying code in GitHub/GitLab does not mean much, because the developer could deploy different code in their server. You could be granted a guest session on their server to verify the transparency of the code but, again, the developer could deploy a sophisticated way to trick you. You could monitor the web application from the frontend every second and deploy a surveillance strategy either manually, or with the help of MLto detect suspicious activity. For example, you suddenly notice that a comment has been suddenly modified, but there is no indication of it being edited afterward, so you can be certain that the cheating happened inside the application. However, accusing the developer is not easy, because it's your word against theirs. You could be accused of creating false evidence.

What works is a credible and competent auditor being hired to do the job. The auditor gains access to their web application and has sufficient permission to read database logs and server logs to make sure there is no cheating taking place. This only works if the auditor cannot be bribed and is competent enough to avoid being tricked by the developer. Alternatively, you could use blockchain.

Voting is a vast subject. We haven't implemented the delegation feature in this voting application. What I mean by delegation is similar to democracy in many countries. In some democratic countries, people don't choose their prime minister or president directly. They choose the members of the House of Representatives. After these are elected, the members will choose the prime minister. You can create a voting smart contract that implements a delegation system. Refer to the *Further reading* section if you want to study this further.

On a final note, our voting smart contract is pretty transparent. This can be good or bad depending on the situation. Transparency is good, especially in financial transactions, because you can audit logs to find money laundering cases. However, when it comes to voting, especially in politics, secrecy is a desirable property. If voters don't have secrecy, they may fear being persecuted by others. Secrecy in voting on a smart contract is still at the research stage.

Summary

In this chapter, you have learned how to create a real-world application where blockchain technology can shine. This real-world application is a voting application. From a simple voting smart contract where every account can vote, we gradually created a voting application in which only certain accounts can vote using a token system. When building this voting smart contract, we also learned about how to write a script to deploy a smart contract with constructors. After deploying a smart contract, we also learned a feature from smart contracts, which is an event. In a `web3` script, we subscribe to this event to learn about things that interest us. Finally, we created helper scripts to create many accounts and send money to other accounts for development purposes.

In the next chapter, you are going to create a frontend for your `web3` script. You are going to build a proper decentralized application in the form of a desktop application.

Further reading

- https://www.ethereum.org/dao

3
Section 3: Frontend Decentralized Applications

This section is a hands-on learning guide to building a Twitter-like application with a desktop frontend.

The following chapters will be covered in this section:

- Chapter 7, Frontend Decentralized Applications

7
Frontend Decentralized Application

In this chapter, we are going to learn how to write a decentralized application that has a GUI frontend. This is a desktop decentralized application. People can interact with a smart contract using buttons and text fields. It is a step forward from the Truffle console or a `web3.py` script. While writing this GUI frontend, we will learn about the best practices when dealing with a smart contract, which are how to deal with latency and how to provide added value in a decentralized application.

We are going to learn about the following topics in this chapter:

- Setting up the Qt GUI library
- Installing Qt for Python
- Crash course on Qt for Python
- Writing the smart contract for the Twitter-like application
- Building the GUI for the Twitter-like application

Setting up the Qt GUI library

The Qt library is a C++ framework that was designed to create a multi-platform application. In Linux, this library is the foundation for the KDE desktop. Its counterpart is the GTK+ library, the foundation for Gnome desktop. However, the Qt library has stepped up its game. You can use the Qt library to create applications on Android and iOS. People have sometimes mistaken the Qt library as a library that only creates GUI applications. However, the Qt library comprises non-GUI libraries as well, for example, data storage, multimedia, and networking. The Qt library even contains a threading library! In the past, you could create an open source application for free with the Qt library. However, if you want to create a proprietary application with the Qt library, you must pay for the license. You can now have a bit more flexibility when it comes to using the Qt library.

You can create a proprietary application with the Qt library for free, but only if you provide a relinking mechanism for Qt libraries, provide a license copy, and explicitly acknowledge Qt usage, among other things, as described at `https://www.qt.io/download`.

Choosing a GUI library

Python has a plethora of GUI libraries to choose from. This includes Tkinter, Phoenix (wxPython), PyGObject, PyQt, Qt for Python (PySide2), among many others. Deciding which GUI library should be used for a Python application is sometimes subjective.

Tkinter is a Python GUI library, but the UI is not slick and polished. PyGObject is a good choice only if you want to write a desktop application in Linux, because it uses GTK+. There is support for GTK+ in Windows and Mac, but it's not native.

I am going to choose the Qt for Python (`https://www.qt.io/qt-for-python`) library. This is the official Python binding for the Qt library from Qt itself. Be careful, though; there is another Python binding for the Qt library from another company. This library is called PyQt, and the company is Riverbank. These libraries both support the latest Qt library, which is Qt 5.

There are differences between these two libraries. If you want to write and sell a proprietary application using PyQt, you must purchase a license from Riverbank. However, you don't need to do that with Qt for Python, although that comes with its own set of restrictions. For example, you must provide a relinking mechanism for Qt libraries. There are books written covering PyQt, but there are none for Qt for Python at the time of writing this book.

Previously, the reliable Python binding for Qt could only be obtained from Riverbank. However, in the middle of this year, Qt announced its Python binding for its latest Qt library (Qt 5.11). Qt is quite serious about promoting this Python binding.

Installing Qt for Python

First, you must install Qt 5.11. Go to `https://www.qt.io/download`. While downloading the library, you have two types of license to choose from—commercial and open source. In this case, you must choose the open source option:

1. If you are on the Linux platform, you will download the following file: `qt-unified-linux-x64-3.0.5-online.run`.

   This is an installer. If you run it, you will get the following screen:

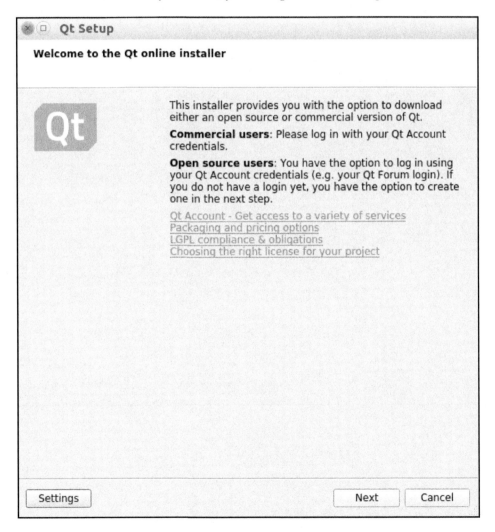

2. Click **Next**. You will then be greeted with a login screen. Create a new account if you don't have one; it's free. After that, log in through the following screen:

3. Then, you will see the installer's welcome screen. From here, click **Next**:

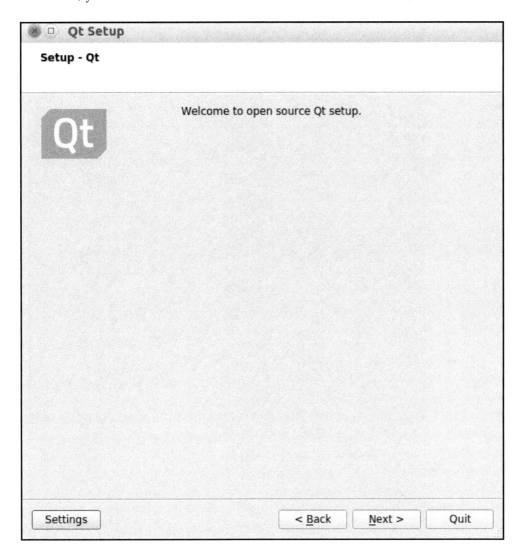

4. Specify where you want to install the Qt library:

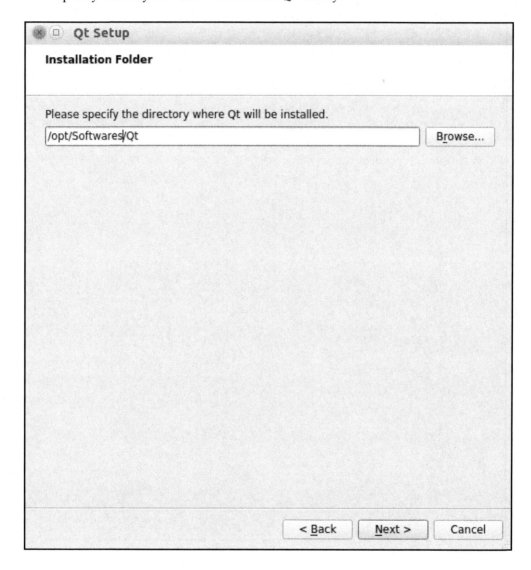

5. Then choose **Qt 5.11.2** or the latest stable release:

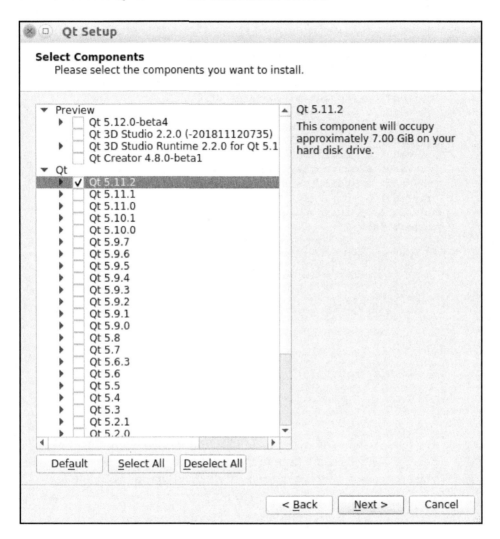

It will be a while before the installer finishes doing its job.

6. Once the Qt 5 installation process is finished, you can install the Python binding to Qt using the following command lines:

```
$ python3.6 -m venv qt-venv
$ source qt-venv/bin/activate
(qt-venv) $ pip install PySide2
```

7. We are going to write a smart contract and a decentralized application with this virtual environment. We need to install the `populus`, `vyper`, and `web3` libraries as usual:

```
(qt-venv) $ pip install eth-abi==1.2.2
(qt-venv) $ pip install eth-typing==1.1.0
(qt-venv) $ pip install py-evm==0.2.0a33
(qt-venv) $ pip install web3==4.7.2
(qt-venv) $ pip install -e
git+https://github.com/ethereum/populus#egg=populus
(qt-venv) $ pip install vyper
(qt-venv) $ mkdir twitter_like_project
(qt-venv) $ cd twitter_like_project
(qt-venv) $ mkdir tests contracts
(qt-venv) $ cp ../qt-
venv/src/populus/populus/assets/defaults.v9.config.json
project.json
```

8. Add Vyper support to `project.json` by changing the value of the `"compilation"` key to the following:

```
"compilation": {
    "backend": {
      "class": "populus.compilation.backends.VyperBackend"
    },
    "contract_source_dirs": [
      "./contracts"
    ],
    "import_remappings": []
},
```

 The latest version of Vyper is 0.1.0b6, and it breaks Populus. The developer needs some time to fix it. If the bug has not been fixed while you are reading this book, you could patch Populus yourself.

9. Check whether the bug has been fixed or not using the following command:

```
(qt-venv) $ cd qt-venv/src/populus
(qt-venv) $ grep -R "compile("
populus/compilation/backends/vyper.py
            bytecode = '0x' + compiler.compile(code).hex()
            bytecode_runtime = '0x' + compiler.compile(code,
bytecode_runtime=True).hex()
```

In our case, the bug has not been fixed.

10. So, let's patch Populus to fix the bug using the following command lines. Make sure you are still in the same directory (`qt-venv/src/populus`):

```
(qt-venv) $ wget
https://patch-diff.githubusercontent.com/raw/ethereum/populus/pull/
484.patch
(qt-venv) $ git apply 484.patch
(qt-venv) $ cd ../../../
```

Crash course on Qt for Python

Let's write a simple application using our GUI library:

1. Create a file named `hello.py`:

```python
import sys
from PySide2.QtWidgets import QApplication, QWidget

app = QApplication(sys.argv)
window = QWidget()
window.resize(400, 400)
window.show()
sys.exit(app.exec_())
```

2. Then run it using the following command:

```
(qt-venv) $ python hello.py
```

You will now see a blank window:

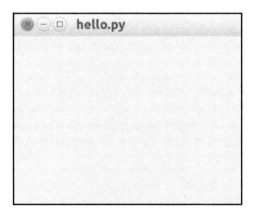

Let's go through this file to better understand Qt for Python:

```
import sys
from PySide2.QtWidgets import QApplication, QWidget
```

The `sys` import is from the standard Python library. This is required because we want to get the arguments from the command line when we launch this GUI application script. Then we import `QApplication` and `QWidget` from `PySide2.QtWidgets`.

What is `PySide2`? It comes from `PySide`, which is a Python binding for Qt 4. `PySide2` is a Python binding for Qt 5. `PySide` was released in 2009 by Nokia (the former owner of Qt). Previously, Nokia failed to reach an agreement with Riverbank to make the `PyQt` license LGPL. Consequently, Nokia decided to create its own Python binding for Qt and named it `PySide`. The ownership of Qt moved from Nokia to the Qt company. The Qt company decided to beef up their effort to develop this Python binding for Qt, especially after Qt 5 was released.

There are two classes we import from `PySide2.QtWidgets`, which are `QApplication` and `QWidget`:

- `QApplication` is a class designed to manage GUI application flows and its settings. It checks your desktop configuration, such as the font, and passes it to the GUI. It also understands the incoming objects from the desktop, for example, when you copy text from the text editor and paste it to the GUI application. There can only be one `QApplication` in your GUI script:

  ```
  app = QApplication(sys.argv)
  ```

  We create an instance of `QApplication` and pass the command-line argument. Most of the time, you would not use any command-line argument. You could pass the command-line argument if you want to tell the GUI application to use a different style or display text from right to left to cater to Arabic users, for example.

- The second class we import from `PySide2.QtWidgets` is `QWidget`. This is the base class of any widget you will ever use when creating a GUI application, such as a button, a text field, a slider, or a label. If you construct the base class, you would get an empty window. This is similar to UIView in iOS. We then resize the window:

  ```
  window = QWidget()
  window.resize(400, 400)
  ```

With the `window.show()` method, we display the window object and then enter the main loop with `app.exec_()`. This is where the `QApplication` will dispatch all events from the desktop to the GUI. We wrap this process inside `sys.exit()` so we can get the return code from `QApplication`:

```
window.show()
sys.exit(app.exec_())
```

Layout

Before we add another widget, we must learn about the concept of layout. We will use two layouts, which are `QHBoxLayout` and `QVBoxLayout`. These two layouts are enough to create a GUI application. There are other layouts, such as `QGridLayout` and `QFormLayout`, among many others, but we do not need them. `QHBoxLayout` and `QVBoxLayout` are like flexbox in CSS. You place widgets in a container that uses `QHBoxLayout`, and then all widgets will be put in a horizontal line. Let's take a look at an example. Name this script `hello_horizontal_layout.py`:

```python
import sys
from PySide2.QtWidgets import QApplication, QWidget, QHBoxLayout,
QPushButton, QLabel

app = QApplication(sys.argv)

hello_button = QPushButton('Hello')
very_label = QLabel('Very Very')
beautiful_button = QPushButton('Beautiful')
world_label = QLabel('World')

layout = QHBoxLayout()
layout.addWidget(hello_button)
layout.addWidget(very_label)
layout.addWidget(beautiful_button)
layout.addWidget(world_label)

window = QWidget()
window.setLayout(layout)
window.resize(200, 200)
window.show()

sys.exit(app.exec_())
```

I'll explain the code line by line. We start by importing the libraries:

```
import sys
from PySide2.QtWidgets import QApplication, QWidget, QHBoxLayout,
QPushButton, Qlabel
```

Other than the classes we imported in the previous script, we import `QHBoxLayout` (the horizontal layout) and two widgets (`QPushButton` and `QLabel`):

```
app = QApplication(sys.argv)

hello_button = QPushButton('Hello')
very_label = QLabel('Very Very')
beautiful_button = QPushButton('Beautiful')
world_label = Qlabel('World')
```

We initialize `QApplication` followed by four widgets (two buttons and two labels). `QPushButton` and `QLabel` receives a string as first argument for their label. Here, we just constructed four widgets, but we haven't displayed them:

```
layout = QHBoxLayout()
layout.addWidget(hello_button)
layout.addWidget(very_label)
layout.addWidget(beautiful_button)
layout.addWidget(world_label)
```

The preceding code constructs the horizontal layout with the `QHBoxLayout` class. Then we will fill the layout with four widgets that we have previously constructed. In this situation, `hello_button` will be the leftmost widget in the layout while `world_label` will be the rightmost widget. Then, we construct a `window` object and tell it to use our horizontal layout:

```
window = QWidget()
window.setLayout(layout)
window.resize(200, 200)
```

This statement will put our widgets inside the window:

```
window.show()

sys.exit(app.exec_())
```

Then, we display the window, execute the `QApplication` instance, and run it using the following command:

```
(qt-venv) $ python hello_horizontal_layout.py
```

You will then see the following result, four widgets displayed from left to right:

To get a vertical layout, create another script and name it hello_vertical_layout.py:

```
import sys
from PySide2.QtWidgets import QApplication, QWidget, QVBoxLayout,
QPushButton, QLabel

app = QApplication(sys.argv)

hello_button = QPushButton('Hello')
very_label = QLabel('Very Very')
beautiful_button = QPushButton('Beautiful')
world_label = QLabel('World')

layout = QVBoxLayout()
layout.addWidget(hello_button)
layout.addWidget(very_label)
layout.addWidget(beautiful_button)
layout.addWidget(world_label)

window = QWidget()
window.setLayout(layout)
window.resize(200, 200)
window.show()

sys.exit(app.exec_())
```

Here, instead of HBoxLayout, you use QVBoxLayout to get a vertical layout. Run the script using the following command:

```
(qt_venv) $ python hello_vertical_layout.py
```

You will then see four widgets displayed in the window from top to bottom:

If you want to combine horizontal and vertical layout, you can embed a horizontal layout inside of the vertical layout, and vice versa. To do this, create a script named hello_vertical_horizontal_layout.py. Refer to the code file in the following GitLab link for the full code: https://gitlab.com/arjunaskykok/hands-on-blockchain-for-python-developers/blob/master/chapter_07/crash_course_qt_for_python/hello_vertical_horizontal_layout.py:

```python
import sys
from PySide2.QtWidgets import QApplication, QWidget, QVBoxLayout,
QHBoxLayout, QPushButton, QLabel

app = QApplication(sys.argv)

hello_button = QPushButton('Hello')
very_label = QLabel('Very Very')
beautiful_button = QPushButton('Beautiful')
world_label = QLabel('World')

...
...

window = QWidget()
window.setLayout(horizontal_layout)
window.resize(200, 200)
window.show()

sys.exit(app.exec_())
```

The thing you need to notice here is that you need to add a nested layout with the `addLayout` method from a layout:

```
vertical_layout = QVBoxLayout()
vertical_layout.addWidget(vertical_hello_button)
vertical_layout.addWidget(vertical_very_label)
vertical_layout.addWidget(vertical_beautiful_button)
vertical_layout.addWidget(vertical_world_label)

horizontal_layout = QHBoxLayout()
horizontal_layout.addWidget(hello_button)
horizontal_layout.addWidget(very_label)
horizontal_layout.addLayout(vertical_layout)
```

Be careful here! You embed a layout into another layout using the `addLayout` method, not `addWidget`.

Run the following script to view the nested layout:

```
(qt-venv) $ python hello_vertical_horizontal_layout.py
```

Doing this will give you the following screen:

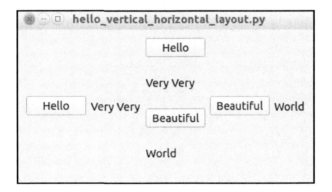

Other widgets

Let's create a script to show more varieties of widgets. To begin, name the script `hello_varieties.py`. Refer to the code file in the following GitLab link for the full code: https://gitlab.com/arjunaskykok/hands-on-blockchain-for-python-developers/blob/master/chapter_07/crash_course_qt_for_python/hello_varieties.py.

The content of the script can be viewed in the following code block:

```
import sys
from PySide2.QtWidgets import (QApplication,
                               QWidget,
                               QVBoxLayout,
                               QHBoxLayout,
                               QGroupBox,
                               QPushButton,
                               QLabel,
                               QSpinBox,
                               QLineEdit,
                               QRadioButton,
                               QComboBox)

...
...

window = QWidget()
window.setLayout(layout)
window.show()

sys.exit(app.exec_())
```

Let's dissect the code line by line. We start by importing libraries using the following lines:

```
import sys
from PySide2.QtWidgets import (QApplication,
                               QWidget,
                               QVBoxLayout,
                               QHBoxLayout,
                               QGroupBox,
                               QPushButton,
                               QLabel,
                               QSpinBox,
                               QLineEdit,
                               QRadioButton,
                               QComboBox)
```

Here, we import many new types of widgets, such as `QGroupBox`, `QSpinBox`, `QLineEdit`, `QRadioButton`, and `QComboBox`. There are a lot of widgets in Qt, we just don't have time to discuss all of them. Then, we initialize all of the widgets:

```
button = QPushButton('Button')
label = QLabel('Label')
spinbox = QSpinBox()
lineedit = QLineEdit()
radio_button1 = QRadioButton('Option 1')
```

```
radio_button2 = QRadioButton('Option 2')
radio_button3 = QRadioButton('Option 3')
combo_box = QComboBox()
combo_box.addItems(["Bitcoin", "Ethereum", "Monero", "Ripple"])
```

These are new types of widget. Let's discuss these new widgets and their unique properties. QSpinBox is a box that you use to choose a number. You can spin this widget by clicking the top or bottom arrow. QLineEdit is a text field, while QRadioButton is a radio button and QComboBox is a select box. Then, we initialize the horizontal layout and the vertical layout:

```
vlayout = QVBoxLayout()
vlayout.addWidget(button)
vlayout.addWidget(radio_button1)
vlayout.addWidget(radio_button2)
vlayout.addWidget(radio_button3)
vlayout.addWidget(spinbox)

hlayout = QHBoxLayout()
hlayout.addWidget(lineedit)
hlayout.addWidget(label)
hlayout.addWidget(combo_box)
```

We put some widgets into the vertical layout and put some other widgets into the horizontal layout. Then, we need to put these layouts in a bigger container:

```
top_groupbox = QGroupBox('Top')
top_groupbox.setLayout(vlayout)
bottom_groupbox = QGroupBox('Bottom')
bottom_groupbox.setLayout(hlayout)
```

We now create two group boxes with the QGroupBox class. The first group box got a vertical layout, while the other group box got a horizontal layout. A group box is like a container with a border. This is similar to <div> in HTML:

```
layout = QVBoxLayout()
layout.addWidget(top_groupbox)
layout.addWidget(bottom_groupbox)

window = QWidget()
window.setLayout(layout)
window.show()

sys.exit(app.exec_())
```

To contain these two group boxes, we need another layout. Here, we use a vertical layout. The rest is as usual. We construct a window, give it a layout, then display it before launching the `QApplication` instance.

Run the following script to see many different types of widget:

(qt_venv) $ python hello_varieties.py

You would then see a screen that looks like this:

Callback

At this point, we have created many widgets and layouts. Now we need to give a widget a job to do, by which I mean what we want a button to do when it is being clicked. Currently, a button would not do anything if it is clicked.

Let's create a simple script to explain how we can give a callback to a button for the clicking event. Name it `hello_connect_simple.py`.

The script contains the following lines of code:

```
import sys
from PySide2.QtWidgets import QApplication, QWidget, QVBoxLayout,
QPushButton, QLabel
from PySide2 import QtCore

app = QApplication(sys.argv)
```

```
hello_button = QPushButton("Hello")
world_label = QLabel("Sun")

layout = QVBoxLayout()
layout.addWidget(hello_button)
layout.addWidget(world_label)

def set_text_in_world_label():
    world_label.setText("World")

hello_button.connect(QtCore.SIGNAL('clicked()'), set_text_in_world_label)

window = QWidget()
window.setLayout(layout)
window.resize(200, 200)
window.show()

sys.exit(app.exec_())
```

Let's go through this code line by line:

```
import sys
from PySide2.QtWidgets import QApplication, QWidget, QVBoxLayout,
QPushButton, QLabel
from PySide2 import QtCore
```

Other than the usual libraries you import, you must import QtCore. QtCore provides a way for widgets to communicate. So, if you want to enable a button to communicate with a label such as "After I have been clicked, please set your label to this string", you need to import QtCore. Then you create widgets and put the widgets inside a layout:

```
app = QApplication(sys.argv)

hello_button = QPushButton("Hello")
world_label = QLabel("Sun")

layout = QVBoxLayout()
layout.addWidget(hello_button)
layout.addWidget(world_label)
```

You instantiate the QApplication class, create a button and a label, then put the widgets inside a vertical layout.

```
def set_text_in_world_label():
    world_label.setText("World")
    hello_button.connect(QtCore.SIGNAL('clicked()'),
set_text_in_world_label)
```

In the preceding lines of code, we create a function to set the text in a label. setText is a method of QLabel for changing the label. In the next line, we connect a clicked signal of a button to this function. This means that if we click QPushButton, set_text_in_world_label will be executed. QPushButton has signals other than clicked, such as pressed and released. Then, we create a window widget, and show it with the following lines of code:

```
window = QWidget()
window.setLayout(layout)
window.resize(200, 200)
window.show()

sys.exit(app.exec_())
```

Run the script to test the callback that we have created:

```
(qt-venv) $ python hello_connect.py
```

After running the script, you will get the following screen:

If you then click the button, the label widget will change the text:

The button does not have a parameter to be sent to the callback function. But another widget may have parameters to be sent to the callback function.

Let's create a script to illustrate this option. Name the script `hello_connect_param.py`. The content of the script can be viewed in the following code block:

```
import sys
from PySide2.QtWidgets import QApplication, QWidget, QVBoxLayout,
QLineEdit, QLabel
from PySide2 import QtCore

app = QApplication(sys.argv)

hello_line_edit = QLineEdit()
world_label = QLabel("")

layout = QVBoxLayout()
layout.addWidget(hello_line_edit)
layout.addWidget(world_label)

def set_world_label(text):
    world_label.setText(text.upper())
    hello_line_edit.textChanged.connect(set_world_label)

window = QWidget()
window.setLayout(layout)
window.resize(200, 200)
window.show()

sys.exit(app.exec_())
```

Focus on these lines to see how we can have a parameter in a callback that a widget has:

```
def set_world_label(text):
    world_label.setText(text.upper())
    hello_line_edit.textChanged.connect(set_world_label)
```

Our callback function has a parameter. The `textChanged` signal of the line edit widget has a parameter. When we change the text in the line edit widget, the text will be sent to the callback function.

This line, `hello_line_edit.textChanged.connect(set_world_label)`, is equivalent to `hello_line_edit.connect(QtCore.SIGNAL('textChanged(QString)'), set_world_label)`.

Run the script to test the callback that has a parameter:

```
(qt_venv) $ python hello_connect_param.py
```

As you type in the line edit, the text in the label widget changes as well:

We use a callback because we want to manipulate the text before we set it to a label widget. However, if you want to send the text parameter from the line edit widget to the label widget directly, you don't have to create a dedicated function, you can use `signal` and `slot`.

To do this, remove the callback, then change this `line` `hello_line_edit.textChanged.connect(set_world_label)` to `hello_line_edit.connect(QtCore.SIGNAL('textChanged(QString)'), world_label, QtCore.SLOT('setText(QString)'))`.

As you type the text in the line edit, your text will be displayed in the label directly.

You can also change that line to `QtCore.QObject.connect(hello_line_edit, QtCore.SIGNAL('textChanged(QString)'), world_label, QtCore.SLOT('setText(QString)'))`.

I hope you see the pattern here. If widget A wants to communicate with widget B, widget A will use `signal` to connect with widget B's `slot`. Of course, you can swap the `slot` part with a custom callback on which you call the API of widget B.

This `signal` and `slot` concept is general and not limited to GUI widgets. It means that you can define a custom `signal` and custom `slot`.

Let's create a script to illustrate this new concept:

```
import sys
from PySide2 import QtCore

@QtCore.Slot(str)
def slot_func(param):
    print(param)

class Simple(QtCore.QObject):
    signal = QtCore.Signal(str)
```

```
simple = Simple()
simple.signal.connect(slot_func)
simple.signal.emit("Hello World")
```

Let's dissect this script. We import the libraries:

```
import sys
from PySide2 import QtCore
```

Slot and signal functionality comes from the `QtCore` class. You can create a `slot` function with the `Slot` decorator:

```
@QtCore.Slot(str)
def slot_func(param):
    print(param)
```

You can also create a class that is a child of `QObject` in order to create a `signal` object:

```
class Simple(QtCore.QObject):
    signal = QtCore.Signal(str)

simple = Simple()
simple.signal.connect(slot_func)
```

You must instantiate this class. `signal` must be part of an instance, not a class. You can then connect it with a `slot` function as follows:

```
simple.signal.emit("Hello World")
```

The last part is to send the parameter from `signal` to `slot`.

Run the script to test whether the callback still works:

```
(qt-venv) $ python hello_custom_signal_slot.py
Hello World
```

Threading

To use a thread in Qt, we can use the `QThread` class from `QtCore`. Hopefully, you can see a pattern here. `QtCore` has many functionalities beyond creating widgets. Threading is important because when building a decentralized application we will have to wait for quite some time for the transaction to be confirmed. Depending on how generous you are with the gas and the traffic in Ethereum, the wait could be anything from a few minutes to half an hour. We don't want the GUI application to freeze for a minute, let alone half an hour.

Let's create a simple script to demonstrate how we create a thread using `QThread`. Name the script `hello_thread.py`:

```python
from PySide2 import QtCore
import time

class SimpleThread(QtCore.QThread):
    def __init__(self, parent=None):
        super(SimpleThread, self).__init__(parent)

    def run(self):
        time.sleep(2) # simulating latency in network
        print("world")

simple_thread = SimpleThread()
simple_thread.start()

print("hello")
simple_thread.wait()
```

You will then subclass `QThread` inside the class where you write what you want to do inside the `run` method. To utilize this threading class, you instantiate the class and then call the `start` method. Then you can do all the things you want to do in the main application while waiting for the threading class to do its job. If you want to wait for the threading class to finish the job, you can call its `wait` method from the threading class.

Threading is a vast subject. We haven't discussed mutex or thread safety, but we will not need to for our decentralized application.

Some people feel dread at the thought of using threading in their application. The alternative is using single-threaded concurrent code using the `asyncio` library. That's perfectly fine, but in this case, we will use threading.

We have everything we need to know about how to use Qt library to build a Python desktop application. Before we write our GUI decentralized application, we need to write a smart contract because without this, there would be no decentralized application.

Writing the smart contract for the Twitter–like application

We are now going to build a censorship resistant, Twitter-like application. This means that even the owner of the smart contract could not delete a tweet from the user of the smart contract. This Twitter-like application is very simple; there is no option of following, liking, or retweeting; it just consists of tweets. In addition, the user cannot delete their tweets and they must be less than 32 bytes, which is even shorter than the original tweet limit in Twitter!

We now come back to our Populus project to modify our `project.json` file. Add this to `project.json`:

```
"ganache": {
  "chain": {
    "class": "populus.chain.ExternalChain"
  },
  "web3": {
    "provider": {
      "class": "web3.providers.HTTPProvider",
      "settings": {
        "endpoint_uri": "http://localhost:7545"
      }
    }
  },
  "contracts": {
    "backends": {
      "JSONFile": {"$ref": "contracts.backends.JSONFile"},
      "ProjectContracts": {
        "$ref": "contracts.backends.ProjectContracts"
      }
    }
  }
}
```

This is the smart contract. Create a `TwitterOnBlockchain.vy` file inside the `twitter_like_projects/contracts` directory:

```
struct Tweet:
    messages: bytes32[10]
    index: int128

tweets: public(map(address, Tweet))

@public
```

```
def write_a_tweet(tweet: bytes32):
    assert self.tweets[msg.sender].index < 10

    index: int128 = self.tweets[msg.sender].index
    self.tweets[msg.sender].messages[index] = tweet
    self.tweets[msg.sender].index += 1
```

This is a very short smart contract.

We start from the struct data type variable declaration and the mapping of the address to this struct data type variable:

```
struct Tweet:
    messages: bytes32[10]
    index: int128

tweets: public(map(address, Tweet))
```

The `tweets` variable is a mapping data type from an address to an array of `messages` and `index`. An array of `messages` has the length of 10 `bytes32` data type variables, which means that each account or address can have a maximum of 10 tweets in this smart contract. `index` is a pointer to the array of `messages`. Each time we create a tweet, `index` is increased by 1 so it can point to the next slot in the array of `messages`.

```
@public
def write_a_tweet(tweet: bytes32):
    assert self.tweets[msg.sender].index < 10
    index: int128 = self.tweets[msg.sender].index
    self.tweets[msg.sender].messages[index] = tweet
    self.tweets[msg.sender].index += 1
```

The `write_a_tweet` function is a method to create a tweet. This simply consists of inserting a tweet inside an array of `messages` with some guards to avoid an overbound error.

Test

This is the test for this smart contract. You can save the test file in `tests/test_twitter_on_blockchain.py`. Refer to the code file in the following GitLab link for the full code: https://gitlab.com/arjunaskykok/hands-on-blockchain-for-python-developers/blob/master/chapter_07/twitter_on_blockchain/tests/test_twitter_on_blockchain.py.

The following code block shows the code:

```
import pytest
import eth_tester

def test_initial_condition(web3, chain):
    twitter_on_blockchain, _ =
chain.provider.get_or_deploy_contract('TwitterOnBlockchain')
    assert
twitter_on_blockchain.functions.tweets__index(web3.eth.coinbase).call() ==
0

...
...

twitter_on_blockchain.functions.tweets__messages(web3.eth.coinbase,0).call(
)[:len(tweet)] == tweet
    assert
twitter_on_blockchain.functions.tweets__messages(web3.eth.coinbase,1).call(
)[:len(tweet2)] == tweet2
```

This test ensures that the `index` starts at zero and will be increased by one after the user tweets in this smart contract. It also checks that the tweet is kept inside the array of `messages`.

Let's reflect on that for a moment. If you look at the smart contract, the owner could not censor the tweets from anyone. The owner could not even delete the smart contract, so neither the government nor the mafia could pressure the owner of the smart contract to censor tweets. Compare this situation to one in which the owner of an application uses a traditional web application. The owner of the application could censor tweets by deleting entries from the database. Alternatively, the government or the mafia could apply pressure to the owner of the application to censor the tweets, or the government or the mafia could take down the hosting server. In the case of blockchain, this means that people need to take down half of the 10,000 nodes to be able to disrupt the Ethereum blockchain in order to destroy the smart contract.

This is one of the things that makes blockchain special—**censorship resistance**. This does not mean it cannot be censored, but it is very hard to be censored. In order to shut down this smart contract, the government would have to ban the Ethereum network itself. Alternatively, they could install spyware in all citizens' computers and make sure they don't access this smart contract. On top of that, censorship resistance does not mean it protects privacy. The government can still figure out who writes what.

To deploy the smart contract, run Ganache, compile the smart contract, and then deploy the smart contract to Ganache using the following command:

```
(qt-venv) $ populus deploy --chain ganache TwitterOnBlockchain
```

Fixtures

Before we develop a decentralized GUI application, let's write a script to put some fixtures in the smart contract. Fixtures are like sample data. This makes developing an application a more pleasurable experience. Call the script `fixtures.py`. Refer to the code file in the following GitLab for the full code: https://gitlab.com/arjunaskykok/hands-on-blockchain-for-python-developers/blob/master/chapter_07/dapp/fixtures.py:

```
from web3 import Web3, HTTPProvider
from populus.utils.wait import wait_for_transaction_receipt
w3 = Web3(HTTPProvider('http://localhost:7545'))

private_keys = ['dummy',
'59e31694256f71b8d181f47fc67914798c4b96990e835fc1407bf4673ead30e2',
'ac1e6abbe002699fbef756a2cbc2bf8c03cfac97adee84ce32f198219be94788']

...
...
        txhash = w3.eth.sendRawTransaction(signed.rawTransaction)
        wait_for_transaction_receipt(w3, txhash)
```

Let's dissect this script line by line. We import the `Web3` class and the `HTTPProvider` class from `web3`. We use `HTTPProvider` because we want to use Ganache. Then we import `wait_for_transaction_receipt` from the `populus` library:

```
from web3 import Web3, HTTPProvider
from populus.utils.wait import wait_for_transaction_receipt

w3 = Web3(HTTPProvider('http://localhost:7545'))
```

Then we have the private keys from the first three accounts:

```
private_keys = ['dummy',
'59e31694256f71b8d181f47fc67914798c4b96990e835fc1407bf4673ead30e2',
'ac1e6abbe002699fbef756a2cbc2bf8c03cfac97adee84ce32f198219be94788']
```

We don't need the private key of the first account or the account that launched the smart contract; we only need the second and the third account:

```
true = True
false = False
abi = [{
        "constant": false,
        "gas": 71987,
        "inputs": [{
                    "name": "tweet",
                    "type": "bytes32"
                }],
        "name": "write_a_tweet",
        "outputs": [],
        "payable": false,
        "type": "function"
    },
...
...
        "payable": false,
        "type": "function"
    }]
```

This is the `abi` that you can get from the compilation of the smart contract:

```
with open('address.txt', 'r') as f:
    address = f.read().rstrip("\n")

TwitterOnBlockchain = w3.eth.contract(address=address, abi=abi)
```

You put the address of the smart contract in the `address.txt` file. You received the address when you deployed the smart contract through Populus.

Then you construct a smart contract object based on the smart contract's address and `abi`:

```
for i in range(1, 3):
    for j in range(1, 11):
        nonce =
w3.eth.getTransactionCount(Web3.toChecksumAddress(w3.eth.accounts[i]))
        txn = TwitterOnBlockchain.functions.write_a_tweet(b'Tweet ' +
str(j).encode('utf-8')).buildTransaction({'gas': 70000, 'gasPrice':
w3.toWei('1', 'gwei'), 'nonce': nonce })
        signed = w3.eth.account.signTransaction(txn,
private_key=private_keys[i])
        txhash = w3.eth.sendRawTransaction(signed.rawTransaction)
        wait_for_transaction_receipt(w3, txhash)
```

For each account, you create 10 tweets. Each tweet is something like 'Tweet 1', 'Tweet 2', and so on. These fixtures enable us to check the tweets without having to create one first. It's beneficial to check the functionality of the application.

Building the GUI frontend for the Twitter–like application

Now let's build a decentralized GUI application. Name the script `twitter_dapp.py`. Refer to the code file in the following GitLab link for the full code: `https://gitlab.com/arjunaskykok/hands-on-blockchain-for-python-developers/blob/master/chapter_07/dapp/twitter_dapp.py`:

```python
from PySide2 import QtCore, QtWidgets
import web3
from web3 import Web3, HTTPProvider
from populus.utils.wait import wait_for_transaction_receipt

w3 = Web3(HTTPProvider('http://localhost:7545'))

...
...

if __name__ == '__main__':
    import sys
    app = QtWidgets.QApplication(sys.argv)
    twitter_dapp = TwitterDapp()
    twitter_dapp.show()
    sys.exit(app.exec_())
```

Let's dissect this script line by line. Here, we import the necessary classes and set our `web3` object to Ganache, which serves the smart contract in port `7545` of localhost:

```python
from PySide2 import QtCore, QtWidgets
import web3
from web3 import Web3, HTTPProvider
from populus.utils.wait import wait_for_transaction_receipt

w3 = Web3(HTTPProvider('http://localhost:7545'))
true = True
false = False

abi = [{
        "constant": false,
        "gas": 71987,
```

```
    "inputs": [{
                    "name": "tweet",
                    "type": "bytes32"
             }],
    "name": "write_a_tweet",
    "outputs": [],
    "payable": false,
    "type": "function"
},
...
...
    "payable": false,
    "type": "function"
}]
```

Then, we define the `abi` as usual:

```
with open('address.txt', 'r') as f:
    address = f.read().rstrip("\n")

TwitterOnBlockchain = w3.eth.contract(address=address, abi=abi)
```

We then create a smart contract object by providing the address of the smart contract and the `abi`.

This is a helper function that removes `'\x00'` from a string:

```
def strip_x00_from_tweet(tweet):
    null_index = tweet.find(b'\x00')
    return tweet[:null_index]
```

Remember, our tweet data type in a smart contract is `bytes32`, which will append `\x00` until it reaches 32 bytes. Consequently, if you set this `bytes32` variable a `'messi'` string that has 5 bytes, it will be `'messi\x00\x00\x00\x00...\x00'`. This utility function will strip `\x00` from the string so that we can get `'messi'` back. Then , we move into the threading class definition:

```
class Web3ReadTweetsThread(QtCore.QThread):
    fetched_posts = QtCore.Signal(list)
    account = ''

    def __init__(self, parent=None):
        super(Web3ReadTweetsThread, self).__init__(parent)

    def setAccount(self, account):
        self.account = account
```

```
          def run(self):
              try:
                  index =
TwitterOnBlockchain.functions.tweets__index(self.account).call()
              except web3.exceptions.ValidationError:
                  return
              tweets = []
              for i in range(index):
                  tweet =
TwitterOnBlockchain.functions.tweets__messages(self.account, i).call()
                  tweets.append(tweet.decode('utf-8'))
              self.fetched_posts.emit(tweets)
```

This is a thread class that aims to read the data from the blockchain. But isn't reading data supposed to be fast, because we are using Ganache and we don't need to involve the miners? If your blockchain node is in the same computer as your GUI frontend script, then this threading class is not needed. However, what if you put your blockchain node in the cloud? Perhaps you don't have enough space in your local computer, and that makes you do this. This kind of setup will introduce latency in your program, so it is a good idea to use a thread to wait for the result from the blockchain in the cloud.

fetched_posts is a signal that will send the list of tweets to a slot that we will define later. Inside the run method, we get the index first so we know how many tweets the tweeter has posted. Due to the fact that what we get from the smart contract is a byte, we decode it first before we send the tweet to the slot function.

The following code is a thread class that we use for creating a transaction in the smart contract. To use this thread class, we need a private key. Remember, we need to sign a transaction with a private key. However, we also need the address so we can get the nonce. We can ask the user to input the address as well, but it will be superfluous. We can derive the address from the private key by using the account = w3.eth.account.privateKeyToAccount('0x'+self.private_key) method:

```
    class Web3WriteATweetThread(QtCore.QThread):
        write_a_tweet = QtCore.Signal()
        private_key = ''
        tweet = ''

    ...
    ...

    w3.eth.sendRawTransaction(signed.rawTransaction)
            wait_for_transaction_receipt(w3, txhash)
            self.write_a_tweet.emit()
```

After getting the address, we get the `nonce` with this line:

```
nonce = w3.eth.getTransactionCount(Web3.toChecksumAddress(account.address))
```

As usual, we then build the transaction, sign the transaction, and send the transaction to the blockchain. We then wait for the transaction to be confirmed. After that, we emit the signal to the `slot` function, which we will define later.

```
class TwitterDapp(QtWidgets.QWidget):
    private_key = '0x0'
    account = ''
    bookmark_file = 'bookmark.txt'
    addresses = []

    def __init__(self):
        super(TwitterDapp, self).__init__()

...
...
self.web3_write_a_tweet_thread.write_a_tweet.connect(self.successfullyWrite
ATweet)
```

Now, it's time to create a GUI. We set the window title, subclass the `QWidget`, and set up the private group box where we will request private key from a user. We will add a writing button widget and configure a group box to display tweets. We then prepare a group box to display bookmarks and add all of them to a vertical layout. In addition, we create two threading instances. For each threading instance, we connect their signals to the `slot` functions:

```
    def createPrivateKeyGroupBox(self):
        self.private_key_group_box = QtWidgets.QGroupBox("Account")
        self.private_key_field = QtWidgets.QLineEdit()
        self.welcome_message = QtWidgets.QLabel()

        layout = QtWidgets.QFormLayout()
        layout.addRow(QtWidgets.QLabel("Private key:"),
self.private_key_field)
        button_box =
QtWidgets.QDialogButtonBox(QtWidgets.QDialogButtonBox.Ok)
button_box.button(QtWidgets.QDialogButtonBox.Ok).clicked.connect(self.check
PrivateKey)
        layout.addRow(button_box)
        layout.addRow(self.welcome_message)

        self.private_key_group_box.setLayout(layout)
```

In this method, we create a group box on which we place line edits to receive the private key. We also put a label to display a notice when the private key that's entered is valid. Here, we use `QFormLayout`, not `QHBoxLayout` or `QVBoxLayout`. `QFormLayout` is very useful for creating a two-column layout. The first column is usually used as a container for labels, while the second column is usually used as container for inputs, such as line edits. So with this layout, we use the `addRow` method, and this accepts one or two arguments. If the number of arguments is two, then the arguments will be the widget on the left column and the widget on the right column. We then add a private key label and a line edit, followed by an OK dialog button and a notice label. For the dialog button, we connect the clicked signal to a method called `checkPrivateKey`.

In the following method, we create a push button inside a horizontal layout. We connect the clicked signal to a method called `writeANewTweet`:

```
def createWritingTweetGroupBox(self):
    self.tweet_button = QtWidgets.QPushButton("Write a new tweet")
    self.tweet_button.setMaximumSize(200,40)
    self.write_button_layout = QtWidgets.QHBoxLayout()
    self.write_button_layout.addWidget(self.tweet_button)
    self.connect(self.tweet_button, QtCore.SIGNAL('clicked()'),
self.writeANewTweet)
```

In the following method, we create a group box to show tweets. First, there is a line edit to accept the address of the tweeter. This is accompanied by a button for fetching tweets and bookmarking the address. The callbacks will be defined later. We also put a layout inside the layout to display all the tweets:

```
def createTweetsGroupBox(self):
    self.tweets_group_box = QtWidgets.QGroupBox("Tweets")
    self.account_address = QtWidgets.QLineEdit()
    self.fetch_button = QtWidgets.QPushButton("Fetch")
    self.add_to_bookmark_button = QtWidgets.QPushButton("Bookmark it!")
    ...
    ...
    self.tweets_main_layout.addLayout(account_address_layout)
    self.tweets_main_layout.addSpacing(20)
    self.tweets_main_layout.addLayout(self.tweets_layout)
    self.tweets_group_box.setLayout(self.tweets_main_layout)
```

In the following method, we create a group box to display bookmarks. This bookmarks layout is just a normal vertical layout. We read the bookmarks from the text file, and then we process the lines. Basically, the process is to remove the new lines from the text line:

```
def createBookmarkGroupBox(self):
    self.bookmark_group_box = QtWidgets.QGroupBox("Bookmark")
    self.bookmark_layout = QtWidgets.QVBoxLayout()
```

```
        self.bookmark_group_box.setLayout(self.bookmark_layout)
        with open(self.bookmark_file) as f:
            addresses = f.readlines()
        self.addresses = list(map(lambda x: x.rstrip(), filter(lambda x:
len(x) > 1, addresses)))
        self.fillBookmark()
```

This is the `slot` function for fetching the tweets. It uses threading to do the job:

```
@QtCore.Slot()
def fetchTweets(self):
    account = self.account_address.displayText()
    self.web3_read_tweets_thread.setAccount(account)
    self.web3_read_tweets_thread.start()
```

This is the `slot` function that adds the address of the tweeter to the bookmark text file. After adding the bookmark to the bookmark the text file, it updates the bookmark layout:

```
@QtCore.Slot()
def bookmarkAddress(self):
    account = self.account_address.displayText()
    if account:
        self.addresses.append(account)
        self.addresses = list(set(addresses))
    with open(self.bookmark_file, 'w') as f:
        for address in self.addresses:
            f.write(address)
    self.fillBookmark()
```

In this method, we launch an input dialog that has only one line edit. After getting the input, we send the input to the threading class before running it:

```
@QtCore.Slot()
def writeANewTweet(self):
    text, ok = QtWidgets.QInputDialog.getText(self, "Write a new
tweet", "Tweet:", QtWidgets.QLineEdit.Normal, "")
    if ok and text != '':
        self.web3_write_a_tweet_thread.setPrivateKey(self.private_key)
        self.web3_write_a_tweet_thread.setTweet(text)
        self.web3_write_a_tweet_thread.start()
```

This is a callback function that checks whether the private key is valid or not. If it is valid (the address can be derived from the private key), we set the notice label to success:

```
def checkPrivateKey(self):
    self.private_key = self.private_key_field.displayText()
    try:
        self.account =
```

```
w3.eth.account.privateKeyToAccount('0x'+self.private_key)
      except ValueError:
          QtWidgets.QMessageBox.warning(self, 'Error', 'Private key is
invalid.')
          return
      self.welcome_message.setText('Welcome, ' + self.account.address +
'!')
      self.private_key_field.clear()
```

These two methods are to be used to fill tweets in the tweets layout. First, we clear the tweets in the vertical layout. We can get each widget from the layout with `takeAt` method. There is no method to delete all child widgets of the layout; we have to iterate them one by one. If the widget exists, we can delete it. After clearing all the tweets from the layout, we fill the layout with new tweets using the `addWidget` method. The same strategy is being used when dealing with bookmarks:

```
def clearTweetsField(self):
    while True:
        label_item = self.tweets_layout.takeAt(0)
        if label_item is None:
            break
        else:
            label_item.widget().close()

def fillPosts(self, posts):
    self.clearTweetsField()
    for post in posts:
        label_field = QtWidgets.QLabel(post)
        self.tweets_layout.addWidget(label_field)
```

The same strategy is used in the two following methods. We clear the bookmark widgets from the bookmarks layout by iterating them one by one and deleting the widget. Then we fill the bookmarks inside the bookmarks layout through the `addWidget` method. One difference between dealing with tweets and bookmarks is that we configure the label in the bookmark section so it can be selected using the mouse. The method responsible for this is the `setTextInteractionFlags` method.

The parameter is the current flag of the label that's masked with the `Qt.TextSelectableByMouse` flag. If you use this code without masking it with the previous value, `label_field.setTextInteractionFlags(QtCore.Qt.TextSelectableByMouse)`, you can delete all current label selection configuration flags that the label widget has. Most of the time, you don't want to do that:

```python
    def clearBookmarkField(self):
        while True:
            label_item = self.bookmark_layout.takeAt(0)
            if label_item is None:
                break
            else:
                label_item.widget().close()

    def fillBookmark(self, addresses):
        self.clearBookmarkField()
        for address in addresses:
            label_field = QtWidgets.QLabel(address)
label_field.setTextInteractionFlags(label_field.textInteractionFlags() |
QtCore.Qt.TextSelectableByMouse)
            self.bookmark_layout.addWidget(label_field)
```

This is a callback to set the success message in the label widget:

```python
    def successfullyWriteATweet(self):
        self.welcome_message.setText('You have successfully written a new
tweet!')
```

Then, finally we launch the GUI frontend:

```python
if __name__ == '__main__':
    import sys
    app = QtWidgets.QApplication(sys.argv)
    twitter_dapp = TwitterDapp()
    twitter_dapp.show()
    sys.exit(app.exec_())
```

Type the second address into Ganache to fetch the tweets that we set when executing the fixtures script:

Type the private key and click **OK**:

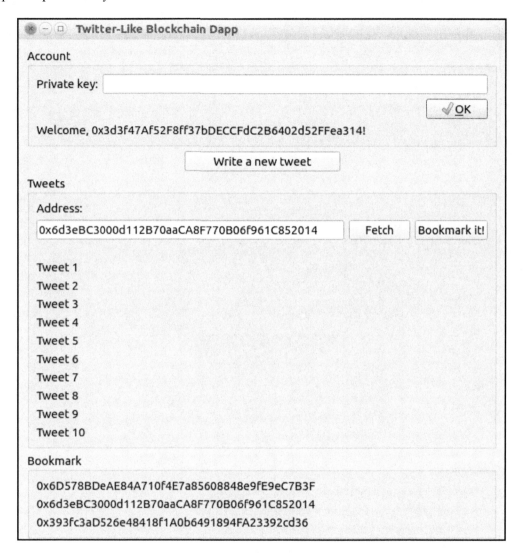

Click on **Write a new tweet** button. It will launch a dialog box. Then type in your tweet and click on **OK**:

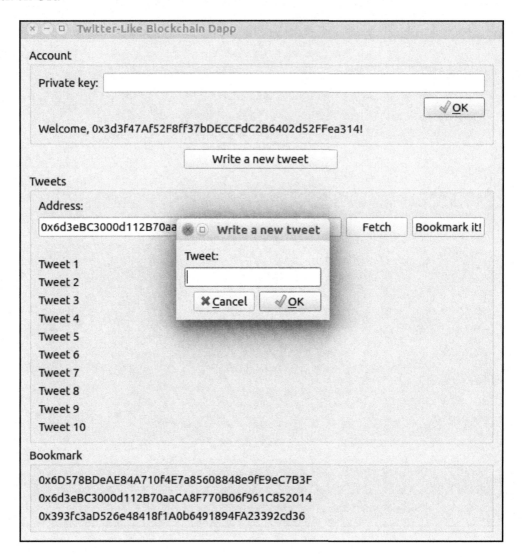

After typing a new tweet and confirming it, you will get a success message. Then you can click the button (**Bookmark it!**) to save the address into the `bookmarks` text file:

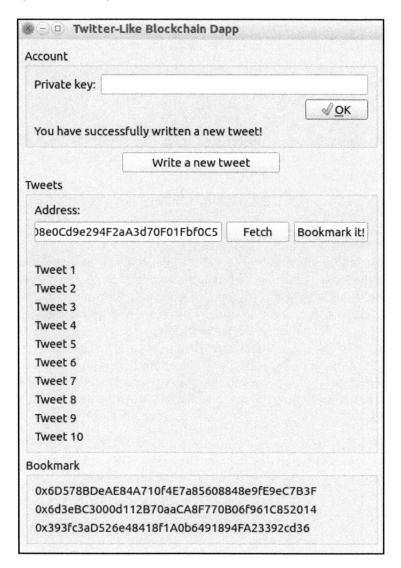

If you want to build a frontend for a smart contract or a decentralized application, you need to keep two things in mind. First, handle the blocking function (sending transactions to the blockchain and waiting for them) gracefully either using threading or single-threaded coroutines (using the `asyncio` library). Secondly, while the smart contract handles the core things (censorship resistance messages), you could add more value to your decentralized application. The added value in our example application is the bookmark utility. Can you add a bookmark functionality in the smart contract? Of course you can. But if you put the functionality in the smart contract, you lose privacy, because everyone can read your bookmarks.

In a nutshell, you cannot put every feature in the smart contract because of the limitations of the smart contract. So if you want to add sentiment analysis using machine learning, it is best to do this outside the smart contract.

Summary

In this chapter, we learned how to build a GUI frontend for a smart contract and how to use Qt for Python or the `PySide2` library, which utilizes the Qt 5 library. We set time aside to learn how to build a GUI application using Qt for Python. Starting with a simple application, we took into the layout, various widgets, signals and slots, and threading, and we finally gained an understanding of how to use the `PySide2` library. We built our smart contract to simulate Twitter in a simple way, delighting in the censorship resistance of this Twitter-like application. Next, we built the GUI frontend. This GUI application uses all the concepts you have learned so far. We used threading to connect to the blockchain so that the GUI would not freeze. We also added additional value through the ability to bookmark in our GUI application.

In the next chapter, you are going to learn how to create an ERC20 token. This is what makes Ethereum popular among developers. Tokens can be used as a substitute for money in certain environments.

Section 4: Cryptocurrency and Wallets

4

This section is a hands-on learning guide to launching your own cryptocurrency and building the wallet to handle it.

The following chapters will be covered in this section:

- Chapter 8, Creating Token in Ethereum
- Chapter 9, Cryptocurrency Wallet

8
Creating Token in Ethereum

In this chapter, you are going to learn how to create a token on top of Ethereum. Tokens have a variety of uses; it may be for local currency in a local community, it may represent a physical good, it may be virtual money in a game, or it may be loyalty points. With this token, you can build a new cryptocurrency. While Ethereum is a cryptocurrency itself, you can build a new cryptocurrency on top of it. Ethereum makes it far easier to create a new token, and this fueled the creation of many new cryptocurrencies in 2017.

This chapter will cover the following topics:

- How to create a simple token smart contract
- ERC 20 (Ethereum token standard)
- How to sell your token
- How to customize your token

Token smart contract

Creating a token on top of Ethereum with Vyper is easy. Let's follow the initial steps to prepare our development environment before we build a token.

Start by ensuring that you have geth installed and that the `geth` program is in the `$PATH` environment variable (meaning that you can call `geth` without its full path):

```
$ virtualenv -p python3.6 token-venv
$ source token-venv/bin/activate
(token-venv) $ pip install eth-abi==1.2.2
(token-venv) $ pip install eth-typing==1.1.0
(token-venv) $ pip install py-evm==0.2.0a33
(token-venv) $ pip install web3==4.7.2
(token-venv) $ pip install -e
git+https://github.com/ethereum/populus#egg=populus
(token-venv) $ pip install vyper
(token-venv) $ mkdir token_project
```

```
(token-venv) $ cd token_project
(token-venv) $ mkdir tests contracts
(token-venv) $ cp ../token-
venv/src/populus/populus/assets/defaults.v9.config.json project.json
```

Add Vyper support to `project.json` by changing the value of the `compilation` key to the following:

```
"compilation": {
    "backend": {
      "class": "populus.compilation.backends.VyperBackend"
    },
    "contract_source_dirs": [
      "./contracts"
    ],
    "import_remappings": []
},
```

 The latest version of Vyper is 0.1.0b6 and it breaks Populus. The developer needs some time to fix this problem. If the bug has still not been fixed by the time you are reading this book, you can patch Populus yourself.

First, check whether the bug has been fixed by using the following command:

```
(token-venv) $ cd voting-venv/src/populus
(token-venv) $ grep -R "compile(" populus/compilation/backends/vyper.py
 bytecode = '0x' + compiler.compile(code).hex()
 bytecode_runtime = '0x' + compiler.compile(code,
bytecode_runtime=True).hex()
```

In our case here, the bug has not been fixed. So, let's patch Populus to fix the bug. Make sure you are still in the same directory (`token-venv/src/populus`):

```
(token-venv) $ wget
https://patch-diff.githubusercontent.com/raw/ethereum/populus/pull/484.patc
h
(token-venv) $ git apply 484.patch
(token-venv) $ cd ../../../
```

Inside the `token_project` directory, run the following command:

```
(token-venv) $ populus chain new localblock
```

Then, initialize the private chain using the `init_chain.sh` script:

```
(token-venv) $ ./chains/localblock/init_chain.sh
```

Edit `chains/localblock/run_chain.sh` and change the value of `--ipcpath` to `/tmp/geth.ipc`.

Then, run the blockchain:

```
(voting-venv) $ ./chains/localblock/run_chain.sh
```

Now, edit the `project.json` file. `chains` has one object that has four keys: `tester`, `temp`, `ropsten`, and `mainnet`. Add one key named `localblock` with its value to this object:

```
"localblock": {
  "chain": {
    "class": "populus.chain.ExternalChain"
  },
  "web3": {
    "provider": {
      "class": "web3.providers.ipc.IPCProvider",
    "settings": {
      "ipc_path":"/tmp/geth.ipc"
    }
    }
  },
  "contracts": {
    "backends": {
      "JSONFile": {"$ref": "contracts.backends.JSONFile"},
      "ProjectContracts": {
        "$ref": "contracts.backends.ProjectContracts"
      }
    }
  }
}
```

Mist

In Chapter 2, *Smart Contract Fundamentals*, and Chapter 3, *Implementing Smart Contracts Using Vyper*, you used the Truffle console to interact with the smart contract. Now, we are going to use another software to interact with the smart contract. The software we will use is Mist, an Ethereum wallet.

For this, go to `https://github.com/ethereum/mist/releases`. If you use Linux Ubuntu, download the `Mist-linux64-0-11-1.deb` file.

Ensure that `geth` is already installed and that the path of `geth` is in the `$PATH` environment variable, so that you can call `geth` from anywhere.

You can then install Mist, as follows:

```
$ dpkg -i Mist-linux64-0-11-1.deb
```

Next, run the application, as follows:

```
$ ethereumwallet --rpc /tmp/geth.ipc
```

Notice the `--rpc /tmp/geth.ipc` flag. We use this flag because we run the private blockchain with the socket file defined in `/tmp/geth.ipc`.

You will see this screen after you run the application. You can create an Ethereum blokchain account by clicking the **ADD ACCOUNT** button:

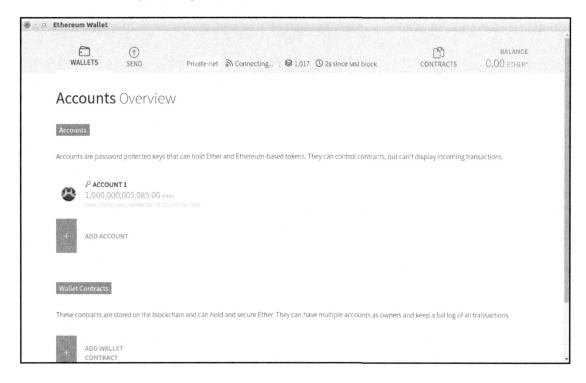

Just as you did in the `geth` console, you need to supply a password to create a new account:

Once your wallet account has been created, you can send some money from the first account to this new account by clicking the **SEND** tab:

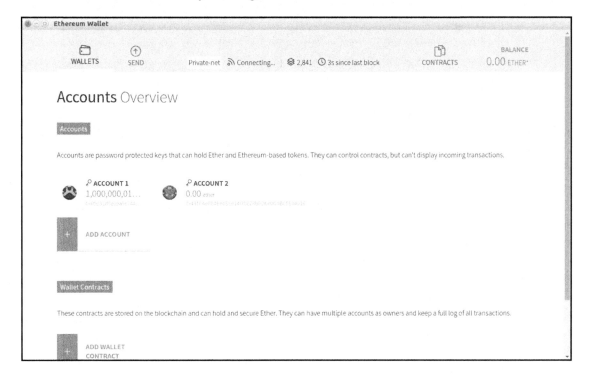

Then, you can insert your new account's address in the **TO** field. Don't forget to include the amount of ether you want to send, and then click the **SEND** button at the bottom of the window:

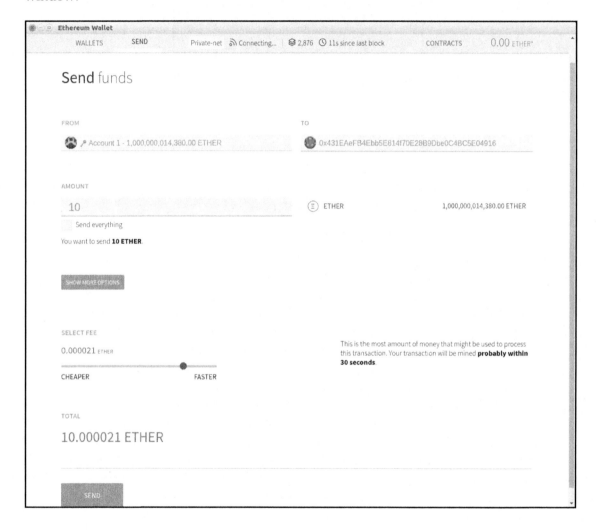

You must fill in the password to create a transaction. The password of the default account can be found in the `chains/localblock/password` file:

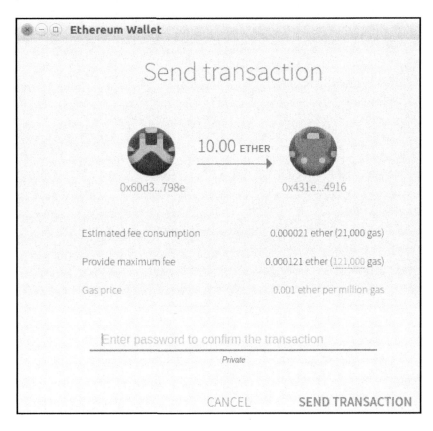

Soon, your transaction will be confirmed in the blockchain:

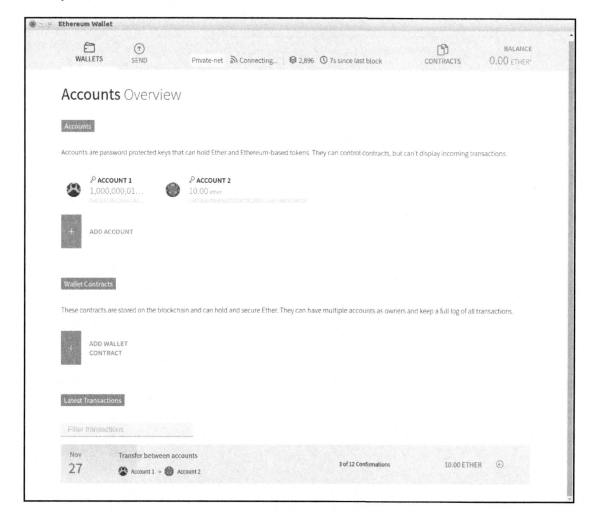

Let's create a simple token smart contract inside the `token_project/contracts` directory:

```
balances: public(map(address, uint256))

@public
def __init__():
    self.balances[msg.sender] = 10000

@public
def transfer(_to: address, _amount: uint256) -> bool:
    assert self.balances[msg.sender] >= _amount

    self.balances[msg.sender] -= _amount
    self.balances[_to] += _amount

    return True
```

This smart contract digitally creates 10,000 coins of the token and gives all of them to the owner of the smart contract. Then, the owner can forward the coins to other accounts using the `transfer` method.

This simple smart contract is special in comparison to creating a simple token traditional web application because, once this smart contract is deployed, the owner cannot change the token amount, no matter how desperate they are. If the owner has just executed the `transfer` method to transfer some coins to another account's address, they cannot take it back again. Other people can verify the rule of the play in the smart contract before interacting with it.

Compare this with the simple token we created in the traditional web application. Once you create 10,000 coins here, you can change the number of tokens by updating the number of coins in the database. You can change the rule as you like, which places other people who want to interact with this application at a disadvantage.

You can also add a method to increase the number of token coins in the smart contract:

```
balances: public(map(address, uint256))
owner: address

@public
def __init__():
    self.balances[msg.sender] = 10000
    self.owner = msg.sender
```

```
@public
def transfer(_to: address, _amount: uint256) -> bool:
    assert self.balances[msg.sender] >= _amount

    self.balances[msg.sender] -= _amount
    self.balances[_to] += _amount

    return True

@public
def mint(_new_supply: uint256):
    assert msg.sender == self.owner
    self.balances[msg.sender] = _new_supply
```

Look at the `mint` method. This can be used to increase the token coins in the owner's balance.

The difference is that you cannot change the rule of the game after you deploy the smart contract. If you deploy this version of the smart contract, people could ask for the source and the compiler's version to verify the code. If you don't give the source code, people could turn away from your smart contract. If you do give the source code, people can check and see that you have a method that can increase your coins any time you like. Whether they accept this rule is up to them, but at least with a smart contract, there is transparency.

The following code block is the test for this simple token smart contract; this test is not exhaustive, but it gives you a good start. The importance of a test for a token smart contract is paramount. To begin with, name the test `test_simple_token.py` and put it inside the `token_project/tests` directory. Refer to the code file in the following GitLab link for the full code: https://gitlab.com/arjunaskykok/hands-on-blockchain-for-python-developers/blob/master/chapter_08/token_project/tests/test_simple_token.py:

```
import pytest
import eth_tester


def test_balance(web3, chain):
    simple_token, _ = chain.provider.get_or_deploy_contract('SimpleToken')

    ...
    ...

    with pytest.raises(eth_tester.exceptions.TransactionFailed):
        simple_token.functions.transfer(web3.eth.coinbase,
10).transact({'from': account2})
```

Let's deploy our simple token smart contract (the first one, without the `mint` function) to the blockchain using Mist.

To do this, click on the **CONTRACTS** tab, and then click on the **DEPLOY NEW CONTRACT** button:

In the **Deploy contract** screen, choose the account you want to deploy from, and then click on the **CONTRACT BYTE CODE** tab. Insert our simple token smart contract's bytecode there. You can get our simple token's bytecode from `token_project/build/contracts.json` after compiling the smart contract's source code first, of course. Find the value with the `bytecode` key and copy the value without the double quote, pasting it into the **CONTRACT BYTE CODE** tab. After doing this, click the **DEPLOY** button (not visible in the following screenshot; you will have to scroll down) and fill in the password as usual in a password dialog:

Soon, your smart contract creation will be confirmed in the blockchain.

Then, to interact with the smart contract, click the **CONTRACTS** tab, followed by the **WATCH CONTRACT** button. A dialog will then appear. Fill in the address of the smart contract and then the name of the smart contract itself. You can apply any name you like here. Next, fill in the `json` interface of the smart contract inside the **JSON INTERFACE** field. You can get the `json` interface from `token_project/build/contracts.json` (in the `contracts.json` file, locate the value of the `abi` key). The form for watching a smart contract looks like the following screen:

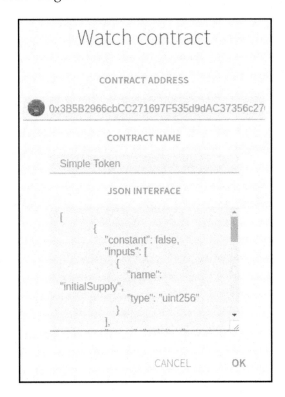

Now, your simple token smart contract will appear on the screen. Click the **SIMPLE TOKEN** label to get into this smart contract's screen:

You can read the balance of the owner of the smart contract using the `Balances` method (Mist likes to capitalize methods). Insert the address of the owner's account in the **Arg 0 - address** field and press Enter. From this, you will get 10,000 as the output.

Now, let's transfer some token coins. Pick a function. Right now, there is only one function: `Transfer` (the capitalized version of the `transfer` method). Choose **Account 1** in the **Execute from** field, choose the **Account 2** address in **to,** and insert 20 in the **amount** field. Finally, click the **EXECUTE** button:

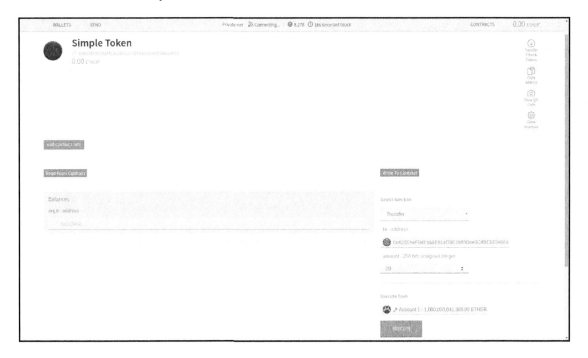

Wait for confirmation before checking the balance of the destination account. Type the destination address into the **Balance** field and then press **Enter**. This will give you 20 as the output:

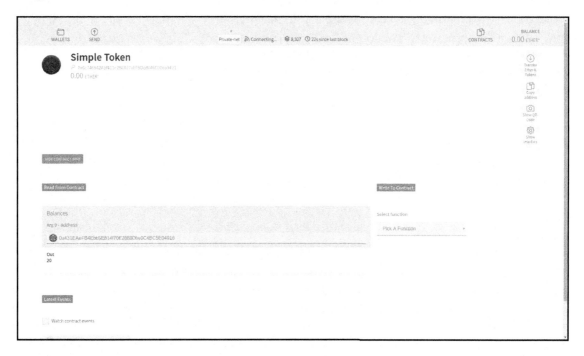

ERC20

More than likely, you will have heard of ERC20. When a new cryptocurrency is out, the first question that usually arises is—is it an ERC20 token? People assume incorrectly regarding the ERC20 token; they think it is a cryptocurrency based on Ethereum. Well, technically speaking, this is true, but it does not tell the whole story. ERC20 is a standard in Ethereum for creating a token. The simple token that we have just created does not fulfill the ERC20 standard. Yes, it is a digital token smart contract, but it is not an ERC20 token. ERC20 is one of many reasons why we have seen an increase in the number of new cryptocurrencies in 2017. However, ERC20 is not a requirement for creating a token on top of Ethereum.

To create an ERC20 token, you must implement the following methods:

```
function totalSupply() public view returns (uint256)
function balanceOf(address _owner) public view returns (uint256 balance)
function transfer(address _to, uint256 _value) public returns (bool
success)
function transferFrom(address _from, address _to, uint256 _value) public
returns (bool success)
function approve(address _spender, uint256 _value) public returns (bool
success)
function allowance(address _owner, address _spender) public view returns
(uint256 remaining)
event Transfer(address indexed _from, address indexed _to, uint256 _value)
event Approval(address indexed _owner, address indexed _spender, uint256
_value)
```

These methods use Solidity syntax. There are optional methods, given in the following code block, that you can implement too:

```
function name() public view returns (string)
function symbol() public view returns (string)
function decimals() public view returns (uint8)
```

So what is so special about this ERC20 token? Is this an obligation when creating a token smart contract? Why can't we create a digital token without fulfilling the ERC20 standard?

Actually, you don't have to follow this standard; there is no law that forces you to create an ERC20 token. For example, the ERC20 standard expects you to tell users the overall amount of tokens in the `totalSupply` method. However, you could create a method named `taylorSwiftIsTheBest` to return the total supply of the token, and then you could create a document to explain this method.

However, there are some advantages if you follow the ERC20 token standard:

- First, it makes it easier for users to audit your smart contract.
- Second, your ERC20 token would be recognized automatically by an Ethereum wallet, such as `Mist` (the one we used just now) and Metamask (the Ethereum wallet is a `Firefox/Opera/Chrome` plugin).
- Third, it is easier for cryptocurrency exchange to list your token. Basically, it makes everyone's lives easier.

However, you should treat the ERC20 standard as guidance, and not strict law. You don't have to follow the ERC20 standard to 100%. Not all popular tokens built on top of Ethereum are 100% ERC20-compliant. One such example is the Golem token smart contract. This does not implement the `approve` method, among other things. You can read the source code of the Golem token smart contract at the following link: `https://etherscan.io/token/0xa74476443119A942dE498590Fe1f2454d7D4aC0d#readContract`.

Having said that, let's create an ERC20 token. This code has been modified from the official example included in the Vyper project (`https://github.com/ethereum/vyper/blob/master/examples/tokens/ERC20.vy`). Refer to the code file in the following GitLab link for the full modified code: `https://gitlab.com/arjunaskykok/hands-on-blockchain-for-python-developers/blob/master/chapter_08/token_project/contracts/ERC20Token.vy`:

```
Transfer: event({_from: indexed(address), _to: indexed(address), _value:
uint256})
Approval: event({_owner: indexed(address), _spender: indexed(address),
_value: uint256})


...
...


@public
@constant
def allowance(_owner: address, _spender: address) -> uint256:
    return self.allowed[_owner][_spender]
```

Let's describe this smart contract line by line:

```
Transfer: event({_from: indexed(address), _to: indexed(address), _value:
uint256})
Approval: event({_owner: indexed(address), _spender: indexed(address),
_value: uint256})
```

You must define two kinds of events, `Transfer` and `Approval`. You can define more events if you wish. A `Transfer` event is used when the transfer of coins occurs, so users of the smart contract can subscribe to this event. An `Approval` event is used when you approve of an amount to spend for an account:

```
name: public(bytes[10])
symbol: public(bytes[3])
totalSupply: public(uint256)
decimals: public(uint256)
balances: map(address, uint256)
allowed: map(address, map(address, uint256))
```

There are six variables. The first variable is the name of the token. I used `bytes[10]` as the data type because the name of my token is less than 10 bytes. Feel free to change the length. The second variable is the symbol of the token; the name and symbol are different. For example, the name of the Ethereum cryptocurrency is Ethereum, but the symbol is ETH. Usually, the symbol's character length is 3. The third variable is `totalSupply`, which is the total amount of tokens, and the fourth variable is decimals. You know that 1 bitcoin is 100,000,000 satoshis, so there will be 21,000,000 bitcoins being created in total in the Bitcoin algorithm. Therefore, we can say that the total supply in the Bitcoin algorithm is 2,100,000,000,000,000. The decimal is 8 (because 1 bitcoin is 100,000,000, or 10^8). Furthermore, the fifth variable is `balances`. This is the variable that keeps track of the balance of the account's address. The final variable is `allowed`, which is a nested mapping. This is designed to keep track of accounts that have been approved to spend ethers from another account's balance up to a certain amount. If this is still not clear, we'll talk about it in depth later. Now, we will move on to the initialization method of this ERC20 token smart contract, as demonstrated in the following code block:

```
@public
def __init__():
    _initialSupply: uint256 = 1000
    _decimals: uint256 = 3
    self.totalSupply = _initialSupply * 10 ** _decimals
    self.balances[msg.sender] = self.totalSupply
    self.name = 'Haha Coin'
    self.symbol = 'HAH'
    self.decimals = _decimals
    log.Transfer(ZERO_ADDRESS, msg.sender, self.totalSupply)
```

This is how we initialize the token in the smart contract. We create the token in the air, and then give all of the token's coins to the owner. Then, we set the name and the symbol of the token as well as the decimal number. Finally, we emit the event of the transfer. The address is `ZERO_ADDRESS` is `0x0000000000000000000000000000000000000000`. This is an indicator that the owner of the smart contract has transferred coins from nowhere:

```
@public
@constant
def balanceOf(_owner: address) -> uint256:
    return self.balances[_owner]
```

This method is used to return the balance of a specific account:

```
@public
def transfer(_to: address, _amount: uint256) -> bool:
    assert self.balances[msg.sender] >= _amount
    self.balances[msg.sender] -= _amount
    self.balances[_to] += _amount
    log.Transfer(msg.sender, _to, _amount)

    return True
```

This is the method for transferring the coin. First, you make sure that the balance of the sender has enough coins to spend. Then, you just subtract the balance of the sender from the number of transfer processes and add that amount to the balance of the destination. Don't forget to log this transaction with the event:

```
@public
def transferFrom(_from: address, _to: address, _value: uint256) -> bool:
    assert _value <= self.allowed[_from][msg.sender]
    assert _value <= self.balances[_from]

    self.balances[_from] -= _value
    self.allowed[_from][msg.sender] -= _value
    self.balances[_to] += _value
    log.Transfer(_from, _to, _value)

    return True

@public
def approve(_spender: address, _amount: uint256) -> bool:
    self.allowed[msg.sender][_spender] = _amount
    log.Approval(msg.sender, _spender, _amount)

    return True
```

Let's take a look at the `approve` method first. So each account has a mapping called `allowed`, but what is this mapping for? It's how each account can let other accounts spend its money. For example, let's say there are 5 accounts—account A, account B, account C, account D, and account E.

Account A has a balance of 50 coins and a mapping variable called `allowed` that has account B, account C, account D, and account E keys. The values of this mapping are as follows:

Account B → 3 coins
Account C → 7 coins

Account D → 2 coins
Account E → 3 coins

This means that at most, account B can spend 3 coins from the balance of account A, account C can spend at most 7 coins from the balance of account A, account D can spend at most 2 coins from the balance of account A, and account E can spend at most 3 coins from the balance of account A.

Inside the `approve` method, we have the following line:

```
self.allowed[msg.sender][_spender] = _amount
```

To ensure that account B can spend 3 coins from the balance of account A, account A called the `approve` method, with _spender set to account B's address, and _amount is set to 3 coins. Don't forget to log this approval.

Then, if account B wants to spend some or all of the 3 coins, account B can call the `transferFrom` method, as follows:

```
assert _value <= self.allowed[_from][msg.sender]
```

The first assertion inside the `transferFrom` method is to make sure that account B does not spend more than 3 coins:

```
assert _value <= self.balances[_from]
```

We make sure that account A has at least 3 coins in its balance as follows:

```
self.balances[_from] -= _value
self.allowed[_from][msg.sender] -= _value
self.balances[_to] += _value
log.Transfer(_from, _to, _value)
```

Then, we subtract the amount of spending from the balance of account A, and the allowance of account A to account B. After this, we increase the balance of the destination account. Don't forget to log this transaction as a `Transfer` event.

The last method is to check the mapping of this allowance:

```
@public
@constant
def allowance(_owner: address, _spender: address) -> uint256:
    return self.allowed[_owner][_spender]
```

This is designated to establish how much account B can spend from the balance of account A.

At this point, you may ask what the point of this method is. Why don't we just transfer the amount of coins to account B if we want to allow account B to spend some ethers in the name of account A? For example, if account A allows account B to spend 5 coins from the balance of account A, this means that account A lets account B send 5 coins from the balance of account A to the address of account B directly. So, why doesn't account A send 5 coins directly to the address of account B to save the hassle? If account B changes their mind, they could refund the amount of tokens to account A.

Normally, we would not allow a normal account to spend on our behalf. However, we do allow the smart contract to do this. There are a number of valid reasons why we want to allow a smart contract to spend our money. One of these reasons is the decentralized exchange smart contract case, in which you want to let the decentralized exchange smart contract sell your token. Let's say that you have created 1,000 HHH coins, and then you want to sell some of them in decentralized exchange. So, you allow this decentralized exchange to spend some coins on your behalf. Perhaps you approve the decentralized exchange to spend 30 HHH coins. This decentralized exchange can try to sell 30 HHH coins on your behalf. You wouldn't allow the decentralized exchange smart contract to have access to all of the coins in your balance just because you only want to sell 30 HHH coins. Although you could audit the smart contract to make sure the smart contract does not try to steal your coins, it's better to have another layer of security. The `approve` method is such a layer.

Compile your token smart contract and deploy it, just like before.

After doing this, go to the **CONTRACTS** tab and click the **WATCH TOKEN** button. In the **Add token** window, insert your ERC20 smart contract's address. Then, other fields such as **TOKEN NAME**, **TOKEN SYMBOL**, and **DECIMAL PLACES OF SMALLEST UNIT** will be filled in automatically. This is one of the reasons why we should implement the ERC20 standard:

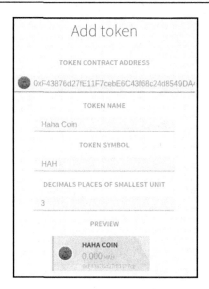

After adding the token, you should see the **HAHA COIN** label on the **CONTRACTS** screen:

Then, in the **SEND** tab, choose the owner of the ERC20 smart contract and then choose **Haha Coin** instead of ether. Send 1,000 Haha coins to Account 2, and then await confirmation:

Now, choose **Account 2** in the same tab; you will see that **Account 2** now has 1,000 Haha coins:

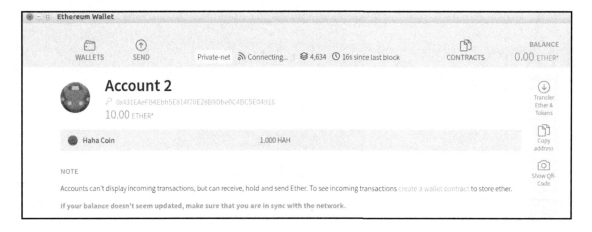

All ERC20 compatible wallets, such as Mist and MetaMask, can recognize and interact with your token easily. The people behind cryptocurrency exchange would not have any technical difficulties either in integrating your ERC20 coins into their exchange. Imagine that you don't follow the ERC20 standard, and that you name a method to transfer coins as `tailorSwiftTransferCoin`. In this case, you must build a custom wallet for users before they can interact with your token.

Here is the test for this ERC20 token. Remember, this test is not comprehensive. Refer to the code file in the following GitLab link for the full code: `https://gitlab.com/arjunaskykok/hands-on-blockchain-for-python-developers/blob/master/chapter_08/token_project/tests/test_erc20_token.py`:

```
import pytest
import eth_tester

def test_balance(web3, chain):
    erc20_token, _ = chain.provider.get_or_deploy_contract('ERC20Token')

    token_name = erc20_token.functions.name().call()
    token_symbol = erc20_token.functions.symbol().call()
    decimals = erc20_token.functions.decimals().call()
    total_supply = erc20_token.functions.totalSupply().call()
    balance = erc20_token.functions.balanceOf(web3.eth.coinbase).call()

...
...

    assert balance_account1 == 999990
    assert balance_account2 == 0
    assert balance_account3 == 10
    assert allowance == 90
```

As well as transferring coin methods, this test also tests the `approval` and `transferFrom` methods.

Selling a token

Now that we have a token, it's time to sell the coins. We want to sell our custom token for ethers. A crowdsourcing token is very easy do create on the Ethereum platform compared to the Bitcoin platform. You already know how to create a method in a smart contract to accept ethers. You also know how to increase the token balance of some accounts. To sell tokens, you must combine those two things. That's all.

This is the core of the **Initial Coin Offering (ICO)**. The currency of Ethereum is valuable. Although the price of ether fluctuates, 1 ether is valued at around USD 100. People would pay real money for some ethers, but not our custom token. To make our custom token worthy, we have to make it useful first, or at least make it appear useful. But to do that, we need capital. So why not sell some of our tokens (say 60%) to early adopters? They can then purchase our custom token with ethers. Then, we can withdraw ethers before changing it to fiat money, so we can hire more programmers and rent an office to develop our new cryptocurrency. This is the basic idea. Of course, because ICO involves a lot of money, it also attracts predators.

This is the crowdsale token smart contract. This is the same as our previous ERC20 token smart contract's source code, but with slight variations. Name this smart contract `CrowdSaleToken.vy` and save it inside the `token_project/contracts` directory. Refer to the code file in the following GitLab link for the full code: `https://gitlab.com/arjunaskykok/hands-on-blockchain-for-python-developers/blob/master/chapter_08/token_project/contracts/CrowdSaleToken.vy`:

```
Transfer: event({_from: indexed(address), _to: indexed(address), _value:
uint256})
Approval: event({_owner: indexed(address), _spender: indexed(address),
_value: uint256})
Payment: event({_buyer: indexed(address), _value: uint256(wei)})

name: public(bytes[10])
symbol: public(bytes[3])
totalSupply: public(uint256)
decimals: public(uint256)
balances: map(address, uint256)
ethBalances: public(map(address, uint256(wei)))
allowed: map(address, map(address, uint256))

...
...

@public
@constant
def allowance(_owner: address, _spender: address) -> uint256:
    return self.allowed[_owner][_spender]
```

Let's discuss this smart contract line by line:

```
Transfer: event({_from: indexed(address), _to: indexed(address), _value:
uint256})
Approval: event({_owner: indexed(address), _spender: indexed(address),
_value: uint256})
Payment: event({_buyer: indexed(address), _value: uint256(wei)})
```

We add one event named `Payment` on top of another two events. This event will be called when someone pays for the token with ethers:

```
name: public(bytes[10])
symbol: public(bytes[3])
totalSupply: public(uint256)
decimals: public(uint256)
balances: map(address, uint256)
ethBalances: public(map(address, uint256(wei)))
allowed: map(address, map(address, uint256))

beneficiary: public(address)
minFundingGoal: public(uint256(wei))
maxFundingGoal: public(uint256(wei))
amountRaised: public(uint256(wei))
deadline: public(timestamp)
price: public(uint256(wei))
fundingGoalReached: public(bool)
crowdsaleClosed: public(bool)
```

We add a couple of new variables, which are `ethBalances`, `beneficiary`, `minFundingGoal`, `maxFundingGoal`, `amountRaised`, `deadline`, `price`, `fundingGoalReached`, and `crowdsaleClosed`.

`ethBalances` is a variable that's designed to keep track of how many ethers a buyer has spent in this smart contract. We want to keep track of this number because we want to refund the ethers if we cannot raise the necessary amount. `beneficiary` is a variable that's used to track who launches this smart contract. This `beneficiary` variable is the only account that is able to withdraw the ethers.

`minFundingGoal` and `maxFundingGoal` are variables that were designed to make sure that the amount that's raised is greater than the minimum funding goal and lower than the maximum funding goal.

`amountRaised` is a variable that's designed to track how many ethers we have raised in this smart contract.

`deadline` is a variable that's used to track the deadline of this crowdsale process.

`price` is how we want to value our digital token in terms of ethers. This variable is designed to answer how many coins of our token the buyer can get with 1 ether.

`fundingGoalReached` is a `boolean` variable stating whether our smart contract has reached our target.

`crowdsaleClosed` is a `boolean` variable stating whether our smart contract still receives the buying process. We'll start from the initialization method:

```
@public
def __init__():
    _initialSupply: uint256 = 100
    _decimals: uint256 = 2
    self.totalSupply = _initialSupply * 10 ** _decimals
    self.name = 'Haha Coin'
    self.symbol = 'HAH'
    self.decimals = _decimals
    self.beneficiary = msg.sender
    self.balances[msg.sender] = self.totalSupply
    self.minFundingGoal = as_wei_value(30, "ether")
    self.maxFundingGoal = as_wei_value(50, "ether")
    self.amountRaised = 0
    self.deadline = block.timestamp + 3600 * 24 * 100 # 100 days
    self.price = as_wei_value(1, "ether") / 100
    self.fundingGoalReached = False
    self.crowdsaleClosed = False
```

The total coin supply in this smart contract is 10,000. We want to raise at least 30 ethers, up to a maximum of 50 ethers.

The deadline is set to 100 days from the time when the smart contract is deployed on the blockchain. `block.timestamp` is approximately the current time, or the time when the block containing this smart contract code is confirmed.

The price of 1 coin is set to `0.01` ether. This means that 1 ether can buy 100 coins of our token. Then, we move into a default function in a smart contract:

```
@public
@payable
def __default__():
    assert msg.sender != self.beneficiary
    assert self.crowdsaleClosed == False
    assert self.amountRaised + msg.value < self.maxFundingGoal
    assert msg.value >= as_wei_value(0.01, "ether")
    self.ethBalances[msg.sender] += msg.value
    self.amountRaised += msg.value
    tokenAmount: uint256 = msg.value / self.price
    self.balances[msg.sender] += tokenAmount
    self.balances[self.beneficiary] -= tokenAmount
    log.Payment(msg.sender, msg.value)
```

This is the method that the user can use to buy the token. __default__ is a default, fallback function. If someone does not execute a method on the smart contract and pays ethers, this function will be executed. Actually, we don't have to use the default function to accept the payment. You can use the standard method, just like you have done in previous smart contracts. We simply use the default function to explain this concept.

In this payment method, we ensure that the buyer is not the beneficiary, that the crowdsale is still happening, and that the amount that has been raised with the ethers sent into this method does not exceed the maximum funding goal of 50 ethers. Lastly, each purchasing action must be at least 0.01 ether. Then, we increase the balance of ethers for this buyer as well as increasing the amount of ethers raised. We then check the amount of coins they purchased by dividing the amount of ethers by the price of 1 coin.

Finally, we have to increase the balance of the token for this buyer and decrease the balance of the token for the owner of the smart contract. Don't forget to log this event. Then, we move onto the method where we can check whether we have reached our target:

```
@public
def checkGoalReached():
    assert block.timestamp > self.deadline
    if self.amountRaised >= self.minFundingGoal:
        self.fundingGoalReached = True
    self.crowdsaleClosed = True
```

First, we make sure that this method can only be executed successfully if the deadline has passed. If the amount raised is more than the minimum funding goal, we set the fundingGoalReached variable to true. Then, finally, we set the crowdsaleClosed variable to true.

For the sake of simplicity, we only check whether the block.timestamp variable is larger than the deadline. However, the timestamp in the block could be filled with anything the miner likes; it does not have to be the current time that the block is confirmed. But, of course, if the miner gave the past timestamp as the value to block.timestamp, all other miners would reject it. Similarly, if the miner gives the future timestamp, which is really far away (for example, a year ahead), as the value for block.timestamp, all other miners would also reject it. To make checking the deadline process more secure, you have to combine it with block.number to check how many blocks have been confirmed since this smart contract launched. Then, we move into the method where the manager of the smart contract can withdraw ethers that have accumulated in the smart contract:

```
@public
def safeWithdrawal():
    assert self.crowdsaleClosed == True
    if self.fundingGoalReached == False:
```

```
        if msg.sender != self.beneficiary:
            if self.ethBalances[msg.sender] > 0:
                self.ethBalances[msg.sender] = 0
                self.balances[self.beneficiary] +=
self.balances[msg.sender]
                self.balances[msg.sender] = 0
                send(msg.sender, self.ethBalances[msg.sender])
    if self.fundingGoalReached == True:
        if msg.sender == self.beneficiary:
            if self.balance > 0:
                send(msg.sender, self.balance)
```

The `safeWithdrawal` method runs differently, depending on whether the funding goal is attained. Inside the preceding method, we make sure that the crowdsale is already closed. If the funding goal is not reached, we make sure that every buyer can get their ethers back. If the funding goal is reached, then we make sure that the beneficiary can withdraw all ethers in the smart contract. The remainder of the methods are the same as in the previous smart contract. However, we add a number of assertions to make sure that these methods can only be executed after the crowdsale is closed.

The following code block is the test for this crowdsale smart contract. Refer to the code file in the following GitLab link for the full code file: https://gitlab.com/arjunaskykok/hands-on-blockchain-for-python-developers/blob/master/chapter_08/token_project/tests/test_crowd_sale_token.py:

```
import pytest
import eth_tester
import time

def test_initialization(web3, chain):
    crowd_sale_token, _ =
chain.provider.get_or_deploy_contract('CrowdSaleToken')


    ...
    ...


    assert abs(beforeCrowdsaleEthBalanceAccount2 -
afterCrowdsaleEthBalanceAccount2 - web3.toWei('40', 'ether')) <
web3.toWei('1', 'gwei')
    assert abs(afterCrowdsaleEthBalanceAccount1 -
beforeCrowdsaleEthBalanceAccount1 - web3.toWei('40', 'ether')) <
web3.toWei('1', 'gwei')
```

Take a look at `test_withdrawal` and `test_refund`, especially these lines:

```
# move forward 101 days
web3.testing.timeTravel(int(time.time()) + 3600 * 24 * 101)
web3.testing.mine(1)
```

Rather than waiting for 100 days, we want to manipulate the clock in the test to believe that the deadline has been reached (101 days from now). Consequently, we pretend that we have passed 101 days and then we confirm 1 block. Therefore, the `block.timestamp` variable inside the smart contract would be 101 days from now.

Stable coin

You have created a digital token that can be sold autonomously. However, you should not restrict yourself to the generic token. You could be more creative in your token smart contract by adding more methods to spice up your smart contract. What methods you should add are dependent on your smart contract's purpose. The token smart contract that is used in a game as currency will have different methods to the token smart contract that is used in a supply chain tracking system.

Let's create a stable coin smart contract. This is a token smart contract that is pegged to fiat money, such as the US dollar. We also want this smart contract to be a bank where we, as an owner, can freeze an account.

We can base our work on an ERC 20 token smart contract. We just need to add three methods—a method to freeze an account, a method to add some coins, and a method to throw away some coins.

This is the smart contract. You can refer to the code file in the following GitLab link for the full code file: `https://gitlab.com/arjunaskykok/hands-on-blockchain-for-python-developers/blob/master/chapter_08/token_project/contracts/StableCoin.vy`:

```
Transfer: event({_from: indexed(address), _to: indexed(address), _value:
uint256})
Approval: event({_owner: indexed(address), _spender: indexed(address),
_value: uint256})
Freeze: event({_account: indexed(address), _freeze: bool})

name: public(bytes[10])
symbol: public(bytes[3])
totalSupply: public(uint256)
decimals: public(uint256)
balances: map(address, uint256)
```

```
allowed: map(address, map(address, uint256))
frozenBalances: public(map(address, bool))
owner: public(address)

...
...

@public
@constant
def allowance(_owner: address, _spender: address) -> uint256:
    return self.allowed[_owner][_spender]
```

Let's discuss the smart contract line by line:

```
Transfer: event({_from: indexed(address), _to: indexed(address), _value:
uint256})
Approval: event({_owner: indexed(address), _spender: indexed(address),
_value: uint256})
Freeze: event({_account: indexed(address), _freeze: bool})
```

We need to add another event for freezing an account action in the preceding code.

We add two new variables on top of variables from the ERC20 token smart contract, which are `frozenBalances` and `owner`:

```
name: public(bytes[10])
symbol: public(bytes[3])
totalSupply: public(uint256)
decimals: public(uint256)
balances: map(address, uint256)
allowed: map(address, map(address, uint256))
frozenBalances: public(map(address, bool))
owner: public(address)
```

`frozenBalances` is a mapping variable to track which accounts have been frozen. `owner` is a variable to track the owner of the smart contract.

In this initialization method, we set the `owner` variable as the account that launched this smart contract:

```
@public
def __init__():
    _initialSupply: uint256 = 1000
    _decimals: uint256 = 3
    self.totalSupply = _initialSupply * 10 ** _decimals
    self.balances[msg.sender] = self.totalSupply
    self.name = 'Haha Coin'
    self.symbol = 'HAH'
```

```
self.decimals = _decimals
self.owner = msg.sender
log.Transfer(ZERO_ADDRESS, msg.sender, self.totalSupply)
```

In the following method, we make sure that only the owner can call this method:

```
@public
def freezeBalance(_target: address, _freeze: bool) -> bool:
    assert msg.sender == self.owner
    self.frozenBalances[_target] = _freeze
    log.Freeze(_target, _freeze)

    return True
```

Then, we set the value of the `frozenBalances` mapping variable. The true value means that the account is frozen. Don't forget to call the `Freeze` event.

The next method is to increase the coins:

```
@public
def mintToken(_mintedAmount: uint256) -> bool:
    assert msg.sender == self.owner
    self.totalSupply += _mintedAmount
    self.balances[msg.sender] += _mintedAmount
    log.Transfer(ZERO_ADDRESS, msg.sender, _mintedAmount)

    return True
```

We increase the total supply and the balance of the owner's account as well.

The following method is designed to burn the coins:

```
@public
def burn(_burntAmount: uint256) -> bool:
    assert msg.sender == self.owner
    assert self.balances[msg.sender] >= _burntAmount
    self.totalSupply -= _burntAmount
    self.balances[msg.sender] -= _burntAmount
    log.Transfer(msg.sender, ZERO_ADDRESS, _burntAmount)

    return True
```

This is similar to the previous method, but its purpose is to decrease the amount of coins from the total supply. Why do you want to annihilate coins? There are a number of valid reasons for this. Suppose you are tracking US dollars with this smart contract. Let's say you have 10,000 US dollars in your pocket. So, the total supply in the smart contract is 10,000 (1 coin is pegged to 1 US dollar), but one day, USD 2,000 of your USD 10,000 is stolen by a thief. To make sure the smart contract is consistent, you burn 2,000 coins with this method.

The remainder of the methods are exactly the same as under the ERC20 token smart contract, with two exceptions: `transfer` and `transferFrom`. We have additional assertions in those methods:

```
assert self.frozenBalances[msg.sender] == False
```

The following code block is the test for this smart contract. You can refer to the code file in the following GitLab link for the full code: https://gitlab.com/arjunaskykok/hands-on-blockchain-for-python-developers/blob/master/chapter_08/token_project/tests/test_stable_token.py:

```python
import pytest
import eth_tester
import time

def test_initialization(web3, chain):
    stable_coin, _ = chain.provider.get_or_deploy_contract('StableCoin')

...
...

    new_total_supply = stable_coin.functions.totalSupply().call()
    assert new_total_supply == 999900
```

Summary

In this chapter, you have learned how to create a token on top of Ethereum. You used Mist an Ethereum wallet, to deploy the contract and interact with the token smart contract. Then, you implemented the ERC 20 standard in creating the token smart contract by creating implementations of certain methods. You also saw how these standard methods help Mist to recognize your token. Then, you created a method to sell tokens for ethers. You put a deadline in this smart contract and then you used a time travel method to simulate the expired deadline in the test of the smart contract. Finally, you added other methods to freeze and unfreeze other accounts. The example you used is a stable coin that pegs coins to real-world assets, such as fiat.

In the next chapter, you are going to create a cryptocurrency wallet that can handle ethers and ERC20 tokens.

Further reading

- https://github.com/ethereum/EIPs/blob/master/EIPS/eip-20.md
- https://ethereum.org/token

9
Cryptocurrency Wallet

In this chapter, you are going to learn how to build a desktop cryptocurrency wallet. You will still use the same GUI library, Qt for Python or PySide2 to create a desktop application. This cryptocurrency wallet can send ethers as well as ERC20 tokens. Before building this cryptocurrency wallet, you will learn advanced features of the PySide2 library, such as tabs, comboboxes, size policy, and adding stretch to control the distribution of widgets in a layout. On top of that, you will integrate testing into applications.

In this chapter, we are going to cover the following topics:

- Advanced features of the PySide2 library
- Pytest Qt, a library to test a Qt for a Python application
- How to build a cryptocurrency wallet
- Some considerations when building a cryptocurrency wallet

Advanced features of the PySide2 library

This chapter requires the reader to have some knowledge of the PySide2 library. You should read Chapter 7, *Frontend Decentralized Application*, first if you have not done so, as this chapter is based on that one. If you have familiarized yourself with building a GUI with PySide2, you are equipped with the necessary skills to build a desktop cryptocurrency wallet, at least from the **User Interface (UI)** persepective. However, the application that you build will be jarring to users. For example, if you incorporated a button in a horizontal layout and that button is the only widget in the horizontal layout, when you resize the window that has the horizontal layout, the button will be stretched to the right and left. If this is not what you want to happen, you need a way to tell the button to keep its width.

So, let's learn other features from the `PySide2` library, such as tab, size policy, and grid layout, so that we have the skills to make the UI of our application more attractive. Our application will not win the *Apple Best Design Award*, but at least it will be less jarring for users.

In addition, in `Chapter 7`, *Frontend Decentralized Application*, we neglected testing. Since a cryptocurrency wallet application is an application that handles people's money, errors are costly. Consequently, we need to catch any errors before users do. We should therefore write proper testing for our cryptocurrency wallet. However, we will focus on testing for the UI part of the cryptocurrency wallet. We will not focus on testing inner methods. In other words, our testing will be integration testing.

 Install the `Qt` library if you haven't already done so. Please read `Chapter 7`, *Frontend Decentralized Application*, for guidance on how to do this. After doing so, create a virtual environment for your project using the following command:

```
$ virtualenv -p python3.6 wallet-venv
$ source wallet-venv/bin/activate
(wallet-venv) $ pip install PySide2
(wallet-venv) $ pip install web3==4.7.2
```

We also want to install a test library to test our application, which can be done by means of the following command:

```
(wallet-venv) $ pip install pytest-qt
```

Now that all the libraries have been set up, let's write a simple application so we can test it.

Testing application

Create a directory named `advanced_course_qt`. We can put all of our tutorial files here. Name the first script `button_and_label.py` and use the following code to create a button and a label for that button (refer to the code file on the following GitLab link for the full code: `https://gitlab.com/arjunaskykok/hands-on-blockchain-for-python-developers/blob/master/chapter_09/advanced_course_qt/button_and_label.py`):

```python
from PySide2.QtWidgets import QWidget, QApplication, QLabel, QPushButton,
QVBoxLayout
from PySide2.QtCore import Qt
import sys

class ButtonAndLabel(QWidget):
```

```
. . .
. . .

if __name__ == "__main__":

    app = QApplication(sys.argv)
    button_and_label = ButtonAndLabel()
    button_and_label.show()
    sys.exit(app.exec_())
```

Run the preceding code to see what this application is about. The application consists of a **button** and a **label**:

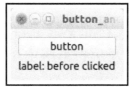

If you click the **button**, the text on the label will change, as shown in the following screenshot:

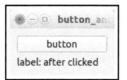

So let's test this application. Name the test `test_button_and_label.py` and put it in the same directory. Use the following code block for the test application:

```
from button_and_label import ButtonAndLabel
from PySide2 import QtCore


def test_button_and_label(qtbot):
    widget = ButtonAndLabel()
    qtbot.addWidget(widget)

    assert widget.label.text() == "label: before clicked"

    qtbot.mouseClick(widget.button, QtCore.Qt.LeftButton)

    assert widget.label.text() == "label: after clicked
```

Run the test using the following command:

```
(wallet-venv) $ pytest test_button_and_label.py
```

Be aware that the `(wallet-venv) $ python test_button_and_label.py` command is a negligible error often used to run the test. Don't fall for it!

In this test script, we import our `widget` class. Then, we create a test method that has a name starting with `test_`. This method has a parameter named `qtbot`. Don't change its name: `qtbot` is a special name and must not be changed. Inside this method, `qtbot` can be used to interact with the `widget` class.

First of all, we instantiate a `widget` class that we want to test. Then, we add that `widget` instance using the `addWidget` method from `qtbot`:

```
qtbot.addWidget(widget)
```

Then, we test the `text` on the `label` variable before clicking the button:

```
assert widget.label.text() == "label: before clicked"
```

As you can see, we can access `label` from `widget`. This is made possible because we declared the `label` variable in `button_and_label.py` using the following code:

```
self.label = QLabel("label: before clicked")
```

If you declare the label in `button_and_label.py` with the following code:

```
label = QLabel("label: before clicked")
```

Then you would not be able to access `label` from the instance of `widget` in the test. Of course, you could circumvent that situation by creating a variable to hold the text of the label. However, making the `label` a `widget` instance property is the easiest thing to do in order to test the text of the label. You will use this strategy in all further tests. In a nutshell, if you want to test widgets (such as a label, button, or combobox), make that `widget` a property of its parent widget instance. Then, we move on to how we click the button widget:

```
qtbot.mouseClick(widget.button, QtCore.Qt.LeftButton)
```

To click a button during testing, you use the `mouseClick` method from `qtbot`. The first parameter of the `mouseClick` method of `qtbot` is a button widget, or something that accepts a clicking event. The second parameter is an option to detect the nature of the mouse click event. The test in this case will only accept a left button click.

The following code is to test and display the text of a label after clicking the button:

```
assert widget.label.text() == "label: after clicked"
```

In building a GUI application, on occasion, we have to display a list of objects. In our cryptocurrency wallet, the list could hold accounts. So let's write a test for that scenario. First, however, we have to create a script to display a list of objects. Name the script `button_and_list.py` and use the following code block for the script (refer to the code file on the following GitLab link for the full code: `https://gitlab.com/arjunaskykok/hands-on-blockchain-for-python-developers/blob/master/chapter_09/advanced_course_qt/button_and_list.py`):

```python
from PySide2.QtWidgets import QWidget, QApplication, QLabel, QPushButton,
QVBoxLayout
from PySide2.QtCore import Qt
import sys


class ButtonAndList(QWidget):
    ...
    ...

if __name__ == "__main__":

    app = QApplication(sys.argv)
    button_and_list = ButtonAndList()
    button_and_list.show()
    sys.exit(app.exec_())
```

Run the script to see how the application appears. The following shows the screenshot of the button prior to clicking it:

And the following shows the result of clicking the button:

You have a single button here and if you click it, a new label should appear with text that simply reads 1. If you click the button for a second time, a new label will appear at the bottom with text that reads 2, and so on.

The new label that shows up after we click the button is part of the vertical box layout. This means that we need to make that vertical box layout the widget instance's property so that we can access it in the test.

Let's write a test for this GUI script, as shown in the following code block, and name it test_button_and_list.py:

```
from button_and_list import ButtonAndList
from PySide2 import QtCore


def test_button_and_list(qtbot):
    widget = ButtonAndList()
    qtbot.addWidget(widget)

    qtbot.mouseClick(widget.button, QtCore.Qt.LeftButton)
    qtbot.mouseClick(widget.button, QtCore.Qt.LeftButton)
    qtbot.mouseClick(widget.button, QtCore.Qt.LeftButton)

    label_item = widget.v_layout.takeAt(2)
    assert label_item.widget().text() == "3"

    label_item = widget.v_layout.takeAt(1)
    assert label_item.widget().text() == "2"

    label_item = widget.v_layout.takeAt(0)
    assert label_item.widget().text() == "1"
```

As we can see in the preceding code block, after the third execution of the `mouseClick` method of `qtbot`, we grab the label from the vertical box layout using the following code:

```
label_item = widget.v_layout.takeAt(2)
```

We take the child widget of a widget by means of the `takeAt` method. The parameter that we use in this case is 2. This means that we want to grab the third child, the last one. Then, we test the text of the widget using the following code:

```
assert label_item.widget().text() == "3"
```

Let's create a more complicated scenario. Hitherto, everything we have tested has been inside one window, but what if we have an input dialog? How do we test a dialog?

Let's create a GUI script that has a dialog and name it `button_and_dialog.py`: (refer to the code file on the following GitLab link for the full code: `https://gitlab.com/arjunaskykok/hands-on-blockchain-for-python-developers/blob/master/chapter_09/advanced_course_qt/button_and_dialog.py`):

```python
from PySide2.QtWidgets import QWidget, QApplication, QLabel, QPushButton,
QVBoxLayout, QInputDialog, QLineEdit
from PySide2.QtCore import Qt
import sys


class ButtonAndDialog(QWidget):

    ...
    ...

if __name__ == "__main__":

    app = QApplication(sys.argv)
    button_and_dialog = ButtonAndDialog()
    button_and_dialog.show()
    sys.exit(app.exec_())
```

Run the code to view the application. There is a button and empty space beneath it:

Click **button** and a dialog will appear, after which you should type any text in the input dialog and click **OK**:

The text you have inputted will appear beneath the button:

Let's take a look at another test script in the following code block in order to understand how to handle the flow involving two different windows. In this test method, we have another parameter besides `qtbot`, called `monkeypatch`. Name the test file `test_button_and_dialog.py`:

```python
from button_and_dialog import ButtonAndDialog
from PySide2.QtWidgets import QInputDialog
from PySide2 import QtCore


def test_button_and_dialog(qtbot, monkeypatch):
    widget = ButtonAndDialog()
    qtbot.addWidget(widget)

    monkeypatch.setattr(QInputDialog, 'getText', lambda *args: ("New Text",
True))
    qtbot.mouseClick(widget.button, QtCore.Qt.LeftButton)

    assert widget.label.text() == "New Text"
```

`monkeypatch` is used to override a dialog input. This means that the `getText` method of `QInputDialog` would return a (`"New Text"`, `True`) tuple when we launch the dialog in the test. Remember the API of `QInputDialog`? This returns a tuple. This tuple contains two parameters—the text that we type in the dialog, and whether we click the **OK** or **Cancel** buttons.

The `getText` method of `QInputDialog` accepts four parameters: the window instance that this dialog is based upon, the title, the label before the input field, and the type of input field. When you type text, such as `To the moon!` in the input field, and clicked the **OK** button, it returns a tuple consisting of the string `To the moon!` and the `boolean` value of whether you click the **OK** button:

```
new_text, ok = QInputDialog.getText(self, "Write A Text", "New Text:",
QlineEdit.Normal)
```

However, `monkeypatch` patches this method so in the testing, no dialog would be launched. We bypass them. It's as if the launching dialog line is replaced with the following line of code:

```
new_text, ok = ("New Text", True)
```

For all of these tests, we always use a button-type widget to initiate something (changing the text on the label). Let's use another type of widget to change the label, as given in the following code block, and name the script `combobox_and_label.py`:

```
from PySide2.QtWidgets import QWidget, QApplication, QLabel, QComboBox,
QVBoxLayout
from PySide2.QtCore import Qt
import sys


class ComboBoxAndLabel(QWidget):

    def __init__(self):
        super(ComboBoxAndLabel, self).__init__()

        self.combobox = QComboBox()
        self.combobox.addItems(["Orange", "Apple", "Grape"])
        self.combobox.currentTextChanged.connect(self.comboboxSelected)

        self.label = QLabel("label: before selecting combobox")

        layout = QVBoxLayout()
        layout.addWidget(self.combobox)
        layout.addWidget(self.label)

        self.setLayout(layout)

    def comboboxSelected(self, value):
        self.label.setText(value)


if __name__ == "__main__":
```

```
app = QApplication(sys.argv)
combobox_and_label = ComboBoxAndLabel()
combobox_and_label.show()
sys.exit(app.exec_())
```

This GUI script uses **combobox** to change the text on the **label**. It sets the text on the label with the text from the selected option of the label. Run the script to see how it appears:

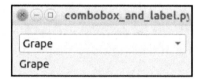

Now, let's create a test script to test this combobox widget and name it `test_combobox_and_label.py`:

```
from combobox_and_label import ComboBoxAndLabel
from PySide2 import QtCore


def test_combobox_and_label(qtbot):
    widget = ComboBoxAndLabel()
    qtbot.addWidget(widget)

    assert widget.label.text() == "label: before selecting combobox"

    qtbot.keyClicks(widget.combobox, "Grape")

    assert widget.label.text() == "Grape"
```

The key point that we can take here is the way we change the selected option of `combobox` with `qtbot`:

```
qtbot.keyClicks(widget.combobox, "Grape")
```

The method's name is not intuitive; it accepts two parameters. The first one is the widget, or the combobox in this case. The second one is the option text in the combobox. This `keyClicks` method is not just for selecting an option in combobox. It could also be used to type text in the line edit. Just put the line edit widget in the first parameter.

This test knowledge is sufficient for testing our cryptocurrency wallet. Before we jump into building our cryptocurrency wallet, let's learn about some other features of PySide2, including grid layout, tab, and size policy.

Advanced features of Qt for Python or PySide2

The first thing that we want to learn about here is stretching. We know how to add widgets to a box layout (vertical or horizontal). However, we can configure to some extent how to distribute these widgets that we added into a box layout. Should we stretch the widgets, put the widgets on top for the horizontal layout, and let the space devour the rest?

Let's create a script to explain this configuration of widget distribution in a box layout and name the script add_stretch.py (refer to the code file on the following GitLab link for the full code: https://gitlab.com/arjunaskykok/hands-on-blockchain-for-python-developers/blob/master/chapter_09/advanced_course_qt/add_stretch.py):

```
from PySide2.QtWidgets import QFrame, QLabel, QWidget, QApplication,
QPushButton, QHBoxLayout, QVBoxLayout, QSizePolicy, QSizePolicy
from PySide2.QtCore import Qt
import sys


class AddStretch(QWidget):

    ...
    ...

if __name__ == "__main__":

    app = QApplication(sys.argv)
    widget = AddStretch()
    widget.resize(500, 500)
    widget.show()
    sys.exit(app.exec_())
```

Run the script to see how it looks:

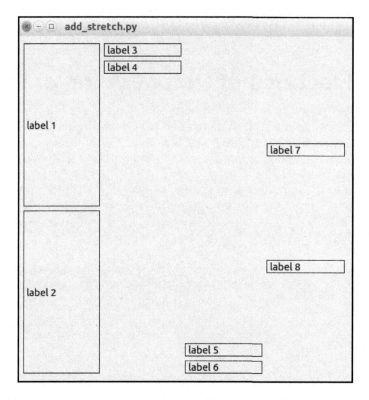

If you add stretching to the end of the vertical container, it would push the widgets to the beginning of the vertical container and let the rest be an empty space. If you add stretching in the beginning, it would push the widgets to the end of the vertical container and let the rest be an empty space. If you don't add any stretching, the widgets would be distributed equally across the layout.

In terms of the functionality of the application, it does not make any difference. However, it can make the UI more attractive if you choose the right options.

We always use the box layout (vertical box layout or horizontal box layout). The box layout suffices in most cases. Occasionally, however, you want to use a more complicated layout. Qt has a grid layout that is more powerful than the box layout.

Let's create a script to explore the power of the grid layout and name the script `create_grid_window.py` (refer to the code file on the following GitLab link for the full code: `https://gitlab.com/arjunaskykok/hands-on-blockchain-for-python-developers/blob/master/chapter_09/advanced_course_qt/create_grid_window.py`):

```python
from PySide2.QtWidgets import QWidget, QApplication, QLabel, QGridLayout
from PySide2.QtCore import Qt
import sys


class GridWindow(QWidget):

    . . .
    . . .

if __name__ == "__main__":

    app = QApplication(sys.argv)
    gridWindow = GridWindow()
    gridWindow.show()
    sys.exit(app.exec_())
```

Run the script to see how the grid layout manages its child window:

A grid is like a table or spreadsheet. Instead of adding a widget to a row with a horizontal layout, or a column with a vertical layout, you add a widget to a table that is composed of rows and columns.

If you want to add the widget to the first row and the first column, use the following statement:

```python
layout.addWidget(label, 0, 0)
```

The first parameter indicates a row. The second parameter indicates a column. So if you want to add the widget to the second row and the first column, use the following statement:

```
layout.addWidget(label, 1, 0)
```

The `addWidget` method of the grid layout accepts optional third and fourth parameters. The third parameter indicates how many rows you want this widget to extend to. The fourth parameter indicates how many columns you want this widget to extend to:

```
layout.addWidget(label, 1, 1, 2, 2)
```

If you stretch the window, you will see something similar to the following screenshot:

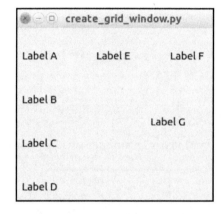

Take a look at **Label G**. This stretches up to two rows and two columns.

Now, let's talk about what happens to the widget if we increase the size of the parent window that contains the widget. Should the widget resize along with it? Should the widget stay still, and allow the margin to become wider? You can decide on the resizing configuration with the size policy. Let's create a script named `button_with_sizepolicy.py` to demonstrate size configuring this policy (refer to the code file on the following GitLab link for the full code: `https://gitlab.com/arjunaskykok/hands-on-blockchain-for-python-developers/blob/master/chapter_09/advanced_course_qt/button_with_sizepolicy.py`):

```python
from PySide2.QtWidgets import QWidget, QApplication, QPushButton,
QVBoxLayout, QSizePolicy
from PySide2.QtCore import Qt
import sys


class ButtonWithSizePolicy(QWidget):
```

```
. . .
. . .

if __name__ == "__main__":

    app = QApplication(sys.argv)
    button_with_size_policy_widget = ButtonWithSizePolicy()
    button_with_size_policy_widget.resize(500, 200)
    button_with_size_policy_widget.show()
    sys.exit(app.exec_())
```

Run the script to see how each button appears differently with a different size policy:

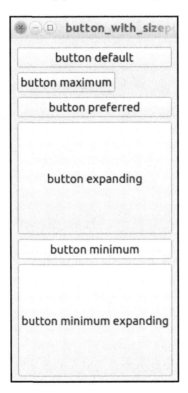

Then, try to resize the window to make sense of the size policy configuration:

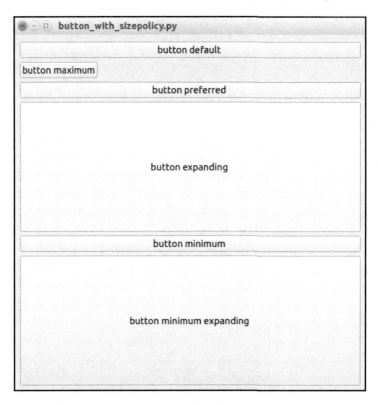

`QSizePolicy.Maximum` indicates that the widget cannot be bigger than the size hint, or the content of the button in this case. If you want your button to stick to its original size, use this size policy. `QSizePolicy.Preferred` indicates that it prefers a size hint but it can be larger or smaller. `QSizePolicy.Expanding` indicates that the widget should expand as much as possible. `QSizePolicy.Minimum` indicates that the widget can be expanded, but it cannot be smaller than the size hint. `QSizePolicy.MinimumExpanding` indicates that the widget cannot be smaller than the size hint, but it expands as much as possible.

 In creating a GUI application, most of the time you would not put all of your functionalities/widgets in a single window. Otherwise, the window would be bigger than the screen resolution of the monitor.

You could launch a dialog with a button to hold more functionalities/widgets. That certainly works. But what you really want is something like a controller. In Qt, you have **StackView**. StackView can contain many windows, but it displays a maximum of one window at one time.

We wouldn't use StackView directly. Instead, we use tabbed view. Tabbed view uses StackView behind the scenes. Let's create a script to use tabbed view and name it `tabbed_window.py`:

```
from PySide2.QtWidgets import QTabWidget, QApplication, QWidget
import sys
from button_and_label import ButtonAndLabel


class TabbedWindow(QTabWidget):

    def __init__(self, parent=None):
        super(TabbedWindow, self).__init__(parent)
        widget1 = QWidget()
        self.widget2 = ButtonAndLabel()
        widget3 = QWidget()
        self.addTab(widget1, "Tab 1")
        self.addTab(self.widget2, "Tab 2")
        self.addTab(widget3, "Tab 3")


if __name__ == "__main__":

    app = QApplication(sys.argv)
    tabbedWindow = TabbedWindow()
    tabbedWindow.show()
    sys.exit(app.exec_())
```

This tabbed window has three tabs. Each tab holds a widget. The second tab even holds a widget that we created in a separate script, `button_and_label.py`. This widget, which is in the second tab, has a button and a label. To add a tab to a tabbed window, you use the `addTab` method. The first parameter is the widget, and the second parameter is the title of the tab.

Run the script to see how tabbed view works. In the following screenshot, we see **Tab 1**:

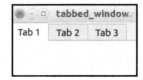

In the following screenshot, we see **Tab 2** and the widget from `button_and_label.py`:

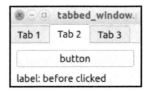

Building a cryptocurrency wallet

Now that you have an understanding of other features of Qt for Python library, let's start to build a desktop cryptocurrency wallet. Since this is a complex application, we should not put everything in one file; instead, we will separate it into many files. We even separate the many files into different directories. We also want to keep this application basic enough for the purpose of a tutorial. Consequently, we will not put a lot of features in this application. This cryptocurrency wallet can create new accounts, send ethers to another account, and watch ERC20 tokens so that we can later send some token coins to another account. However, it will not have complete features that you would expect from a proper cryptocurrency wallet.

First, let's create a project directory and its inner directory using the following commands:

```
$ mkdir wallet
$ mkdir wallet/icons
$ mkdir wallet/images
$ mkdir wallet/tests
$ mkdir wallet/tools
$ mkdir wallet/wallet_threads
$ mkdir wallet/wallet_widgets
```

The main application, main library, and its configuration files are put in the main directory, which is the `wallet` directory. Some icons to spice up the UI of the application are put inside the `icons` directory. The avatar images are put inside the `images` directory. The test files are put inside the `tests` directory. The library files that are not related to blockchain and the UI are put inside the `tools` directory. The thread classes are put inside the `wallet_threads` directory. Finally, the child widgets of the main widget are put inside the `wallet_widgets` directory.

Blockchain class

Let's create a blockchain interface code in `wallet` and name the script `blockchain.py`. This file is responsible for connecting to the blockchain. Its responsibilities include checking the balance of the account, getting local accounts, sending transactions, and getting token information. By putting all blockchain functions inside one class or file, it is easier for us to debug the problem, to test the implementations, and to develop the functionalities. Go to `https://gitlab.com/arjunaskykok/hands-on-blockchain-for-python-developers/tree/master/chapter_09/wallet` and refer to the `blockchain.py` code file for this section.

This blockchain class has 10 methods to interact with the blockchain. In addition, it also has the generic `json` interface of the ERC20 token.

Let's discuss this blockchain class file on a line-by-line basis:

```
from web3 import Web3, IPCProvider
from web3.exceptions import ValidationError
from populus.utils.wait import wait_for_transaction_receipt
from collections import namedtuple
from os.path import exists
import json


SendTransaction = namedtuple("SendTransaction", "sender password
destination amount fee")
TokenInformation = namedtuple("TokenInformation", "name symbol totalSupply
address")
```

After importing the required libraries, we create two named tuples. So, why do we want to create these named tuples? Basically, we do this to avoid errors. Having errors in a cryptocurrency wallet is expensive.

Imagine you have the following function:

```
def send_transaction(sender, password, destination, amount, fee):
    // the code to create transaction
```

You execute the function as follows:

```
send_transaction("427af7b53b8f56adf6f13932bb17c42ed2a53d04", "password",
"6ad2ffd2e08bd73f5c50db60fdc82a58b0590b99", 3, 2)
```

If you swap the sender and the destination, in the worst case scenario, you get an unhandled exception and the program stops because the private key does not match the sender. However, what if you swap the amount and the fee? In this case, you send the small amount to someone with a very high fee. There are many ways to avoid this mistake. For example, you could use a keyword argument, as given in the following code block, or you could use a named tuple:

```
send_transaction(SendTransaction(sender="0xaksdfkas", password="password",
destination="0xkkkkkk", amount=3, fee=2))
```

Now, let's move on to the `json` interface of the ERC20 token smart contract. This is not required when we want to send ethers: it is only required when we want to send token coins:

```
true = True
false = False
erc20_token_interface = [
        {
            "anonymous": false,
            "inputs": [
                {
                    "indexed": true,
                    "name": "_from",
                    "type": "address"
                },
                {
                    "indexed": true,
                    "name": "_to",
                    "type": "address"
                },
                {
                    "indexed": false,
                    "name": "_value",
```

```
                    "type": "uint256"
                }
            ],
            "name": "Transfer",
            "type": "event"
        },
    ...
```

As you are aware, in order to interact with a smart contract, you need the `json` interface (`abi`) of the smart contract. You may be wondering how we get this `json` interface. This is achieved through the compilation output of the ERC20 token smart contract. It does not matter what the name, decimal number, and the symbol are. As long as the interface is from the smart contract that fulfills the ERC20 standard, we should get the correct interface. I decided to put the interface in the same file as the `Blockchain` class in order to simplify matters. However, you could put the interface in the `json` file, and then load the `json` file in the `Blockchain` class file. Then, we move on to the definition of the `Blockchain` class:

```
class Blockchain:

    tokens_file = 'tokens.json'

    def __init__(self):
        self.w3 = Web3(IPCProvider('/tmp/geth.ipc'))
```

Here, we start the `Blockchain` class. In its initialization method, we construct a `w3` variable to connect to blockchain. We hardcode the connection to blockchain with an IPC provider. You can change this configuration if you use `HTTPProvider`, for example, or use a different `IPC` file path. The `tokens_file` variable is the file that holds all the tokens that we watch.

Let's take a look at the following lines of code:

```
    def get_accounts(self):
        return map(lambda account: (account,
    self.w3.fromWei(self.w3.eth.getBalance(account), 'ether')),
    self.w3.eth.accounts)
```

We get all local accounts with `w3.eth.accounts`, and then we get the balance from each account using `w3.eth.getBalance`. The local accounts are the accounts you created in the local node. Usually, the files are kept in the `keystore` directory.

The following code is used to create a new account in the local blockchain node:

```
    def create_new_account(self, password):
        return self.w3.personal.newAccount(password)
```

The account file will be encrypted with the password we supply. To see the private key, we need to decrypt the account file with the password. However, this is not necessary except for backup purposes.

Use the following code to get the balance from an address:

```
def get_balance(self, address):
    return self.w3.fromWei(self.w3.eth.getBalance(address), 'ether')
```

The balance is in wei. Then, we convert the balance in wei to the balance in ethers.

The following code block is designed to obtain the balance of ERC20 tokens, but not the balance of ethers:

```
def get_token_balance(self, account_address, token_information):
    try:
        token_contract =
self.w3.eth.contract(address=token_information.address,
abi=erc20_token_interface)
        balance =
token_contract.functions.balanceOf(account_address).call()
    except ValidationError:
        return None
    return balance
```

First, we get the contract's object that accepts two parameters – the address of the smart contract and the json interface. If you remember what you learned in Chapter 8, *Creating Token in Ethereum*, the ERC20 token needs to have a `balanceOf` method. The purpose of this method is to get the balance of the token from the account's address.

The following code block is used for creating a transaction of sending ethers:

```
def create_send_transaction(self, tx):
    nonce = self.w3.eth.getTransactionCount(tx.sender)
    transaction = {
      'from': tx.sender,
      'to': Web3.toChecksumAddress(tx.destination),
      'value': self.w3.toWei(str(tx.amount), 'ether'),
      'gas': 21000,
      'gasPrice': self.w3.toWei(str(tx.fee), 'gwei'),
      'nonce': nonce
    }

    tx_hash = self.w3.personal.sendTransaction(transaction,
tx.password)
    wait_for_transaction_receipt(self.w3, tx_hash)
```

First, you get the `nonce`, and then you construct a transaction object. To send this transaction using a password, and not a private key, you need to use the `sendTransaction` method from the `w3.personal` object. Then, you wait until the transaction is confirmed.

After learning about transactions involving the sending of ethers, let's move on to the following code block, which is a method for creating a transaction whereby ERC20 tokens are sent:

```
def create_send_token_transaction(self, tx, token_information):
    nonce = self.w3.eth.getTransactionCount(tx.sender)
    token_contract =
self.w3.eth.contract(address=token_information.address,
abi=erc20_token_interface)
    transaction = token_contract.functions.transfer(tx.destination,
int(tx.amount)).buildTransaction({
                'from': tx.sender,
                'gas': 70000,
                'gasPrice': self.w3.toWei(str(tx.fee), 'gwei'),
                'nonce': nonce
        })

    tx_hash = self.w3.personal.sendTransaction(transaction,
tx.password)
    wait_for_transaction_receipt(self.w3, tx_hash)
```

First, you get the `nonce`, and then construct a contract object. Then, you call the `transfer` method of this smart contract object. Remember that the ERC20 token needs to have a `transfer` method to transfer token coins that accepts two parameters—the destination and the amount of token coins. Then, you execute this method by building a transaction from this method before passing it to the `sendTransaction` method from the `w3.personal` object. Finally, we wait for this transaction to be confirmed.

The following code block is used to obtain the information from the token smart contract:

```
def get_information_of_token(self, address):
    try:
        token_contract = self.w3.eth.contract(address=address,
abi=erc20_token_interface)
        name = token_contract.functions.name().call()
        symbol = token_contract.functions.symbol().call()
        total_supply = token_contract.functions.totalSupply().call()
    except ValidationError:
        return None
    token_information = TokenInformation(name=name.decode('utf-8'),
                                        symbol=symbol.decode('utf-8'),
```

```
                                           totalSupply=total_supply,
                                           address=address)
        return token_information
```

First, we create a contract object. Then, to get the name, symbol and total supply, we access the `name`, `symbol`, and `totalSupply` methods from the smart contract. Because the name and symbol are byte objects, we need to decode it to string. We wrap this information in a tuple named `TokenInformation`.

The following code is a convenient way of wrapping a token information dictionary inside a named `tuple`:

```
def get_token_named_tuple(self, token_dict, address):
    return TokenInformation(name=token_dict['name'],
                            totalSupply=token_dict['total_supply'],
                            symbol=token_dict['symbol'],
                            address=address)
```

The following code is used to get all tokens that we're watching from the configuration file:

```
def get_tokens(self):
    tokens = {}
    if exists(self.tokens_file):
        with open(self.tokens_file) as json_data:
            tokens = json.load(json_data)
    return tokens
```

There are many smart contracts for tokens out there, but we only want to use some of these. Consequently, we save the information pertaining to these token smart contracts into a `json` file. Then, we go to the last line of the file, which is constructing a `Blockchain` class instance:

```
blockchain = Blockchain()
```

We do this so that any file that imports this module would get the blockchain object straight away and two different files would get the same object. This is similar to a singleton pattern.

Thread classes

Now, let's write thread objects in order to access the blockchain. When creating a transaction in a blockchain, you usually want to use a thread or non-blocking function. Consequently, every time we want to broadcast a transaction, we use these thread classes. These thread classes will use the blockchain object that we have described previously.

Use the following code block to create a `balance_thread.py` file in the `wallet_threads` directory:

```
from PySide2.QtCore import QThread, Signal
from time import sleep
from blockchain import blockchain


class BalanceThread(QThread):

    get_balance_transaction = Signal(map)

    def __init__(self, parent=None):
        super(BalanceThread, self).__init__(parent)
        self.quit = False

    def kill(self):
        self.quit = True

    def run(self):
        while True:
            sleep(2)
            if self.quit:
                break
            accounts = blockchain.get_accounts()
            self.get_balance_transaction.emit(accounts)
```

This thread class is not creating any transaction in the blockchain; its purpose is to read the balance of the ethers in every account. So, why do we need a thread to read the balance? Is reading the balance supposed to be fast? Imagine you launch your cryptocurrency wallet, and you see your balance is 10 ethers. Then, someone sends you some ethers. You want your balance to be reflected as soon as possible, right? That is the purpose of this thread; it will check the balance of every account every 2 seconds. The `kill` method is designed to shut down the application and stop the thread from working. It is not mandatory, but if you don't do this, you would get an annoying warning stating that the application is destroyed while the thread is still running when you close your application.

Now, let's create another thread class inside the `wallet_threads` directory and name it `send_thread.py`:

```
from PySide2.QtCore import QThread, Signal
from blockchain import blockchain


class SendThread(QThread):
```

```
        send_transaction = Signal()

    def __init__(self, parent=None):
        super(SendThread, self).__init__(parent)

    def prepareTransaction(self, tx):
        self.tx = tx

    def run(self):
        blockchain.create_send_transaction(self.tx)
        self.send_transaction.emit()
```

The purpose of this thread class is to call the `create_send_transaction` method of the blockchain object. Before we run the thread, we need to call the `prepareTransaction` method of this thread class with a `tuple` parameter named `SendTransaction`.

Now, let's create another thread class inside the `wallet_threads` directory and name it `send_token_thread.py`:

```
from PySide2.QtCore import QThread, Signal
from blockchain import blockchain


class SendTokenThread(QThread):

    send_token_transaction = Signal()

    def __init__(self, parent=None):
        super(SendTokenThread, self).__init__(parent)

    def prepareTransaction(self, tx, token_information):
        self.tx = tx
        self.token_information = token_information

    def run(self):
        blockchain.create_send_token_transaction(self.tx,
    self.token_information)
        self.send_token_transaction.emit()
```

This is similar to the `SendThread` class. The purpose of this thread is to call the `create_send_token_transaction` method, which accepts two parameters this time, one tuple named `SendTransaction`, and another tuple named `TokenInformation`.

Identicon and Icons

Now, let's understand what the identicon library is. The purpose of the identicon library is to generate a custom avatar image (such as fractal) based on the hash of a specific string. If you log in to StackOverflow and you don't set your profile image, your avatar would be generated by the identicon library.

The screenshot will appear like this:

Or it will appear like this:

This is optional. Our cryptocurrency wallet could run fine without these avatar images. This is just to spice up the UI.

Download the file from `https://gitlab.com/arjunaskykok/hands-on-blockchain-for-python-developers/blob/master/chapter_09/wallet/tools/identicon.py` into the `tools` directory. This is fine work on the part of Shin Adachi. I have modified it so that it works with Python 3. You don't have to understand this file; treat it like a third-party library.

Then, create a file inside the `tools` directory, using the following code block to utilize this library, and name it `util.py`:

```
from os.path import isdir, exists
from os import mkdir
from tools.identicon import render_identicon


def render_avatar(code):
    code = int(code, 16)
```

```
img_filename = 'images/%08x.png' % code
if exists(img_filename):
    return img_filename
img = render_identicon(code, 24)
if not isdir('images'):
    mkdir('images')
img.save(img_filename, 'PNG')
return img_filename
```

Basically, this method can render an avatar image using the account address. This serves to make an application a bit more attractive. Consequently,when you create an account, you get an avatar that is unique according to your address.

Then, download a number of icons in the `icons` folder. You need two of these: `ajax-loader.gif` and `copy.svg`. You can download `copy.svg` from the free icon website. Any icon showing a copying action should do just fine. Then, you can download `ajax-loader.gif` from `http://ajaxload.info/`.

Building widgets

Let's create our main application using the following code block. This is the main entry for our cryptocurrency wallet. Name it `wallet.py`:

```python
from PySide2.QtWidgets import QTabWidget, QApplication
import sys

from wallet_widgets.account_widget import AccountWidget
from wallet_widgets.send_widget import SendWidget
from wallet_widgets.token_widget import TokenWidget


class WalletWidget(QTabWidget):

    def __init__(self, parent=None):
        super(WalletWidget, self).__init__(parent)
        self.account_widget = AccountWidget()
        self.send_widget = SendWidget()
        self.token_widget = TokenWidget()
        self.addTab(self.account_widget, "Account")
        self.addTab(self.send_widget, "Send")
        self.addTab(self.token_widget, "Token")

    def killThreads(self):
        self.account_widget.kill()
```

```
if __name__ == "__main__":

    app = QApplication(sys.argv)
    wallet_widget = WalletWidget()
    wallet_widget.show()
    return_app = app.exec_()
    wallet_widget.killThreads()
    sys.exit(return_app)
```

`WalletWidget` is a tabbed window. There are three tabs:

- The first tab is designed to hold an account widget. This widget is responsible for managing accounts (listing accounts and creating a new account).
- The second tab is designed to hold a widget that a user can use to create a transaction to send ethers or ERC20 tokens. Anything to do with sending ethers or tokens is done in this widget.
- The third tab is used to hold token widgets. This widget is responsible for watching ERC20 tokens. Watching ERC20 tokens means getting the information from the ERC20 custom token smart contract and making these tokens capable of being spent in the sending transaction widget.

These three widgets will be defined in other files that will be discussed later.

The `killThreads` method is optional. If you don't use this method, you will get alerts after you close the application because the thread that the application created has not finished its business.

Account widget

Now, let's create the first widget in the first tab of this tabbed window. Put the file inside the `wallet_widgets` directory and name it `account_widget.py`. You will then get the full code file from the following link: `https://gitlab.com/arjunaskykok/hands-on-blockchain-for-python-developers/tree/master/chapter_09/wallet/wallet_widgets`.

As mentioned previously, this widget will show up in the first tab of the wallet tabbed window. In this tab, you will acquire listing accounts and create new account functionalities.

Use the following code to import many types of widgets and classes from `PySide2`:

```
from PySide2.QtWidgets import (QWidget,
                               QGridLayout,
                               QVBoxLayout,
                               QHBoxLayout,
                               QPushButton,
                               QLabel,
                               QInputDialog,
                               QLineEdit,
                               QToolTip,
                               QApplication,
                               QSizePolicy)
from PySide2.QtCore import Slot, SIGNAL, QSize
from PySide2.QtGui import QPixmap, QIcon, QCursor, QClipboard
from time import sleep
from blockchain import blockchain
from tools.util import render_avatar
from wallet_threads.balance_thread import BalanceThread
```

We also import the `blockchain` object and the `render_avatar` method, among other things. In addition, we will use the `balance_thread` instance, which is a thread to update our account's balance.

Use the following code block to create a button that allows us to create an account within the widget:

```
class AccountWidget(QWidget):

    balance_widgets = {}

    def __init__(self, parent=None):
        super(AccountWidget, self).__init__(parent)

        self.create_account_button = QPushButton("Create Account")
        self.create_account_button.setSizePolicy(QSizePolicy.Maximum,
QSizePolicy.Maximum)
        self.connect(self.create_account_button, SIGNAL('clicked()'),
self.createNewAccount)

        self.accounts_layout = QVBoxLayout()

        accounts = blockchain.get_accounts()

        for account, balance in accounts:
            self._addAccountToWindow(account, balance)

        layout = QGridLayout()
```

```
layout.addWidget(self.create_account_button, 0, 0)
layout.addLayout(self.accounts_layout, 1, 0)

self.setLayout(layout)

self.balance_thread = BalanceThread()
self.balance_thread.get_balance_transaction.connect(self._updateBalances)
self.balance_thread.start()
```

All of these accounts will be put in the accounts_layout vertical box layout. We get all
local accounts from the blockchain object, and then we use the addAccountToWindow
method to put this account in the accounts layout. After this, we put the button and
accounts_layout in the main layout. Lastly, we connect the slot for the BalanceThread
thread instance to the _updateBalances method and run the thread.

Use the following code to launch the input dialog and request the password:

```
@Slot()
def createNewAccount(self):
    password, ok = QInputDialog.getText(self, "Create A New Account",
            "Password:", QLineEdit.Normal)
    if ok and password != '':
        new_account = blockchain.create_new_account(password)
        self._addAccountToWindow(new_account, 0, resize_parent=True)
```

Here, we call the create_new_account method of the blockchain object. The address of
the new account will be sent to the _addAccountToWindow method, which will include the
new account information in the vertical box layout.

Next, we use the following code block to copy the address of the account to the clipboard:

```
def copyAddress(self, address):
    QToolTip.showText(QCursor.pos(), "Address %s has been copied to
clipboard!" % address)
    clipboard = QApplication.clipboard()
    clipboard.setText(address)
```

Here, we get the clipboard object and copy the content to it. Consequently, in every piece of
account information, there will a button that is connected to this method. First, however,
we will show the information for this copying action in a tooltip. Qcursor.pos() is the our
mouse's position. The showText method of QtoolTip is used to show the tooltip.

There are four main widgets—the account's address label, the button to copy the address of the account, the balance of this account's label, and the avatar image. To display the avatar image, we can use a label. But instead of the `setText` method, we use the `setPixmap` method, as provided in the following code block:

```
def _addAccountToWindow(self, account, balance, resize_parent=False):
    wrapper_layout = QVBoxLayout()
    account_layout = QHBoxLayout()
    rows_layout = QVBoxLayout()
    address_layout = QHBoxLayout()
    account_label = QLabel(account)
...
...

    avatar.setPixmap(pixmap)
    account_layout.addWidget(avatar)
    account_layout.addLayout(rows_layout)
    wrapper_layout.addLayout(account_layout)
    wrapper_layout.addSpacing(20)
    self.accounts_layout.addLayout(wrapper_layout)

    if resize_parent:
        sizeHint = self.sizeHint()
        self.parentWidget().parentWidget().resize(QSize(sizeHint.width(),
        sizeHint.height() + 40))
```

`setPixmap` accepts the `Qpixmap` object. If `resize_parent` is true, then we will increase the height of the window. We access the main window, which is the tabbed window, with a method called `parentWidget`. This has to be chained and called twice, like `self.parentWidget().parentWidget()`. The first parent widget is the stack view. A tabbed widget is built using the stack view.

Use the following code to call the `kill()` method of the `BalanceThread` instance:

```
def kill(self):
    self.balance_thread.kill()
    sleep(2)
```

This will tell the thread to stop its task.

The next method is used by the thread instance to update the balance:

```
@Slot()
def _updateBalances(self, accounts):
    for account, balance in accounts:
        self.balance_widgets[account].setText('Balance: %.5f ethers' %
balance)
```

`balance_widgets[account]` holds a balance label for a specific account.

Sending a transaction widget

The second widget is `SendWidget`. Create a file named `send_widget.py` inside the `wallet_widgets` directory. This widget is responsible for sending ethers or coins from the ERC20 token. For the full code in this section, go to the following GitLab link: `https://gitlab.com/arjunaskykok/hands-on-blockchain-for-python-developers/tree/master/chapter_09/wallet/wallet_widgets`.

This widget is the most complex in the tabbed window. In this widget, we need to select the account of the sender, and then, based on that account, we need to display the balance of ethers or coins relative to the ERC20 token for this account. Whether or not the balance is displayed in ethers or ERC20 tokens is decided based on whether Ethereum or the ERC20 token is selected in another part of this widget. We also need to add a line edit so people can fill in the destination address. In addition, we need a way to choose the fee because sometimes, people don't mind paying a higher fee so that their transaction is processed faster. Then, there is a button to launch an input dialog that requests the password so we can create a transaction.

To import widgets and classes from the `PySide2` library, use the following code block:

```
from PySide2.QtWidgets import (QWidget,
                               QGridLayout,
                               QVBoxLayout,
                               QHBoxLayout,
                               QPushButton,
                               QLabel,
                               QInputDialog,
                               QLineEdit,
                               QToolTip,
                               QComboBox,
                               QApplication,
                               QSlider,
                               QSizePolicy)
from PySide2.QtCore import Slot, SIGNAL, QSize, Qt
from PySide2.QtGui import QPixmap, QMovie, QPalette, QColor
```

```
from os.path import isdir, exists
from os import mkdir
from tools.util import render_avatar
from blockchain import blockchain, SendTransaction
from wallet_threads.send_thread import SendThread
from wallet_threads.send_token_thread import SendTokenThread
```

We also imported other things as well, such as tools to render an avatar, methods to interact with the blockchain, and the thread classes that create transactions and retrieve information regarding tokens.

Use the following code to initialize the SendWidget class:

```
class SendWidget(QWidget):

    tokens_file = 'tokens.json'

    def __init__(self, parent=None):
        super(SendWidget, self).__init__(parent)

        self.token_name = 'Ethereum'

        self.setupSenderSection()
        self.setupDestinationSection()
        self.setupTokenSection()
        self.setupProgressSection()
        self.setupSendButtonSection()
        self.setupFeeSection()

        self.send_thread = SendThread()
        self.send_thread.send_transaction.connect(self.sendTransactionFinished)
        self.send_token_thread = SendTokenThread()
        self.send_token_thread.send_token_transaction.connect(self.sendTransactionFinished)

        layout = QGridLayout()

        layout.addLayout(self.sender_layout, 0, 0)
        layout.addLayout(self.destination_layout, 0, 1)
        layout.addLayout(self.progress_layout, 1, 0, 1, 2, Qt.AlignCenter)
        layout.addLayout(self.token_layout, 2, 0)
        layout.addLayout(self.send_layout, 2, 1)
        layout.addLayout(self.slider_layout, 3, 0)

        self.setLayout(layout)
```

`tokens_file` holds the `tokens.json` file. This configuration file is the file that contains all ERC20 tokens that we watch. `token_name` is set to `Ethereum` initially because, by default, our cryptocurrency wallet is supposed to handle Ethereum transactions, and not ERC20 tokens. In this widget, we can send ethers or custom tokens. Then, we call six methods to establish six inner layouts. This widget is composed of six layouts. The sender layout is used to choose the account of a sender. The destination layout is a field designed to hold the destination account of the transaction. The progress layout, which is hidden by default, is used to show that the transaction is still being confirmed after just sending the transaction. The token layout is used to choose whether you want to send ERC20 token or ethers. In addition, the send layout is used to hold the send button, and the slider layout is used to hold the slider to choose the transaction fee. We also create two thread instances—the first is used to send ethers, while the second is used to send ERC20 tokens. For the main layout, we use the grid layout. This layout is used because it is easier to lay out our widgets.

The following code block is a method that can be used to set up the sender layout section for creating a transaction widget:

```
def setupSenderSection(self):
    accounts = blockchain.get_accounts()

    sender_label = QLabel("Sender")
    sender_label.setSizePolicy(QSizePolicy.Maximum,
QSizePolicy.Maximum)

    self.balance_label = QLabel("Balance: ")
    self.balance_label.setSizePolicy(QSizePolicy.Maximum,
QSizePolicy.Maximum)

    self.avatar = QLabel()

    self.sender_combo_box = QComboBox()
    self.sender_items = []
    for account, balance in accounts:
        self.sender_items.append(account)
    self.sender_combo_box.addItems(self.sender_items)
    self.sender_combo_box.setSizePolicy(QSizePolicy.Maximum,
QSizePolicy.Maximum)
    self.sender_combo_box.currentTextChanged.connect(self.filterSender)

    first_account = self.sender_items[0]
    self.filterSender(first_account)
    self.setAvatar(first_account, self.avatar)

    self.sender_layout = QVBoxLayout()
    sender_wrapper_layout = QHBoxLayout()
```

```
sender_right_layout = QVBoxLayout()
sender_right_layout.addWidget(sender_label)
sender_right_layout.addWidget(self.sender_combo_box)
sender_right_layout.addWidget(self.balance_label)
sender_wrapper_layout.addWidget(self.avatar)
sender_wrapper_layout.addLayout(sender_right_layout)
sender_wrapper_layout.addStretch()

self.sender_layout.addLayout(sender_wrapper_layout)
self.sender_layout.addStretch()
```

Here, you have a combobox to choose the local account, an avatar image, and a balance label. If you change the value of the combobox, this would automatically change the text on the balance label and the avatar image.

The following code block is the method used to set up the destination layout section:

```
def setupDestinationSection(self):
    self.destination_layout = QVBoxLayout()

    destination_label = QLabel("Destination")
    destination_label.setSizePolicy(QSizePolicy.Maximum,
QSizePolicy.Maximum)

    self.destination_line_edit = QLineEdit()
    self.destination_line_edit.setFixedWidth(380);
    self.destination_line_edit.setSizePolicy(QSizePolicy.Maximum,
QSizePolicy.Maximum)

    self.destination_layout.addWidget(destination_label)
    self.destination_layout.addWidget(self.destination_line_edit)
    self.destination_layout.addStretch()
```

This method mainly holds a line edit. You paste or type the destination's address in this line edit.

The following code block is a method for setting up the token layout section:

```
def setupTokenSection(self):
    token_label = QLabel("Token")
    token_label.setSizePolicy(QSizePolicy.Maximum, QSizePolicy.Maximum)

    token_combo_box = QComboBox()

    tokens = blockchain.get_tokens()
    first_token = 'Ethereum'
    items = [first_token]
    self.token_address = {'Ethereum':
```

```
'0xcccccccccccccccccccccccccccccccccccccccc'}
        self.token_informations = {}

    for address, token_from_json in tokens.items():
        token_information =
blockchain.get_token_named_tuple(token_from_json, address)
        self.token_informations[token_information.name] =
token_information
        self.token_address[token_information.name] =
token_information.address
        items.append(token_information.name)

    self.amount_label = QLabel("Amount (in ethers)")

    token_combo_box.addItems(items)
    token_combo_box.setSizePolicy(QSizePolicy.Maximum,
QSizePolicy.Maximum)
    token_combo_box.currentTextChanged.connect(self.filterToken)

    self.token_avatar = QLabel()

    self.filterToken(first_token)
    token_address = self.token_address[first_token]
    self.setAvatar(token_address, self.token_avatar)

    self.token_layout = QVBoxLayout()
    token_wrapper_layout = QHBoxLayout()
    token_right_layout = QVBoxLayout()
    token_right_layout.addWidget(token_label)
    token_right_layout.addWidget(token_combo_box)
    token_wrapper_layout.addWidget(self.token_avatar)
    token_wrapper_layout.addLayout(token_right_layout)
    token_wrapper_layout.addStretch()
    self.token_layout.addLayout(token_wrapper_layout)
```

This section has an avatar for a token, the combobox to choose Ethereum or other ERC20 tokens, and the total supply of the ERC20 token. If we change the value of combobox, it will change the avatar and the total supply label. The avatar of the token is derived from the address of the token smart contract. However, Ethereum does not have the address, since it is the platform itself. So, for Ethereum, we use the following dummy address: 0xcccccccccccccccccccccccccccccccccccccccc.

The following code block is the method used to set up the progress layout section:

```
def setupProgressSection(self):
    self.progress_layout = QHBoxLayout()
    progress_vertical_layout = QVBoxLayout()
    progress_wrapper_layout = QHBoxLayout()
    self.progress_label = QLabel()
    movie = QMovie('icons/ajax-loader.gif')
    self.progress_label.setMovie(movie)
    movie.start()
    self.progress_label.setSizePolicy(QSizePolicy.Maximum,
QSizePolicy.Maximum)
    self.progress_description_label = QLabel()
    self.progress_description_label.setText("Transaction is being
confirmed. Please wait!")
    self.progress_description_label.setSizePolicy(QSizePolicy.Maximum,
QSizePolicy.Maximum)
    progress_wrapper_layout.addWidget(self.progress_label)
    progress_wrapper_layout.addWidget(self.progress_description_label)
    progress_vertical_layout.addLayout(progress_wrapper_layout, 1)
    self.progress_layout.addLayout(progress_vertical_layout)
    self.sendTransactionFinished()
```

Basically, this is a label used to show that the transaction is being confirmed. In this section, there is a label used to display the loading activity indicator. First, we initialize the QMovie object that accepts a `gif` file. Then, you set this `Qmovie` to a label by calling the `setMovie` method of that label.

The following code block is a method to set up the send layout section of the widget to create a transaction:

```
def setupSendButtonSection(self):
    self.send_layout = QVBoxLayout()
    self.amount_line_edit = QLineEdit()
    self.send_button = QPushButton("Send")
    self.send_button.setSizePolicy(QSizePolicy.Maximum,
QSizePolicy.Maximum)
    self.send_button.clicked.connect(self.sendButtonClicked)
    pal = self.send_button.palette()
    pal.setColor(QPalette.Button, QColor(Qt.green))
    self.send_button.setAutoFillBackground(True)
    self.send_button.setPalette(pal)
    self.send_button.update()
    self.send_layout.addWidget(self.amount_label)
    self.send_layout.addWidget(self.amount_line_edit)
    self.send_layout.addWidget(self.send_button)
```

This section is used to hold a send button, which is connected to a callback. This send button is customized to make it appear more attractive by using background colors. The way you change the color for the button is simple:

Use the following code to get the palette object from the button and then set the color to that palette object:

```
pal = self.send_button.palette()
pal.setColor(QPalette.Button, QColor(Qt.green))
```

Here, we use predefined colors.

The following code block is used to create a slider and a label indicating what value we choose in a slider:

```
def setupFeeSection(self):
    self.slider_layout = QVBoxLayout()
    fee_label = QLabel("Fee")
    self.fee_slider = QSlider(Qt.Horizontal)
    self.fee_slider.setRange(1, 10)
    self.fee_slider.setValue(3)
    self.fee_slider.valueChanged.connect(self.feeSliderChanged)
    self.gwei_label = QLabel()
    self.feeSliderChanged(3)
    self.slider_layout.addWidget(fee_label)
    self.slider_layout.addWidget(self.fee_slider)
    self.slider_layout.addWidget(self.gwei_label)
```

The purpose of the slider is to choose the fee of the transaction. If you choose the bigger fee, the transaction will be processed faster.

The following code block is used to choose Ethereum or the ERC20 token:

```
def filterToken(self, token_name):
    address = self.token_address[token_name]
    token_information = None
    if token_name != 'Ethereum':
        token_information = self.token_informations[token_name]
        self.amount_label.setText("Amount")
    else:
        self.amount_label.setText("Amount (in ethers)")
    self.updateBalanceLabel(token_name, self.sender_account,
token_information)
    self.setAvatar(address, self.token_avatar)
    self.token_name = token_name
```

This is the callback that will be executed if we change the value of the token combobox. We update the balance of ethers or the token of the account here. After doing so, we change the avatar of the token. We also update the total supply of the token.

The following code block is used to choose the sender account:

```
def filterSender(self, account_address):
    self.sender_account = account_address
    token_information = None
    if self.token_name != 'Ethereum':
        token_information = self.token_informations[self.token_name]
    self.updateBalanceLabel(self.token_name, account_address,
token_information)
    self.setAvatar(account_address, self.avatar)
```

This is the callback that will be executed if we change the value of the sender combobox. Here, we update the balance of ethers or tokens of the account and then we change the avatar of the account based on the address.

The following code block is the method used to set the balance of the account to the label:

```
def updateBalanceLabel(self, token_name, account_address,
token_information=None):
    if token_name == 'Ethereum':
        self.balance_label.setText("Balance: %.5f ethers" %
blockchain.get_balance(account_address))
    else:
        self.balance_label.setText("Balance: %d coins" %
blockchain.get_token_balance(account_address, token_information))
```

In this `updateBalanceLabel` method, we set the text for `balance_label` with the `get_balance` method from the `blockchain` object if we are working with Ethereum. If we are working with ERC20 tokens, we use the `get_token_balance` method from `blockchain`.

The following code block is the method used to set the avatar:

```
def setAvatar(self, code, avatar):
    img_filename = render_avatar(code)
    pixmap = QPixmap(img_filename)
    avatar.setPixmap(pixmap)
```

This method is used to set the avatar of both the token and the account.

The following code block is the callback that will be executed when we change the value of the fee slider:

```
def feeSliderChanged(self, value):
    self.gwei_label.setText("%d GWei" % value)
    self.fee = value
```

The following code block is the method that will be executed when we click the **Send** button:

```
def sendButtonClicked(self):
    password, ok = QInputDialog.getText(self, "Create A New
Transaction",
            "Password:", QLineEdit.Password)
    if ok and password != '':
        self.progress_label.setVisible(True)
        self.progress_description_label.setVisible(True)
        tx = SendTransaction(sender=self.sender_account,
                            password=password,
destination=self.destination_line_edit.text(),
                            amount=self.amount_line_edit.text(),
                            fee=self.fee)
        token_information = None
        if self.token_name != 'Ethereum':
            token_information =
self.token_informations[self.token_name]
            self.send_token_thread.prepareTransaction(tx,
token_information)
            self.send_token_thread.start()
        else:
            self.send_thread.prepareTransaction(tx)
            self.send_thread.start()
```

Here, we will be asked to provide the password in an input dialog. If we hit **Ok,** then we will set the progress label and loading activity indicator as visible. We construct a tuple named `SendTransaction` and then send it to the thread class objects that handle sending transactions either for Ethereum or ERC20 tokens. Finally, we run the thread.

The following code block is used to hide the progress label (loading indicator) when the transaction is finished:

```
def sendTransactionFinished(self):
    self.progress_label.setVisible(False)
    self.progress_description_label.setVisible(False)
```

This method will be called by the thread instance after finishing the job (either by sending ethers or coins as ERC20 tokens).

Token widget

The last widget is the token widget. This widget is responsible for watching the ERC20 token. Create `token_widget.py` inside the `wallet_widgets` directory. Go to the following GitLab link provided for the full code file in this section: `https://gitlab.com/arjunaskykok/hands-on-blockchain-for-python-developers/tree/master/chapter_09/wallet/wallet_widgets`.

This last widget is in the third tab of the main widget. The purpose here is to watch the ERC20 token and list all ERC20 tokens that have been watched. There is a button to launch an input dialog, a button to ask for the address of the ERC20 smart contract token, and then there is a vertical layout that displays all ERC20 tokens:

```python
from PySide2.QtWidgets import (QWidget,
                               QGridLayout,
                               QVBoxLayout,
                               QHBoxLayout,
                               QPushButton,
                               QLabel,
                               QInputDialog,
                               QLineEdit,
                               QToolTip,
                               QComboBox,
                               QApplication,
                               QSlider,
                               QSizePolicy)
from PySide2.QtCore import Slot, SIGNAL, QSize, Qt
from PySide2.QtGui import QPixmap, QMovie, QPalette, QColor
from os.path import isdir, exists
from os import mkdir
from time import sleep
import json
from tools.util import render_avatar
from blockchain import blockchain, SendTransaction, TokenInformation
```

As usual, we import many things, such as rendering the avatar tool, the blockchain object to establish information regarding tokens from the blockchain, and a number of libraries to deal with filesystems. On top of that, we also import UI classes from `PySide2`, such as many types of widgets, and classes to attach the callback to widgets. Beside UI classes, we import non-UI classes from PySide2, such as `slot` and `signal`.

Use the following code block for the initialization method:

```
class TokenWidget(QWidget):

    tokens_file = 'tokens.json'

    def __init__(self, parent=None):
        super(TokenWidget, self).__init__(parent)

        self.watch_token_button = QPushButton("Watch Token")

        tokens = blockchain.get_tokens()
...
...

        self.watch_token_button.setSizePolicy(QSizePolicy.Maximum,
QSizePolicy.Maximum)
        self.connect(self.watch_token_button, SIGNAL('clicked()'),
self.watchNewToken)

        layout.addWidget(self.watch_token_button, 0, 0)
        layout.addLayout(self.tokens_layout, 1, 0)

        self.setLayout(layout)
```

In this initialization method, we create a button that is linked to the `watchNewToken` method, and then a vertical box layout to hold all token information. We also declare the `tokens_file` object, which holds the `tokens.json` configuration file. This file keeps track of all ERC20 token-related information.

Use the following code block to create an avatar image, a token name label, a token symbol label, and a token total supply label for each piece of token information:

```
def _addTokenToWindow(self, token_information, resize_parent=False):
        wrapper_layout = QVBoxLayout()
        token_layout = QHBoxLayout()
        rows_layout = QVBoxLayout()
        token_label = QLabel(token_information.name)
...
...
        if resize_parent:
            sizeHint = self.size()
self.parentWidget().parentWidget().resize(QSize(sizeHint.width(),
sizeHint.height() + 100))
```

If `resize_parent` is true, this means we add token information through a dialog. In other words, we ask the parent window to increase its height. If `resize_parent` is `false`, this means that this method is called from the start.

The following code block is a method used to request the address of the smart contract with a dialog:

```
@Slot()
def watchNewToken(self):
    address, ok = QInputDialog.getText(self, "Watch A New Token",
            "Token Smart Contract:", QLineEdit.Normal)
    if ok and address != '':
        token_information =
blockchain.get_information_of_token(address)
        self._addTokenToWindow(token_information, resize_parent=True)
        token_data = {}
        if exists(self.tokens_file):
            with open(self.tokens_file) as json_data:
                token_data = json.load(json_data)
        token_data[token_information.address] = {'name':
token_information.name,
                                                  'symbol':
token_information.symbol,
                                                  'total_supply':
token_information.totalSupply}
        with open(self.tokens_file, 'w') as outfile:
            json.dump(token_data, outfile)
```

If a user confirms the address of the smart contract, we get the token information using the `get_information_of_token` method of the `blockchain` object. This token's information is then put in the vertical box layout. Later, we save the token's information in the json file. This is done so that we can load this token information when we restart the application.

Before you can launch your cryptocurrency wallet, make sure you run a private chain first and then deploy one or two ERC20 smart contracts in this private chain. You can use the ERC20 smart contract source code in Chapter 8, *Creating Token in Ethereum*. After doing this, run the desktop cryptocurrency wallet using the following command:

```
(wallet-venv) $ python wallet.py
```

You will get the final output shown in the following screenshot:

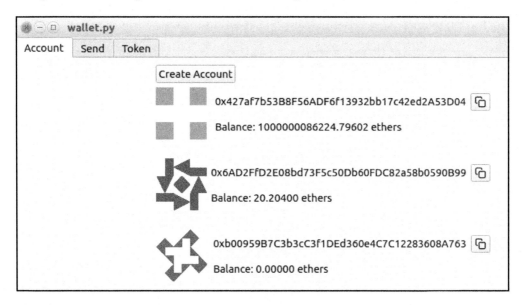

In the preceding screenshot, we see the **Account** tab showing the balance of each account. Make sure you have at least two accounts. If not, create one from this tab by clicking the **Create Account** button.

The following screenshot shows the **Send** tab, where we can send ethers to any account we choose:

In the second tab, try to send ethers. It will take some time before the transaction is confirmed. Consequently, try sending ERC20 tokens to another account (but you have to add the ERC20 token first in the third tab), as shown in the following screenshot:

Finally, in the third tab, try to watch a token smart contract. Put the address of the smart contract address in the dialog when you click the **Watch Token** button:

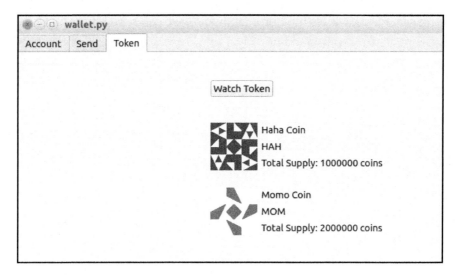

Your token will be reflected in the second tab.

Test

Let's write tests for this GUI application. These tests should not be exhaustive. We will create three tests, one for each tab. We will not create a test for the non-UI part of the application. This section is simply here to demonstrate how to test a UI application.

The first test for the first tab is an account widget test. Name the test `test_account.py` and save it inside the `tests` directory. The following code block is the test script:

```python
import sys, os
sys.path.append(os.path.realpath(os.path.dirname(__file__)+"/.."))

from wallet import WalletWidget
from PySide2.QtWidgets import QInputDialog
from PySide2 import QtCore


def test_account(qtbot, monkeypatch):
    wallet = WalletWidget()
    qtbot.addWidget(wallet)

    old_accounts_amount = wallet.account_widget.accounts_layout.count()

    monkeypatch.setattr(QInputDialog, 'getText', lambda *args: ("password",
True))
    qtbot.mouseClick(wallet.account_widget.create_account_button,
QtCore.Qt.LeftButton)

    accounts_amount = wallet.account_widget.accounts_layout.count()
    assert accounts_amount == old_accounts_amount + 1

    wallet.killThreads()
```

In this test, we test how many children the accounts layout has before we click a button, launch a dialog, fill in a password, and then click **OK**. Then, we check the number of children again after we create a new account. The number should have increased by one. For this test, we patch the dialog to make it easier for testing.

 This test is not comprehensive. We did not test the fail case. I will leave that as an exercise for the reader.

The test for the second tab is a sending transaction widget test. Name the test file `test_send.py` and save it inside the `tests` directory. The test script is given in the following code block (refer to the code file in the following GitLab link for the full code: `https://gitlab.com/arjunaskykok/hands-on-blockchain-for-python-developers/blob/master/chapter_09/wallet/tests/test_send.py`):

```
import sys, os
sys.path.append(os.path.realpath(os.path.dirname(__file__)+"/.."))
from time import sleep

from wallet import WalletWidget
from PySide2.QtWidgets import QInputDialog
from PySide2 import QtCore


...
...

    qtbot.keyClicks(wallet.send_widget.sender_combo_box, second_account)
    balance_of_second_account =
int(float(wallet.send_widget.balance_label.text().split()[1]))

    assert balance_of_second_account - old_balance_of_second_account == 10

    wallet.killThreads()
```

In this test, we check the balance of the second account in the combobox. This second account will be the destination account. Here, we read the balance from the label and then we change the value of the combobox back to the first account, which will be the sender. After that, we set the destination account's address to the destination line edit. We then set the amount of ethers in the amount line edit and click the **Send** button, but remember, we need to patch the input dialog. Finally, we wait around 20 seconds before changing the account combobox's value again to be the second account. We retrieve the balance from the label and then we compare the difference between the old value and the new value, which should be 10 ethers.

The test for the third tab is for testing a token widget. Name this `test_token.py` and save it inside the `tests` directory. The test script for this test is given in the following code block:

```
import sys, os
sys.path.append(os.path.realpath(os.path.dirname(__file__)+"/.."))

from wallet import WalletWidget
from PySide2.QtWidgets import QInputDialog
from PySide2 import QtCore
```

```
def test_token(qtbot, monkeypatch):
    wallet = WalletWidget()
    qtbot.addWidget(wallet)

    old_tokens_amount = wallet.token_widget.tokens_layout.count()

    address = None
    with open('address.txt') as f:
        address = f.readline().rstrip()

    monkeypatch.setattr(QInputDialog, 'getText', lambda *args: (address,
True))
    qtbot.mouseClick(wallet.token_widget.watch_token_button,
QtCore.Qt.LeftButton)

    tokens_amount = wallet.token_widget.tokens_layout.count()
    assert tokens_amount == old_tokens_amount + 1

    wallet.killThreads()
```

First, we load the address of the token smart contract in the address.txt file because we
don't want to hardcode it in the test file. The strategy is the same as in the test of the
account widget. We check how many children the vertical box layout has. After that is
done, we click the button, launch a dialog, fill in the address of the smart contract, and then
click **OK**. Next, we check again how many children the vertical box layout has. The number
should have increased by 1 again.

 Like I said, this test is actually not complete. We should test the token
information as well. However, this test is a good start.

You can run the preceding tests by using the following command:

```
(wallet-venv) $ pytest tests
```

Considerations when building a cryptocurrency wallet

You have now created a desktop cryptocurrency wallet. However, this wallet is not yet complete. A cryptocurrency wallet is a vast topic that changes so often that a book could be written on this topic alone. There are other features you can implement into a cryptocurrency wallet application, such as how many blocks have been confirmed for this transaction. In our application, we only wait for one transaction, but some users may want to confirm a couple of blocks first. If the transaction is confirmed with only one block, there is a slight chance that it could be replaced with a longer block. However, after 12 blocks, the transaction in the block is pretty much secure and irreversible, as explained in the following link: `https://ethereum.stackexchange.com/questions/319/what-number-of-confirmations-is-considered-secure-in-ethereum`.

Our cryptocurrency wallet is a pure cryptocurrency wallet. However, you could also add other features to our cryptocurrency wallet that are unrelated to the wallet functionality. For example, the Mist cryptocurrency wallet is not just a wallet; it is a decentralized application explorer as well. It can also compile a smart contract's source code and deploy it to the blockchain.

There are many features that you should implement if you want to make a fully-fledged cryptocurrency wallet. A number of ideas include generating a QR code, an option to export an encrypted private key, importing a private key, using a seed phrase to generate accounts, the validation of input, and remembering a password for a short period of time.

Here, we are building a desktop cryptocurrency wallet. A desktop application can have the luxury of a lot of memory and storage. However, if you are building a mobile cryptocurrency wallet, this is a different story. For example, a Bitcoin desktop cryptocurrency wallet can access the full node locally. However, you cannot put a full Bitcoin node on a mobile phone as it is just too big. You could, of course, put the full Bitcoin node on the cloud and let the mobile cryptocurrency wallet application access that. However, most people don't want to set up a full node on the cloud. As a result, any developer of a Bitcoin mobile cryptocurrency wallet usually uses **Simplified Payment Verification (SPV)**. In this way, the Bitcoin mobile cryptocurrency wallet does not require a full Bitcoin node to be stored on the phone.

If you want to build a cryptocurrency wallet or contribute to existing cryptocurrency wallets, you need to bear two things in mind: security and the **user experience (UX)**.

Security

A cryptocurrency wallet handles money, so you need to make it secure. Security is a complex topic that we will discuss briefly here.

Don't install a third-party library just because you can; every library is another vector attack. Be conservative in bundling third-party libraries in your application. Our cryptocurrency wallet uses libraries from Ethereum GitHub, such as web3.py and Populus. That should be fine because they are core libraries. We also use the `PySide2` library from the Qt company. This library is a must because without a GUI library, there cannot be a GUI application. We also use a third-party library to generate an identicon avatar image. We need to be careful here. The library is a single file, and I have read it fully to ensure there is no hidden malware. Because of that, I can integrate it confidently into our application.

Use a minimum number of confirmations before declaring that the transaction is complete. How many confirmations is good enough depends on your threat and risk modelling. Usually, 12 confirmations make the reversing transaction impractical. The Mist wallet uses 12 confirmations, while the ZCash wallet uses 10 confirmations.

You could also force the user to create a good password when creating an account in a cryptocurrency wallet, because most users have a tendency to create an account with a bad password. But be careful here; you don't want to annoy them too much.

User experience

If an application is very secure but very hard to use, it is of no use. As a consequence, we need to make it less intimidating for users. The creator of Bitcoin, Satoshi Nakamoto, put a lot of thought into user experience when building the software. Previously, people used base64 format to convert binary to text. However, Satoshi used base58 to represent the Bitcoin address. Base58 is like base64, but without characters that cause confusion when it gets printed, such as I (capital i) and l (lower L).

Zcash has released a UX guide for designing a cryptocurrency wallet, and this can be found at the following link: `https://zcash.readthedocs.io/en/latest/rtd_pages/ux_wallet_checklist.html`. Not everything can be implemented here because Zcash has a private transaction that Ethereum does not have. However, other suggestions can be implemented; for example, market information. Like it or not, people peg the cryptocurrency price to fiat money and it is a good idea to show people what the market price of 1 ether is. If the network is congested, you should inform the user as well. You can suggest that the user waits or increases the transaction fee.

If you build an iOS cryptocurrency wallet, you should follow the Apple Human Interface Guideline. If you are building an Android cryptocurrency wallet, you should follow the Material Design guidelines. Be careful when choosing typography and the color to be used. You should do the user interview when designing a cryptocurrency wallet. UX is a broad subject. Balancing UX and security is a delicate art. You should not ignore UX when building a cryptocurrency wallet.

Summary

In this chapter, we have familiarized ourselves with the tabbed view, size policy, and the grid layout of `PySide2`. Then, we also learned how to test Qt applications. Next, we started to build a desktop cryptocurrency wallet. We divided the application into many parts: the blockchain, the thread, the widget, the identicon tool, and the test. The blockchain part of the cryptocurrency wallet is based on the `web3` and `Populus` libraries and its purpose is to read and create transactions in the blockchain. The thread is a middleman between the UI part and the blockchain object when creating a transaction. The identicon tool is used to create an avatar image based on a specific string (usually the address of the account or the token smart contract's address). The widget part is a tabbed widget that has three tabs. The first tab is the account widget, the second tab is the sending transaction widget, and the third tab is the token widget. Lastly, we created tests for this application.

In the next chapter, we will start learning a topic beyond the scope of blockchain technology. This technology is called IPFS. It is still part of the decentralized technology, but this technology will overcome the weakness associated with the blockchain technology; in other words, its storage is expensive.

Section 5: Decentralized Filesystem

5

This section is an introduction to InterPlanetary File System, where people can store files in a distributed manner. We are also going to build a decentralized Youtube-like application.

The following chapters will be covered in this section:

- Chapter 10, InterPlanetary – A Brave New File system
- Chapter 11, Using ipfsapi to Interact with IPFS
- Chapter 12, Implementing a Decentralized Application Using IPFS

InterPlanetary - A Brave New File System

10

In this chapter, we are going to learn about the **InterPlanetary File System** (**IPFS**). The IPFS is not actually part of the blockchain technology; instead, it complements it. IPFS with blockchain is a match made in heaven. As you have learned in previous chapters, storage in a blockchain is expensive. Usually, people save links to files in a blockchain and save the actual files in normal storage, such as cloud storage. But this strategy suffers the fate of centralization. IPFS offers blockchain developers a way to avoid this.

In this chapter, you are going to learn about the following:

- The motivation behind IPFS
- Merkle DAG
- Peer-to-peer networking

The motivation behind IPFS

IPFS is not a normal filesystem, such as `fat32`, `ntfs`, or `ext3`. It is more similar to Dropbox. It is a cross-device filesystem. You can save a file in this filesystem and people around the world can access it as easily as if the file were on their own computer. If Ethereum can be thought of as the world's singleton operating system, IPFS can be considered as the world's singleton storage!

The slogan of the IPFS website is *IPFS is the Distributed Web*. IPFS tries to replace, or at least supplement, HTTP. The HTTP protocol has served us for a long time, over 20 years, but it is not considered sufficient for upcoming challenges, such as increasing bandwidth demands or redundancy of files. HTTP uses a client-server model. You can only choose one of these two roles: either to be a server or a client.

There are a couple of problems with this architecture:

- The first problem is that to pick up the server role, we have to have sufficient resources. If not, if the server is flooded with a lot of requests, it could go down rapidly. The resources required to handle one million requests per minute is out of reach for many common people.
- The second problem is that the server-and-client architecture is not efficient in some situations. Imagine that you are sat beside a grandma in a park and both of you are watching the same video of a cute panda from the same URL (something like `https://example.com/cute_panda.mp4`). Let's say that the size of this video is 20 MB. This means the server must send a 20 MB file twice to two different locations, even though these two different locations are located closely together with a proximity of one meter. In other words, the server uses 40 MB of bandwidth. Imagine, however, if you could pull the file not from the server, but from the grandma who sits beside you (in this case, let's assume grandma has watched the cute panda video two minutes before you). Wouldn't this be more efficient?

Juan Benet was inspired to build IPFS in late 2013. Back then, he was working with knowledge tools, a term that refers to software that can be used to efficiently gather knowledge from papers. Let's say, for example, that a scientist reads a lot of papers. It would be better if that scientist could get this knowledge faster. Benet came across the problem that datasets required too much effort to distribute. There was no easy way to handle the versioning of datasets. He looked at various tools, such as Git and BitTorrent, and wondered if they could be combined to solve this problem. As a result, IPFS was born. BitTorrent inspired IPFS with regard to distributing files and finding files among the nodes. Git inspired IPFS with regard to keeping the integrity of files and converting saved files into storage.

IPFS is a peer-to-peer hypermedia protocol that makes the web faster, safer, and more open. The goal of IPFS is pragmatic and idealistic. Besides saving bandwidth, another of its aims is to increase the longevity of a file. Keeping a file in a server for a very long time (such as a decade) requires a huge amount of resources. The reason why we might want a file to stay alive is usually because it has some kind of economic benefit for the owner of the server; for example, it could be monetized with ads if it is a blog post. If not, there is a possibility that the file will be destroyed by the owner of the storage server. This happened when Geocities was shut down.

Geocities was a website that allowed people to create their own personal website. It was similar to `wordpress.com` and `medium.com`. Some owners of servers would keep files alive even without ads, like Wikipedia, which works thanks to donations. Other than that, however, the files are not so lucky.

The other goals of IPFS are more idealistic and involved democratizing how we provide content. Right now, content is heavily centralized. We usually go to just a few websites, such as Facebook, Instagram, Reddit, Medium, Netflix, Amazon, Google, Wikipedia, and so on. This oligopoly of information hinders innovation on the internet because information is controlled literally by a few companies. Apart from Wikipedia, most, if not all, companies are beholden to rich shareholders. This situation is in stark contrast to 10 years ago, when the internet was considered a great equalizer of wealth and information, similar to printing press technology.

The other disadvantage of this heavy centralization is that the information that's provided is susceptible to censorship. For example, Google is a company based in Mountain View, California, and is therefore subject to US law. Most people who have the power to make decisions (senior executives and C-levels) are American and therefore have an American bias in their perception of the world. Things that are fine in most countries in Europe could be censored in the name of American morals. This could include content that is disliked by the state because it is considered blasphemous or dangerous. The founder of the IPFS project likened this situation to the case of burning books that were considered dangerous by the state or powerful institutions. One of the goals of the IPFS project was to increase the resistance of documents to censorship. IPFS makes it easier for people to mirror and serve dangerous documents. We'll discuss how IPFS achieves this goal in a later section of this chapter.

The final goal of IPFS, which is more pragmatic, concerns our fragile internet infrastructure, which is composed of computer networks and core routers connected by fiber-optic cables. If the connecting cable is damaged accidentally or deliberately, a block or area could go offline. In 2011, a woman with a shovel damaged the cable that brought internet to Armenia when she was digging looking for metal to sell. The IPFS project does not solve this problem completely, but it can mitigate the damage to some extent.

You can find the incident about the woman and her shovel here: `https://web.archive.org/web/20141225063937/http://www.wsj.com/articles/SB10001424052748704630004576249013084603344`.

Merkle DAG

If you have learned about the internals of Git, Merkle **Directed Acyclic Graph (DAG)** shouldn't be too foreign. As a version control system software, Git is required to keep many versions of a file and distribute them easily to other people. It also needs to be able to check the integrity of the file very quickly.

There are two words that make up Merkle DAG: Merkle and DAG. Let's discuss Merkle first. Actually, the full word of Merkle in this context is Merkle tree. A Merkle tree is a fast way to check whether partial data has been tampered with or not.

Merkle tree

Let's take a look at an example of a Merkle tree in order to understand it. Let's say you have eight pieces of data. In this case, we will use the names of animals for our data, but in Bitcoin, which uses a Merkle tree, the pieces of data are usually transactions. Back to Merkle trees: put the data in order, so in this case, cat is the first piece of data, dog is the second, ant is the third, and so on:

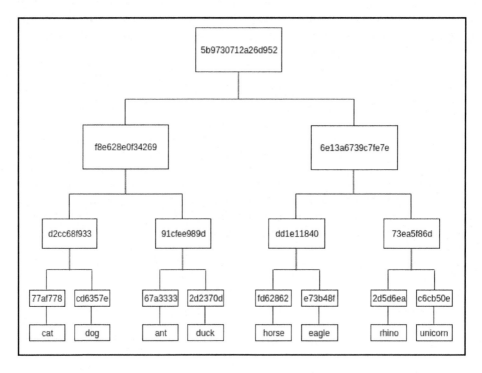

We take the hash of each piece of data, in this case, cat, dog, ant, and so on. For this demonstration, we use the hash function SHA256. Because of limited space, we have truncated the full hash result in the diagram. For now, we will order the data from left to right, so the hash of the "cat" string is Data 1, the hash of the "dog" string is Data 2, the hash of the "ant" string is Data 3, and so on.

Here's come the interesting part. For Data 1 and Data 2, we combine the hash and hash the result. Combining the hash means concatenating it. Do this for Data 3 and Data 4, Data 5 and Data 6, Data 7 and Data 8 as well.

This might remind you of a knockout competition. We are now in the semi-final phase. We now have Hash 1 (from Data 1 and Data 2), Hash 2 (from Data 3 and Data 4), Hash 3 (from Data 5 and Data 6), and Hash 4 (from Data 7 and Data 8).

We then concatenate Hash 1 and Hash 2, hash the result, and name this Hash 5. We then do the same thing for Hash 3 and Hash 4. Name the result Hash 6.

We are now in the final phase. Combine Hash 5 and Hash 6, then hash the result. The result is the Root Hash. This Root Hash can guarantee the integrity of all the pieces of data (from Data 1 to Data 8). If you change any of the data, Root Hash would be different.

You may be asking why we don't just concatenate all the data (from Data 1 to Data 8) from the beginning and then hash the result. It turns out, however, that Merkle trees has some benefits over just concatenating all the data together and then hashing it (this technique is called a **hash list**, and it is used in some situations). One of the benefits is that it is easier and cheaper to check the integrity of the partial data when we use a Merkel tree.

In a Merkle tree, to check the integrity of Data 5, you only need to download Data 5, Data 6, Hash 4, Hash 5, and the Root Hash, as shown in the following diagram. You don't need to download all the data:

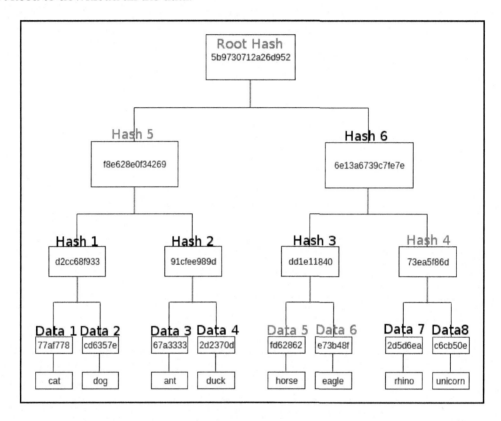

If you use a naive approach, you need to download all the hashes of the data (Data 1 to Data 8) and the Root Hash. In this example, we only have eight pieces of data. Imagine if we had 100 and you had to download the entire dataset. Merkle trees makes this process more efficient because we don't need to download the full set of data.

If we had an odd number of nodes, such as seven, the general rule (the one that Bitcoin implements) is to clone the last node, so Data 8 is a copy of Data 7. You could use another rule, however; I have seen an implementation of a Merkle tree in which a single piece of data (Data 7 in our example) is simply promoted to the top. In this case, Hash 4 is just Data 7.

This is what Bitcoin does when people use Simplified Payment Verification. With a mobile app, downloading the full node is difficult. In order to send Bitcoin transactions, the user downloads only the important parts of the node instead of the full node. Merkle tree enables this process.

In the next section, we will move on to learn about DAGs.

Directive Acrylic Graphs (DAGs)

Directive Acrylic Graphs (DAGs), as its name suggests, are graphs in which each vertex (or node) can have edges pointing to other vertexes, as shown in the following diagram:

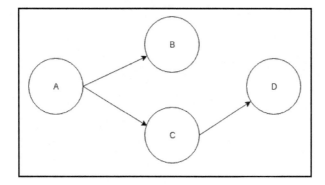

The direction of the arrow does not matter, as long as you make it consistent:

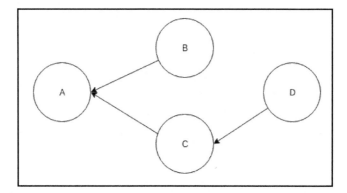

The rule is that these edges should not make a cycle. In the following figure, we can see that vertexes A, C, and D make a cycle, which is against the rules of a DAG:

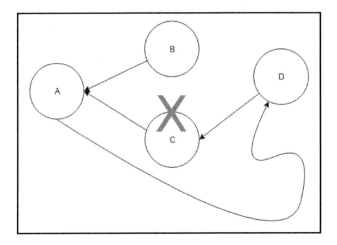

Now, if you combine a Merkle tree and DAG, you get a Merkle DAG. This is the data structure that is used by Git and IPFS.

In a Merkle tree, only the leaf nodes hold data. In a Merkle DAG, however, any node could hold the data. In a Merkle tree, the tree has to be balanced, but there is no such limitation in a Merkle DAG.

Before we jump into Merkle DAGs, let's learn about content addressing, because Merkle DAGs are dependent on this feature.

Content addressing

In a linked list, you chain together nodes (or blocks) with a pointer. A pointer is a data type that points to memory. For example, let's say we have two nodes, node A and node B. Node A is the head and node B is the tail. The structure of the node has two important components. The first component is the data component where you store the data. In Git, this data could be the content of the file. The second component is a link to another node. In a linked list, this is the pointer to a node's address.

But with content addressing, instead of just a pointer, we also add the hash of the target (in this case, node B). You may recognize this concept; this is exactly what happens in blockchain. A Merkle DAG, however, is not a linked list that spans linearly in one straight line. A Merkle DAG is a tree that can have branches.

This is a linked list. It is used in a blockchain's data structure:

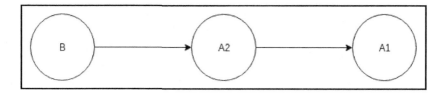

Now, consider this case. We have three nodes: nodes A1 and A2 are both heads that point to node B. Instead of putting the pointers on node A1 and node A2, we put the pointers on node B. Node B now has two pointers. Node B hashes nodes A1 and A2, then concatenates both hashes before hashing the result again. In this way, node B can keep the integrity of the content of node A1 and node A2. If somebody changes the content of node A1 or the content of node A2, the hash kept by node B would be invalid:

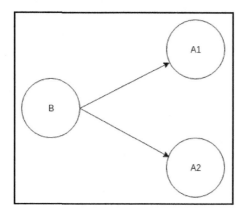

IPFS is different to HTTP in terms of how it fetches a document. HTTP uses links, which work like pointers. For example, let's say we have the following link: `https://example.com/cute_panda.png`. This uses a location to fetch a document called `cute_panda.png`. Only one provider could serve this document, which is `example.com`. IPFS, however, does not use a URL link. Instead, it uses a hash link, such as `ipfs://QmYeAiiK1UfB8MGLRefok1N7vBTyX8hGPuMXZ4Xq1DPyt7`. When you access this hash link, the IPFS sofware will find the document that, when hashed, will give you the same hash output. Because hashing is a one-way function, IPFS must have some other information to locate the document. Basically, it broadcasts the request to nodes that are nearby the document that has this hash output. If the nearby nodes don't have these files, they forward the requests to their nearby nodes. This peer-finding request is quite complex. IPFS uses S/Kademlia Distributed Hash Tables, which we will discuss in a later section of this chapter.

The interesting thing is that when you use content addressing, there may be multiple providers that can serve this document. In the case of the `cute_panda.png` document, there could be more than four nodes that can serve this document. We can pick the nearest node to make the download process more efficient. This property also makes censorship much more difficult. In the case of HTTP, an actor could ban the server `https://example.com`. In the case of IPFS, however, anyone could launch a new node and serve the document. Right now, IPFS is transparent, perhaps too much so. The node that requests the document can see the IP address of the node serving the document, and vice versa. The actor could ban the IP address to forbid this document being spread. The development to make IPFS work with Tor, software that allows users to browse websites anonymously, however, is still in its early days.

If you download a document from `https://example.com/cute_panda.png`, the document that you get at that moment may be different to the document that your friend downloaded from the same URL yesterday. It could be that the admin of the server changed the document before you downloaded it today.

With the content addressing system, however, the document that you get from the IPFS hash link, `ipfs://QmYeAiiK1UfB8MGLRefok1N7vBTyX8hGPuMXZ4Xq1DPyt7`, will always be the same, no matter when or where you download it. This hash link guarantees that nobody can tamper with the document. If you change the document and upload it to IPFS, the IPFS URL or hash would be different.

We can create a simple Python script to illustrate this case. Create a directory called `ipfs_tutorial`. Create three sample files in this directory. The first sample file is `hello.txt`, which has the content `I am a good boy.\n`. The second sample file is `hello2.txt`, which has the content `I am a good girl.\n`. The third sample file is `hello3.txt`, which has the content `I am a good horse.\n`. The fourth sample file is `hello4.txt`, which has the content `I am a good girl.\n`. The fact that the second and fourth files have the same content is deliberate. You can create different files, if you wish, but make sure that at least two of them have the same content.

Create a Python script as shown in the following code block and name it `create_hash_from_content.py`:

```
from os import listdir
from hashlib import sha256


files = [f for f in listdir('.') if 'hello' in f]

hashes = {}
```

```
for file in files:
    with open(file) as f:
        content = f.read().encode('utf-8')
        hash_of_content = sha256(content).hexdigest()
        hashes[hash_of_content] = content

content =
hashes['20c38a7a55fc8a8e7f45fde7247a0436d97826c20c5e7f8c978e6d59fa895fd2']
print(content.decode('utf-8'))

print(len(hashes))
```

This script lists all files in the same directory that have a name that starts with `hello`. You can modify this part if your sample files don't start with `hello`. The long hash is the hash of the content of `hello2.txt`.

When you run the script, you will get the following result:

```
I am a good girl.

3
```

As you can see, there are four files, but the final output is three, not four. This is because there are three files with unique content, not four. This is how content addressing works. It does not care about the filename, it only cares about the content. It doesn't matter whether the file is called `hello1.txt` or `hello2.txt` or `hello4.txt`, it only matters that the content, `I am a good girl.\n`, is the same. Technically speaking, this is a **white lie**; there is a situation when IPFS must consider the filename and cannot ignore it. I'll explain the truth of this matter later in this chapter.

What we have seen in the preceding example is normal hashing. There is no Markle DAG or even Merkle tree. Let's now create a more complicated scene with a big file. Hashing a big file is not efficient. Usually, we split the file into multiple smaller pieces of the same size. For example, a 900 KB file would turn into four files. The first, second, and third files would have a size of 250 KB. The fourth file would have a size of 150 KB. Then, we hash each smaller file and combine it with a Merkle tree.

For illustration purposes, we won't use a large file, but we will make some imaginary limitations. We don't want to hash content that spans more than one line. If the text file has four lines, we would split them into four smaller files.

Inside your project directory, create a file called `hello_big.txt` and enter the following lines:

```
I am a big boy.
I am a tall girl.
I am a fast horse.
I am a slow dragon.
```

Before we create a script to hash this big file, let's create a very simple Merkle tree library and name it `merkle_tree.py`. Refer to the GitLab link for the complete code file: `https://gitlab.com/arjunaskykok/hands-on-blockchain-for-python-developers/tree/master/chapter_10`.

Let's discuss this Merkle tree library, starting from its initialization:

```python
def __init__(self, leaf_nodes : List[str]):
    self.hash_nodes : List[str] = []
    self.leaf_nodes : List[str] = leaf_nodes
    self._turn_leaf_nodes_to_hash_nodes()
    if len(leaf_nodes) < 4:
        self.root_hash = self._hash_list()
    else:
        self.root_hash = self._build_root_hash()
```

We make sure there are at least four nodes. If not, we might as well use the hash list technique. The `leaf_nodes` are original data nodes. They are string lists, such as `['cat', 'dog', 'unicorn', 'elephant']`. The `hash_nodes` are the hash list of the data nodes, such as `[hash of 'cat', hash of 'dog', hash of 'unicorn', hash of 'elephant']` or `['77af778...', 'cd6357e...', 'c6cb50e...', 'cd08c4c...']`.

We use the `_hash_list()` method to hash list the data if there are less than four nodes. We concatenate all the pieces of data before hashing them:

```python
def _hash_list(self):
    long_node = "".join(self.hash_nodes)
    return self._hash(long_node.encode('utf-8'))
```

In the `_turn_leaf_nodes_to_hash_nodes()` method, we fill the `hash_nodes` based on the `leaf_nodes`. This is one-to-one mapping:

```python
def _turn_leaf_nodes_to_hash_nodes(self):
    for node in self.leaf_nodes:
        self.hash_nodes.append(self._hash(node.encode('utf-8')))
```

In the _hash() method, we wrap the sha256 hashing function. This is to make the customization of the class easier, since we may want to use a different hashing function:

```
def _hash(self, data : bytes) > bytes:
    return sha256(data).hexdigest()
```

The following code block shows how we can get the root nodes from the hash nodes:

```
def _build_root_hash(self) > bytes:
    parent_amount = ceil(len(self.hash_nodes) / 2)
    nodes : List[str] = self.hash_nodes

    while parent_amount > 1:
        parents : List[bytes] = []
        i = 0
        while i < len(nodes):
            node1 = nodes[i]
            if i + 1 >= len(nodes):
                node2 = None
            else:
                node2 = nodes[i+1]
            parents.append(self._convert_parent_from_two_nodes(node1,
node2))

            i += 2
        parent_amount = len(parents)
        nodes = parents

    return parents[0]
```

Here, we are carrying out multiple iterations on hash nodes. It jumps two steps on each iteration. For each iteration, it works on two nodes. It concatenates the hash of these two nodes, then hashes the result. The resulting hash is the parent of these two nodes. This parent becomes part of the hash nodes that will be iterated over again. This parent, along with its neighbor, will be concatenated again before being hashed, and so on. If there is an odd number of hash nodes, the last node will be concatenated with itself before being hashed. If there is only one parent, we return the hash of that, which is the **root hash**:

```
def _convert_parent_from_two_nodes(self, node1 : bytes, node2) ->
bytes:
    if node2 == None:
        return self._hash((node1 + node1).encode('utf-8'))
    return self._hash((node1 + node2).encode('utf-8'))
```

The _convert_parent_from_two_nodes() method allows us to get the parent hash from the two child nodes. We concatenate the two nodes and hash them. If the second node is None, meaning there is an odd number of nodes or we are processing the last node, we just concatenate the node with itself before hashing it.

Now that the Merkle tree library is ready, we will create a Python script to hash the `hello_big.txt` file and name it `hash_big_file.py`:

```python
from os import listdir
from hashlib import sha256
from merkle_tree import MerkleTree


hashes = {}

file = 'hello_big.txt'
with open(file) as f:
    lines = f.read().split('\n')
    hash = []
    hash_of_hash = []
    merkle_tree = MerkleTree(lines)
    root_hash = merkle_tree.root_hash

hashes[root_hash] = []
for line in lines:
    hashes[root_hash].append(line)

print(hashes)
```

If you execute this Python script, you will get the following output:

```
{'ba7a7738a34a0e60ef9663c669a7fac406ae9f84441df2b5ade3de1067c41808': ['I am
a big boy.', 'I am a tall girl.', 'I am a fast horse.', 'I am a slow
dragon.', '']}
```

If the file is big, you would not hash it directly, because this could cause you to run out of memory. Instead, you split the file. Here, we split the text file based on the new lines. If you handle the binary file, you read the file chunk by chunk and save that chunk into a smaller file. Of course, before feeding them into a Merkle tree, you need to serialize the binary data into the text data. Once you have done that, you can feed the pieces of data into a Merkle tree. You get the root hash, which will protect the integrity of the original file. If you alter a single bit in a piece of data, the root hash would be different.

The Merkle DAG data structure

We have used content addressing to handle a file. If the file is big, we can split it and get the root hash with a Merkle tree. In this case, we only care about the content of the file; we don't even save its name.

There is a situation, however, where the name of the file does matter. For example, let's say that you want to save a file directory that contains 100 images of cute pandas. The names of the files in this case don't matter; what we care about is the content, the pictures of the cute pandas! If this is a directory of a programming project, however, the names of the files do matter. If one Python file tries to import another Python library that is contained in a different file, we have to keep the name of the file. Let's say that we have a Python file called `main.py` that has the following content:

```
from secret_algorithm import SuperSecretAlgorithm

# execute it
SuperSecretAlgorithm()
```

The `main.py` file is dependent on another file in the same directory called `secret_algorithm.py`. It is not just the content of the `secret_algorithm.py` file that matters, but also its name. If the filename changes, `main.py` will not be able to import the library.

In order to save the content and the filename, we need to use a Merkle DAG data structure. As mentioned before, one of the differences between a Merkle DAG and a Merkle tree is that any node in a Merkle DAG can hold data, not just a leaf node, as is the case in a Merkle tree.

Let's create a sample directory that contains sample files and a nested directory that also contains files:

```
$ mkdir sample_directory
$ cd sample_directory
$ // Create some files
$ mkdir inner_directory
$ cd inner_directory
$ // Create some files
```

Then, create a Python script to explain this new data structure. Create a file called `merkle_dag.py` in your project directory. Refer to the GitLab link for the complete code file: https://gitlab.com/arjunaskykok/hands-on-blockchain-for-python-developers/tree/master/chapter_10.

Let's discuss the `MerkleDAGNode` class, starting from its initialization method:

```
def __init__(self, filepath : str):
    self.pointers = {}
    self.dirtype = isdir(filepath)
    self.filename = Path(filepath).name
    if not self.dirtype:
```

```
                with open(filepath) as f:
                    self.content = f.read()
                self.hash = self._hash((self.filename +
    self.content).encode('utf-8'))
            else:
                self.content = self._iterate_directory_contents(filepath)
                nodes_in_str_array = list(map(lambda x: str(x), self.content))
                if nodes_in_str_array:
                    self.hash = self._hash((self.filename +
    MerkleTree(nodes_in_str_array).root_hash).encode('utf-8'))
                else:
                    self.hash = self._hash(self.filename.encode('utf-8'))
```

The _init_() method accepts a file path as an argument. This could be a path to a file or a directory. We make an assumption that this is a valid path and not a symbolic link. self.pointers will be explained later on in the section with the _iterate_directory_contents() method. self.dirtype is used to differentiate between the directory or the file. self.filename is used to hold the name of the file or the name of the directory.

If the argument is the path to the file (not the directory), we read the content into self.content. For demonstration purposes, we assume the content of the file is small and we don't try to split the files like we did before. Then, we calculate the hash based on the filename and the content.

If the argument is the path to the directory, the content would be an array of MerkleDAGNode objects of the inner files inside that directory. To calculate the hash, we use a Merkle tree to get the root hash of its children. However, we need to concatenate this with the name of the directory before hashing it again:

```
        def _hash(self, data : bytes) -> bytes:
            return sha256(data).hexdigest()
```

_hash() is a wrapper method of the sha256 hashing function.

The _iterate_directory_contents() method is used to iterate over the inner children of the directory. We convert every file or directory inside this directory to a MerkleDAGNode object. The self.pointers object is used to make it easier to access the MerkleDAGNode based on the filename. Basically, it is like a recursive function, especially when we hit a directory:

```
        def _iterate_directory_contents(self, directory : str):
            nodes = []
            for f in listdir(directory):
                merkle_dag_node = MerkleDAGNode(directory + '/' + f)
```

```
            nodes.append(merkle_dag_node)
            self.pointers[f] = merkle_dag_node
      return nodes
```

The `_repr_()` method is used to make it easier to print objects for debugging:

```
      def __repr__(self):
          return 'MerkleDAGNode: ' + self.hash + ' || ' + self.filename
```

The `_eq_()` method is needed so that we can compare the `MerkleDAGNode` object with other `MerkleDAGNode` objects. This is useful during the testing process:

```
      def __eq__(self, other):
          if isinstance(other, MerkleDAGNode):
              return self.hash == other.hash
          return False
```

Let's create a `hash_directory.py` file to demonstrate the power of this data structure:

```
from merkle_dag import MerkleDAGNode


outer_directory = 'sample_directory'

node = MerkleDAGNode(outer_directory)
print(node)
print(node.content)
```

You would get the following result if you execute the script:

```
MerkleDAGNode:
ec618189b9de0dae250ab5fa0fd9bf1abc158935c66ff8595446f5f9b929e037 ||
sample_directory
[MerkleDAGNode:
97b97507c37bd205aa15073fb65367b45eb11a975fe78cd548916f5a3da9692a ||
hello2.txt, MerkleDAGNode:
8ced218a323755a7d4969187449177bb2338658c354c7174e21285b579ae2bca ||
hello.txt, MerkleDAGNode:
c075280aef64223bd38b1bed1017599852180a37baa0eacce28bb92ac5492eb9 ||
inner_directory, MerkleDAGNode:
bc908dfb86941536321338ff8dab1698db0e65f6b967a89bb79f5101d56e1d51 ||
hello3.txt]
```

The output is the schema of the Merkle DAG node.

This is how Git keeps the files. Our implementation is just for education purposes and would not be fit for production purposes. In the real world, you should have many optimizations. One of the optimizations that you could implement is using a reference for the data, just like Git. If there are two different files that have the same content (but different filenames), the content would be saved just once. The other optimization is that Git uses compression. The following diagram illustrates the concept of Git, where we have two files, **file B** and **file D**. These both have the same content, **content xxx**. File B is saved just once in **directory A**. File D is saved at **directory C** with **file E**, which has a different content, **content yyy**. **Directory C** is also saved in **directory A**. But the content of **File B** and **File D**, which is **content xxx**, is saved only once:

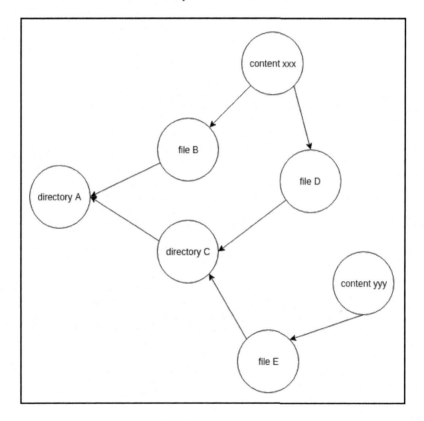

Now that we know how to save a directory of files with Merkle DAG, what if we want to change the content of the file? Should we abandon this Merkle DAG node and create a totally new node? A more efficient way to solve this problem would be to use a versioning system. A file could have version 1, version 2, version 3, and so on. The easiest way to implement versioning is to use a linked list, as illustrated in the following diagram:

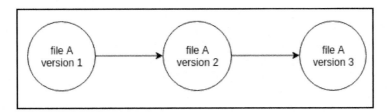

Peer-to-peer networking

We understand how to save files in IPFS. The key is the **hash**. The value is the name of the file or directory and the content of the file or directory. If we were building a centralized system, our story would be finished. We would just need to add a few other things to create a piece of software to save files and search them based on the hash. This software would be similar to a database, such as SQLite or LevelDB. IPFS is neither of those; it is a peer-to-peer filesystem that is like a database but spread all over the place. In other words, it is a distributed hash table.

IPFS uses S/Kademlia, an extended version of Kademlia, as a distributed hash table. Before we discuss Kademlia, let's discuss its predecessor.

First, imagine a hash table, which is like a dictionary in Python, as shown in the following table:

Key	Value
2	Cat
5	Unicorn
9	Elephant
11	Horse
4	Rhino
101	Blue Parrot
33	Dragon

In IPFS, the key is the hash, not a number. But for demonstration purposes, let's make it a simple integer. The value is just a simple name of animal, not the content of the file or the content of the files inside a directory.

Now, imagine you have four nodes. A node could be a computer that is located in a different continent to the rest of the nodes.

Let's define which node holds which keys:

Node	Keys
A	2, 9, 11
B	5
C	4, 33
D	101

You keep this table in a central server. One of the nodes will be the central node. This means that if someone wants to access key five, they have to ask the central server before receiving the answer, node B. After that, the request can be directed to node B. Node B would return "Unicorn" to the data requester.

This method is very efficient; no time is wasted. Napster, the peer-to-peer music sharing system, uses this approach. The drawback is that the central server is a single point of failure. An adversary (someone who does not like this information being spread; in the case of Napster, this could be a big music labels) could attack the central server.

One solution would be to ask all nodes about which node holds the key instead of keeping this information in the central node. This is what Gnutella does. This setup is resilient to censorship and attacks from adversaries but it makes life hard for nodes and people who request the data. The node must work hard when receiving many requests. This setup is called **flooding**. It is suitable for Bitcoin, but not for IPFS.

This is why the distributed hash table technology was created. There are a couple of distributed hash table algorithms, one of which is Kademlia. This algorithm was created by Petar Maymounkov and David Mazières in 2002. It was later used by the eDonkey file sharing platform.

The notion of closeness of data and nodes

In a distributed hash table, we don't put the data in every node. We put the data in certain nodes according to the notion of closeness. We want to put the data in nearby nodes. This means that we have the concept of distance not just between nodes, but also between the data and the nodes.

Imagine that every node launched or created in this distributed hash table is given an ID between 1 and 1000. Every node ID is unique, so there can be a maximum of 1,000 nodes. There are likely to be more than 1,000 nodes in a real-world setting, but this will work as an example. Let's say that we have 10 nodes:

Node ID
5
13
45
48
53
60
102
120
160
220

We also have some data. To make it simple, the data in this case is just some strings:

Data
Unicorn
Pegasus
Cat
Donkey
Horse

To be able to say whether this data is close to or far from certain nodes, we need to convert this data into a number between 1 and 1000. In the real world, you could hash the data. But for our practical demonstration, we will just allocate a random number:

Key	Data
54	Unicorn
2	Pegasus
100	Cat
900	Donkey
255	Horse

If we want to store the Unicorn data in the four nearest nodes (four is just a configuration number), this can be done as follows. First, you check the key, which is 54. Then, we want to get the nearest four nodes to 54. If you check the node ID list, the nearest four nodes are 45, 48, 53, and 60. So, we store the Unicorn data in these four nodes. If we want to store the Cat data, the nearest neighbors from its key, 100, are 53, 60, 102, and 120, so we store the Cat data in these four nodes.

We treat data as a node when calculating the distance. This is how we look up data in a distributed hash table. The data and the nodes share the same space.

XOR distance

However, in Kademlia, we don't measure distance by decimal subtraction. To make it clear, decimal subtraction is just normal subtraction. The distance between 45 and 50 is 5. The distance between 53 and 63 is 10.

In Kademlia, measuring distance is done by XOR distance. The XOR distance between 3 and 6 is 5, not 3. Here's how to count it:

The binary version of 3 is 011. The binary version of 6 is 110. What I mean by binary version is the number in base 2. XOR means *exclusive or*. Using the XOR operation, 1 XOR 0 is 1, 1 XOR 1 is 0, 0 XOR 0 is 0, and 0 XOR 1 is 1. If two operands are same, the result is 0. If two operands are different, the result is 1.

```
011
110
---xor
101
```

101 is the binary version of 5.

The XOR distance has a few useful properties that prompted the author of the Kademlia paper to choose the XOR distance to measure the distance between the nodes.

The first property is that the XOR distance of a node to itself is 0. The closest node to a node with an ID of 5 is another node with an ID 5, or itself. The binary version of 5 is 0101:

```
0101
0101
----xor
0000
```

The 0 distance is only possible if we measure the distance between a node and itself.

The second property is that the distance between different nodes is symmetrical. The XOR distance between 4 and 8 is same as the XOR distance between 8 and 4. The binary version of 4 is 0100 and the binary version of 8 is 1000. So, if we calculate the distance between them using their binary value, we get the same value. The XOR distance between 4 and 8 is as follows:

```
0100
1000
----xor
1100
```

The XOR distance between 8 and 4 is as follows:

```
1000
0100
----xor
1100
```

If you are used to working with decimal subtraction distances, this will be intuitive to you.

The last useful property is that the distance between node X and node Z is less than or equal to the distance between node X and node Y plus the distance between node Y and Z. This last property is important because a node in a Kademlia distributed hash table does not save all the other nodes' addresses. It only saves some nodes' addresses. But a node can reach another node through intermediate nodes. Node X knows the address of node Y, but does not know the address of node Z. Node Y does know the address of node Z. Node X can query the neighbor nodes of node Y from node Y. Then, node X can reach node Z knowing that the distance to node Z is less than or equal to the distance of node X and node Y added to the distance of node Y and node Z.

If this property were not true, the longer node X searches for a node, the further the distance a particular node will be, which is not what we wanted. But with this property, the addresses of neighbor nodes from other nodes may be smaller than, if not the same as, the combined distances.

When you think about using XOR distance, you should think that the more prefixes shared by two numbers, the shorter the distance between those two numbers. For example, if the numbers share three common prefixes, such as five and four, the distance is one:

```
0101
0100
----xor
0001
```

Likewise, for numbers 14 and 15, the distance is also 1:

```
1110
1111
----xor
0001
```

But, if the bit differences are on the left side, such as is the case for 5 and 13, the distance might be large, in this case eight:

```
0101
1101
----xor
1000
```

The XOR distance between 4 and 5 is 1 but the XOR distance between 5 and 6 is 3. This is counter-intuitive if you are accustomed to decimal subtraction distances. To make this concept easier to explain, let's create a binary tree that is composed of numbers from 1 to 15:

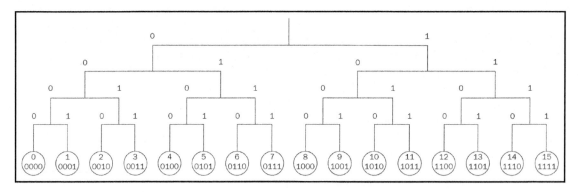

Look at this tree carefully. The XOR distance between 4 and 5 is 1, but the XOR distance between 5 and 6 is 3. If you look at the picture, 4 and 5 are under an immediate branch, whereas 5 and 6 is under a larger branch, which implies a larger distance. The immediate branch corresponds to the bit on the right. The parent branch of that immediate branch corresponds to the second-most right bit. The top branch corresponds to the bit on the left. So, if the number is separated by a top branch, the distance is at least 8. The binary version of 8 is 1000.

This is just for understanding purposes; it is not a rigorous mathematical definition. If you look at the journey from 5 to 11 and 5 to 13, you should get roughly the same distance, but this is not the case. The XOR distance of 5 and 13 is 8 but the XOR distance of 5 and 11 is 14.

In Python, you can XOR two numbers with the ^ operator:

```
>> 5 ^ 11
14
```

You can turn any decimal number to its binary version using the bin function:

```
>>> bin(5)
'0b101'
```

Then, if you want to convert the binary number back to a decimal number, use the int function:

```
>>> int('0b101', 2)
5
```

The second argument of the int function indicates which base the first argument is. Binary is base 2.

Buckets

Now that we have gone through XOR distances, we will take a look at how a node saves other nodes' addresses. A node does not save all other nodes in a distributed hash table. The number of nodes a node can save depends on the number of bits in a node and the *k* configuration number. Let's discuss these one by one.

Remember the tree picture we saw previously? It has 16 leaves. Now imagine the smallest tree:

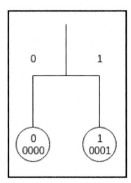

It has two leaves. Let's double the tree:

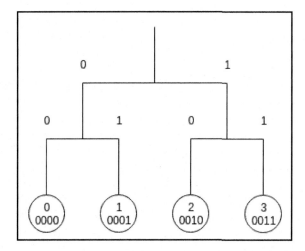

The tree now has four leaves. Let's double it again:

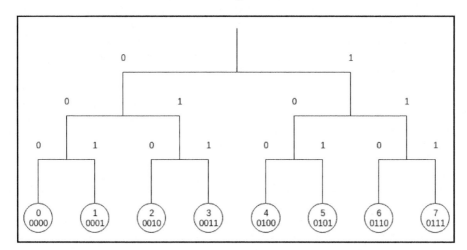

The tree now has eight leaves. If you double it again, you would have a tree like our previous tree, which has 16 leaves.

The progression we can see is 2, 4, 8, 16. If we continue the journey, the numbers would be 32, 64, 128, and so on. This can be written as $2^1, 2^2, 2^3, 2^4, 2^5 \ldots 2^n$.

Let's focus on a tree with 16 leaves. When we represent the leaf number, we must use a 4-bit binary number, such as 0001 or 0101, because the biggest number is 15, or 1111. If we use a tree with 64 leaves, we must use a 6-bit number, such as 000001, 010101 because the biggest possible number is 63 or 111111. The bigger the bit number, the larger the amount of nodes a node must save in its address book.

Then, we have the *k* configuration number. *k* decides the maximum amount of nodes a node can save in a bucket. The number of buckets is the same as the number of bits used in a distributed hash table. In a tree with 16 leaves, the number of buckets is 4. In a tree with 64 leaves, the number of buckets is 6. Each bucket corresponds to a bit. Let's say we have a tree with 16 leaves, so each number has 4 bits, such as 0101 or 1100. This means the node has four buckets.

The first bucket corresponds to the first bit from the left. The second bucket corresponds to the second bit from the left. The third bucket corresponds to the third bit from the left. The fourth bucket corresponds to the fourth bit from the left.

Let's take a look at example of a node with ID 3 in a tree with 16 leaves. For now, we assume we have 16 nodes in a tree that has 16 leaves. In the real world, the tree would be sparse and a lot of branches would be empty.

In the paper that describes Kademlia, the authors used 160 buckets or a 160-bit address. The number of leaves in this tree is vast. For comparison, 2^{78} is the number of atoms in visible universe. The k configuration number is chosen as 20 in this paper, so a node can have a maximum of 3,200 nodes in its address book.

For this example, let's say that the k number is 2. This means for every bucket, the node saves two other nodes. The first bucket, which corresponds to the first bit, corresponds to the other half of the tree, where the node does not reside. We have eight nodes in this half of the tree but we can only save two of them because the k number is 2. Let's choose nodes 11 and 14 for this bucket. How we choose which nodes go in which buckets will be described later.

Then, let's divide the half of the tree where the node resides, so we have two branches. The first branch consists of a node with ID 0, a node with ID 1, a node with ID 2, and a node with ID 3. The second branch consists of a node with ID 4, a node with ID 5, a node with ID 6, and a node with ID 7. This second branch is the second bucket. There are four nodes in this branch, but we can only save two nodes. Let's choose the node with ID 4 and the node with ID 5.

Then, let's divide the branch where our node (the node with ID 3) resides so we have two small branches. The first small branch consists of a node with ID 0 and a node with ID 1. The second small branch consists of a node with ID 2 and a node with ID 3. So the third bucket is the first small branch. There are only two nodes, a node with ID 0 and node with ID 1, so we save both.

Finally, let's divide the the small branch where our node (the node with ID 3) resides so we have two tiny branches. The first branch consists of a node with ID 2 and the second branch consists of a node with ID 3. The fourth bucket, or the last bucket, would be the branch that consists of node 3.

We save this one node because it is less than the k configuration number:

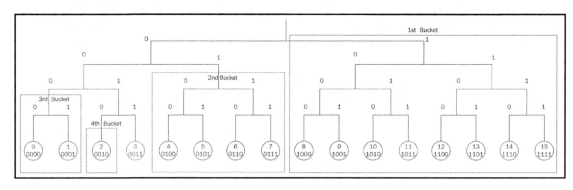

The following diagram shows the full four buckets. Each bucket is half of the branch in which the source node does not reside. The bucket configuration of different nodes are different. The node with ID 11 could have a bucket configuration that looks as follows:

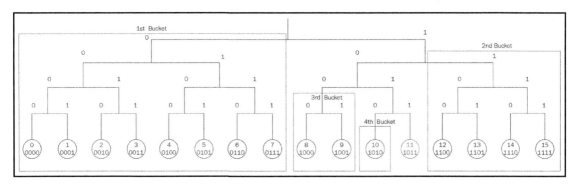

Let's take a look at an example of how a certain node could find another node that does not reside in its address book. Imagine the *k* configuration number is 1. The source node is the node with the ID 3 in a tree with 16 leaves. For the first bucket (the largest branch that consists of the nodes from ID 8 to ID 15), the node with ID 3 saves the node with ID 10. But the node with ID 3 wants to find the node with ID 13. The node with ID 3 contacts the node with ID 10 with a request, "Can you help me find the node with ID 13?". The node with ID 10 has saved the node with ID 14 in its corresponding bucket (the branch that consists of nodes with IDs 12, 13, 14, and 15). The node with ID 10 gives the node with ID 14 to the node with ID 3. The node with ID 3 asks the same question to the node with ID 14, "Can you help me find the node with ID 13?". The node with ID 14 does not have it, but it has the node with ID 12 in its bucket (the branch that consists of the node with ID 12 and the node with ID 13). The node with ID 14 gives the node with ID 12 to the node with ID 3. The node with ID 3 asks the same question again to the node with ID 12. This time, the node with ID 12 can give the destination node or the node with ID 13 to the node with ID 3. A happy ending!

The following diagram shows the nodes:

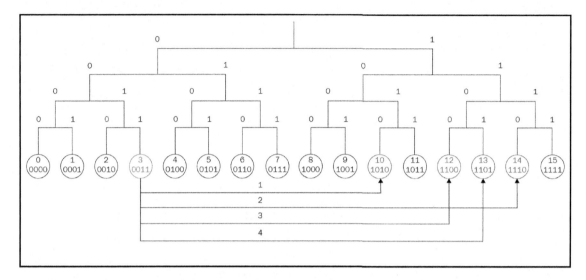

Did you notice how many times the node ID 3 must repeat the request? Four times. If this number sounds familiar, that is because this tree has 16 leaves, which is 2^4. In computer science, the worst case scenario of the amount of hopping required before getting to the destination is $2 \log n + c$. n is how many leaves the tree has and c is constant number.

The tree you have just seen has full nodes; there are no empty leaves or empty branches. In the real world, however, there are empty branches and empty leaves. Imagine that you have a tree with 1,024 (2^{10}) leaves and the k number is 3. You launch the first node with the ID 0. This node will be the source node. We will see the tree from the lens of the node with ID 0:

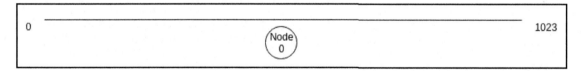

Then, you launch the node with ID 800:

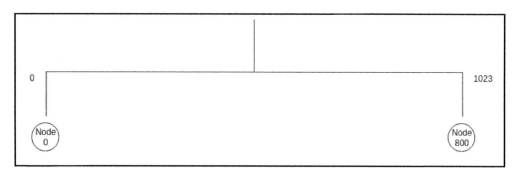

The tree will be split into two buckets. Then, you launch the node with ID 900 and the node with ID 754:

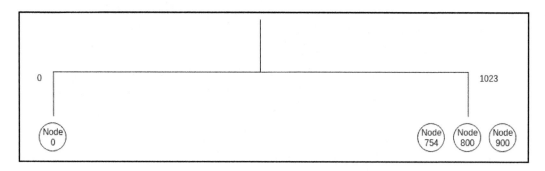

What if we add another node to the bucket? Let's launch the node with ID 1011. The node with ID 0 will ping the least recently used node, which is the node with ID 800, to see if it is still alive. If it is, it will check the other nodes. If the node with ID 754 is not alive, then this node will be replaced with the node with ID 1011. If all the nodes are still alive, then the node with ID 1011 will be rejected from the bucket. The reason for this is to avoid new nodes swamping the system. We assume that the nodes with longer uptimes are trustworthy and we prefer these nodes to new nodes. Let's say we reject the node with ID 1011.

First, we launch the node with ID 490. Then, we split the branch where the node with ID 0 resides:

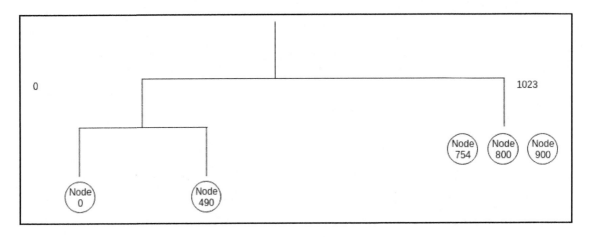

Now, let's add the node with ID 230:

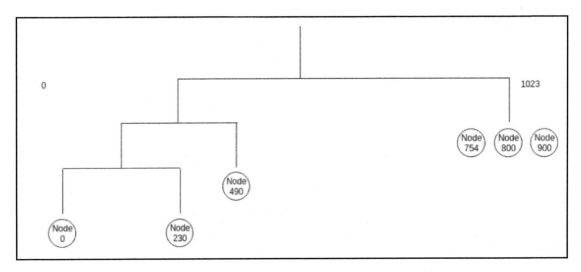

Let's add the node with ID 60:

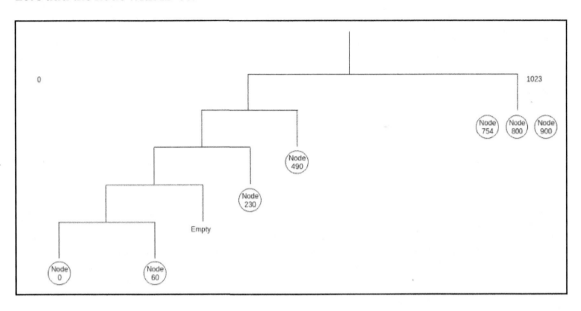

...and so on. Every time we add a node in a branch where the source node resides, it will split the bucket into two until it reaches the lowest level. If we add a node in other branch on which the source node does not live, we add nodes until we reach the *k* number.

You now have a basic understanding of how Kademlia works. This is not, however, the whole story. If a node is inserted, a node needs to tell the older nodes of its existence. That node also needs to get the contacts from the old node. I mentioned that the branch is split when a node is inserted to a branch on which the source node resides, but there is a case where the branch is split even when the source node does not reside there. This happens because a node is required to keep all valid nodes in a branch that has at least *k* nodes if that means the branch in which the source node does not reside has to be split.

There are other important aspects of Kademlia other than routing algorithms. A node is required to republish the key and the value (the data) every hour. This is to anticipate the old nodes leaving and the new nodes joining the system. These nodes are nearer, so they are more suited to keep the data. There is also an accelerated lookup algorithm so that we can use fewer steps when a node is looking for another node.

 You can refer to the Kademlia paper for the full specification. `https://pdos.csail.mit.edu/~petar/papers/maymounkov-kademlia-lncs.pdf`.

IPFS uses S/Kademlia, an extended version of Kademlia. It differs from the original Kademlia algorithm in that S/Kademlia has some security requirements. Not all nodes join the Kademlia distributed hash table with a noble purpose. So, in S/Kademlia, to generate the ID of a node, it requires the node to generate a cryptography key pair, so it is very difficult to tamper with the communication between the nodes. Other requirements include the fact that proof-of-work (like in Bitcoin and Ethereum) is used before a node is able to generate its ID. There is also some adjustment in the routing algorithm to make sure a node can communicate with other nodes in the midst of adversaries, such as nodes that spam the network.

Summary

In this chapter, we have studied IPFS. We started by looking at the motivations of the IPFS project and its history. Although IPFS is not a part of the blockchain technology, it is similar to blockchain because it complements blockchain technology. We then learned about the data structure of the content that we saved in the IPFS filesystem. This data structure is Merkle **Directed Acyclic Graph** (**DAG**), which is based on the Merkle tree. We created simple Merkle tree and Merkle DAG libraries to understand the uniqueness of these data structures. Merkle trees provide an easy way to check the integrity of partial data, while Merkle DAGs are used when we want to save a directory with files and we want to keep the filenames. Then, we learned about the peer-to-peer networking aspect of a Kademlia distributed hash table. The distance between nodes is based on the XOR distance. The nodes also are kept in buckets, which corresponds to bit addressing. Finally, we showed how a node can find others nodes by hopping through the buckets.

In the next chapter, we are going to use the IPFS software and interact with it programmatically.

11
Using ipfsapi to Interact with IPFS

In this chapter, we are going to learn how to interact with IPFS programmatically with Python. There are a couple of interactions that we can do here, such as adding files, retrieving files, hosting mutable files, subscribing to topics, publishing topics, and copying files to the **Mutable File System** (**MFS**). First, we have to install the IPFS software and launch it. Then, we will learn how to install the IPFS Python library and learn about most of its API.

In this chapter, we are going to cover the following topics:

- Installing the IPFS software and it's library
- Content hashing
- The ipfsapi API

Installing the IPFS software and its library

At the time of writing, there are only two IPFS implementations: `go-ipfs` (written in the Go language) and `js-ipfs` (written in JavaScript). There is no IPFS implementation written in Python as of yet. The Go implementation is the more popular one, so we will use that.

Go to, `https://dist.ipfs.io/#go-ipfs`, and download the software for your platform. For Ubuntu Linux, the file is named `go-ipfs_v0.4.18_linux-amd64.tar.gz`.

Extract this using the following command line:

```
$ tar xvfz go-ipfs_v0.4.18_linux-amd64.tar.gz
```

Then, install the binary using the following command:

```
$ cd go-ipfs
$ sudo ./install.sh
```

This step is optional. Here, we export the IPFS_PATH environment variable to our shell:

```
$ export IPFS_PATH=/path/to/ipfsrepo
```

This is where the ipfs stores the files. You can store this statement in ~/.bashrc. By default (without this environment variable), the ipfs would use ~/.ipfs (the .ipfs directory in the home directory) as the place to store data.

After setting up the environment variable, initialize the ipfs local repository. You only perform this step once:

```
$ ipfs init
```

If you run the ipfs in the cloud (such as Amazon Web Services, Google Cloud Platform, Digital Ocean, or Azure), you should use a server profile flag:

```
$ ipfs init --profile server
```

If not, you will get a pesky warning letter from the cloud provider because the IPFS daemon, by default (without a server profile flag), would do something resembling port scanning.

Then, launch daemon, as follows:

```
$ ipfs daemon
```

By default, the API server is listening on port 5001. We will interact with the IPFS programmatically through this port. By default, it only listens in localhost. Be careful if you want to open this port to the outside world. There is no **Access Control List** (**ACL**) in the IPFS. Anyone who has access to this port can upload data to the IPFS.

By default, the Gateway server is listening on port 8080. We download the file from the IPFS peer-to-peer file system using this port. The Swarm, by default, is listening on port 4001. This is how other nodes download the file from our storage. All of these ports can be changed.

The IPFS has a dashboard that can be accessed at the following link: `http://localhost:5001/webui`. The following is a screenshot of the dashboard:

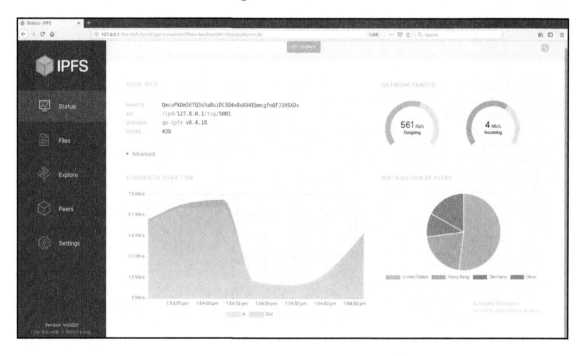

As you can see, most IPFS nodes are located in the US, China, and Germany.

Click on the **Peers** tab to see the distribution of IPFS nodes according to their IP address, as shown in the following screenshot:

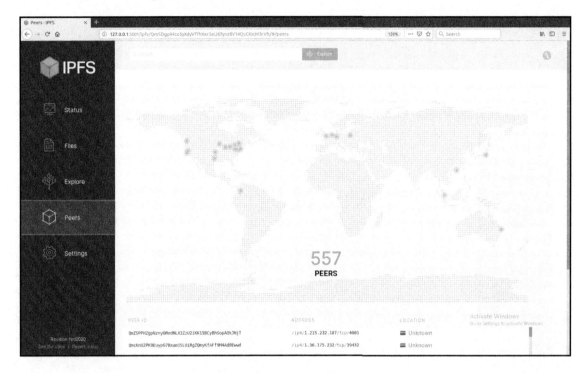

The nodes can be seen in this tab, including their IP addresses. If you are concerned about the privacy of nodes, bear in mind that the development of the privacy feature is still in its infancy.

You can configure the IPFS setting in the **Settings** tab, as shown in the following screenshot:

Now that our IPFS daemon has been launched, let's install our `ipfs` Python library.

Open a new Terminal since we don't want to disturb our daemon. Then, run the following command:

```
$ virtualenv -p python3.6 ipfs-venv
$ source ipfs-venv/bin/activate
(ipfs-venv) $ pip install ipfsapi
```

Previously, the `ipfs` Python library was called `py-ipfs-api`, but it has since been renamed to `ipfsapi`.

Content hashing

In the IPFS quick start documentation (`https://docs.ipfs.io/introduction/usage`), the first thing that they teach you is to download the cute cat picture. Use the following code to do this:

```
$ ipfs cat /ipfs/QmW2WQi7j6c7UgJTarActp7tDNikE4B2qXtFCfLPdsgaTQ/cat.jpg
>cat.jpg
$ eog cat.jpg
```

When you run the preceding code, the cat picture will be downloaded and you will get the following as output:

 `eog` is an image viewer in Ubuntu.

To respect the tradition, let's create a Python script to download the preceding image programmatically with Python and name the script `download_cute_cat_picture.py`:

```
import ipfsapi


c = ipfsapi.connect()
cute_cat_picture = 'QmW2WQi7j6c7UgJTarActp7tDNikE4B2qXtFCfLPdsgaTQ/cat.jpg'
c.get(cute_cat_picture)
```

After executing this script, the image will be named `cat.jpg` in your directory.

As you may have noticed, there is a `cat.jpg` filename after the long hash. Technically speaking, what we are doing here is downloading a file inside a directory that contains a cute cat picture. You can try this if you like. To do so, create another script and name it `download_a_directory_of_cute_cat_picture.py` and then run the following code:

```
import ipfsapi


c = ipfsapi.connect()
directory = 'QmW2WQi7j6c7UgJTarActp7tDNikE4B2qXtFCfLPdsgaTQ'
c.get(directory)
```

After executing this script, you will get a directory named `QmW2WQi7j6c7UgJTarActp7tDNikE4B2qXtFCfLPdsgaTQ` in the directory that contains this script. If you peek inside this directory, you will find the cat picture file.

Let's take a look at the script line by line to understand the usage of the `ipfsapi` library. You can use the following code to import the library:

```
import ipfsapi
```

The following code is used to get a connection object to IPFS daemon:

```
c = ipfsapi.connect()
```

The `connect` method accepts a couple of parameters. The two most important parameters are `host` and `port`:

```
c = ipfsapi.connect(host="ipfshost.net", port=5001)
```

By default, we connect to localhost with port 5001:

```
c.get(cute_cat_picture)
```

Then, we use the methods of the IPFS HTTP API from the *c* object. `get` is one of the methods that's used to interact with IPFS daemon. For this method, there is usually an equivalent argument with the `ipfs` client software:

```
$ ipfs get QmW2WQi7j6c7UgJTarActp7tDNikE4B2qXtFCfLPdsgaTQ/cat.jpg
```

You may notice that we use the `ipfs cat` command in the command-line interface before we created our first Python script. However, in the script, we use the `get` method. There is also a `cat` method in the `ipfsapi` library.

The `get` method is used to download the file, while the `cat` method is used to get the content of the file.

Let's create a script that uses the `cat` method and name it `cat_cute_cat.py`:

```
import ipfsapi


c = ipfsapi.connect()
result = c.cat('QmW2WQi7j6c7UgJTarActp7tDNikE4B2qXtFCfLPdsgaTQ/cat.jpg')
with open('cat.jpg', 'wb') as f:
    f.write(result)
```

The `cat` method returns the bytes object of the content of the file. It accepts two optional parameters, `offset` and `length`. `offset` is a starting position in the file where you want to start to get the content. `length` is the length of the content you want to get starting from the `offset` position. These parameters are important if you want to build a download manager (with pausing and resuming capabilities) or a video streaming player. You may not always want to download the whole file.

Now, let's add a file to the IPFS. To do this, create a simple file and name it `hello.txt`. This is the content of the file:

```
I am a good unicorn.
```

Make sure you have a new line after the string:

```
$ cat hello.txt
I am a good unicorn.
$
```

If the command prompt comes after the line of the string, then all is well. You can carry on.

However, Let's say the command prompt comes on the right of the string, as shown in the following code block:

```
$ cat hello.txt
I am a good unicorn.$
```

This means you don't have the new line and you need to add this after the string.

Now, let's create a script to add this file to the IPFS and name it `add_file.py`:

```
import ipfsapi


c = ipfsapi.connect()
result = c.add('hello.txt')
print(result)
```

Executing this code will give you the following output:

```
(ipfs-venv) $ python add_file.py
{'Name': 'hello.txt', 'Hash':
'QmY7MiYeySnsed1Z3KxqDVYuM8pfiT5gGTqprNaNhUpZgR', 'Size': '29'}
```

We can retrieve the content of the file, which is I am a good unicorn.\n, by using the cat or get method. Let's use the cat method in the script named get_unicorn.py, as given in the following code block:

```
import ipfsapi


c = ipfsapi.connect()
result = c.cat('QmY7MiYeySnsed1Z3KxqDVYuM8pfiT5gGTqprNaNhUpZgR')
print(result)
```

Running this will give you the following output:

```
(ipfs-venv) $ python get_unicorn.py
b'I am a good unicorn.\n'
```

As we mentioned in Chapter 10, *InterPlanetary – A Brave New File System*, we get the content of the file through the hash. Through this, we only retrieve the content, not the name of the file.

But how do you turn b'I am a good unicorn.\n' into 'QmY7MiYeySnsed1Z3KxqDVYuM8pfiT5gGTqprNaNhUpZgR'? Is it just by hashing the content? For example, to hash the content of the file, you could use the SHA-256 hash function:

```
import hashlib
the_hash = hashlib.sha256(b'I am a good unicorn.\n').hexdigest()
```

Not so fast! It turns out you need to learn about protobuf, multihash, and base58 first to understand the process. Let's discuss these in the following sections.

Protobuf

If you have tried to install Google open source software such as Tensorflow, you would encounter protobuf because it is used by Tensorflow. Protobuf is a serialization library. If you learned about Python from the official documentation, you would know that Pickle as a way to serialize data. If you learned about web development programming, most likely, you would use .json or .xml as data serialization.

Before we pass `b'I am a good unicorn.\n'` to the IPFS, we wrap our data in a data structure. Let's create a script to prove my claim and name the script `get_unicorn_block.py`:

```
import ipfsapi


c = ipfsapi.connect()
result = c.block_get('QmY7MiYeySnsed1Z3KxqDVYuM8pfiT5gGTqprNaNhUpZgR')
print(result)
```

Running the script will allow you to see that the content of the file is wrapped by other stuff:

```
(ipfs-venv) $ python get_unicorn_block.py
b'\n\x1b\x08\x02\x12\x15I am a good unicorn.\n\x18\x15'
```

We can see that we still have our content of the file intact, `b'I am a good unicorn.\n'`, between the cryptic strings. What are the junk characters on the left and on the right? This is the data structure of a data node in the IPFS.

Before we unserialize this serialized data, let's quickly learn how to use `protobuf`:

1. Install the `protobuf-compiler` using the following command:

   ```
   $ sudo apt-get install protobuf-compiler
   ```

   Your `protobuf` compiler is `protoc`:

   ```
   $ protoc --version
   libprotoc 2.6.1
   ```

2. Then, let's install the Python `protobuf` library using the following command:

   ```
   (ipfs-venv) $ pip install protobuf
   ```

3. Before serializing data with `protobuf`, you need to create a data structure format first. The format must be saved in a file. Let's name the format file `crypto.proto` and use the following script:

   ```
   syntax = "proto2";

   package crypto;

   message CryptoCurrency {
     required string name = 1;
     optional int32 total_supply = 2;
   ```

```
enum CryptoType {
BITCOIN = 0;
ERC20 = 1;
PRIVATE = 2;
} required CryptoType type = 3 [default = ERC20];
}
```

When you look at this data structure, it's like a struct or class without methods. After declaring the syntax you use, you declare the `package` to avoid a name collision. `message` is just like a class or struct keyword in another mainstream programming language. This `message` is an encapsulation of many data types. In our case, they are `string`, `int32`, and `enum`.

4. Before we can serialize data with protobuf in Python, we need to convert this `.proto` file into a Python module file:

   $ protoc crypto.proto --python_out=.

The `python_out` parameter is used to indicate in which directory you want to output this Python file.

You should get the `crypto_pb2.py` file generated for you. Refer to the code file in GitLab link for the script: https://gitlab.com/arjunaskykok/hands-on-blockchain-for-python-developers/tree/master/chapter_11.

If you did not read the comment on the top of the file, let me read it for you: Do not edit the file directly. If you want to change the data structure in a serialization process, you modify the `.proto` file and then compile it. Now that you have this `Python` library file generated for you, you can throw away the `.proto` file. However, it's a good idea to keep it for documentation.

Now, let's test the serialization and unserialization processes with a Python script. Name the script `serialize_crypto_data.py`:

```
import crypto_pb2

cryptocurrency = crypto_pb2.CryptoCurrency()
cryptocurrency.name = 'Bitcoin Cash'
cryptocurrency.total_supply = 21000000
cryptocurrency.type = crypto_pb2.CryptoCurrency.BITCOIN

serialized_data = cryptocurrency.SerializeToString()
print(serialized_data)

cryptocurrency2 = crypto_pb2.CryptoCurrency()
```

```
cryptocurrency2.ParseFromString(serialized_data)
print(cryptocurrency2)
```

If you execute the script, you will get the following output:

```
(ipfs-venv) $ python serialize_crypto_data.py
b'\n\x0cBitcoin Cash\x10\xc0\xde\x81\n\x18\x00'
name: "Bitcoin Cash"
total_supply: 21000000
type: BITCOIN
```

The serialized output, b'\n\x0cBitcoin Cash\x10\xc0\xde\x81\n\x18\x00', resembles our unicorn data block in the IPFS. If you parse this binary data, you should get the original Python object.

Now that you understand the basic usage of protobuf, let's get back to our block data in the IPFS:

```
(ipfs-venv) $ python get_unicorn_block.py
b'\n\x1b\x08\x02\x12\x15I am a good unicorn.\n\x18\x15'
```

This is the serialized data in protobuf. Before we unserialize it, we need to get the related .proto files. Apparently, we need two .proto files, unixfs.proto and merkledag.proto.

unixfs.proto can be downloaded from https://github.com/ipfs/go-unixfs/blob/master/pb/unixfs.proto, while merkeldag.proto can be downloaded from https://github.com/ipfs/go-merkledag/blob/master/pb/merkledag.proto.

The following code block is the content of the unixfs.proto file:

```
syntax = "proto2";

package unixfs.pb;

message Data {
    enum DataType {
        Raw = 0;
        Directory = 1;
        File = 2;
        Metadata = 3;
        Symlink = 4;
        HAMTShard = 5;
    }

    required DataType Type = 1;
    optional bytes Data = 2;
```

```
        optional uint64 filesize = 3;
        repeated uint64 blocksizes = 4;

        optional uint64 hashType = 5;
        optional uint64 fanout = 6;
    }

    message Metadata {
        optional string MimeType = 1;
    }
```

The following code block is the content of the `merkledag.proto` file:

```
    package merkledag.pb;

    import "code.google.com/p/gogoprotobuf/gogoproto/gogo.proto";

    option (gogoproto.gostring_all) = true;
    option (gogoproto.equal_all) = true;
    option (gogoproto.verbose_equal_all) = true;
    option (gogoproto.goproto_stringer_all) = false;
    option (gogoproto.stringer_all) =  true;
    option (gogoproto.populate_all) = true;
    option (gogoproto.testgen_all) = true;
    option (gogoproto.benchgen_all) = true;
    option (gogoproto.marshaler_all) = true;
    option (gogoproto.sizer_all) = true;
    option (gogoproto.unmarshaler_all) = true;


    . . .
    . . .


    // An IPFS MerkleDAG Node
    message PBNode {

      // refs to other objects
      repeated PBLink Links = 2;

      // opaque user data
      optional bytes Data = 1;
    }
```

To simplify the process, you should remove the following lines in the `merkledag.proto` file:

```
    import "code.google.com/p/gogoprotobuf/gogoproto/gogo.proto";

    option (gogoproto.gostring_all) = true;
```

```
option (gogoproto.equal_all) = true;
option (gogoproto.verbose_equal_all) = true;
option (gogoproto.goproto_stringer_all) = false;
option (gogoproto.stringer_all) =  true;
option (gogoproto.populate_all) = true;
option (gogoproto.testgen_all) = true;
option (gogoproto.benchgen_all) = true;
option (gogoproto.marshaler_all) = true;
option (gogoproto.sizer_all) = true;
option (gogoproto.unmarshaler_all) = true
```

Then, compile both .proto files using the following command:

```
$ protoc unixfs.proto merkledag.proto --python_out=.
```

After doing this, you will get the unixfs_pb2.py and merkledag_pb2.py files that were generated as the output.

Let's create a script to decode our block data, b'\n\x1b\x08\x02\x12\x15I am a good unicorn.\n\x18\x15', and name the script unserialize_unicorn.py:

```python
import unixfs_pb2
import merkledag_pb2

outer_node = merkledag_pb2.PBNode()
outer_node.ParseFromString(b'\n\x1b\x08\x02\x12\x15I am a good
unicorn.\n\x18\x15')
print(outer_node)

unicorn = unixfs_pb2.Data()
unicorn.ParseFromString(outer_node.Data)
print(unicorn)
```

Run the script. This will give you the following output:

```
(ipfs-venv) $ python unserialize_unicorn.py
Data: "\010\002\022\025I am a good unicorn.\n\030\025"

Type: File
Data: "I am a good unicorn.\n"
filesize: 21
```

Let's dissect what's happening here. Our original data, `b'I am a good unicorn.\n'`, is wrapped in `Data` from the `unixfs` proto module, and is then wrapped again in `PBNode` from the `merkledag` proto module. That's why we unserialize the serialized data in the script with `PBNode` first. Then, we unserialize the result with `Data`.

Multihash

Now, let's hash the serialized data. IPFS uses multihash to hash the data. This means it is not just outputting the hash output, but it also outputs the hash function that it uses, the length of the hash output from that hash function, and the hash output from that hash function.

Let's take a look at an example of the usage of multihash. Suppose the data that we want to hash is `b'i love you'`. We choose `sha256` as a hash function, as follows:

```
>>> from hashlib import sha256
>>> sha256(b'i love you').hexdigest()
'1c5863cd55b5a4413fd59f054af57ba3c75c0698b3851d70f99b8de2d5c7338f'
```

Let's check out the length of this hash output:

```
>>> len('1c5863cd55b5a4413fd59f054af57ba3c75c0698b3851d70f99b8de2d5c7338f')
64
```

Since a number in hexadecimal format always takes two characters, the length of the hash output is 32 (64 / 2). However, we want the hexadecimal version of 32, which is 0x20 or `20`.

 There is a hash function table that lists all hash functions that multihash supports (sha1, shake, blake, keccak, and so on). This can be seen here: https://github.com/multiformats/multicodec/blob/master/table.csv.

As you can see, `sha256` is given the number `12`.

Now, we combine them using the following command:

```
Hash function + the length of hash output from hash function + hash output
from hash function
12 + 20 + 1c5863cd55b5a4413fd59f054af57ba3c75c0698b3851d70f99b8de2d5c7338f
```

Alternatively, we can use the following command:

```
12201c5863cd55b5a4413fd59f054af57ba3c75c0698b3851d70f99b8de2d5c7338f
```

Let's do this again, but using another function, which is `sha1`:

```
>>> from hashlib import sha1
>>> sha1(b'i love you').hexdigest()
'bb7b1901d99e8b26bb91d2debdb7d7f24b3158cf'
>>> len('bb7b1901d99e8b26bb91d2debdb7d7f24b3158cf')
40
```

The hex version of 20 (40 / 2) is 0x14, or `14`.

The `sha1` hash function is given the number 0x11 or `11` from the hash functions table. Hence, the output is as follows:

```
11 + 14 + bb7b1901d99e8b26bb91d2debdb7d7f24b3158cf
1114bb7b1901d99e8b26bb91d2debdb7d7f24b3158cf
```

So, why would you want to use multihash and not just a normal hash function, such as `sha1`, `sha256`, or `keccak256`? The argument is sometimes that the hash function is broken, meaning that someone could find two different inputs with the same hash output in a reasonable time. If this happens, it is very dangerous. Hashing is used for integrity checks. Imagine I sent you a secret document to create a cure for cancer. To make sure it is not tampered with, we hash this document and then broadcast the hash output. Consequently, anyone who wants to learn this document needs to verify the hash of the document first before reading and executing it. However, imagine my enemy could create a different document. Now, instead of a cure for cancer, this document is a guide to creating a virus, but it still has the same hash output. If you hash the wrong document, you will innocently execute the file and create the virus.

If a hash function is broken (and it happened, the `sha1` hash function is already broken), programmers need to upgrade their system. However, they will encounter difficulties because usually, they make assumptions regarding the hash function. For example, if they use the `sha1` function, they would expect the output from the hash function to be 20 numbers in length. If they choose to upgrade the hash function to `sha256`, they need to replace all the code that anticipates a length of 20 characters when dealing with the old hash function, which is cumbersome.

With `multihash`, we expect the upgrade process to be simplified because the function and the length of the output of the hash function is embedded in the output of the `multihash` function. We no longer make assumptions regarding the length of hashing output.

If you still cannot get your head around the motivation of `multihash`, let's experiment with it using the following code:

```
(ipfs-venv) $ pip install pymultihash
(ipfs-venv) $ python
>>> import multihash
>>> the_universal_hash = multihash.digest(b'i love you', 'sha1')
>>> the_universal_hash.verify(b'i love you')
True
```

Did you observe that when we want to check the integrity of the `b'i love you'` data, we don't make assumptions regarding the length of the hash output? We then discovered the bad news that the `sha1` hash function is broken. To upgrade our system, what we need to do is merely replace the `'sha1'` string with the `'sha2_256'` string:

```
>>> the_universal_hash = multihash.digest(b'i love you', 'sha2_256')
>>> the_universal_hash.verify(b'i love you')
True
```

By using multihash, upgrading the hash function in the IPFS software becomes an easy task. The hash function is just a matter of configuration.

Base58

The last thing we need to learn is `base58`. Base58 is a modified version of `base64`. This is usually used to encode the binary data as an ASCII string. The following code block is used to encode `b'i love you'` as an ASCII string:

```
>>> import base64
>>> base64.b64encode(b'i love you')
b'aSBsb3ZlIHlvdQ=='
```

The `base64` module is part of the Python standard library.

Usually, you will not encode another ASCII string with `base64`. Instead, you will encode binary data, such as an image file. If you open `cat.jpg` with the text editor, you would get gibberish text similar to the text that's shown in the following screenshot:

This is a perfect example of encoding with `base64`. Why would you want to encode binary data with `base64`? One of the use cases is if you want to attach a cute cat picture in an email to your friend. Email protocol does not allow binary data. The following code block shows what the result will be if we attach the picture:

```
>>> c = None
>>> with open('cat.jpg', 'rb') as f:
...     c = f.read()
...
>>> import base64
>>> base64.b64encode(c)
```

b'/9j/4AAQSkZJRgABAQIAJQAlAAD/2wBDAAEBAQEBAQEBAQEBAQEBAQEBAQEBAQEBA
QEBAQEBAQEBAQEBAQEBAQEBAQEBAQEBAQEBAQEBAQH/2wBDAQEBAQEBAQEBAQEBAQEB
AQEBAQEBAQEBAQEBAQEBAQEBAQEBAQEBAQEBAQEBAQEBAQEBAQEBAQEBAQH/wAARCAMgBQA
DASIAAhEBAxEB/8QAHwAAAAYDAQEBAAAAAAAAAAAAQFBgcIAgMJCgEL/8QAbhAAAAQCBgQJCA

YHBQQGBQIXAgMEBQEGAAcREhMhFCMxQQgiJDNRYXGB8BUyNEORobHBQkRT0eHxCRYlUlRjczViZ
HSDF3KEkyZFgpSjszZVZZKkw9MKGHWitMRWhdTj5Eay8xkndoaVlsLS4v/EABwBAAAEFAQEBAAAA
AAAAAAAAAACAwQFBgcBCP/EAEwRAAAEBAIIBAUDAgQFAgUCBwECAxEABCExQVEEEhBhcYGR8KKG
xwdEGFCIj4TIz8SRDBxVCUzREUmJjFnNUco............s0fQyVCRRbpSW0yyylf5pKJGnOLT1
ixICLAcYL6fZ25/hSCW3hIrDGFOwjWKFEvluXlXQ8Mosvyoe Vg4umYFuP8AV4psrOiyiO8V8M5x
Bw1BwcG8WAJeNhmW5/du25QypGNKzQKJcAEXxthvCtWiuBRPVVA9twcApcfLHKP/2Q=='

The process of encoding with `base64` (how you turn `b'i love you'` into `b'aSBsb3ZlIHlvdQ=='`) is beyond the scope of this book. You can look into the `base64` specification if you are curious enough.

Now that you are familiar with `base64`, `base58` will be very simple. In `base58` encoding, the ambiguous letters when printed, such as 0, O, I, and l, are removed. The + (plus) and / (slash) characters are also removed. This `base58` encoding was designed by Satoshi Nakamoto to encode large integers. A Bitcoin address is just a very large integer in a nutshell. If you have ever transferred any amount in cryptocurrency (not necessarily Bitcoin), you would most likely have double checked the address to make sure the address is correct. For example, you want to transfer 1 Bitcoin to your grandma's Bitcoin address, and her address is `1BvBMSEYstWetqTFn5Au4m4GFg7xJaNVN2`. If you are like most people, you would verify the correctness of the address a couple of times to make sure the address is not incorrect. By removing ambiguous characters such as 0, O, I, and l, you would find it easier to make sure this address is what it is supposed to be. Base58 is one of the good UX designs in software that is used to solve this problem.

So, `base58` is not designed to encode a cute cat picture. You would use `base64` encoding for that purpose.

Let's install the `base58` library to experiment with it:

```
>>> import base58
>>> base58.b58encode(b'i love you')
b'6uZUjTpoUEryQ8'
```

By using `base58`, we can create a long hexadecimal string that can be checked and verified with ease using our own eyes.

Combining protobuf, multihash, and base58

Now that you have learned about protobuf, multihash, and base58, we can finally make sense of the puzzle of how the content of the `b'I am a good unicorn.\n'` file turned into `'QmY7MiYeySnsed1Z3KxqDVYuM8pfiT5gGTqprNaNhUpZgR'`.

The b'I am a good unicorn.\n' data is wrapped in an IPFS node and serialized with protobuf into b'\n\x1b\x08\x02\x12\x15I am a good unicorn.\n\x18\x15'. Here's how to do it in Python.

Create a script and name it serialize_unicorn.py:

```
import unixfs_pb2
import merkledag_pb2

precious_data = b'I am a good unicorn.\n'

unicorn = unixfs_pb2.Data()
unicorn.Type = unixfs_pb2.Data.File
unicorn.Data = precious_data
unicorn.filesize = len(precious_data)

serialized_unicorn_node = unicorn.SerializeToString()

outer_node = merkledag_pb2.PBNode()
outer_node.Data = serialized_unicorn_node
print(outer_node.SerializeToString())
```

Run it. You should get the following output:

```
(ipfs-venv) $ python serialize_unicorn.py
b'\n\x1b\x08\x02\x12\x15I am a good unicorn.\n\x18\x15'
```

Then, this protobuf-serialized data is hashed with sha256 (the multihash in the IPFS uses the sha256 hashing function by default) into '912d1af8f0013cd12a514859d20e9a196eb2845981408a84cf3543bb359a4536'.

Here's how to do it in Python:

```
>>> import hashlib
>>> hashlib.sha256(b'\n\x1b\x08\x02\x12\x15I am a good
unicorn.\n\x18\x15').hexdigest()
'912d1af8f0013cd12a514859d20e9a196eb2845981408a84cf3543bb359a4536'
```

The number of sha256 functions in the multihash table used by the IPFS is 12. The table can be seen here: https://github.com/multiformats/multicodec/blob/master/table.csv.

The length of the hash output is 32, or 0x20 in hexadecimal. One hex number occupies two characters:

```
>>> len('912d1af8f0013cd12a514859d20e9a196eb2845981408a84cf3543bb359a4536')
// 2
32
>>> hex(32)
'0x20'
```

Let's concatenate them:

```
12 + 20 + 912d1af8f0013cd12a514859d20e9a196eb2845981408a84cf3543bb359a4536
1220912d1af8f0013cd12a514859d20e9a196eb2845981408a84cf3543bb359a4536
```

If you encode this output in base58 encoding, you should get
`'QmY7MiYeySnsed1Z3KxqDVYuM8pfiT5gGTqprNaNhUpZgR'`.

Here's how you do it in Python. The `b58encode()` method only accepts byte objects, not hexadecimal objects, so you have to convert hexadecimal string into byte objects first:

```
>>> import codecs
>>>
codecs.decode('1220912d1af8f0013cd12a514859d20e9a196eb2845981408a84cf3543bb
359a4536', 'hex')
b'\x12 \x91-
\x1a\xf8\xf0\x01<\xd1*QHY\xd2\x0e\x9a\x19n\xb2\x84Y\x81@\x8a\x84\xcf5C\xbb5
\x9aE6'
```

`codecs` is part of the Python standard library.

Upon executing the code, you will get the following output:

```
>>> base58.b58encode(b'\x12 \x91-
\x1a\xf8\xf0\x01<\xd1*QHY\xd2\x0e\x9a\x19n\xb2\x84Y\x81@\x8a\x84\xcf5C\xbb5
\x9aE6')
b'QmY7MiYeySnsed1Z3KxqDVYuM8pfiT5gGTqprNaNhUpZgR'
```

Voilà! The puzzle has finally been solved.

The ipfsapi API

Let's go back to the API of ipfsapi. We have added a file with IPFS API and received the hash that we use to refer to the content of the file. But if we add a big file, this will be split into many chunks. This is for efficiency purposes.

Let's download quite a big image file from Unsplash. Go to, `https://unsplash.com/photos/UBtUB4Qc-_4` to download an image file. The name of the downloaded file is `milada-vigerova-1284157-unsplash.jpg`. Put this in the same directory as your IPFS Python script files. You could use any image file for this, but make sure its size is at least 1 MB. However, if you use another image file, you should get a different hash.

Create a script named `add_image_file.py` using the following code block:

```
import ipfsapi


c = ipfsapi.connect()
result = c.add('dose-juice-1184429-unsplash.jpg')
print(result)
```

Run it. You should get the following output:

```
(ipfs-venv) $ python add_image_file.py
{'Name': 'milada-vigerova-1284157-unsplash.jpg', 'Hash':
'QmV5KPoHHqbq2NsALniERnaYjCJPi3UxLnpwdTkV1EbNZM', 'Size': '2604826'}
```

Next, create another script to list all blocks from this block and name the script `list_blocks.py`:

```
import ipfsapi
import pprint


c = ipfsapi.connect()
blocks = c.ls('QmV5KPoHHqbq2NsALniERnaYjCJPi3UxLnpwdTkV1EbNZM')
pp = pprint.PrettyPrinter(indent=2)
pp.pprint(blocks)
```

`pprint` is part of the Python standard library.

Run the script. You should get the following output:

```
(ipfs-venv) $ python list_blocks.py
{ 'Objects': [ { 'Hash': 'QmV5KPoHHqbq2NsALniERnaYjCJPi3UxLnpwdTkV1EbNZM',
 'Links': [ { 'Hash': 'Qmahxa3MABVtHWh7b2cbQb9hEfiuvwKeYceaqrW8pZjemV',
 'Name': '',
 'Size': 262158,
 'Type': 2},
 { 'Hash':
 . . .
 . . .
 'QmbSa1vj3c1edyKFdTCaT88pYGTLS9n2mpRuL2B2NLUygv',
```

```
'Name': '',
'Size': 244915,
'Type': 2}]}]}
```

As I have explained in Chapter 10, *InterPlanetary – A Brave New File System*, a big file would not be hashed straight away because of memory concerns. Instead, it will be divided into many chunks. Each chunk has a size of 262,158 bytes, except for the last one. However, you can configure the size of the chunk. Each chunk would be hashed separately. Then, the root hash of the content of the file is the combination of these hashes. The IPFS uses the Merkle tree to calculate the root hash. Of course, however, you must wrap each chunk inside the IPFS node before serializing it with protobuf. Then, there will be the container node that contains all of the links to these chunks.

You can reverse engineer the following IPFS block without `.proto` files:

```
{'Name': 'milada-vigerova-1284157-unsplash.jpg', 'Hash':
'QmV5KPoHHqbq2NsALniERnaYjCJPi3UxLnpwdTkV1EbNZM', 'Size': '2604826'}
```

Remember the hash from this image file. Get the IPFS block of this file content. You can use Python script or the IPFS command-line utility to do so:

```
$ ipfs block get QmV5KPoHHqbq2NsALniERnaYjCJPi3UxLnpwdTkV1EbNZM > block.raw
```

We save the block, which is in binary format, to a binary file. Then, we can decode this binary file using the protoc compiler.

```
$ protoc --decode_raw < block.raw
```

You should get the following result:

```
2 {
  1 {
    2:
"\267\301\242\262\250qw\216+\237\301\273\'\360%\"\2022\201#R\364h\262$\357\
227\2355\244>x"
  }
  2: ""
  3: 262158
}
...
...
1 {
  1: 2
  3: 2604197
  4: 262144
  4: 262144
...
```

```
...
   4: 262144
   4: 244901
}
```

You may be familiar with this structure. When you decode the serialized data in protobuf without proto files, the problem is that you have to guess what 1, 2, 3, and 4 means inside a certain block. If you have proto files, this line, `3: 2604197`, would turn into `filesize: 2604197`. Consequently, it is a good idea to get the proto files before decoding serialized data in protobuf.

We can reconstruct the original file from these chunks. Let's create the script and name it `construct_image_from_blocks.py`:

```python
import ipfsapi


c = ipfsapi.connect()

images_bytes = []

blocks = c.ls('QmV5KPoHHqbq2NsALniERnaYjCJPi3UxLnpwdTkV1EbNZM')
for block in blocks['Objects'][0]['Links']:
    bytes = c.cat(block['Hash'])
    images_bytes.append(bytes)

images = b''.join(images_bytes)
with open('image_from_blocks.jpg', 'wb') as f:
    f.write(images)
```

After running the script, if you open `image_from_blocks.jpg`, you will view the original image file.

We have added one file. Now, let's try to add a directory of files.

Create a directory named `mysite`. Inside this directory, create a directory named `img`. Put the `cat.jpg` image file inside this `img` directory. Then, adjacent to the `img` directory, create a file named `index.html`.

The following code block is the content of `index.html`:

```html
<html>
  <head>
    <link
href="https://stackpath.bootstrapcdn.com/bootstrap/4.2.1/css/bootstrap.min.
css" rel="stylesheet" integrity="sha384-
GJzZqFGwb1QTTN6wy59ffF1BuGJpLSa9DkKMp0DgiMDm4iYMj70gZWKYbI706tWS"
```

```
crossorigin="anonymous">
  </head>
  <body>
    <img src="img/cat.jpg" class="rounded-circle" />
  </body>
</html>
```

Then, create a README.md file adjacent to the img directory as well. The following code block is the content of the README.md file:

```
This is Readme file.
```

Now, create a Python script to add this directory to the IPFS and name the script add_directory.py:

```
import ipfsapi
import pprint


c = ipfsapi.connect()
result = c.add('mysite', True)

pp = pprint.PrettyPrinter(indent=2)
pp.pprint(result)
```

Running the, script will give you the following output:

```
(ipfs-venv) $ python add_directory.py
[ { 'Hash': 'QmWhZDjrm1ncLLRZ421towkyYescK3SUZdWEM5GxApfxJe',
    'Name': 'mysite/README.md',
    'Size': '29'},
  { 'Hash': 'QmUni2ApnGhZ89JEbmPZQ1QU9wcinnCoujjrYAy9TCQQjj',
    'Name': 'mysite/index.html',
    'Size': '333'},
  { 'Hash': 'Qmd286K6pohQcTKYqnS1YhWrCiS4gz7Xi34sdwMe9USZ7u',
    'Name': 'mysite/img/cat.jpg',
    'Size': '443362'},
  { 'Hash': 'QmW2WQi7j6c7UgJTarActp7tDNikE4B2qXtFCfLPdsgaTQ',
    'Name': 'mysite/img',
    'Size': '443417'},
  { 'Hash': 'QmZamPcNnfZjjTkoyrYjYMEA8pp29KmpmkuSvkicSGiZDp',
    'Name': 'mysite',
    'Size': '443934'}]
```

The second argument of the add method concerns recursive arguments. The IPFS uses the Merkle DAG data structure to save this directory of files.

We can open our website in a browser with the following URL:
`http://localhost:8080/ipfs/QmZamPcNnfZjjTkoyrYjYMEA8pp29KmpmkuSvkicSGiZ`
`Dp/`. The following screenshot is how the website will appear in a browser:

You could also access the IPFS path from another gateway (using another node) using the
following URL: `https://ipfs.io/ipfs/`
`QmZamPcNnfZjjTkoyrYjYMEA8pp29KmpmkuSvkicSGiZDp/`. Depending on your internet
connection, this could take some time because a node in the ipfs.io server needs to locate
the content in your computer.

IPNS

Being able to publish a file or a directory of files in which their integrities are guarded by
hashes is wonderful. Occasionally, however, you may want to be able to publish a dynamic
file with the same link. What I mean here is that a hash link would generate different
content at different times. One of the use cases is that you want to publish news. Depending
on the situation, news can change every minute or hour.

The way you do that is by using the **Interplanetary Name System (IPNS)**. The hash link is derived from the cryptography key in our IPFS node. When we launch the IPFS daemon, we become one node among many in IPFS peer-to-peer networks. Our identity is based on a cryptography key.

Let's create two horoscope predictions. The predictions here should change over time. The first filename is `horoscope1.txt`, and the content of this file is given in the following code block:

```
You will meet the love of your life today!
```

The second filename is `horoscope2.txt`, and the content of this file is given in the following code block:

```
You need to be careful when going outside!
```

Let's add those two files using this Python script, named `add_horoscope_predictions.py`:

```
import ipfsapi


c = ipfsapi.connect()
result = c.add('horoscope1.txt')
print(result)
result = c.add('horoscope2.txt')
print(result)
```

Running this will give you the following output:

```
(ipfs-venv) $ python add_horoscope_predictions.py
{'Name': 'horoscope1.txt', 'Hash':
'QmTG4eE6ruUDhSKxqwofJXXqDFAmNzQiGdo4Z7WvVdLZuS', 'Size': '51'}
{'Name': 'horoscope2.txt', 'Hash':
'Qme1FUeEhA1myqQ8C1sCSXo4dDJzZApGD6StE26S72ZqyU', 'Size': '51'}
```

Note these two hashes that we obtained in the output.

Now, create a script to list all of our keys and name the script `keys_list.py`:

```
import ipfsapi


c = ipfsapi.connect()
print(c.key_list())
```

Running the preceding script will give you the following output:

```
(ipfs-venv) $ python keys_list.py
{'Keys': [{'Name': 'self', 'Id':
'QmVPUMd7mFG54zKDNNzPRgENsr5VTbBxWJThfVd6j9V4U8'}]}
```

Now, let's publish our first horoscope prediction. Create a Python script named
publish_horoscope1.py using the following code block:

```
import ipfsapi

c = ipfsapi.connect()
peer_id = c.key_list()['Keys'][0]['Id']
c.name_publish('QmY7MiYeySnsed1Z3KxqDVYuM8pfiT5gGTqprNaNhUpZgR')
result = ipfs.cat('/ipns/' + peer_id)
print(result)
```

Running this may take a while. Publishing a file in the IPNS is a little slow. If you are
patient enough, you will get the following output:

```
(ipfs-venv) $ python publish_horoscope1.py
b'You will meet the love of your life today!\n'
```

You publish content with the name_publish() method. It accepts a hash link of the
content (IPFS path, not the filename) as the first argument.

Then, to access the content from the IPFS, you can use the cat or get methods. Here, we
are using the cat method. The argument for the cat method is not a hash link or IPFS path,
but an IPNS path, which is just a key that you can get from the keys_list.py script. You
must prefix this with the '/ipns/' string. Consequently, the IPNS path is '/ipns/
QmVPUMd7mFG54zKDNNzPRgENsr5VTbBxWJThfVd6j9V4U8'.

Now, let's publish more data. Create a script named publish_horoscope2.py using the
following code block:

```
import ipfsapi

c = ipfsapi.connect()
peer_id = c.key_list()['Keys'][0]['Id']
c.name_publish('Qme1FUeEhA1myqQ8C1sCSXo4dDJzZApGD6StE26S72ZqyU')
result = ipfs.cat('/ipns/' + peer_id)
print(result)
```

Running this will give you a different result from the previous one:

```
(ipfs-venv) $ python publish_horoscope2.py
b'You need to be careful when going outside!\n'
```

The IPNS path, which is `'ipns/`
`QmVPUMd7mFG54zKDNNzPRgENsr5VTbBxWJThfVd6j9V4U8'`, is still the same, but we got a different result.

This is very interesting, but are we limited to a single IPNS path? No. You could generate another key so that you can have another IPNS path.

Create a Python script named `generate_another_key.py` using the following code block:

```
import ipfsapi

c = ipfsapi.connect()
print(c.key_list())
c.key_gen('another_key', 'rsa')
print(c.key_list())
```

Running the preceding script will give you the following output:

```
(ipfs-venv) $ python generate_another_key.py
```

```
{'Keys': [{'Name': 'self', 'Id':
'QmVPUMd7mFG54zKDNNzPRgENsr5VTbBxWJThfVd6j9V4U8'}]}

{'Keys': [{'Name': 'self', 'Id':
'QmVPUMd7mFG54zKDNNzPRgENsr5VTbBxWJThfVd6j9V4U8'}, {'Name': 'another_key',
'Id': 'QmcU8u2Koy4fdrSjnSEjrMRYZVPLKP5YXQhLVePfUmjmkv'}]}
```

Your new IPNS path from `'another_key'` is `'/ipns/`
`QmcU8u2Koy4fdrSjnSEjrMRYZVPLKP5YXQhLVePfUmjmkv'`.

Then, when you want to publish content on the IPNS path, just use the `key` argument in `name_publish()`. Create a script named `publish_horoscope1_in_another_ipns.py` using the following code block:

```
import ipfsapi


c = ipfsapi.connect()
peer_id = c.key_list()['Keys'][1]['Id']
c.name_publish('QmTG4eE6ruUDhSKxqwofJXXqDFAmNzQiGdo4Z7WvVdLZuS',
key='another_key')
result = c.cat('/ipns/' + peer_id)
print(result)
```

Run it. You should get the first horoscope prediction. As you may have observed, we use another peer ID. Notice the index 1 in `peer_id = c.key_list()['Keys'][1]['Id']`. Previously, we used the index 0.

Publishing in the IPNS would not store it forever. By default, it stores the IPFS file for 24 hours. You could change the duration by using the `lifetime` keyword in `name_publish()`. For example, if you want to publish the IPFS file in the IPNS for `5h`, you could do this instead:

```
c.name_publish('QmTG4eE6ruUDhSKxqwofJXXqDFAmNzQiGdo4Z7WvVdLZuS',
key='another_key', lifetime='5h')
```

Pinning

What if you want to delete the file on the IPFS? Let's say you accidentally add a nude picture of yourself using the `ipfs add` command:

```
$ ipfs add nude_picture.jpg
added QmWgMcTdPY9Rv7SCBusK1gWBRJcBi2MxNkC1yC6uvLYPwK nude_picture.jpg
2.64 MiB / 2.64 MiB [==================================================]
100.00%
```

How do you remove your nude picture? There is no such thing as `ipfs rm QmPCqvJHUs517pdcFNZ7EJMKcjEtbUBUDYxZcwsSijRtBx` because this command does not make any sense. What is it supposed to do? Tell every node that holds your nude picture to delete the picture? That would defeat the noble purpose of IPFS. What you can do is remove the picture on your IPFS local storage. The term for removing the local file in IPFS is called *removing the pin*. After removing the pin of your nude picture file, the content is still in IPFS local storage. But when the garbage collector of the IPFS works to clean up objects, it would remove the content of your nude picture file. Hopefully, no one has had the opportunity to pin (download) this sensitive file on their nodes!

Let's create a script to remove the pin and ask the garbage collector to do its job. Name the script `removing_nude_picture.py`:

```
import ipfsapi


c = ipfsapi.connect()
c.pin_rm('QmWgMcTdPY9Rv7SCBusK1gWBRJcBi2MxNkC1yC6uvLYPwK')
c.repo_gc()
```

Run the script. Then, if you try to get the content of your nude picture, it will fail:

```
(ipfs-venv) $ ipfs get QmWgMcTdPY9Rv7SCBusK1gWBRJcBi2MxNkC1yC6uvLYPwK
```

Of course, if someone has already pinned your nude picture in another node, then you would still get the content of your nude picture.

The nude picture in this example is basically a nude picture of a panda, which can be downloaded from the Unsplash website from: `https://unsplash.com/photos/IgdVdJCmzf4`. If you use this picture in this example, be prepared that there are other people who will use it as well. To test whether deleting a pin really works, you could use a truly unique file that no one in this world has. There is a way to check whether the file has been deleted on your local storage by dissecting the `LevelDB` file in the IPFS store path. However, that is beyond the scope of this book.

Pubsub

The IPFS has an experimental feature, which is **Publish-Subscribe**, or **pubsub**. Basically, a node in the IPFS can subscribe to a topic. Let's say this topic is a Bitcoin topic. A node in the IPFS can publish a *To the moon!* message to a bitcoin topic. Then, any node that subscribes to the 'bitcoin' topic could get the message.

Because pubsub is an experimental feature, you need to run IPFS daemon with a particular flag. Run IPFS daemon with the `--enable-pubsub-experiment` flag using the following command:

```
$ ipfs daemon --enable-pubsub-experiment
```

Both the subscriber and the publisher need to run the daemon with this particular flag.

Let's create a script to subscribe to a certain topic and name the script `subscribe_topic.py`:

```
import ipfsapi
from base64 import b64decode


c = ipfsapi.connect()
with c.pubsub_sub('bitcoin') as sub:
    for message in sub:
        string = b64decode(message['data'])
        print(string)
        break
```

The method to subscribe to a topic is `pubsub_sub`. The first argument is a topic we want to subscribe to. When we receive data from our subscription, we will also get the information about the sender. However, for now, we only care about the message. This message is in `base64` encoding, so we have to decode it first.

Run the script. This will wait until any message is received before exiting.

Let's create a script to publish to this topic and name the script `publish_topic.py`:

```
import ipfsapi


c = ipfsapi.connect()
c.pubsub_pub('bitcoin', 'To the moon!')
```

 It would be better if you run this script in another computer so you can marvel at the wonder of the decentralized technology. Don't forget that you must run the IPFS daemon with a particular flag. But if you are lazy, you could run this script in the same computer.

While the subscribing script is running, run the publishing script.

Then, in the Terminal where you run the subscribing script, you should get the following output:

```
(ipfs-venv) $ python subscribe_topic.py
b'To the moon!'
```

So, what is pubsub good for? To start with, you could build a notification system. Imagine you run a home file-sharing system for your family. When you add a picture of your daughter, you want to give notice to all of your family members. Not just a notification; you could build a decentralized chatting system (something such as IRC or Slack). When combined with other technologies, such as a content-free replicated data type, you could even build a decentralized online pair programming system on top of the IPFS!

Beware that pubsub are still experimental features. The developers of the IPFS have many interesting plans in the pipeline. Among the most interesting is the plan to add an authentication system to the top of the pubsub system based on a cryptography key. Now, everyone can publish and subscribe to a topic.

Mutable File System

The IPFS has a feature called Mutable File System (MFS). The MFS is different from your OS file system. Let's create a script to explore this feature and name the script `exploring_mfs.py`:

```python
import ipfsapi
import io


c = ipfsapi.connect()

print("By default our MFS is empty.")
print(c.files_ls('/')) # root is / just like Unix filesystem

print("We can create a directory in our MFS.")
c.files_mkdir('/classical_movies')

print("We can create a file in our MFS.")
c.files_write('/classical_movies/titanic',
              io.BytesIO(b"The ship crashed. The end."),
              create=True)

print("We can copy a file in our MFS.")
c.files_cp('/classical_movies/titanic',
           '/classical_movies/copy_of_titanic')

print("We can read the file.")
print(c.files_read('/classical_movies/titanic'))

print("We can remove the file.")
print(c.files_rm('/classical_movies/copy_of_titanic'))

print("Now our MFS is not empty anymore.")
print(c.files_ls('/'))
print(c.files_ls('/classical_movies'))

print("You can get the hash of a path in MFS.")
print(c.files_stat('/classical_movies'))

print("Then you can publish this hash into IPNS.")
```

Running this will give you the following output:

```
(ipfs-venv) $ python exploring_mfs.py
By default our MFS is empty.
{'Entries': None}
We can create a directory in our MFS.
We can create a file in our MFS.
We can copy a file in our MFS.
We can read the file.
b'The ship crashed. The end.'
We can remove the file.
[]
Now our MFS is not empty anymore.
{'Entries': [{'Name': 'classical_movies', 'Type': 0, 'Size': 0, 'Hash':
''}]}
{'Entries': [{'Name': 'titanic', 'Type': 0, 'Size': 0, 'Hash': ''}]}
You can get the hash of a path in MFS.
{'Hash': 'QmNUrujevkYqRtYmpaj2Af1DvgR8rt9a7ApyiyXHnF5wym', 'Size': 0,
'CumulativeSize': 137, 'Blocks': 1, 'Type': 'directory'}
Then you can publish this hash into IPNS
```

You may wonder what the point of this feature is. There is nothing that you can do in your MFS that you cannot do in your OS file system. In terms of this particular example, yes, you are right that this feature is pointless. But there is one subtle difference between MFS and your OS file system when copying files. Let's create a script to prove this assertion and name the script copy_in_mfs.py:

```
import ipfsapi


c = ipfsapi.connect()
c.files_cp('/ipfs/QmY8zTocoVNDJWUr33nhksBiZ3hxugFPhb6qSzpE761bVN',
'/46MB_cute_bear.mp4')

print(c.files_ls('/'))
```

Running the script will give you the following output:

```
(ipfs-venv) $ python copy_in_mfs.py
{'Entries': [{'Name': '46MB_cute_bear.mp4', 'Type': 0, 'Size': 0, 'Hash':
''}, {'Name': 'classical_movies', 'Type': 0, 'Size': 0, 'Hash': ''}]}
```

The file with the hash link `QmY8zTocoVNDJWUr33nhksBiZ3hxugFPhb6qSzpE761bVN` is a cute bear video that can be downloaded from: `https://videos.pexels.com/videos/bear-in-a-forest-855113`. You can download this with the following command: `ipfs get QmY8zTocoVNDJWUr33nhksBiZ3hxugFPhb6qSzpE761bVN` (assuming my IPFS node is online, you could download the video from that URL and pin the video yourself in another computer to test the script if no other IPFS nodes pinning this video are online). The file size is 46 MB, but the script was executed very quickly. The runtime of the script is too fast considering we have to download the video file. That happened because we do not download the video to our storage. The path of `/46MB_cute_bear.mp4` in our MFS is not a genuinely traditional file, as in our OS file system. You can say it's like a symbolic link to a real file in the IPFS, pinned by some nodes in the IPFS ecosystem.

That means you could copy 100 TB files from IPFS paths to your MFS and it would not take any storage (except for some metadata).

If you think like a computer scientist, the IPFS file system is like a giant graph database.

Other APIs

There are other methods of the IPFS HTTP API that we don't have room to discuss here. The complete reference can be found in `https://docs.ipfs.io/reference/api/http/`. There are APIs to bootstrap your nodes (which is useful if you want to construct your nodes list based on certain existing nodes), to find nearby nodes from a node, to connect to a particular node, to configure the IPFS, to shutdown IPFS daemon, and so on.

Summary

In this chapter, you have learned about interacting with the IPFS through the HTTP API using Python. First of all, you installed IPFS software and ran the daemon. You started this by adding a file to the IPFS and studied how to get the hash of the content of the file, which is based on protobuf, multihash, and base58. Then, you saw that a big file would be divided into many chunks if added to the IPFS. You could also add a directory of files into the IPFS. Based on this ability, you could host a static website on the IPFS. Then, you learned about publishing IPFS files in the IPNS on which you could have dynamic content. After this, you learned about the MFS, where you could copy a large file from the IPFS without incurring any significant costs in your local storage.

In the next chapter, you will combine the IPFS and smart contracts to build a decentralized application.

Further reading

The following are the references to the various sites associated with this chapter:

- `https://github.com/ipfs/py-ipfs-api`
- `https://docs.ipfs.io/`

12
Implementing a Decentralized Application Using IPFS

In this chapter, we are going to combine a smart contract with the **InterPlanetary File System (IPFS)** to build a decentralized video-sharing application (similar to YouTube but decentralized). We will use a web application as the frontend for the blockchain and IPFS. As stated previously, IPFS is not a blockchain technology. IPFS is a decentralized technology. However, in a blockchain forum, meetup, or tutorial, you may hear IPFS being mentioned quite often. One of the main reasons for this is that IPFS overcomes the weakness of blockchain, which is that its storage is very expensive.

In this chapter, we will cover the following topics:

- Architecture of the decentralized video-sharing application
- Writing the video-sharing smart contract
- Building the video-sharing web application

Architecture of the decentralized video-sharing application

This is how our application will look after it is finished—first, you go to a website, where you will see a list of videos (just like YouTube). Here, you can play videos in your browser, upload videos to your browser so that people can watch your cute cat video, and like other people's videos.

On the surface, this is like a normal application. You build it with your favorite Python web framework, such as Django, Flask, or Pyramid. Then you use MySQL or PostgreSQL as the database. You could choose NGINX or Apache as the web server in front of the Gunicorn web server. For caching, you can use Varnish for full page caching and Redis for template caching. You will also host the web application and videos on the cloud, such as **Amazon Web Service (AWS)** or **Google Cloud Platform (GCP)**, Azure. Then you will use a content delivery network to make it scalable worldwide. For the frontend side, you could use the JavaScript framework, with React.js, Angular.js, Vue.js, or Ember. If you are an advanced user, you could use machine learning for video recommendations.

However, the key point here is that what we want to build is a decentralized video sharing application with blockchain technology, not a centralized application.

Let's discuss what we mean by building a decentralized video-sharing application with blockchain technology.

We cannot store video files on the Ethereum blockchain as it is very expensive; even storing a picture file costs an arm and a leg on the Ethereum blockchain. Someone has done the math on this for us at the following link: `https://ethereum.stackexchange.com/questions/872/what-is-the-cost-to-store-1kb-10kb-100kb-worth-of-data-into-the-ethereum-block`.

The cost of storing 1 KB is roughly 0.032 ETH. A decent image file is about 2 MB. 1 MB is 1,000 KB if you ask hard drive manufacturers, or 1,024 KB if you ask an operating system. We simply round this to 1,000 because it does not make any difference to our calculation. Consequently, the cost of storing a 2 MB file on Ethereum is around 2,000 multiplied by 0.032 ETH, which is equal to 64 ETH. The price of ETH is always changing. At the time of writing, the cost of 1 ETH is around 120 US dollars. This means that to store a 2 MB picture file (a normal size stock picture file on the Unsplash website) you need to spend 7,680 US dollars. A one-and-a-half-minute video file in MP4 format is roughly 46 MB. Consequently, you need to spend 176,640 US dollars to store this video file on Ethereum.

Instead of paying this, blockchain developers will usually store the reference of a video file on the blockchain and store the video file itself on normal storage, such as on AWS. In a Vyper smart contract, you can use the `bytes` data type:

```
cute_panda_video: bytes[128]
```

Then, you could store the link of the video that you store in AWS S3 (`https://aws.amazon.com/s3/`) in the smart contract:

```
cute_panda_video =
"http://abucket.s3-website-us-west-2.amazonaws.com/cute_panda_video.mp4"
```

This approach is all fine and dandy, but the problem is that you are dependent on AWS. If the company does not like your cute panda video, they could delete it, and the URL that is present in the smart contract becomes invalid. You could of course change the value of the `cute_panda_video` variable on the smart contract (unless you forbid it from doing so). However, this situation causes inconveniences in our application. If you use the service from a centralized company, your faith is dependent on the whim of that company.

We can mitigate this problem by using decentralized storage, such as IPFS. Instead of an URL, we could store the IPFS path (or IPFS hash) as the value of the `cute_panda_video` variable, similar to the following example:

```
cute_panda_video = "/ipfs/QmWgMcTdPY9Rv7SCBusK1gWBRJcBi2MxNkC1yC6uvLYPwK"
```

Then, we can launch our IPFS daemon on AWS and other places, such as GCP. Consequently, if AWS censors our cute panda video, the IPFS path of our cute panda video is still valid. We could serve the video from other places, such as GCP. You could even host the video on the computer at your grandma's house. People who are addicted to cute panda videos could even pin the video, and help us serve the cute panda video.

Other than hosting a cute panda video in a decentralized fashion, there are other values of the decentralized video sharing application. This value relates to blockchain technology. Suppose we want to build a **like** (thumbs up) video feature. We could store the like value on the blockchain. This prevents corruption. Imagine we want to build a voting contest for the cutest panda video with a prize of 10 BTC. If our contest application is done in a centralized fashion (using a table to keep the like value on a SQL database such as MySQL or PostgreSQL), we, as a centralized admin, could hijack the winner using the following code:

```
UPDATE thumbs_up_table SET aggregate_voting_count = 1000000 WHERE video_id
= 234;
```

Of course, it is not this easy to cheat. You need to cover your tracks with database logs by ensuring that the aggregate counts match individual counts. This needs to be done subtly. Instead of adding a whopping number of votes, such as 1 million at once, you could add the aggregate count to a random number between 100 and 1,000 in an hour. This is not to suggest that you cheat the users, I am merely getting my point across.

With blockchain, we can prevent the corruption of the integrity of data via the centralized admin. The like value is kept in the smart contract, and you let people audit the smart contract's source code. Our like feature on the decentralized video sharing application increases the number of likes on a video through an honest process.

Other than the integrity of data, we could build a crypto economy. What I mean is, we could have economic activities (such as selling, buying, bidding, and so on) in our smart contract. We could build tokens in the same smart contract. The coin of this token could be spent on liking the video, so that liking videos is no longer free. The owner of the video could cash this out like money into their pocket. This dynamic could incentivize people to upload better videos.

On top of that, a decentralized application guarantees the independence of APIs. The nature of the decentralization of the application prevents APIs from being disturbed or harassed in a similar way to the Twitter API fiasco. A long time ago, developers could develop an interesting application on top of the Twitter API with a lot of freedom, but then Twitter imposed heavy restrictions on how developers could use their API. One such example is that Twitter once shut down API access to Politwoops, which preserved politicians' deleted tweets. Access has been reactivated, though. By making our application decentralized, we could increase the democratic nature of the API.

For educational purposes, our application has two main features. Firstly, you can see a list of videos, play videos, and upload videos. These are normal things that you do on YouTube. Secondly, you can like a video, but only with a coin or token.

Before we jump into building the application, let's design the architecture of the smart contract and the architecture of the web application.

Architecture of a video-sharing smart contract

Our application starts with the smart contract. There are a few things that our smart contract needs to do here, and these are as follows:

- Keep track of videos that have been uploaded by a user
- Utilize a token and its standard operation (ERC20)
- Provide a way for a user to like a video using a coin or token
- The coin used for liking a video will be transferred to the video owner

That's it. We always strive to keep the smart contract as short as possible. The more the lines of code, the bigger the chances of a bug showing up. And a bug in the smart contract can't be fixed.

Before writing this smart contract, let's think about how we want to structure our smart contract. The structure of the smart contract includes the data structure. Let's look at an example of what data structure we want to use to track a user's videos.

We definitely want to use a mapping variable with an address data type as the key. The difficult part here is choosing what data type we want to use as the value for this mapping data type. As we learned in `Chapter 3`, *Implementing Smart Contracts Using Vyper*, there is no infinite size array in Vyper. If we use a `bytes32` array, we are limited to a certain size of array as the value for this mapping. This means a user can have a maximum size of videos. We can use a `bytes32` array to hold a list of videos that is very large in size, such as 1 million videos. What is the chance someone will upload more than 1 million videos? If you upload one video per day, you will only upload 3,650 videos in ten years. However, the problem with the `bytes32` array is, that it cannot accept data more than 32 bytes in size. The IPFS path, such as `QmWgMcTdPY9Rv7SCBusK1gWBRJcBi2MxNkC1yC6uvLYPwK`, has a length of 44 characters. Consequently, you must use at least a `bytes[44]` data type, but we round this up to `bytes[50]`.

Instead, we want to have another mapping data type variable (let's call this mapping z) as the value of this mapping data type variable, which has been described in the previous paragraph. Mapping z has an integer as the key and a struct that contains a `bytes[50]` data type variable to keep the IPFS path and the `bytes[20]` data type variable to keep the video title as the value. There is an integer tracker to initiate the value of the key in mapping z. This integer tracker is initialized with the value 0. Every time we add a video (IPFS path and video title) to mapping z, we increase this integer tracker by one. So the next time we add another video, the key of mapping z is not 0 anymore, but 1. This integer tracker is unique for each account. We could create another mapping of the account to this integer tracker.

After taking care of videos, we focus on likes. How do we store the fact that user A likes video Z? We need to make sure that a user cannot like the same video more than once. The easiest way to do this is to create a mapping with a `bytes[100]` data type as the key and a `boolean` data type as the value. The `bytes[100]` data type variable is a combination of using the video liker's address, the video uploader's address, and the index of videos. The `boolean` data type variable is used to indicate whether the user has already liked the video or not.

On top of that, we need an integer data type to keep the aggregate count of the number of likes a video has. The aggregate likes is a mapping with a `bytes[100]` data type as the key and an `integer` data type as the value. The `bytes[100]` data type variable is a combination of the video uploader's address and the index of the videos.

The downside of this approach is that it is very hard to keep track of which users have liked particular videos in the smart contract. We could create another mapping to keep track of which users have liked a certain video. However, that would complicate our smart contract. Previously, we went the extra mile to create a mapping dedicated to keeping track of all videos that a user has uploaded. That is necessary because we want to get a list of a user's videos. This is what we call a core feature. However, keeping track of which users have liked a video is not what I call a core feature.

As long as we can make the video-liking process honest, we don't need to keep track of which users have liked a video. If we are really itching to keep track of these users, we can use events in a smart contract. Every time a user likes a video, it triggers an event. Then, on the client side with the web3.py library, we could filter these events to get all users who like a particular video. This will be an expensive process and should be done separately to the main application. We can use background jobs using Celery, at which point the result can be stored on a database such as SQlite, PostgreSQL, or MySQL. Building a decentralized application does not mean completely negating a centralized approach.

 The topic of tokens has been discussed thoroughly in Chapter 8, *Creating Token in Ethereum*.

Architecture of a video-sharing web application

We will develop a Python web application to use as the frontend for our smart contract. This means we need a proper server to become the host for the Python web application. For this, we at least need a Gunicorn web server. In other words, we need to host our Python web application in a centralized server, such as in AWS, GCP, or Azure. This is actually fine for viewing videos, but the problem arises when a user wants to upload a video because that requires accessing a private key. Users may become concerned that our Python web application on a centralized server would steal their private keys.

So, the solution is to post the source code of our Python web application on GitHub or GitLab, then tell a user to download it, install it, and run it on their computer. They can audit our Python web application's source code to make sure there is no pesky code trying to steal their private keys. However, if they need to audit the source code every time, then we add another commit on our Git repository.

Or better still, we could store our Python web application's source code on IPFS. They can download this from IPFS and be sure that our application's source code could not be tampered with. They only need to audit the source code once before using it.

However, while we could host a static website on IPFS, we could not do the same with dynamic web pages such as Python, PHP, Ruby, or Perl web applications. Such dynamic websites need a proper web server. Consequently, anyone who downloads our Python web application's source code needs to install the right software before executing our application. They need to install the Python interpreter, the web server (Gunicorn, Apache, or NGINX), and all of the necessary libraries.

However, only desktop users can do that. Mobile users cannot execute our application because there are no proper Python interpreters or web servers on the Android or iOS platforms.

This is where JavaScript shines. You could create a static website that is dynamic so that you can have interactivity in the web pages. You could also create a complex JavaScript web application using React.js, Angular.js, Ember.js, or Vue.js and deploy it on IPFS. A desktop user and a mobile user could execute the JavaScript web application. Because this is a book about Python, we will still look at creating a Python web application. However, you should keep the advantages of JavaScript compared to Python in mind.

No matter how good JavaScript is, it still cannot save the plight of mobile users. Computing power on the mobile platform is still less powerful than computing power on the desktop platform. You still cannot run a full Ethereum node on a mobile platform in the same way that you cannot run IPFS software on a mobile platform.

Let's design our web application. This has a few utilities:

- Playing a video
- Uploading a video
- Liking a video
- Listing recent videos from many users
- Listing videos from one specific user

Listing all videos from a user is moderately easy because we have an unlimited size array (which is basically a mapping with integer as key and another integer tracker) of videos that we can get based on a user in the smart contract. The controller of the page accepts a user (or basically an address in the smart contract) as parameter.

Playing a video accepts the video uploader's address and the index of the videos as parameters. If the video does not yet exist on our storage, we download it from IPFS. Then we serve the video to the user.

Uploading a video requires interacting with an Ethereum node. This method or functionality to upload a video accepts an argument of the account's address to be used, an argument of a password for the encrypted private key, an argument of the video file, and an argument of the video title. We store the video file first on IPFS. Then if it succeeds, we can store the information about this video on the blockchain.

Liking a video also requires interacting with an Ethereum node. This method or functionality to like a video accepts an argument of the video liker's address to be used, an argument of a password for the encrypted private key, an argument of the video uploader's address, and an argument of the videos index. After making sure that the user has not liked the video previously, we store the information on the blockchain.

Listing recent videos from many users is a bit tricky. The effort involved is quite tremendous. In a smart contract, we don't have a variable to track all participating users. We also don't have a variable to track all videos from different users. However, we can create an event through the method of storing video information on the blockchain. After doing so, we can find all recent videos from this event.

Now it's time to build the decentralized video-sharing application.

Writing the video-sharing smart contract

Without further ado, let's set up our smart contract development platform:

1. First things first, we set up our virtual environment as follows:

```
$ virtualenv -p python3.6 videos-venv
$ source videos-venv/bin/activate
(videos-venv) $
```

2. Then we install Web3, Populus, and Vyper:

```
(videos-venv) $ pip install eth-abi==1.2.2
(videos-venv) $ pip install eth-typing==1.1.0
(videos-venv) $ pip install py-evm==0.2.0a33
(videos-venv) $ pip install web3==4.7.2
(videos-venv) $ pip install -e
git+https://github.com/ethereum/populus#egg=populus
(videos-venv) $ pip install vyper
```

The latest version of Vyper is 0.1.0b6, which breaks Populus. The developer needs some time to fix this. If the bug has not been fixed by the time you are reading this book, you could patch Populus yourself.

3. Check whether this library has fixed the bug or not using the following command:

```
(videos-venv) $ cd videos-venv/src/populus
(videos-venv) $ grep -R "compile("
populus/compilation/backends/vyper.py
            bytecode = '0x' + compiler.compile(code).hex()
            bytecode_runtime = '0x' + compiler.compile(code,
bytecode_runtime=True).hex()
```

In our case, the bug has not been fixed.

4. So, let's patch Populus to fix the bug. Make sure you are still in the same directory (videos-venv/src/populus):

```
(videos-venv) $ wget
https://patch-diff.githubusercontent.com/raw/ethereum/populus/pull/
484.patch
(videos-venv) $ git apply 484.patch
(videos-venv) $ cd ../../../
```

5. After patching Populus, we will create our smart contract project directory:

```
(videos-venv) $ mkdir videos-sharing-smart-contract
```

6. Then, we will initialize the directory as a Populus project directory:

```
(videos-venv) $ cd videos-sharing-smart-contract
(videos-venv) $ mkdir contracts tests
```

7. Next, we will download the Populus configuration file inside the Populus project directory:

```
(videos-venv) $ wget
https://raw.githubusercontent.com/ethereum/populus/master/populus/a
ssets/defaults.v9.config.json -O project.json
```

8. We will now open the `project.json` configuration file for Populus and override the value of the `compilation` key, as shown in the following code block:

```
"compilation": {
  "backend": {
    "class": "populus.compilation.backends.VyperBackend"
  },
  "contract_source_dirs": [
    "./contracts"
  ],
  "import_remappings": []
},
```

9. Then we write our smart contract code in `videos-sharing-smart-contract/contracts/VideosSharing.vy` as shown in the following code block (refer to the code file at the following GitLab link for the full code: `https://gitlab.com/arjunaskykok/hands-on-blockchain-for-python-developers/blob/master/chapter_12/videos_sharing_smart_contract/contracts/VideosSharing.vy`):

```
struct Video:
    path: bytes[50]
    title: bytes[20]

Transfer: event({_from: indexed(address), _to: indexed(address), _value:
uint256})
Approval: event({_owner: indexed(address), _spender: indexed(address),
_value: uint256})
UploadVideo: event({_user: indexed(address), _index: uint256})
LikeVideo: event({_video_liker: indexed(address), _video_uploader:
indexed(address), _index: uint256})


...
...


@public
@constant
def video_aggregate_likes(_user_video: address, _index: uint256) ->
uint256:
    _user_video_str: bytes32 = convert(_user_video, bytes32)
    _index_str: bytes32 = convert(_index, bytes32)
    _key: bytes[100] = concat(_user_video_str, _index_str)

    return self.aggregate_likes[_key]
```

Now, let's discuss our smart contract bit by bit:

```
struct Video:
    path: bytes[50]
    title: bytes[20]
```

This is a struct of video information that we want to keep on the blockchain. The path of the Video struct stores the IPFS path, which has a length of 44. The IPFS path will be a different length if we use another hashing function. Remember that IPFS uses multihash when hashing objects. If you use the more expensive hashing function, such as SHA512, in your IPFS configuration, then you need to double the size of the bytes[] array data type. For example, bytes[100] should be sufficient. The title of the Video struct stores the video title. Here, I use bytes[20] because I want to keep the title short. You could use lengthier bytes such as bytes[100] if you want to store a lengthier title. However, remember that the more bytes you store on the blockchain, the more gas (money!) you have to spend. Of course, you could add more information in this struct, such as a video description or video tags, as long as you know the consequences, which is more gas needed to execute the method to store the video information.

We are now moving to the list of events:

```
Transfer: event({_from: indexed(address), _to: indexed(address), _value:
uint256})
Approval: event({_owner: indexed(address), _spender: indexed(address),
_value: uint256})
UploadVideo: event({_user: indexed(address), _index: uint256})
LikeVideo: event({_video_liker: indexed(address), _video_uploader:
indexed(address), _index: uint256})
```

Transfer and Approval are part of ERC20 standard events. You can read more about ERC20 in Chapter 8, *Creating Token in Ethereum*. The UploadVideo event is triggered when we upload video information in our smart contract. We save the video uploader's address and the index of videos. The LikeVideo event is triggered when we like a video in our smart contract.

We save the video liker's address, the video uploader's address, and the index of videos:

```
user_videos_index: map(address, uint256)
```

This is the integer tracker for our unlimited array. So if user_videos_index[address of user A] = 5, it means user A has uploaded four videos already.

The following is part of the ERC20 standard:

```
name: public(bytes[20])
symbol: public(bytes[3])
totalSupply: public(uint256)
decimals: public(uint256)
balances: map(address, uint256)
allowed: map(address, map(address, uint256))
```

Refer to `Chapter 8`, *Creating Token in Ethereum* for more information about ERC20.

We move on to the next line:

```
all_videos: map(address, map(uint256, Video))
```

This is the core variable to keep all videos from all users. The `address` data type key is used to hold a user's address. The `map(uint256, Video)` data type value is our infinite array. The `uint256` key in `map(uint256, Video)` starts from 0 and then is tracked by the `user_videos_index` variable. `Video` struct is our video information.

The next two lines of code are used for the likes:

```
likes_videos: map(bytes[100], bool)
aggregate_likes: map(bytes[100], uint256)
```

The `likes_videos` variable is a variable that's used to check whether a certain user has liked a particular video or not. The `aggregate_likes` variable is a variable used to show how many likes this particular video has got already.

We are now done with defining variables and will move on to the code shown in the following code block:

```
@public
def __init__():
    _initialSupply: uint256 = 500
    _decimals: uint256 = 3
    self.totalSupply = _initialSupply * 10 ** _decimals
    self.balances[msg.sender] = self.totalSupply
    self.name = 'Video Sharing Coin'
    self.symbol = 'VID'
    self.decimals = _decimals
    log.Transfer(ZERO_ADDRESS, msg.sender, self.totalSupply)

...
...

@public
```

```
@constant
def allowance(_owner: address, _spender: address) -> uint256:
    return self.allowed[_owner][_spender]
```

This is standard ERC20 code that you can learn about in Chapter 8, *Creating Token in Ethereum*. However, I made a small adjustment to the code, as shown in the following code block:

```
@private
def _transfer(_source: address, _to: address, _amount: uint256) -> bool:
    assert self.balances[_source] >= _amount
    self.balances[_source] -= _amount
    self.balances[_to] += _amount
    log.Transfer(_source, _to, _amount)

    return True


@public
def transfer(_to: address, _amount: uint256) -> bool:
    return self._transfer(msg.sender, _to, _amount)
```

In this smart contract, I extracted the inner code of the transfer method to the dedicated private method. The reason for this is that the transferring coins functionality would be used in the method to like a video. Remember, when we like a video, we must pay coins to the video uploader. We cannot call public function inside another public function. The rest of the code is the same (other than the name of the token):

```
@public
def upload_video(_video_path: bytes[50], _video_title: bytes[20]) -> bool:
    _index: uint256 = self.user_videos_index[msg.sender]

    self.all_videos[msg.sender][_index] = Video({ path: _video_path, title: _video_title })
    self.user_videos_index[msg.sender] += 1

    log.UploadVideo(msg.sender, _index) aggregate_likes

    return True
```

This is the method used to store video information on the blockchain. We call this method after we upload the video to IPFS. _video_path is the IPFS path, and _video_title is the video title. We get the latest index from the video uploader (msg.sender). Then we set the value of the Video struct to all_videos based on video uploader's address and the latest index.

We then increase the integer tracker (`user_videos_index`). Don't forget to log this event.

```
@public
@constant
def latest_videos_index(_user: address) -> uint256:
    return self.user_videos_index[_user]

@public
@constant
def videos_path(_user: address, _index: uint256) -> bytes[50]:
    return self.all_videos[_user][_index].path

@public
@constant
def videos_title(_user: address, _index: uint256) -> bytes[20]:
    return self.all_videos[_user][_index].title
```

The methods in the preceding code block are convenient ways to get the latest video index, the video IPFS path, and the video title for clients using web3. Without these methods, you could still get the information about the video, but accessing a struct variable inside a nested mapping data type variable with web3 is not straightforward.

The following code shows the method used to like a video. It accepts the video uploader's address and the videos index. Here, you create two keys—one for `likes_videos` and the other for `aggregate_likes`. The key for `likes_videos` is a combination of the video liker's address, the video uploader's address, and the videos index. The key for `aggregate_likes` is a combination of the video uploader's address and the video's index. After creating keys, then we make sure the video liker cannot like the same video in the future and the video liker has not liked this particular video before. Liking a video merely sets a `True` value to `likes_videos` variable with the key that we have created. Then we increase the value of `aggregate_likes` with the key that we have created by one. Finally, we transfer one coin of the token from the video liker to the video uploader. Don't forget to log this event:

```
@public
def like_video(_user: address, _index: uint256) -> bool:
    _msg_sender_str: bytes32 = convert(msg.sender, bytes32)
    _user_str: bytes32 = convert(_user, bytes32)
    _index_str: bytes32 = convert(_index, bytes32)
    _key: bytes[100] = concat(_msg_sender_str, _user_str, _index_str)
    _likes_key: bytes[100] = concat(_user_str, _index_str)
  a particular
    assert _index < self.user_videos_index[_user]
    assert self.likes_videos[_key] == False

    self.likes_videos[_key] = True
```

```
    self.aggregate_likes[_likes_key] += 1
    self._transfer(msg.sender, _user, 1)

    log.LikeVideo(msg.sender, _user, _index)

    return True
```

The following lines of code are convenience methods used to check whether a video has been liked by a particular user and how many likes this particular video has already:

```
@public
@constant
def video_has_been_liked(_user_like: address, _user_video: address, _index:
uint256) -> bool:
    _user_like_str: bytes32 = convert(_user_like, bytes32)
    _user_video_str: bytes32 = convert(_user_video, bytes32)
    _index_str: bytes32 = convert(_index, bytes32)
    _key: bytes[100] = concat(_user_like_str, _user_video_str, _index_str)

    return self.likes_videos[_key]

@public
@constant
def video_aggregate_likes(_user_video: address, _index: uint256) ->
uint256:
    _user_video_str: bytes32 = convert(_user_video, bytes32)
    _index_str: bytes32 = convert(_index, bytes32)
    _key: bytes[100] = concat(_user_video_str, _index_str)

    return self.aggregate_likes[_key]
```

Let's write a test in
`videos_sharing_smart_contract/tests/test_video_sharing.py`. Refer to the code file at the following GitLab link for the full code: `https://gitlab.com/arjunaskykok/hands-on-blockchain-for-python-developers/blob/master/chapter_12/videos_sharing_smart_contract/tests/test_videos_sharing.py`.

```
import pytest
import eth_tester


def upload_video(video_sharing, chain, account, video_path, video_title):
    txn_hash = video_sharing.functions.upload_video(video_path,
video_title).transact({'from': account})
    chain.wait.for_receipt(txn_hash)

def transfer_coins(video_sharing, chain, source, destination, amount):
    txn_hash = video_sharing.functions.transfer(destination,
```

```
amount).transact({'from': source})
    chain.wait.for_receipt(txn_hash)

...
...

    assert events[1]['args']['_video_liker'] == video_liker2
    assert events[1]['args']['_video_uploader'] == video_uploader
    assert events[1]['args']['_index'] == 0

    with pytest.raises(eth_tester.exceptions.TransactionFailed):
        like_video(video_sharing, chain, video_liker, video_uploader, 0)
```

Let's discuss the test script in detail, bit by bit. In the following code block, after importing necessary libraries, we created three convenient functions—a function to upload video, a function to transfer coins, and a function to like a video:

```
import pytest
import eth_tester


def upload_video(video_sharing, chain, account, video_path, video_title):
    txn_hash = video_sharing.functions.upload_video(video_path,
video_title).transact({'from': account})
    chain.wait.for_receipt(txn_hash)

def transfer_coins(video_sharing, chain, source, destination, amount):
    txn_hash = video_sharing.functions.transfer(destination,
amount).transact({'from': source})
    chain.wait.for_receipt(txn_hash)

def like_video(video_sharing, chain, video_liker, video_uploader, index):
    txn_hash = video_sharing.functions.like_video(video_uploader,
index).transact({'from': video_liker})
    chain.wait.for_receipt(txn_hash)
```

As the following code block shows, before uploading a video, we make sure that the latest videos index is 0. Then, after we upload one video, we should check the latest video's index, which should have increased by one. Of course, we check the video path and the video title as well. Then we upload one video again and check the latest video's index, which should be 2 by now. We also check the video path and the video title. Finally, we check the events and make sure they have been created correctly:

```
def test_upload_video(web3, chain):
    video_sharing, _ =
chain.provider.get_or_deploy_contract('VideosSharing')
```

```
    t = eth_tester.EthereumTester()
    video_uploader = t.get_accounts()[1]

    index =
video_sharing.functions.latest_videos_index(video_uploader).call()
    assert index == 0

...
...

    assert events[0]['args']['_user'] == video_uploader
    assert events[0]['args']['_index'] == 0

    assert events[1]['args']['_user'] == video_uploader
    assert events[1]['args']['_index'] == 1
```

Let's look at the next part of the test script:

```
def test_like_video(web3, chain):
    video_sharing, _ =
chain.provider.get_or_deploy_contract('VideosSharing')

    t = eth_tester.EthereumTester()
    manager = t.get_accounts()[0]
    video_uploader = t.get_accounts()[1]
    video_liker = t.get_accounts()[2]
    video_liker2 = t.get_accounts()[3]

    transfer_coins(video_sharing, chain, manager, video_liker, 100)
    transfer_coins(video_sharing, chain, manager, video_liker2, 100)
    transfer_coins(video_sharing, chain, manager, video_uploader, 50)
    upload_video(video_sharing, chain, video_uploader, b'video-ipfs-path',
b"video title")

...
...

    with pytest.raises(eth_tester.exceptions.TransactionFailed):
        like_video(video_sharing, chain, video_liker, video_uploader, 0)
```

First, we transfer some coins from the manager account (the one that launched the smart contract) to different accounts, then we upload a video. Before liking a video, we should ensure that accounts' token balances are what they should be, the testing accounts have not liked this video, and the aggregate likes number is still 0.

After doing this, we like a video from a particular account. The balance of a token for the video liker should be decreased by one and the balance of a token for the video uploader should be increased by one. This means that the smart contract has recorded that this account has liked the video and the aggregate likes of this video should be increased by 1.

Then, we like a video from another account. The balance of the token for the video liker should be decreased by one and the balance of token for the video uploader should be increased by one again. The smart contract has recorded that this other account has liked this video, at which point the aggregate likes of this video should be increased by 1 again, making it 2.

Then, we make sure the events of liking a video are triggered.

Lastly, we make sure the video liker cannot like the same video more than once.

We will not discuss the testing of ERC20 part of this smart contract. Refer to `Chapter 8`, *Creating Token in Ethereum,* to learn how to test the ERC20 token smart contract.

To execute the test, run the following statement:

```
(videos-venv) $ py.test tests/test_videos_sharing.py
```

Launching a private Ethereum blockchain

Let's launch our private Ethereum blockchain using geth. We will not use Ganache here, because events are not supported in the stable version of Ganache yet (however, the beta version of Ganache (v 2.0.0 beta 2) already supports events):

1. We will use the following code block to launch the block:

```
(videos-venv) $ cd videos_sharing_smart_contract
(videos-venv) $ populus chain new localblock
(videos-venv) $ ./chains/localblock/init_chain.sh
```

2. Now edit `chains/localblock/run_chain.sh`. Find `--ipcpath`, then change the value (the word after `--ipcpath`) to `/tmp/geth.ipc`.

3. Then edit the `project.json` file. The `chains` object points to four keys: `tester`, `temp`, `ropsten`, and `mainnet`. Add another key, `localblock`, in the `chains` object:

```
"localblock": {
  "chain": {
    "class": "populus.chain.ExternalChain"
  },
```

```
"web3": {
  "provider": {
    "class": "web3.providers.ipc.IPCProvider",
    "settings": {
      "ipc_path":"/tmp/geth.ipc"
    }
  }
},
"contracts": {
  "backends": {
    "JSONFile": {"$ref": "contracts.backends.JSONFile"},
    "ProjectContracts": {
      "$ref": "contracts.backends.ProjectContracts"
    }
  }
}
}
```

4. Run the blockchain using the following command:

   (videos-venv) $ ./chains/localblock/run_chain.sh

5. Compile our smart contract using the following command:

   (videos-venv) $ populus compile

6. Then, deploy our smart contract to our private blockchain using the following command:

   (videos-venv) $ populus deploy --chain localblock VideosSharing

Write down the address in which our smart contract is deployed in address.txt. This file must be adjacent to videos_sharing_smart_contract directory.

Creating a bootstrap script

This script is used to load data to make the development of our application easier. We can download free videos from https://videos.pexels.com/. Create a stock_videos directory adjacent to the videos_sharing_smart_contract directory and download some MP4 files to that stock_videos directory. In my case, I downloaded more than 20 videos.

After downloading some data, we will create a script called `bootstrap_videos.py`. Refer to the code file at the following GitLab link for the full code: `https://gitlab.com/ arjunaskykok/hands-on-blockchain-for-python-developers/blob/master/chapter_12/ bootstrap_videos.py`:

```python
import os, json
import ipfsapi
from web3 import Web3, IPCProvider
from populus.utils.wait import wait_for_transaction_receipt


w3 = Web3(IPCProvider('/tmp/geth.ipc'))

common_password = 'bitcoin123'
accounts = []
with open('accounts.txt', 'w') as f:
...
...
    nonce = w3.eth.getTransactionCount(Web3.toChecksumAddress(account))
    txn = VideosSharing.functions.upload_video(ipfs_path,
title).buildTransaction({
                'from': account,
                'gas': 200000,
                'gasPrice': w3.toWei('30', 'gwei'),
                'nonce': nonce
            })
    txn_hash = w3.personal.sendTransaction(txn, common_password)
    wait_for_transaction_receipt(w3, txn_hash)
```

Let's discuss the script in detail, bit by bit. In the following code block, after importing the necessary libraries, we create an object named w3, which is a connection object to our private blockchain:

```python
import os, json
import ipfsapi
from web3 import Web3, IPCProvider
from populus.utils.wait import wait_for_transaction_receipt


w3 = Web3(IPCProvider('/tmp/geth.ipc'))
```

In the following lines of code, we create new accounts with the `w3.personal.newAccount()` method. Then we put the new account's address in the `accounts.txt` file and the `accounts` variable. All accounts use `'bitcoin123'` as their password:

```python
common_password = 'bitcoin123'
```

```
accounts = []
with open('accounts.txt', 'w') as f:
    for i in range(4):
        account = w3.personal.newAccount(common_password)
        accounts.append(account)
        f.write(account + "\n")
```

Remember: we save our smart contract's address in the `address.txt` file after deploying it on our private blockchain. Now it's time to load the content of the file to the `address` variable:

```
with open('address.txt', 'r') as f:
    address = f.read().rstrip("\n")

with open('videos_sharing_smart_contract/build/contracts.json') as f:
    contract = json.load(f)
    abi = contract['VideosSharing']['abi']
```

Then we load the `abi` or the interface of our smart contract that we can get from `contracts.json` in the `build` directory of our Populus project directory: `videos_sharing_smart_contract`. We load the JSON to the `contract` variable with the `json.load()` method. The `abi` is from the `'abi'` key of the `'VideosSharing'` key from the `json` object.

Then we initialize the smart contract object with the address and the interface with `w3.eth.contract()` method. Then we get the IPFS connection object with the `ipfsapi.connect()` method:

```
VideosSharing = w3.eth.contract(address=address, abi=abi)

c = ipfsapi.connect()
```

Next, we want to transfer ether to our new accounts. By default, the first account (`w3.eth.accounts[0]`) gets all the rewards from the mining, so it has plenty of ether to share. The default password is `'this-is-not-a-secure-password'`:

```
coinbase = w3.eth.accounts[0]
coinbase_password = 'this-is-not-a-secure-password'
# Transfering Ethers
for destination in accounts:
    nonce = w3.eth.getTransactionCount(Web3.toChecksumAddress(coinbase))
    txn = {
            'from': coinbase,
            'to': Web3.toChecksumAddress(destination),
            'value': w3.toWei('100', 'ether'),
            'gas': 70000,
```

```
                    'gasPrice': w3.toWei('1', 'gwei'),
                    'nonce': nonce
            }
        txn_hash = w3.personal.sendTransaction(txn, coinbase_password)
        wait_for_transaction_receipt(w3, txn_hash)
```

Sending ether is done via the `w3.personal.sendTransaction()` method, which accepts a dictionary containing the sender (`'from'`), destination (`'to'`), amount of ether (`'value'`), gas, price of gas (`'gasPrice'`), nonce as the first argument, and a password as the second argument. Then we wait for the transaction to be confirmed with the `wait_for_transaction_receipt()` method.

After transferring ether, we transfer some ERC20 coins of our token to new accounts. This is necessary because, to like a video, we need coins of our ERC20 token:

```
# Transfering Coins
for destination in accounts:
    nonce = w3.eth.getTransactionCount(coinbase)
    txn = VideosSharing.functions.transfer(destination,
100).buildTransaction({
                'from': coinbase,
                'gas': 70000,
                'gasPrice': w3.toWei('1', 'gwei'),
                'nonce': nonce
            })
    txn_hash = w3.personal.sendTransaction(txn, coinbase_password)
    wait_for_transaction_receipt(w3, txn_hash)
```

We build a transaction object, `txn`, for transferring token methods (`VideosSharing.functions.transfer`), which accepts the destination account and the amount of coins with the `buildTransaction` method. This accepts a dictionary of the sender (`'from'`), gas, the price of gas (`'gasPrice'`), and nonce. We create a transaction using the `w3.personal.sendTransaction()` method then wait for the transaction to be confirmed with the `wait_for_transaction_receipt()` method.

We list all files from the `stock_videos` directory with the `os.listdir()` method. You have downloaded some MP4 files to this directory. After doing this, we iterate over these files:

```
# Uploading Videos
directory = 'stock_videos'
movies = os.listdir(directory)
length_of_movies = len(movies)
for index, movie in enumerate(movies):
    account = accounts[index//7]
    ipfs_add = c.add(directory + '/' + movie)
```

```
        ipfs_path = ipfs_add['Hash'].encode('utf-8')
        title = movie.rstrip('.mp4')[:20].encode('utf-8')

        nonce = w3.eth.getTransactionCount(Web3.toChecksumAddress(account))
        txn = VideosSharing.functions.upload_video(ipfs_path,
    title).buildTransaction({
                     'from': account,
                     'gas': 200000,
                     'gasPrice': w3.toWei('30', 'gwei'),
                     'nonce': nonce
                 })
        txn_hash = w3.personal.sendTransaction(txn, common_password)
        wait_for_transaction_receipt(w3, txn_hash)
```

We want every account to upload seven videos (`account = accounts [index//7]`). Consequently, the first seven videos will be uploaded by the first account, while the second batch of seven videos will be uploaded by the second account. Then we add the MP4 file to IPFS (`ipfs_add = c.add(directory + '/' + movie)`). We get the IPFS path and convert it to a bytes object (`ipfs_path = ipfs_add['Hash'].encode('utf-8')`), strip the MP4 filename to 20 characters and convert it to a bytes object because the title in the smart contract has a data type of `bytes[20]`.

Then we call the `upload_video` method of our smart contract (`VideosSharing.functions.upload_video`). We have to build the transaction object before sending it as argument to the `w3.personal.sendTransaction()` method. We wait for the transaction to be confirmed as usual with the `wait_for_transaction_receipt()` method.

However, you must be careful with the `upload_video` method because it saves the video path, which has a `bytes[50]` data type, and video title, which has a `bytes[20]` data type on the blockchain. It also increases the video's index and logs the event. The gas and gas price needed is much more than the transferring coins or token method. To transfer token coins, you can get away with a gas price of 1 gwei and 70,000 gas. However, this would fail for our `upload_video` method. For this method, I use gas price of 30 gwei and 200,000 gas. Remember, storage is expensive in blockchains. Even some strings could raise the gas and gas price needed for the operation.

1. Make sure you have launched your private blockchain, then launch the IPFS daemon:

    ```
    $ ipfs daemon
    ```

Refer to `Chapter 11`, *Using ipfsapi to Interact with IPFS*, if you don't know how to install and launch IPFS.

2. Now, we need to install the IPFS Python library in our virtual environment:

```
(videos-venv) $ pip install ipfsapi
```

3. Then, we run our bootstrap script using the following command:

```
(videos-venv) $ python bootstrap_videos.py
```

It will take some time. You could test whether your bootstrap script succeeds or not by accessing the smart contract and checking whether the videos have been uploaded or not.

4. Create a script named `check_bootstrap.py`:

```python
import json
from web3 import Web3, IPCProvider


w3 = Web3(IPCProvider('/tmp/geth.ipc'))

with open('accounts.txt', 'r') as f:
    account = f.readline().rstrip("\n")

with open('address.txt', 'r') as f:
    address = f.read().rstrip("\n")

with open('videos_sharing_smart_contract/build/contracts.json') as f:
    contract = json.load(f)
    abi = contract['VideosSharing']['abi']

VideosSharing = w3.eth.contract(address=address, abi=abi)

print(VideosSharing.functions.latest_videos_index(account).call())
```

5. Run the script. If you get 0 as the output, your bootstrap script failed. If you get some output other than 0, then your video information has been uploaded into the blockchain successfully.

Building the video-sharing web application

It's time to build the frontend of our smart contract. Previously, in Chapter 7, *Frontend Decentralized Application*, and Chapter 9, *Cryptocurrency Wallet*, we have created a desktop application using Qt for Python or the Pyside2 library. This time we are going to build a web application using the Django library:

1. Without further ado, let's install Django:

   ```
   (videos-venv) $ pip install Django
   ```

2. We also need the OpenCV Python library to get the thumbnail of our videos:

   ```
   (videos-venv) $ pip install opencv-python
   ```

3. Now let's create our Django project directory. This will create a skeleton Django project with its settings files:

   ```
   (videos-venv) $ django-admin startproject decentralized_videos
   ```

4. Inside this new directory, create a static media directory:

   ```
   (videos-venv) $ cd decentralized_videos
   (videos-venv) $ mkdir static media
   ```

5. Still in the same directory, create a Django application named videos:

   ```
   (videos-venv) $ python manage.py startapp videos
   ```

6. Then update our Django project settings file. The file is located in decentralized_videos/settings.py. Add our new application, videos, to INSTALLED_APPS variable. Make sure there is a comma between the 'videos' and 'django.contrib.staticfiles' strings. We need to add every Django application to this variable in order for the Django project to recognize it. A Django project can be composed of many Django applications:

   ```
   INSTALLED_APPS = [
       'django.contrib.admin',
       'django.contrib.auth',
       'django.contrib.contenttypes',
       'django.contrib.sessions',
       'django.contrib.messages',
       'django.contrib.staticfiles',
       'videos'
   ]
   ```

7. Then, in the same file, add the following lines of code:

```
STATIC_URL = '/static/'

STATICFILES_DIRS = [
    os.path.join(BASE_DIR, "static"),
]

MEDIA_URL = '/media/'
MEDIA_ROOT = os.path.join(BASE_DIR, 'media')
```

The `STATIC_URL` variable defines how we access a static URL. With this value, we can access static files with this URL: `http://localhost:8000/static/our_static_file`. The `STATICFILES_DIRS` variable refers to where we keep our static files in the filesystem. We simply store the videos in the `static` directory inside our Django project directory. `MEDIA_URL` has the same purpose as `STATIC_URL`, but for media files. Media files are what users upload into the Django project, while static files are what we as developers put into the Django project.

Views

Now let's create the view file of the `videos` application. A view is a controller that is like an API endpoint. The file is located in `decentralized_videos/videos/views.py`. Refer to the code file at the following GitLab link for the full code: `https://gitlab.com/arjunaskykok/hands-on-blockchain-for-python-developers/blob/master/chapter_12/decentralized_videos/videos/views.py`:

```
from django.shortcuts import render, redirect
from videos.models import videos_sharing


def index(request):
    videos = videos_sharing.recent_videos()
    context = {'videos': videos}
    return render(request, 'videos/index.html', context)
...
...
def like(request):
    video_user = request.POST['video_user']
    index = int(request.POST['index'])
    password = request.POST['password']
    video_liker = request.POST['video_liker']
    videos_sharing.like_video(video_liker, password, video_user, index)
    return redirect('video', video_user=video_user, index=index)
```

Let's discuss the code bit by bit. First, we import all the required libraries using the following lines of code:

```
from django.shortcuts import render, redirect
from videos.models import videos_sharing
```

The `render` and `redirect` methods are convenience functions from Django library that render templates (such as HTML files) and redirect them from a view to another view. `videos_sharing` is a custom instance that we will create soon in our `models` file.

Next, we will create the method that will be the view for our homepage:

```
def index(request):
    videos = videos_sharing.recent_videos()
    context = {'videos': videos}
    return render(request, 'videos/index.html', context)
```

We retrieve recent videos from our model instance. We will build this class and its methods. We render the `'videos/index.html'` template, which we will create later with a context containing a `videos` object. The `request` parameter is the representation of POST parameters and GET parameters, among other things.

Then, we have the following lines of code for the page, which lists all the videos from a specific video uploader:

```
def channel(request, video_user):
    videos = videos_sharing.get_videos(video_user)
    context = {'videos': videos, 'video_user': video_user}
    return render(request, 'videos/channel.html', context)
```

This method accepts a `video_user` parameter, which represents the address of the video uploader. We get the videos from the `videos_sharing.get_videos` method, which accepts the address of the video uploader. Then we render the `'videos/channel.html'` template file with a context containing the videos and the address of the video uploader.

In the following method, we have the view for the page on which a video will be played:

```
def video(request, video_user, index):
    video = videos_sharing.get_video(video_user, index)
    context = {'video': video}
    return render(request, 'videos/video.html', context)
```

This method accepts the `video_user` parameter, which represents the address of the video uploader, and the `index` parameter, which represents the video's index. We get a specific video from the `videos_sharing.get_video` method, which accepts the `video_user` and `index` parameters. Following this, we render `'videos/video.html'` with a contract containing this video.

Then, we have the view that we call when we upload a video file, its title, the address of the video uploader, and the password:

```
def upload(request):
    context = {}
    if request.POST:
        video_user = request.POST['video_user']
        title = request.POST['title']
        video_file = request.FILES['video_file']
        password = request.POST['password']
        videos_sharing.upload_video(video_user, password, video_file,
title)
        context['upload_success'] = True
    return render(request, 'videos/upload.html', context)
```

To retrieve the POST parameter, we can use `request.POST` property. However, to access the file we are uploading, we use the `request.FILES` property. This view is used for the page to upload the file and to process the file itself. We store video information to the blockchain with the `videos_sharing.upload_video` method. At the end of this method, we render `'videos/upload.html'` with `context` containing a success notification if we have uploaded a video successfully.

> For educational purposes, I made the uploading code simpler without validating it. On top of that, this web application is used by one person. However, if you intend to build a web application that serves many strangers, you need to validate uploaded files. You should also use the Django form to handle POST parameters instead of doing it manually.

Then, in the following method, we have the view to like the video:

```
def like(request):
    video_user = request.POST['video_user']
    index = int(request.POST['index'])
    password = request.POST['password']
    video_liker = request.POST['video_liker']
    videos_sharing.like_video(video_liker, password, video_user, index)
    return redirect('video', video_user=video_user, index=index)
```

When we want to like a video, we retrieve all the necessary information, such as the address of the video liker, the address of the video uploader, the video's index, and the password, so we can get the specific video. Then we use the `videos_sharing.like_video` method to do the job. After liking a video, we redirect to the `video` view.

Models

Let's create our models file in `decentralized_videos/videos/models.py`. Most logic and heavy operations happen here. Calling a smart contract's methods and storing files into IPFS also happen here. Refer to the code file at the following GitLab link for the full code: `https://gitlab.com/arjunaskykok/hands-on-blockchain-for-python-developers/blob/master/chapter_12/decentralized_videos/videos/models.py`:

```
import os.path, json
import ipfsapi
import cv2
from web3 import Web3, IPCProvider
from populus.utils.wait import wait_for_transaction_receipt
from decentralized_videos.settings import STATICFILES_DIRS, STATIC_URL,
BASE_DIR, MEDIA_ROOT


class VideosSharing:
...
...
        txn_hash = self.w3.personal.sendTransaction(txn, password)
        wait_for_transaction_receipt(self.w3, txn_hash)


videos_sharing = VideosSharing()
```

Let's discuss the core functionalities of our Django project bit by bit. First, we import convenience methods from the Python standard library, the IPFS Python library, OpenCV Python library, the web3 library, the Populus library, and some variables from the Django settings file:

```
import os.path, json
import ipfsapi
import cv2
from web3 import Web3, IPCProvider
from populus.utils.wait import wait_for_transaction_receipt
from decentralized_videos.settings import STATICFILES_DIRS, STATIC_URL,
BASE_DIR, MEDIA_ROOT
```

Then, we start with the initialization code of the `VideosSharing` model:

```
class VideosSharing:

    def __init__(self):
        self.w3 = Web3(IPCProvider('/tmp/geth.ipc'))
        with open('../address.txt', 'r') as f:
            address = f.read().rstrip("\n")

        with open('../videos_sharing_smart_contract/build/contracts.json')
as f:
            contract = json.load(f)
            abi = contract['VideosSharing']['abi']

        self.SmartContract = self.w3.eth.contract(address=address, abi=abi)

        self.ipfs_con = ipfsapi.connect()
```

We initialize this instance by creating a web3 connection object, which is `w3`, create a smart contract object by providing the address of the smart contract and the interface, which is `SmartContract`, and lastly create an IPFS connection object, which is `ipfs_con`.

Then, we have the method that is used in the `index` view:

```
    def recent_videos(self, amount=20):
        events =
self.SmartContract.events.UploadVideo.createFilter(fromBlock=0).get_all_ent
ries()
        videos = []
        for event in events:
            video = {}
            video['user'] = event['args']['_user']
            video['index'] = event['args']['_index']
            video['path'] = self.get_video_path(video['user'],
video['index'])
            video['title'] = self.get_video_title(video['user'],
video['index'])
            video['thumbnail'] = self.get_video_thumbnail(video['path'])
            videos.append(video)
        videos.reverse()
        return videos[:amount]
```

Recent videos can be retrieved from events. If you recall when we uploaded a video in our smart contract, you will remember that we logged an event here. Our event is `UploadVideo`. Because this Django project is a toy application, we get all the events from the starting block. In the real world, you will want to limit it (maybe the last 100 blocks). Furthermore, you probably want to store events to a database in background jobs (such as cron) for easy retrieval. This event object contains the video uploader and the video's index. Based on this information we can get the video path, the video title, and the video thumbnail. We accumulate videos in the `videos` object, reverse it (because we want to get recent videos), and return this object to the caller of the method.

Then, we have the method to get the videos from a specific video uploader:

```
def get_videos(self, user, amount=20):
    latest_index =
self.SmartContract.functions.latest_videos_index(user).call()
    i = 0
    videos = []
    while i < amount and i < latest_index:
        video = {}
        index = latest_index - i - 1
        video['user'] = user
        video['index'] = index
        video['path'] = self.get_video_path(user, index)
        video['title'] = self.get_video_title(user, index)
        video['thumbnail'] = self.get_video_thumbnail(video['path'])
        videos.append(video)
        i += 1
    return videos
```

This is used in the `channel` view. First, we get the latest videos index of this video uploader. Based on this information, we can find out how many videos the video uploader has uploaded. Then, we retrieve the videos one by one from the highest index to the lowest index until the number of videos reaches the number we need.

These are the methods for getting the video path and the video title based on the address of the video uploader:

```
def get_video_path(self, user, index):
    return self.SmartContract.functions.videos_path(user,
index).call().decode('utf-8')

def get_video_title(self, user, index):
    return self.SmartContract.functions.videos_title(user,
index).call().decode('utf-8')
```

And the videos index is defined as follows:

```
def process_thumbnail(self, ipfs_path):
    thumbnail_file = STATICFILES_DIRS[0] + '/' + ipfs_path + '.png'
    if not os.path.isfile(thumbnail_file):
        video_path = STATICFILES_DIRS[0] + '/' + ipfs_path + '.mp4'
        cap = cv2.VideoCapture(video_path)
        cap.set(cv2.CAP_PROP_POS_FRAMES, 0)
        _, frame = cap.read()
        cv2.imwrite(thumbnail_file, frame)
```

We use the `videos_path` and `videos_title` methods from our smart contract. Don't forget to decode the result because the `bytes` object forms our smart contract.

The following code block is the method that gets the video thumbnail:

```
def get_video_thumbnail(self, ipfs_path):
    thumbnail_file = STATICFILES_DIRS[0] + '/' + ipfs_path + '.png'
    url_file = STATIC_URL + '/' + ipfs_path + '.png'
    if os.path.isfile(thumbnail_file):
        return url_file
    else:
        return "https://bulma.io/images/placeholders/640x480.png"
```

When we view a video in the video-playing page, we check whether there is a certain filename with a `.png` file extension. We find this filename pattern inside the `static files` directory. If we can't find the file, we just use a placeholder picture file from the internet.

The following code block is the method to retrieve a specific video:

```
def get_video(self, user, index):
    video = {}
    ipfs_path = self.get_video_path(user, index)
    video_title = self.get_video_title(user, index)
    video_file = STATICFILES_DIRS[0] + '/' + ipfs_path + '.mp4'
    thumbnail_file = STATICFILES_DIRS[0] + '/' + ipfs_path + '.png'
    video['title'] = video_title
    video['user'] = user
    video['index'] = index
    video['aggregate_likes'] =
self.SmartContract.functions.video_aggregate_likes(user, index).call()

    if os.path.isfile(video_file):
        video['url'] = STATIC_URL + '/' + ipfs_path + '.mp4'
    else:
        self.ipfs_con.get(ipfs_path)
```

```
        os.rename(BASE_DIR + '/' + ipfs_path, STATICFILES_DIRS[0] + '/'
+ ipfs_path + '.mp4')
            video['url'] = STATIC_URL + '/' + ipfs_path + '.mp4'

        if not os.path.isfile(thumbnail_file):
            self.process_thumbnail(ipfs_path)

        return video
```

This is used in the `video` view. We need the video path, the video title, the video file, the video thumbnail, and the aggregate likes of this video (which we can get with `video_aggregate_likes` method from our smart contract). We check whether this MP4 file exists or not in our static files directory. If not, we retrieve it from IPFS with the `ipfs_con.get` method. Then we move the file to the static files directory and create a thumbnail image if one does not exist yet.

In the real world, you will want to retrieve the file from IPFS in a background job using Celery and RabbitMQ, for example. For this toy application, we just download a video in a blocking fashion. However, installing and configuring Celery and RabbitMQ is not for the faint of heart, and I think it will be a distraction from our educational purpose here.

The following method demonstrates what happens when we upload a video:

```
    def upload_video(self, video_user, password, video_file, title):
        video_path = MEDIA_ROOT + '/video.mp4'
        with open(video_path, 'wb+') as destination:
            for chunk in video_file.chunks():
                destination.write(chunk)
        ipfs_add = self.ipfs_con.add(video_path)
        ipfs_path = ipfs_add['Hash'].encode('utf-8')
        title = title[:20].encode('utf-8')
        nonce =
self.w3.eth.getTransactionCount(Web3.toChecksumAddress(video_user))
        txn = self.SmartContract.functions.upload_video(ipfs_path,
title).buildTransaction({
                    'from': video_user,
                    'gas': 200000,
                    'gasPrice': self.w3.toWei('30', 'gwei'),
                    'nonce': nonce
                })
        txn_hash = self.w3.personal.sendTransaction(txn, password)
        wait_for_transaction_receipt(self.w3, txn_hash)
```

We save the file in the media directory from our file in memory, and then add the file to IPFS with the `ipfs_con.add` method. We get the IPFS path and prepare the title of the video. Then, we call `upload_video` method from our smart contract. Remember to set enough gas and gas price for this. This is quite an expensive smart contract method. We wait for the transaction to be confirmed. In the real world, you'll want to do all of these steps using a background job.

The following code block shows how to generate a thumbnail from a video:

```python
def process_thumbnail(self, ipfs_path):
    thumbnail_file = STATICFILES_DIRS[0] + '/' + ipfs_path + '.png'
    if not os.path.isfile(thumbnail_file):
        video_path = STATICFILES_DIRS[0] + '/' + ipfs_path + '.mp4'
        cap = cv2.VideoCapture(video_path)
        cap.set(cv2.CAP_PROP_POS_FRAMES, 0)
        _, frame = cap.read()
        cv2.imwrite(thumbnail_file, frame)
```

After ensuring no such file exists, we get the video object. We read the first frame of the object and save this to an image file. This video functionality is from the OpenCV Python library.

Then, we have the method for liking a video:

```python
def like_video(self, video_liker, password, video_user, index):
    if self.SmartContract.functions.video_has_been_liked(video_liker,
video_user, index).call():
        return
    nonce =
self.w3.eth.getTransactionCount(Web3.toChecksumAddress(video_liker))
    txn = self.SmartContract.functions.like_video(video_user,
index).buildTransaction({
            'from': video_liker,
            'gas': 200000,
            'gasPrice': self.w3.toWei('30', 'gwei'),
            'nonce': nonce
        })
    txn_hash = self.w3.personal.sendTransaction(txn, password)
    wait_for_transaction_receipt(self.w3, txn_hash)
```

We make sure this video has not been liked by calling the `video_has_been_liked` method from our smart contract. Then we call the `like_video` method with the required parameters from our smart contract.

And, finally, we create an instance of the `VideosSharing` class so we can import this instance:

```
videos_sharing = VideosSharing()
```

Instead of importing a class, I prefer to import an instance of a class. Consequently, we initialize a class instance here.

Templates

It's time to write our templates. First, let's create a template directory using the following command lines:

```
(videos-venv) $ cd decentralized_videos
(videos-venv) $ mkdir -p videos/templates/videos
```

Then, we create our base layout first using the following lines of HTML. This is the layout that will be used by all our templates. The file is located in `videos/templates/videos/base.html`. You can refer to the code file at the following GitLab link for the full code: `https://gitlab.com/arjunaskykok/hands-on-blockchain-for-python-developers/blob/master/chapter_12/decentralized_videos/videos/templates/videos/base.html`:

```html
<!DOCTYPE html>
<html>
  <head>
    <meta charset="utf-8">
    <meta name="viewport" content="width=device-width, initial-scale=1">
    <title>Decentralized Videos Sharing Application</title>
    <link rel="stylesheet"
href="https://cdnjs.cloudflare.com/ajax/libs/bulma/0.7.2/css/bulma.min.css"
>
  ...
  ...
    </section>
    {% block content %}
    {% endblock %}
  </body>
</html>
```

In the header, we import the Bulma CSS framework and the Font Awesome JavaScript file. In this base layout, we set up our navigation, which holds the home page link and the video upload link. The section between `{% block content %}` and `{% endblock %}` will be filled by our template's content.

 While this book focuses on teaching Python only, avoiding other technologies such as CSS and JavaScript as much as possible, some CSS is necessary to make our web application look decent. You can go to `https://bulma.io` to learn about this CSS framework.

Then, let's create our first template file in `videos/templates/videos/index.html`. Use the following code block to create the template file:

```
{% extends "videos/base.html" %}

{% block content %}
<section class="section">
  <div class="container">
    {% for video in videos %}
      {% cycle '<div class="columns">' '' '' '' %}
        <div class="column">
          <div class="card">
            <div class="card-image">
              <figure class="image is-4by3">
                <img src="{{ video.thumbnail }}" />
              </figure>
            </div>
            <p class="card-footer-item">
              <span><a href="{% url 'video' video_user=video.user
index=video.index %}">{{ video.title }}</a></span>
            </p>
          </div>
        </div>
      {% cycle '' '' '' '</div>' %}
    {% endfor %}
  </div>
</section>
{% endblock %}
```

First things first; we make sure this template extends our base layout. Then we display our video in this template. We use the `card` class div to display the video. The `cycle` method is used to generate the `columns` class div to contain four `column` class divs. The second `cycle` method is used to close this div. In the footer of this `card`, we create a link to the page to play this video. The `url` method accepts the URL name (which we will discuss soon) and its parameters.

Then, we will create our template file to play the video in
`videos/templates/videos/video.html`. You can refer to the code file at the following
GitLab link for the full code: `https://gitlab.com/arjunaskykok/hands-on-blockchain-`
`for-python-developers/blob/master/chapter_12/decentralized_videos/videos/`
`templates/videos/video.html`:

```
{% extends "videos/base.html" %}

{% block content %}
<section class="section">
  <div class="container">
    <nav class="breadcrumb" aria-label="breadcrumbs">
      <ul>
        <li><a href="/">Home</a></li>
        <li><a href="/channel/{{ video.user }}">Channel</a></li>
        <li class="is-active"><a href="#" aria-current="page">{{
video.title }}</a></li>
      </ul>
    </nav>

. . .
. . .

  </div>
</section>
{% endblock %}
```

After extending base layout, we create a `breadcrumb` so a user can go to the video
uploader's channel page. Then we display the video with a `video` HTML tag. Below the
video, we display the aggregate likes number. At the bottom of the page, we create a form
to like the video. This accepts the video liker's address and the password input by the user.
There are hidden inputs to send the video uploader's address and the videos index. Note
that there is a CSRF token named `{% csrf_token %}` inside this form. This is necessary
for avoiding CSRF vulnerabilities.

Then let's create our template file to list all videos from a specific video uploader in
`videos/templates/videos/channel.html`. You can refer to the code file at the
following GitLab link for the full code: `https://gitlab.com/arjunaskykok/hands-on-`
`blockchain-for-python-developers/blob/master/chapter_12/decentralized_videos/`
`videos/templates/videos/channel.html`:

```
{% extends "videos/base.html" %}

{% block content %}
<section class="section">
  <div class="container">
```

```
    <nav class="breadcrumb" aria-label="breadcrumbs">
      <ul>
        <li><a href="/">Home</a></li>
        <li class="is-active"><a href="#">{{ video_user }}</a>
...
...
            </p>
          </div>
        </div>
      {% cycle '' '' '' '</div>' %}
    {% endfor %}
  </div>
</section>
{% endblock %}
```

This template file is the same as the index template, except we have a `breadcrumb` at the top of the list of videos.

Let's create the last template file for uploading videos in `videos/templates/videos/upload.html`. You can refer to the code file at the following GitLab link for the full code: `https://gitlab.com/arjunaskykok/hands-on-blockchain-for-python-developers/blob/master/chapter_12/decentralized_videos/videos/templates/videos/upload.html`:

```
{% extends "videos/base.html" %}

{% block content %}
<section class="section">
  <div class="container">
    <nav class="breadcrumb" aria-label="breadcrumbs">
      <ul>
        <li><a href="/">Home</a></li>
        <li class="is-active"><a href="#" aria-current="page">Uploading
Video</a></li>
      </ul>
    </nav>
    <div class="content">
...
...
</section>
<script type="text/javascript">
var file = document.getElementById("video_file");
file.onchange = function() {
  if(file.files.length > 0) {
    document.getElementById('video_filename').innerHTML =
file.files[0].name;
  }
```

```
};
</script>
{% endblock %}
```

In this template, after extending the base layout, we create the `breadcrumb`. Then, we create a form to upload the video.

This has four inputs—the video title, the video file, the video uploader's address, and the password. The JavaScript code at the bottom of the template is used to set the filename on the label of the file upload field after we have selected a file. Because we are uploading a file, we need to have the `enctype` attribute of the form set to `"multipart/form-data"`.

Urls

The `urls` file is a routing mechanism in Django. Open `decentralized_videos/videos/urls.py`, delete the content, and replace it with the following script:

```
from django.urls import path

from . import views

urlpatterns = [
    path('', views.index, name='index'),
    path('channel/<str:video_user>', views.channel, name='channel'),
    path('video/<str:video_user>/<int:index>', views.video, name='video'),
    path('upload-video', views.upload, name='upload'),
    path('like-video', views.like, name='like'),
]
```

Remember the views file we created previously? Here, we map the views into routing. We access the video-playing page by using `http://localhost:8000/video/0x0000000000000000000000000000000000000000/`
`1`. The parameters will be mapped into the `video_user` variable and the `index` variable. The first parameter of the `path` method is the way we call it in the browser. The second method is the view we use, and the third parameter is the name of the routing that is used in templates.

Then we need to register these `urls` to the project `urls` file. Edit `decentralized_videos/decentralized_videos/urls.py` and add our `videos.urls` path so our web application knows how to route our URL to our `videos` views:

```python
from django.contrib import admin
from django.urls import include, path

urlpatterns = [
    path('', include('videos.urls')),
    path('admin/', admin.site.urls)
]
```

Demo

It's time to enjoy the fruits of your labor. Make sure you are inside the `decentralized_videos` directory before running the server. Don't forget to run the private blockchain and IPFS daemon first:

```
(videos-venv) $ cd decentralized_videos
(videos-venv) $ python manage.py runserver
```

Then open `http://localhost:8000`. Here, you will be greeted with recent videos, as shown in the following screenshot. If you are confused about why I have a thumbnail for some videos, you need to go to the video-playing page to generate the thumbnail:

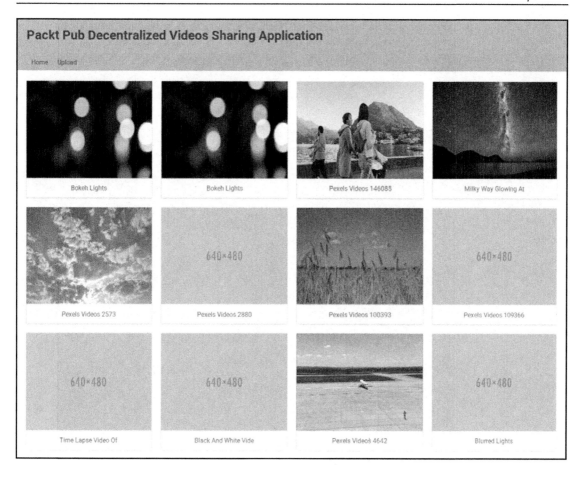

Let's click on one of the videos:

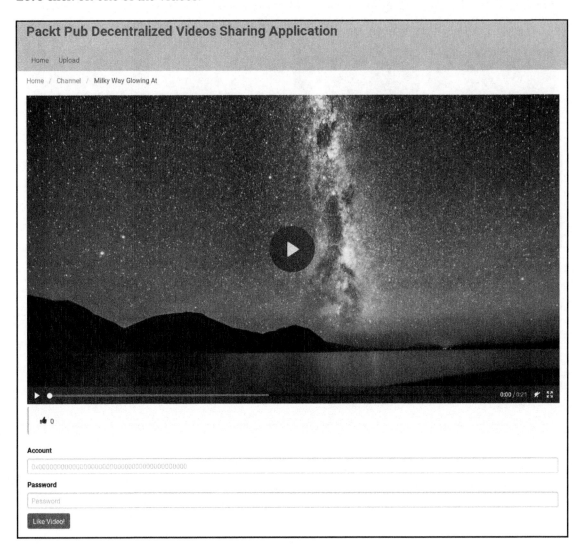

You can play the video here.

 To play HTML5 video on the web, we can use Chrome browser. You can also use Firefox browser, but you need to do additional steps to enable playing video on browser, by following the steps on this following website: https://stackoverflow.com/questions/40760864/how-to-play-mp4-video-in-firefox.

You can also like the video with the form. Let's click on the **Channel** link in the breadcrumb:

This is the list of videos from a specific video uploader. Finally, let's go to the uploading video page. Click the **Upload** link in the navigation menu:

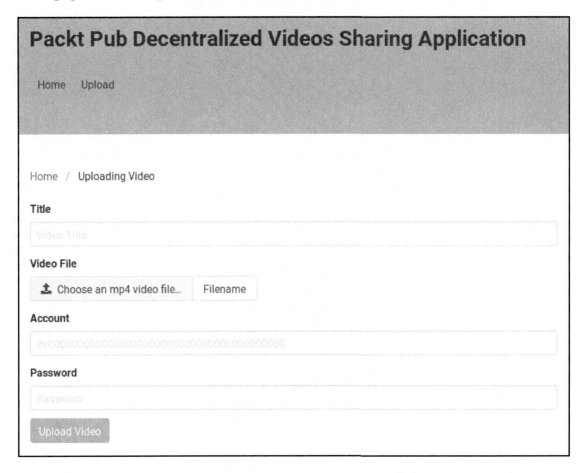

You can upload a video here, as shown in the preceding screenshot.

Note

To make this application perform better in the real world, there are a lot of things that need to be done. You need to add testing, you need to test the model, the views, the templates, and, finally, you need to carry out solid integration tests. You also need to put heavy and long operations (such as calling operations on the smart contract, adding and getting files with IPFS) in the background jobs using Celery and RabbitMQ or Redis. In addition to this, you need to add some JavaScript files in order to notice whether the background jobs have finished or not using a pooling mechanism. You could also use the Django channel to do the job.

Instead of accessing methods of the smart contract in the model, perhaps it is better to put all information from the blockchain in the database in the background task using cron. Then the model can access the database to get necessary information. To upload and like a video, we need to send our address and its password every time. Perhaps, for convenience, we could offer a way to save the address and the password temporarily for the user. We can save this in the session, in cookies, or even in a web3 object.

In our toy application, we assume everyone uploads a valid video file. If someone uploads an invalid video file, we need to handle that situation. Furthermore, if someone uploads an invalid IPFS path of a video, this should also be dealt with accordingly. Should we validate on the smart contract (using more gas)? Should we validate it in the frontend? There are many corner cases we need to take care of. We also need to add pagination. What about searching? We need to crawl the events on the blockchain. Should we only care about the video title, or should we extract the information from the video file itself? These are the questions you need to contemplate if you want to build a decentralized video-sharing application in the real world.

Summary

In this chapter, we combined IPFS technology and smart contract technology. We built a decentralized video-sharing application. First, we wrote a smart contract to store video information and the video titles. We also built in the crypto economics by making the act of liking videos require coins from the ERC20 token. In addition to this, we learned that even storing video information such as a bytes string of the IPFS path and the title requires more gas than usual. After writing a smart contract, we built a web application using the Django library. We created a project, followed by building an application inside this project. Moving forward, we built views, models, templates, and URLs. In the models, we stored the video file in IPFS and then stored the IPFS path on the blockchain. We made the templates more beautiful using the Bulma CSS framework, and then launched the application by executing the functionalities of this web application.

In this book, we have learned what blockchain is and what a smart contract is. We used the Vyper programming language to build many interesting smart contracts, such as a voting smart contract, a Twitter-like application smart contract, an ERC20 token smart contract, and a video-sharing smart contract. We also utilized the web3 library to interact with these smart contracts and built decentralized applications. On top of that, we built our GUI frontend for our decentralized applications using the PySide2 library and the web frontend for our decentralized applications using the Django library. One of the GUI frontend applications is a cryptocurrency wallet that can handle ether and ERC20 tokens. Finally, we also learned about a complementary decentralized technology, IPFS, that can be the storage solution for blockchain applications.

After mastering all of these skills, you are equipped to build many interesting applications on top of the Ethereum platform. But Ethereum is still a nascent technology. Technologies such as sharding, Proof of Stake, and privacy are still being researched and developed in Ethereum. These new technologies may affect the technologies that you have learned, such as Vyper and web3. So you need to be aware of new updates on the Ethereum platform.

Further reading

- We can learn more about upcoming changes on Ethereum on the following website: `https://github.com/ethereum/eth2.0-specs`.

Other Books You May Enjoy

If you enjoyed this book, you may be interested in these other books by Packt:

Blockchain By Example

Bellaj Badr, Richard Horrocks, Xun (Brian) Wu

ISBN: 978-1-78847-568-6

- Grasp decentralized technology fundamentals to master blockchain principles
- Build blockchain projects on Bitcoin, Ethereum, and Hyperledger
- Create your currency and a payment application using Bitcoin
- Implement decentralized apps and supply chain systems using Hyperledger
- Write smart contracts, run your ICO, and build a Tontine decentralized app using Ethereum
- Implement distributed file management with blockchain
- Integrate blockchain into existing systems in your organization

Foundations of Blockchain
Koshik Raj

ISBN: 978-1-78913-939-6

- The core concepts and technical foundations of blockchain
- The algorithmic principles and solutions that make up blockchain and cryptocurrencies
- Blockchain cryptography explained in detail
- How to realize blockchain projects with hands-on Python code
- How to architect the blockchain and blockchain applications
- Decentralized application development with MultiChain, NEO, and Ethereum
- Optimizing and enhancing blockchain performance and security
- Classical blockchain use cases and how to implement them

Leave a review - let other readers know what you think

Please share your thoughts on this book with others by leaving a review on the site that you bought it from. If you purchased the book from Amazon, please leave us an honest review on this book's Amazon page. This is vital so that other potential readers can see and use your unbiased opinion to make purchasing decisions, we can understand what our customers think about our products, and our authors can see your feedback on the title that they have worked with Packt to create. It will only take a few minutes of your time, but is valuable to other potential customers, our authors, and Packt. Thank you!

Index

Printed in Great Britain
by Amazon